DIVINE HORSEMEN
The Living Gods of Haiti

MAYA DEREN

DIVINE HORSEMEN
The Living Gods of Haiti

DOCUMENTEXT

MCPHERSON & COMPANY

DIVINE HORSEMEN: THE LIVING GODS OF HAITI

This Documentext edition is published by McPherson & Company
Post Office Box 1126, Kingston, New York 12401.
Manufactured in the United States of America.
10

Library of Congress Cataloging in Publication Data

Deren, Maya (1917-1961)
Divine Horsemen.

Reprint. Originally published: London; New York:
Thames and Hudson, c1953
"Documentext"
Bibliography: p.
Includes index
1. Voodooism—Haiti   2. Haiti—Religion.   I. Title
BL2530.H3D47   1983   299'.67   83-16228
ISBN 0-914232-64-9
ISBN 0-914232-63-0 (pbk.)

Great Gods cannot ride little horses

(HAITIAN PROVERB)

CONTENTS

vii

ILLUSTRATIONS

Photogravure Plates

ix

Line Drawings

EDITOR'S FOREWORD

MAYA DEREN has performed the feat of delineating the Haitian cult of Voudoun, not anthropologically—as a "relic of primeval ignorance and archaic speculation" (S. Hartland)—but as an experienced and comprehended initiation into the mysteries of man's harmony within himself and with the cosmic process. To some it will be incredible that an illiterate people should preserve in their traditions an arcanum lost to popular Christianity (which is today largely dogmatic rather than initiatory, moral rather than metaphysical), but no one acquainted with the true character of any so-called primitive religion will be surprised. "The content of folklore", wrote Ananda K. Coomaraswamy in one of his penetrating studies of mythology, "is metaphysical. Our failure to recognize this is primarily due to our own abysmal ignorance of metaphysics and of its technical terms.... *So long as the material of folklore is transmitted, so long is the ground available on which the superstructure of full initiatory understanding can be built.*"* All mythology, whether of the folk or of the literati, preserves the iconography of a spiritual adventure that men have been accomplishing repeatedly for millennia, and which, whenever it occurs, reveals such constant features that the innumerable mythologies of the world resemble each other as dialects of a single language. The peculiar interest of Voudoun derives from the fact that a congeries of displaced persons, ravished from various African homelands to the Caribbean hell of Hispaniola, where Spain had already all but annihilated the native Indian population, should have been competent to revivify, out of their own spiritual realizations and with whatever guidance splintered ancestral traditions can have afforded, those perennial symbolic forms.

* Ananda K. Coomaraswamy, *Figures of Speech or Figures of Thought,* Luzac and Co., London, 1946, pp. 216, 220. Italics, Dr. Coomaraswamy's.

This achievement constitutes a chapter in the history of the spirit of man in the New World that is certainly no less notable, though indeed less advertised, than that of the religious imperialism of the elegantly literate slavers. Moreover, in contrast to the ironic destiny of Christianity from the sixteenth to the twentieth centuries—which was, through its radical divorce of spirit from matter and its final reference of all spiritual values back to events clothed in the toga of Rome, to drive the entire modern world, progressively, into a frenzy of absolutely despiritualized materialism—the function and actual effect of Voudoun (despised, traduced, and persecuted) has been to invest the most ravaged victims of the Christian debauch with the living radiance of the timeless symbols, of which the Christian symbols themselves are but a local Near Eastern variant. Whereas God would seem to have hidden his head from the average churchgoer, to the average serviteur of the hounfor he visibly sends, even today, his angels: the gods. And these communicate the same message, which, in times of yore, was communicated to the patriarchs and the seers; namely, that divinity is here, now, and that by proper service and contemplation it may be made apparent even to the intelligence of man. Man, thereby, is given a fifth dimension, which is eternity—beyond the accidents of space and time; and man made aware of this dimension is in the Earthly Paradise— even where the tourist may see only a squalid heathen in a shattered hut.

It is because Christians today recognize, painfully, the limitations of our Western tradition and are seeking earnestly some enlarged base for the formulation of a unified and unifying, yet adequately differentiated, understanding of humanity, that, suddenly—as though promising a revelation—mythology and folklore have acquired a new interest. Few of the earlier studies of the materials can be of direct service, however, since they are based on a concept of the Occidental tradition as supreme (whether in its scriptural or in its scientific stage), whereas we are now striving to detect the tongue of the Spirit in the dialects of our neighbors. The series *Myth and Man* has therefore been conceived, as a conspectus composed by contemporary experts endowed with ears to hear. Dr. C. Kerényi's *The Gods of the Greeks* and Miss Deren's *Divine Horsemen: The Living Gods of Haiti,* published as the openers of the way, reveal the vast scope of the subject, but equally its unity. For the day-to-day epiphanies of Voudoun are experiences of a crisis of becoming ενθεος, "full of the god", such as precipitated much of the mythology preserved in Greek and Roman literary documents. We are not far from Hermes when in the presence of Ghede; not far from Ares when in that of Ogoun; and when with Erzulie, not far from the foam-born Cyprian. The mythological archetypes live on—within the heart of man; so that by knowing them in their various inflections we know man too in his variety, and equally in his glorious unity, discovering no need to unite what is already unitary, but only to understand. From mythology and folklore, therefore, there actually comes the promised revelation, which the world, fatigued with imperialism, requires: of man beyond, though among, the accidents of history. In this apocalypse enemies are brothers, the poor in spirit know the kingdom of heaven, and the pure in heart see God.

Joseph Campbell

New York, 1952

MAYA DEREN'S definition of myth (p. 21) as "the facts of the mind made manifest in a fiction of matter" is the key to both the psychological interest and the moral relevance of her richly informed anthropology. It was just after I had completed work on *The Hero with a Thousand Faces* that I met Miss Deren, fresh back from her first season in Haiti; and it was exactly her perception of the "facts of the mind"—

which are substratal to *all* productions of the human imagination—in the colorful local "matter" of the "fictions" of Haitian Voodoo that immediately struck me with wonder and delight. I had, of course, already read a good deal about Voodoo. The derivation of many of its fundamental gods and rites from the Gold and Slave Coasts of West Africa was already known to me; as was the importance of possession in the context of the cult. But nothing I had read had quite prepared me for the revelation of those "facts of the mind" that opened as Maya Deren spoke of her own experiences of possession, telling of the power of the drums as they drove the god (the *loa,* the *mystère*) into the body of the devotee (the *serviteur*); also, as she described the pranks and characteristics of the various *mystères* when they had "mounted" *(monté),* i.e., taken possession of, a worshiper. Every *loa* had his own drum beat, his own manner of behavior, his own costume (which was immediately installed on the *monté* as soon as the *loa* present was identified), and his own domain of spiritual revelation—through all of which, as Maya talked, I could readily recognize the motifs already familiar to me from the myths of the high religions, not only of antiquity, but also of the modern East and West. And it was then that I suggested to her that this jewel of a book simply *had* to be written and that I wished it to be the first of a series of volumes on the mythologies of mankind that I had just been invited to edit.

"When the anthropologist arrives, the gods depart." So declares, I am told, a Haitian proverb. Maya Deren, on the other hand, was an artist: therein, the secret of her ability to recognize "facts of the mind" when presented through the "fictions" of a mythology. Her avantgarde films, composed before her first trip to Haiti—"Meshes of the Afternoon," "Ritual in Transfigured Time," "Atland," and "Choreography for the Camera"—had already testified to her understanding of the pictorial script of dream, vision, and hallucination. As she describes in her preface (p. 5), she went first to

Haiti as an artist, thinking to make a film in which Haitian dance should be a leading theme. But the manifestations of rapture that there first fascinated and then seized her transported her beyond the bounds of any art she had ever known. She was open, willingly and respectfully, to the messages of that speechless deep, which is, indeed, the wellspring of the *mystères*. And so it was that when I first met her, just following her plunge into what she has named, in her last chapter, "The White Darkness," she was in a state of high exaltation—which even increased in force through the following three years of her sobering toil in the shaping and writing of this book.

There are a number of spheres of interest from which the phenomenology of Haitian Voodoo can be regarded. The first, I would say, is the historical. The marvel of its history lies in the fact that a congeries of displaced persons, torn from various African homelands and tossed together indiscriminately in a totally new environment, should have been able to reconstitute out of the fragments of their differing tribal heritages a single religion, self-consistent and, moreover, of a traditional type. In fact, as my learned Haitian friend Milo Rigaud has demonstrated in his substantial study *La tradition voudoo haïtien: son temple, ses mystères, sa magie* (Paris: Editions Niclaus, 1953), it is even possible to recognize the well-preserved lineaments in Haitian Voodoo of an esoteric philosophy of the Gnostic-Hermetic-Kabbalistic order.

According to Milo Rigaud, there must have been among the Africans transported to the New World a number of those who, in their villages, had been *houngans* ("spirit masters"); and it would have been these, then, who maintained the continuity of the esoteric doctrine. The rôle of the *mystère* named Legba, for example, corresponds to that of Hermes in the Hellenistic mysteries, so many of their symbols being identical that the analogies cannot be dismissed, either as incidental, or as a consequence of what anthropologists term "convergence." They comprise the total image of the god and are, furthermore, symbolically consistent, whether as rendered in the rites and myths, or as interpreted by qualified *houngans*—with a sufficient number of whom Milo Rigaud has been for years well acquainted on the best of terms. In any case, no matter what the explanation may be, the parallels between the myths and cults of contemporary Haiti and those, not only of seventeenth-century Africa, but also of antiquity, are undeniable and abundant.

However, the fascination of the historical approach to the mysteries of Voodoo is even surpassed by the psychological.

"Some psychologists believe," Maya said to me one day, "that possession is a kind of hypnosis. Do you think they could be right?"

"I have never been hypnotized," I answered, "and have never experienced possession. You have experienced possession, but have never been hypnotized. I think you owe it to science, now, to be hypnotized."

"You think so?"

"I do," I said.

"Do you know a hypnotist?"

"I do.

Well, to make a long and amusing story very short, the hypnotist (up to then, my friend) tried every art he knew, without result, so that the question remains unanswered to this hour. As does another: the question as to whether information derived from any such indentification with an alien culture as overcame Maya Deren can be accepted as "scientific"; or, to phrase the problem in psychoanalytic terms: can countertransference to a culture be employed as a methodological tool? Can its "findings" amount to anything more than a projection of personal fantasies?

My own reply to this objection would be that in the science of anthropology the ideal of objectivity has never yet been, and in the nature of things will never be, attained.

Further, as anyone who has ever studied the book review section of an anthropological journal must realize, no two anthropological investigators of any culture whatsoever have ever agreed in their findings, let alone evaluations. Moreoever (and this, in fact, is the great professional secret of the fraternity), *there is no known method of checking, to determine which (if either) of two radically differing "scientific" interpretations of an investigated culture is correct.* In short, as every student of philosophy knows, the object of knowledge is a function of the limitations of the subject; or, as in the Indian Gandharva Tantra, "One should worship a divinity by becoming oneself a divinity. One who has not become a divinity should not worship a divinity. Anyone worshiping a divinity without becoming a divinity will not reap the fruits of that worship." Or again, to repeat the Haitian dictum, "When the anthropologist arrives, the gods depart."

Whose interpretation, then, of the sense and experience of a religion is to be preferred in the name of science: that of the one who has been touched and psychologically transformed by the rites, or that of the one who has not? To whom, for example, do we turn for the sense and experience of Christian worship: to a Dante Alighieri or to Max Weber? It has always been my finding that the poet and the artist are better qualified both by temperament and by training to intuit and interpret the sense of a mythological figure than the university-trained empiricist. And rereading today, after twenty years, Maya Deren's celebration of the gods by whom her own life and personality were transformed, I am reconfirmed in that finding; reconfirmed, also, in my long-held belief that this little volume is the most illuminating introduction that has yet been rendered to the whole marvel of the Haitian *mystères* as "facts of the mind."

J.C.

New York, 1970

DIVINE HORSEMEN

The Living Gods of Haiti

AUTHOR'S PREFACE

IN September 1947 I disembarked in Haiti, for an eight-month stay, with eighteen motley pieces of luggage; seven of these consisted of 16-millimetre motion-picture equipment (three cameras, tripods, raw film stock, etc.), of which three were related to sound recording for a film, and three contained equipment for still photography. Among my papers I carried a certificate of a John Simon Guggenheim Fellowship for "creative work in the field of motion pictures" (as distinguished from documentary film projects), which was a reward for the stubborn effort that had been involved in creating, producing and successfully distributing four previous films with purely private and limited means and in the face of a cinema tradition completely dominated by the commercial film industry on the one hand and the documentary film on the other. Also among my papers was a carefully conceived plan for a film in which Haitian dance, as purely a dance form, would be combined (in montage principle) with various non-Haitian elements. I recite all these facts because they are evidence of a concrete, defined film project undertaken by one who was acknowledged as a resolute and even stubbornly willful individual.

Today, in September 1951 (four years and three Haitian trips later), as I write these last few pages of the book, the filmed footage (containing more ceremonies than dances) lies in virtually its original condition in a fireproof box in the closet; the recordings are still on their original wire spools; the stack of still photographs is tucked away in a drawer labeled "TO BE PRINTED", and the elaborate design for the montaged film is somewhere in my files, I am not quite sure where. (That is unimportant, for a new plan of editing is necessary, and this is my next immediate project.) This disposition of the objects related to my original Haitian project—evidence that this book was written not because I had so intended but in spite of my

5

intentions—is, to me, the most eloquent tribute to the irrefutable reality and impact of Voudoun mythology. I had begun as an artist, as one who would manipulate the elements of a reality into a work of art in the image of my creative integrity; I end by recording, as humbly and accurately as I can, the logics of a reality which had forced me to recognize its integrity, and to abandon my manipulations.

It was only after I had completely conceded my defeat as an artist—my inability to master the material in the image of my own intention—that I became aware of the ambiguous con﹨ sequences of that failure, for, in effect, the reasons for and the nature of my defeat contained, simultaneously, the reasons for and the nature of the victorious forces as well. I have come to believe that if history were recorded by the vanquished rather than by the victors, it would illuminate the real, rather than the theoretical, means to power; for it is the defeated who know best which of the opposing tactics were irresistible. The Russian peasant has another way of saying this: "He who wears the shoe knows best where it pinches."

I feel that the fact that I was defeated in my original intention assures, to a considerable degree, that what I have here recorded reflects not my own integrity which, as an artist's, had been overcome, but that of the reality that mastered it. It is this which encouraged me to undertake this book, for I was well aware of the fact that it is unorthodox for a non﹨professional to speak of matters that are normally the province of trained anthropolo﹨ gists. Since I assumed this responsibility two years ago, I have returned twice to Haiti (bringing to a total of eighteen months the time spent there) specifically to search out and ascertain details which, during my first visit, I had not troubled to note carefully; and during this same period I have also devoted myself to a study of the works of those professionals who have been concerned with Haitian culture: Herskovits, Courlander, Simpson and others. In reading those works, however, I also discovered that my background as an artist and the initial approach to the culture which my film project induced, served to illuminate areas of Voudoun mythology with which the standard anthropological procedure had not concerned itself, or, if so, from a different position entirely. It would seem proper to elaborate upon what was unorthodox in my approach to this subject, so that the reader may, if he wishes, proceed with the appropriate reservations.

To begin with, since film is dependent upon visual impact, I deliberately refrained, at first, from learning anything about the underlying meaning of the dance movements, so that such knowledge should not prejudice my evaluation of their purely visual impact. Once my original premise was destroyed— once I realized that the dance could not be considered indepen- dently of the mythology—I had no other preparation or motivation, no anthropological background (and anticipation) from other ethnic cultures, no systematized approach to an established methodology for collecting data, no plan of questions to ask, which might have created a self-consciousness and distorted the normal distribution of emphasis. But if my specialized concern for film left me unprepared for the culture as a whole, it created, also, a disinterested receptivity to it. And if at first, and for quite a while, I merely retained an amorphous, formless collection of memories which a pro- fessional observer would have systematized as soon as possible, I, having no such commitment, nor professional or intellectual urgency, could permit the culture and the myth to emerge gradually in its own terms and its own form.

I am not suggesting that my attitude was or could be one of complete passivity. Rather, it was a deliberate discretion, reflecting a strong distaste for aggressive inquiry, staring or prying, and which both resulted from and was rewarded by a sense of human bond which I did not fully understand until my first return to the United States. At that moment I became freshly aware of a situation to which I had grown inured and oblivious: that in a modern industrial culture, the artists constitute, in fact, an "ethnic group", subject to the full "native" treatment. We too are exhibited as touristic curiosities on Monday, extolled as culture on Tuesday, denounced as immoral and unsanitary on Wednesday, reinstated for scientific study Thursday, feasted for some obscurely stylish reason Friday, forgotten Saturday, revisited as picturesque Sunday. We too are misrepresented by professional appreciators and subjected to spiritual imperialism, our most sacred efforts are plagiarized for yard goods, our histories are traced, our psyches analysed, and when everyone has taken his pleasure of us in his own fashion, we are driven from our native haunts, our modest dwellings are condemned and replaced by a chromium sky-scraper. Of all persons from a modern culture, it is the artist who, looking at a native looking at a "white" man—whether tourist, industrialist or anthropologist—would mutter the heart-felt phrase: "Brother, I sure know what you're thinking and you can think that thought again!"

My own ordeal as an "artist-native" in an industrial culture made it impossible for me to be guilty of similar effronteries towards the Haitian peasants. It is a sad commentary upon the usual visitor to Haiti that this discretion seemed, to the Haitians, so unique that they early formed the conviction that I was not a foreigner at all, but a prodigal native daughter finally returned. (This conviction was shared by much of the Haitian bourgeoisie who felt that only an element of Negro blood in me would account for the psychological affinity with the peasants, since the city dwellers were only too proud to protest for themselves a psychological alienation.) This affinity—resulting from a situation peculiar to an artist as citizen of an industrial culture—is a basis of communication which is not comprehended in any catalogue of professional field methods.

And if my background as an artist resulted in a discretion which, while creating a general human affinity also closed off avenues of interrogation and explanation, it provided an alternative mode of communication and perception: the sub-jective level which is the particular province of artistic state-ment. I am referring to the communication of concepts and ideas by means addressed to emotional and psychological perceptions rather than in terms of a self-conscious articulation or an address to intellectual analysis: for example, the idea of power conveyed in posture rather than in the label of a name or definition. Since, as an artist, it was my *métier* to deal in such subjective communication, I might have expected it to be of general assistance in any context. But I was not prepared for the fact that such primitive rituals, which, in general, had been represented as yielding their true meanings only to a scholarly investigation of historical origins, would be so directly meaning-ful to me. Indeed, my interpretations of the rituals, based on my immediate experience and without the clues (and mis-guidances) of historical or esoteric research, proved so con-sistently correct that the Haitians began to believe that I had gone through varying degrees of initiation. And this means of perception yielded, not some historical meaning, but the same contemporary meaning which the ordinary serviteur experiences and which motivates him to continue serving that religion.

(I believe that it is not altogether inappropriate to consider that the peculiar and isolated position of the artist in Occidental culture might arise from the fact that he, alone among pro-fessionals, does not—by definition—accept certain beliefs which have so long been the premises of Occidental thought. Is it not worth considering that reverence for "detachment"—whether scientific or scholarly—might be primarily a projection of the notion of a dualism between spirit and matter, or the brain and the body, the belief that physical, sensory—hence, sensual!—experience is at least a lower form, if not a profane one, of human activity and the moral judgement that the highest, most reliable truths can be achieved only by means of a rigid asceticism? Is it valid to use this means to truth in examining Oriental or African cultures which are not based on such a dualism and are, on the contrary, predicated on the notion that truth can be apprehended only when every cell of brain and body —the totality of a human being—is engaged in that pursuit?)

It is probable that any sensitive layman would have had a

generalized emotional response to the rituals and the dances—to their grace, excitement, tension or whatever. But my detailed and precise interpretations were derived specifically from the fact that, as an artist, my predominant professional concern was with *form*. An artist usually recognizes the integrity of a form, whether or not he agrees with it, if only because he would do unto others as he would desperately hope to have them do unto him. He would be the first to insist that what was important about a Cézanne was not that it contained an apple and a pear, but the *form* in which those were conceived and rendered, and that this form was the significant distinction between Cézanne's still-life and one with similar fruit, painted, let us say, by Paul Klee. He would not react to the apple or the pear in terms of what these objects had come to mean to him personally, in terms of his own background (as the layman is inclined to do), but he would be concerned first with the ideas implicit in the *form* in which the objects were rendered—whether analytic, naturalistic, lyric, whimsical, frivolous, etc. —after which he might choose to agree or disagree with those ideas. It is because of this acute sensitivity to form that artists are so frequently involved in disagreements, for they deduce, from formal details and nuances of which others are barely aware, a whole logic of ramifications and connotations which amount to an entire metaphysical system. It was this order of awareness which made it impossible for me to execute the art work I had intended. It became clear to me that Haitian dancing was not, in itself, a dance-form, but part of a larger form, the mythological ritual. And the respect for formal integrity that makes it impossible for me to consider Cézanne's apple as an apple rather than as a Cézanne, made it equally impossible, in Haiti, to ignore the total integrity of cultural form, and to cut up the canvas into apples and pears to be catalogued or compared with other apples and other pears.

It led me, further, to sense, for instance, that the Petro dance and drumming were not merely another ritual—not merely a more violent canvas by the same painter—but that they were of a different character—a canvas by another painter altogether. This distinction arrested my attention and I began to observe the difference in major forms, which eventually led me to look for the possible interpolation of another culture, to investigate the history of the Spanish and Indian period of the islands, and finally, to the determination of the Indian influence as elaborated in the Appendix to this book. What emerges from this research is the fact that the African culture in Haiti was saved by the Indian culture which, in the Petro cult, provided the Negroes with divinities sufficiently aggressive (as was not true of the divinities of the generally stabilized African kingdoms) to be the moral force behind the revolution. In a sense, the Indians took their revenge on the white man through the Negro.

In effect, sensitivity to form provides the artist with a vast area of clues and data that might elude the professional anthro⁄pologist whose training emphasizes, precisely, that "scientific" detachment which may muffle even his normal sensitivity and responsiveness to formal nuance and subtlety, so that he becomes dependent upon the vagaries of informants' memory, intelligence and articulations. (Even in a verbal culture, such as our own, self⁄conscious articulation is not recognized as a completely reliable source of information; how, then, could it be so in a culture where expository formulation is not habitual, in a language which is largely imagistic, and in reference to a religion which is completely couched in ritualistic action and in which the "sermon" is unknown?) And it is this same order of formal data that is also likely to elude the psycho⁄analyst who, on the whole, suspects formal statement as being a mask rather than a projection of meaning, and who would ignore the fact that an African female figure is represented *without nostalgia* and is therefore a statement of progressive generation rather than an ethnic example of the regressive "mom⁄ism" which has become so familiar to him as a prevalent contem⁄porary disorder.

My intention is not to imply that this area of data—a sensi⁄tivity to form and to the clues it provides for meaning and research—has been entirely ignored by the anthropological profession. It is in the form of the artifacts and acts of a culture that the distinguishing *ethos* of a culture is stated, and a major discussion of ethos, in relation to the anthropological analysis of a culture, is contained in *Naven*, a study of the Iatmul tribes, by Gregory Bateson.* Chronologically, it is to Mr. Bateson, in fact, that my first acknowledgements are due. Before I went to Haiti and before this book was ever contemplated, I had the good fortune to have many extended conversations with him concerning the nature of cultural organization particularly in reference to Balinese, British and American culture. It was the non-sectarian quality of his anthropological intelligence—his readiness to engage every sensibility and every possible point of view in the effort to illuminate the structure of society—that, in my eyes, once more reaffirmed anthropology as the *study* of *man*, restoring to both words their major meaning. And those conversations altogether represent an influence which I am sure pervades this book, particularly in that it sharpened my observation of significant details and differences and my respect for the particular ethos of Haitian culture. If Mr. Bateson's influence was to make me more sharply aware of what distinguishes culture from culture, and why, it is my subsequent contact with Joseph Campbell, and my readings in his many writings (particularly *The Hero With A Thousand Faces***), which sharpened my awareness of that which man has in common, as expressed on the cosmic level of mythological concepts; and it was his influence that inspired me to formulate, from the vast accumulation of my observations, the meaningful, metaphysical structure of Haitian mythology. Indeed, this book is dedicated not to the presentation of data, but to the effort to perceive—both in the data of other scholars and in those of my own observations—at once the major human pattern, and the distinctive aspect which it manifests in Haitian culture. Mr. Bateson and Mr. Campbell, then,

* Cambridge University Press, 1936.
** Pantheon Books, Inc., New York, 1949.

represent, in a sense, harmonious polarities, and this book is an effort to unite these points of view according to a third—that of the artist—for which both gentlemen have shown a most gratifying tolerance.

To Mr. Campbell, also, I am profoundly grateful in a more personal context, for his untiring moral support at so many moments when every circumstance seemed to conspire to make this project, already overwhelming, an impossibly difficult undertaking from every point of view. At such moments I was also the beneficiary of assistances of all kinds from friends too numerous to mention. Predominant among these, in Haiti, was Odette Mennesson Rigaud, whose guidances and assis-tances, in respect both to my research and also to an infinite variety of personal and practical problems, I could not begin to enumerate; also, I am specifically indebted to her for the notes on the sacred marriages that are appended to this book, and which are a sample of her enormous annotation and knowledge of Voudoun ritual. I should like also to acknow-ledge my unfortunately brief but stimulating contact with Mr. Milo Rigaud, who impressed me profoundly with the erudi-tion of his esoteric study of those rituals. And I have a profound debt to Charles Pressoir, who gave so unfailingly of his friend-ship in so many difficult situations in Haiti, which I doubt would have been favorably resolved without the presence of his sensitive intelligence, moral support and practical assistance.

These trips to Haiti would have been impossible without, at the same time, the contributing efforts of persons here. I am grateful to Miss Anne Dubs, whose devoted attention to my film distribution, apartment, belongings, business affairs and a thousand other details made it possible for me to absent myself; to Dr. Max Jacobson, for the creative medicine involved in helping me accomplish an appallingly demanding program of work; to my mother, Marie Deren, and my friends—James Merrill, Mr. and Mrs. Alexander Hammid, Miriam Arsham, Leni Hoffman and others—who, each in his own way, helped make it possible for me to write this book. There is, finally, my inestimable debt to my father, and whatever is worthiest in this book—whether the specific psychological insight learned from the example he set as psychiatrist, or the more general intellectual dynamic—is a tribute to his memory. It is clear that, without the Haitian peasants and people who serve Voudoun, this book would not exist. But I am grateful to them not primarily for the existence of this book or for their relationship to it or to me or even for those special kindnesses and friendships which I enjoyed; I am grateful for their sheer existence, and would be so even if it had in no way benefited me personally. I am not sure to what or to whom or in which direction to make such an acknowledgement, but I *am* sure that—despite any faults that it may have—the fact that such a culture exists is, in itself, a good. I am certain, also, that this feeling would be shared by all those who believe that man should exercise to the full the totality of those capacities which make him human in the major sense, and that to be preoccupied with the achievement of this end, whether by art, science or any other means, is to serve the greatest good.

At the time of my first trip to Haiti there was virtually no precedent for the filming of ceremonies; photographing them was altogether a delicate undertaking, for many reasons. When the time came, I broached the subject to a Voudoun priest whose ceremonies I had attended and who had come to know me well. I spoke to him of my desire to capture the beauty and the significance of the ceremonies, so that the rest of the world might become aware. He understood virtually nothing of cinema and I was uncertain of his reaction, since his own standing in the community could be jeopardized by such a permission. Besides, in his culture, the artist as a singular individual did not exist. Could he possibly understand and sympathize with my motivations? He hesitated but a moment. Then, offering his hand as one would to a colleague or collaborator, he said: "Each one serves in his own fashion."

This book is dedicated to all those who serve, each in his own fashion.

INTRODUCTORY NOTE

VOUDOUN is the religion, primarily African in origin, of the vast majority of the inhabitants of the Republic of Haiti in the West Indies. Most of these are also members of the Catholic Church, which is the official state religion. In the larger cities, and particularly in Port-au-Prince, the "middle" and "upper" classes, influenced, no doubt, by conventional criteria of "civilized" cultures, as well as by the pressure of the Catholic Church, have altogether abandoned Voudoun in favor of Christianity. The schism between these classes and the masses of the people is so great that the former are largely ignorant of Voudoun. It is therefore to be clearly understood that the term "Haitian", used in connection with Voudoun, does not include the "middle" and "upper" class segment of the national population.

It is, however, this very class of people which governs the country, and represents it in all its economic, social and political contacts with the world. In deference to its dislike of Voudoun, to its efforts to detach itself publicly from any suggestion that it may share these beliefs and even to deny their existence altogether, it becomes imperative to emphasize that Voudoun is not the religion of the Haitians whom one is likely to encounter in social circumstances, either in Haiti or abroad. It must also be clearly understood that this book does not share the distaste of the "educated" Haitian (as this class has chosen to designate itself) for Voudoun, but, on the contrary, was inspired by the conviction that this is a religion of major stature, rare poetic vision and artistic expression, and that it contains a pantheon of divinities which, in astronomical terminology, could be called a constellation of first magnitude.

Like all religions, Voudoun is built on certain basic premises. Briefly, it proposes that man has a material body, animated by an *esprit* or *gros-bon-ange*—the soul, spirit, psyche

15

or self—which, being non-material, does not share the death of the body. This soul may achieve (by stages elaborated in the discussion immediately following) the status of a *loa*, a divinity, and become the archetypal representative of some natural or moral principle. As such, it has the power to displace temporarily the gros-bon-ange of a living person and become the animating force of his physical body. This psychic phenomenon is known as "possession". The actions and utterances of the possessed person are not the expression of the individual, but are the readily identifiable manifestations of the particular loa of archetypal principle. Since it is by such manifestations that the divinities of the pantheon make known their instructions and desires and exercise their authority, this phenomenon is basic to Voudoun, occurs frequently, and is *normal* both to the religion and to the Haitians. In fact, the Haitian would find it abnormal if it should suddenly cease to occur.

To most readers, however, such religious possession is not only unfamiliar, but carries exotic and sensational overtones. Also, as the most spectacular phenomenon in a religion whose ritual action is disciplinarian, reiterative and replete with detail having no significance for the uninformed, it has frequently inspired in observers an emphasis which isolated it from its context and gave rise to interpretations which distorted its true quality and function. The detailed elaboration and analysis of possession has been reserved for the final chapter of this book, in the hope that, by then, the structure and emotional logic of that total context of which it is a part will have been amply demonstrated and established. In describing Voudoun, however, it will be necessary to make repeated reference to possession. For the purposes of such description the fact will be referred to as precisely what it is sincerely understood and believed to be by those who are involved in the context of the religion. Thus, if a loa possesses a person, it will be assumed that, for the duration of the possession, the actions and attitudes witnessed and described are those of the loa spirit and not of the person proper. If a male loa possesses a female devotee, the name of the loa or the pronoun *he* will be used (as it always is in Voudoun) when referring to the acting subject responsible for all the events transpiring during that possession; and con-versely, if a female loa possesses a male, the pronoun will be *she*.

Similarly, in the interests of retaining and even emphasizing other religious concepts as they are understood by the Haitians themselves, it has been preferable to use the Voudoun terminology frequently, even at the risk of an initial awkward-ness for the reader. To render these terms in English, it would be necessary to determine the closest equivalent in the Christian religion, to use, for example, the word "priest" for *houngan*. But the Christian terms derive their full meaning from the entire context of Christian metaphysics and organizational practices. They automatically evoke a mass of implications, connotations and associations in terms of that context and the culture of which it is a part, and all this, if carried over to the Haitian concepts, would lead to a grave distortion and misunderstand-ing of Voudoun belief. The fact that Haitian informants them-selves transpose their concepts to Christian equivalents without being aware of discrepancies between them accounts for a good deal of the misinterpretation of those beliefs in the litera-ture on Haiti. A houngan, for instance, is like a Catholic priest in that he is responsible for the preservation and performance of complex religious traditions and rituals. But Voudoun is not a centralized church organization, and the houngan has no organizational authority behind him, so that in this respect, the less absolute, relatively informal character of his relationship to the community would be much more accurately suggested by the term "minister". Yet neither of these terms includes one of the houngan's major activities, which is the herbalistic treatment of disease, for which the word "doctor" would be the only proper equivalent. In other words, the concept "houngan" would only be seriously misrepresented by the use of any one of the terms available in our culture. The exclusive

use of the word "soul" (which has moral and mystic connotations) would similarly misrepresent the sense of gros-bon-ange
or esprit, which is understood, in Voudoun, as the invisible,
non-material *self* or character of an individual, as distinguished
from his physical body: i.e., the person John, as a *concept*,
distinct from the physical body of John. As a matter of fact,
the word "psyche", as it is used in modern psychology, conveys
some aspects of the Voudoun gros-bon-ange much more
accurately than the word "soul", which has been used in most
of the literature on Haiti because of its relevant religious associations; and the word "spirit" would approximate the Voudoun
esprit only if understood as a person's "life principle", his
"nature" or "character" (as we understand it in such phrases as
"the spirit of the times") rather than in its exclusively mystic or
spiritual sense. For expediency, the initial use of such Voudoun
terms is immediately defined by the closest equivalent. But the
Haitian term itself is used generally, as a statement and reminder
of the distinctively Haitian concept which is implied, and its
full sense is elaborated in the course of the text.

Voudoun terminology, titles and ceremonies still make use
of the original African words and in this book they have been
spelled out according to usual English phonetics and so as to
render, as closely as possible, the Haitian pronunciation. Most
of the songs, sayings and even some of the religious terms,
however, are in Creole, which is primarily French in derivation (although it also contains African, Spanish and Indian
words). Where the Creole word retains its French meaning, it
has been written out so as to indicate both the original French
word and the distinctive Creole pronunciation.

Finally, it must also be pointed out that since Voudoun is
not a centralized religion, ritualistic detail may differ enormously
from region to region. Rituals that are important in a certain
locality may be entirely unknown in other regions. Even
within a given locality, as within a thirty-mile radius of Port-
au-Prince (where most of the rituals cited in this book were
observed), details may differ from one *bounfor* (parish) to

THE CARDINAL POINTS AND POINTS BETWEEN

another. Any complete documentation of a ritual would there-fore hold true only for that specific hounfor, and such docu-mentation is not the purpose of this book. Nor is it to be inferred that those rituals and details that are cited represent universal practices. The ceremonies, incidents and interpreta-tions here included have been selected not because they indicate universal *practices* but because they seem to be particularly expressive of universal *principles* in Voudoun. Thus, a relatively unusual detail may sometimes be cited (although the typical detail is described for the most part) because it is an especially forceful or illuminating expression of one of the general principles.

The footnote arrangement (some being inserted at the bottom of the page and others grouped at the back of the book) is perhaps unorthodox and even, at first glance, confusing but it has been arrived at in the effort to answer to the interests both of the general lay reader and the professional scholar. The footnotes which are readily accessible at the bottom of the page consist of remarks and references which are relevant to the information and interest of the general reader; the source references, discussions of conflicting data and opinions, addi-tional details and specifications, etc., which are of interest primarily to the student of anthropology, have been grouped together at the end of the book.

The factual data which are included are based on first-hand observation and both conflicting and corroborative data from other observers have been incorporated. But the purpose of this book is not to assemble and present available data on Voudoun practices; it is to delineate the metaphysical principles underlying those practices and to render them in terms of their cultural context in such a way that they may become, for the non-Haitian reader, as real and as reasonable as they are to the Haitian worshipper.

CHAPTER I

The Trinity: Les Morts, Les Mystères, et les Marassa

I

THE POINT OF DEPARTURE

MYTH is the twilight speech of an old man to a boy. All the old men begin at the beginning. Their recitals always speak first of the origin of life. They start by inventing this event which no man witnessed, which still remains mystery. They initiate the history of their race with a fiction. For, whether it was first in the sense of time, life is, for all men, first of miracles in the sense of prime. This is a fact. Myth is the facts of the mind made manifest in a fiction of matter.

The speech of an elder in the twilight of his life is not his history but a legacy; he speaks not to describe matter but to demonstrate meaning. He talks of his past for purposes of his future. This purpose is the prejudice of his memory. He remembers that which has been according to what could and should be, and by this measure sifts the accumulation of his memory: he rejects the irrelevant event, elaborates the significant detail, combines separate incidents of similar principle. Out of physical processes he creates a metaphysical processional. He transposes the chronology of his knowledge into a hierarchy of meanings. From the material circumstances of his experience he plots, in retrospect, the adventure for the mind which is the myth.

This adventure is composed, then, as all fictions are, from the matter of memory at hand—from the specific physical conditions which circumstance imposes and the particular processes which time composes for each individual race. The differences between the tales of the venerable ancients of the

21

various nations are differences, then, between the matter of them. But in all this cosmic variety, the constant is the mind of man. Where it has least to describe outside itself and most to invent out of itself, it displays this constancy most purely, as in the fictions of origins. It is as if the mind, by-passing the particularities of circumstance, the limitations and imprecisions of the senses, arrived, by paths of metaphysical reason, at some common principled truth of the matter.

The fictions begin with a solemn fanfare, less for the Person of the First Source, than for the moment of creation. The metaphors of the diverse myths differ; the nature of the Cosmic Catalyst is the same. It is an energy which, out of the anonymity of void, of chaos, of the wholeness of a Cosmic Egg, crystallizes the major elements, precipitates the primary areas, and finally differentiates the first androgynous life (as the solitary Adam) into the twinned specializations: male and female. This is the fiction of beginnings, couched in the past tense. But the chants are not *in memoriam*. They may be heard as a celebration of each contemporary recapitulation of that first creation. The microcosmic egg rides the red tides of the womb which, like the green tides, still rise and recede with the moon; the latest life, like the first, flows with the seas' chemistry, is first anonymous, then androgynous, becomes differentiated, is beached in a surf, its heart reverberates a life-time with the pounding momentum of the primal sea pulse. The beginning, which no man witnessed, is ever present, ever before us. When we come to perceive the final fact of the matter, we find that it was conceived by the mind in the first fiction of the myth.

But the accomplishment of matter is always as an overture to the major movement of myth, the accomplishment of moral man. Matter creates the matter of man. But this creature, who may intermittently feel hunger and fatigue, would not understand the intervals as time; it might sense itself at first weak, then strong, then weak again, but would not comprehend this change as age; it might come to perceive the logics of matter and might observe, eventually, the reason for the succession of seasons, for natural sequences of natural events. But the reasons in matter are still a property of matter; its meaning, conceived in the marriage of matter and mind, is a property of the human mind. As chaos contained the possibility of matter, so this creature contains the possibility of a mind, like a fifth limb latent in man, structured to make and manipulate meaning as the fist is structured to grasp and finger matter.

The fictions of the old men are their final fecundity. As their flesh once labored to bring forth flesh, so the minds of the elders labor, with a like passion, to bring forth a mind. By rites of initiation they would accomplish the metamorphosis of matter into man, the evolution of a mind for meaning in the animal which is the issue of their flesh. By this they would insure that the race endure as a race of men. The rites of this second birth, into the metaphysical cosmos, everywhere mime the conditions of the first physical birth. The novice is purified of past, relieved of possessions, made innocent, placed nascent in the womb solitude of a dark room. The matter, which is himself, and the myth of the race are joined. His solitary meditation is a gestation and, in the end, a man emerges by ordeal, to be newly named, newly rejoiced in.

But who first informed the ancestral elders of the various nations? What was the common inspiration of their common fanfare for origins, their common fiction of initiation, their common metaphors of metamorphosis? No man has ever witnessed the moment when life begins; it is in the moment of its ending that the limits of life, hence life itself, are manifest. Death, as the edge beyond which life does not extend, delineates a first boundary of being. Thus the ending is, for man, the beginning: the condition of his first consciousness of self as living. Death is life's first and final definition. The fanfare for cosmic origins is followed by this major fugue: the initial figure is a lament of the living for the dead; and the voice which first propounds the major themes of life, love and generation is borne up from the abyss as the flesh was first, and is still, born from the deep seas of chaos. The hero of man's metaphysical adventure—his healer, his redeemer, his guide and guardian—is always a corpse. He is Osiris, or Adonis, or Christ.

But death itself we recognize not so much by what it is as by the fact that it is not life. As the land and the sea define each other at the shore, so life and death define each other by exclusion. These, which are the immediate neighbors in the realm of matter, are separated by a difference which is as a vast distance in the realm of meaning. Myth is the voyage of exploration in this metaphysical space. The point of departure is the first meeting between the quick and the dead.

To enter a new myth is a moment of initiation. One must return to the moment before myth, anterior to all its inventions, when the myth of any man might still become the myth of any other. It is to enter, in one's mind, the room which is both tomb and womb, to become innocent of everything except the motivation for myth, the natural passion of the mind for meaning. It is to meditate upon the common human experience which is the origin of the human effort to comprehend the human condition.

2

THE MORTAL ME: THE IMMORTAL MYSELF

We look at the corpse and we know that it is dead because we know and we remember what it is to be alive. A critical change has occurred. Yet all that is visible is merely the evidence of this event. The root of the difference is invisible. The stillness of the corpse is, in itself, no different from the stillness of a sleeper. We know that it is not sleep because we know that it is forever; but this foreverness, this time, is itself invisible. The stillness, even of the heart, is evidence of death but is not itself death, just as movement—the mobility as of an object moved —is not always evidence of life and is certainly not life itself. So we are forced to conceive of life as an inner power, a force which may be manifest in the movement of the matter which contains it. The moment of death, then, is a separation, forever, of this life force from the flesh, the matter. And this invisible force is, in turn, more than the energy of matter as manifest in movement; it is also an energy of mind, the capacity for memory and meaning, for discrimination and invention. Whether called intelligence, consciousness, spirit or soul, it is the invisible action within man which motivates and molds his visible acts and expressions.

The Haitian myth couches this primary contemplation in its own language. It proposes as basic, a generic distinction between visible matter and les Invisibles. By this term it describes a relationship relative to our senses; but the nature itself of les Invisibles, the forces or spirits whose presence in matter constituted a state of life and whose permanent withdrawal constitutes a state of death, is known as *esprit*. For the Haitian, this "spirit" is not some vague, mystical evanescence. In colloquial speech he says that a man has "pil esprit" (much spirit) and means, by this, that the man has great intelligence. Esprit, then is a reference to the energy and action of the mind which, as a state of consciousness and as a repository of material and moral knowledge and experience, is the source and the act of judgement, decision, desire and of all the motivation and the will projected in a man's visible action.

The energy of matter is common to all living matter. The lament for the dead is not for this fractional diminution of either the cosmic life force or the cosmic consciousness as a vast anonymous generality. Intelligence which, with death, ceases to be manifest, is at once common to all men and is particular to each. It is the source and means of each man's singular identity. We mourn not man, but *a* man; and we lament not for his lot, but for our own. His death is as the closing of a door upon that singular, particular self which, projected through his flesh, nourished the world of substance which we shared. We mourn this man because to us his spirit was not like any other. The moment of death is as a separation of a mold from the form to which it had transferred all the particularities of its configuration. As the integrity of the mold's form is destroyed by the act of separation, so the flesh perishes. But the form, the self which had been cast, is non-material, hence is immortal—an identity, invisible but real, acknowledged in common and known by a name.

This self, this form, the Haitian calls the *gros-bon-ange*.* It is born of the body, and may be imagined as the shadow of a man cast upon the invisible plane of a fourth dimension, or as his reflection in a dark mirror. The gros-bon-ange is the metaphysical double of the physical being, and, since it does not exist in the world of matter, it is the immortal twin who survives the mortal man. It is these immortal twins, these gros-bon-anges of the deceased, who are les Invisibles or les esprits.

The Haitian gros-bon-ange is similar to what we understand by a man's soul, if we think of the soul as duplicating the man and not as a moral force of a "higher" nature. The universal commitment towards good, the notion of truth as desirable, all that conscience which, in our culture, is understood as a function of the soul is, for the Haitian, the function of a third element in man, the *ti-bon-ange*. It is the ti-bon-ange, for example, that cannot lie. But the very impersonality of this conscience, its detachment from the pressures of actuality, its imperviousness both to development and corruption, its changelessness inspires, in the Haitian, a somewhat reciprocal detachment. He accepts the ti-bon-ange as one of the constants of the cosmos. It is as if he said to himself: although all men have a conscience, yet some men do good and some do bad. Therefore, what he does depends on his gros-bon-ange. It is what a man does, and not whether he feels satisfaction or remorse, which is important to other men. Of what consequence is the private sentiment of a man if he has not the necessary knowledge or experience or energy or power to act

---

* Gros-bon-ange is used when referring to the souls of living men; esprit may mean "intelligence" in the living, but when used as "un esprit" or "les esprits" it refers to the immortal souls of the dead, or what was known, during lifetime, as the gros-bon-ange.

upon it? In a collective community, where men are inter-dependent, the collective welfare cannot be entrusted either to the vagaries of subjective conscience, or to the "free" or "natural" development of the gros-bon-ange. The entire Haitian religion is, in fact, structured for the controlled development of a man's gros-bon-ange and the enforcement of a collective morality in action.

So, for the Haitian, the significant morality—that which is manifest in actuality—is the product of the flesh and therefore shares its nature. In Voudoun the cosmic drama of man consists not of a dualism, a conflict of the irreconcilable down-pull of flesh and the up-pull of spirit; it is, rather, an almost organic dynamic, a process by which all that which characterizes divinity—intelligence, power, energy, authority, wisdom—evolves out of the flesh itself. Instead of being eternally separated, the substance and the spirit of a man are eternally and mutually committed: the flesh to the divinity within it and the divinity to the flesh of its origin.

3

THE BIRTH OF A DIVINITY

The gros-bon-ange, as the repository of a man's history, his form and his force, the final resultant of his ability, intelligence and experience, is a precious accumulation. If, after his death, his descendants were able to provide this disembodied soul with some other means of manifestation to substitute for the flesh which perished, they could salvage this valuable legacy. One of the major Voudoun rituals is the ceremony of *retirer d'en bas de l'eau*, the reclamation of the soul of the deceased from the waters of the abyss, the world of les Invisibles. This service for the ancestral dead is not a nostalgia or sentimentality. The poor, and those who live in difficult primitive circumstances, cannot afford superfluous expenditures of either energy or property. It is not a moment of return to the past; it is the procedure by which the race reincorporates the fruit of previous life-processes into the contemporary moment, and so retains the past as a ground gained, upon and from which it moves forward to the future. The living do not serve the dead; it is the dead who are made to serve the living.

The ceremony of reclamation is as the third and final birth of a man. He emerged into the world, for the first time, as an animal. Initiation was his second birth, as a proper man. And this soul which, with death and the perishing of the flesh, was lost to the visible world is brought back into it once more. The clay jar, or *govi*, in which it is placed at this ceremony is a substitute for the vessel of flesh which once contained it. Out of the mouth of that jar issue the counsels and wisdoms by which the deceased continues to aid and advance his descendants.

An undistinguished member of the family may be neglected and the costly ceremony of his reclamation repeatedly post-poned, to be accomplished eventually, without much enthusiasm, only because nothing of heredity's accumulations should be permitted to leak away, to be lost for ever. At the Feast for the Dead, a sense of filial loyalty may induce the immediate descendants to name such departed ones in-dividually; or later, they may be so remembered because of some intimate, personal sympathy. But such individual recognition is rare, and these undistinguished dead become known as that anonymous heritage, les Morts.[1] On the other hand, the person who has been distinguished for his wisdom or power, love or therapies, disciplines or skills—who has perhaps reached the rank of *houngan* (priest), with all the accomplishments that such a rank signified—is reclaimed with elaborate care, so that his special virtues may not be lost.[2]

In due course of time, the parent in the govi becomes grand-parent and the grandparent becomes ancestor. As his con-temporaries die off, and with them all immediate first-hand memories, the flesh of the original human personality withers away, so that there is left within the govi only the distilled, depersonalized, almost abstract essence of the principle that especially characterized him. Thus, in time, *the person becomes principle.* And yet—what once was so real, so substantial, cannot be permitted to end in such rarefaction, to vanish forever into the far reaches of history. This abstraction, to function in reality, must become reality; *the principle must become person.* And so the process of abstraction, as though meeting, finally, the limits of its own extension, curves back toward its origins: those who cannot remember begin to create, building now from the inside outward, as one might be guided by the clues and logic of a skeleton to construct a figure. In time, the ancestor becomes archetype.[3] Where there was once a person, there is now a personage. Transposed to this dimension, the summoned voice in the govi is no longer intimate, advisory; it is an objective oracular authority that booms as if from the bowels of the earth.[4] What was once believed, is now believed in. He who was once respected is now revered. Where once the parent inspired filial devotion, the deity now exacts dedication. The ancestor has been transfigured into a god.

Death had deprived the gros-bon-ange of its own living form; the memory of the living had reclaimed it and given it voice. Time was a distance separating it from its immediate descendants, from the too-intimate prejudice of such proximity. In a sense, it became purified of human ego. Only after such purification could it achieve the powers of divinity. The special power of the *loa*, or les Mysteres, as the Haitian calls those esprits who have achieved some degree of divine elevation, is that of becoming manifest in a living form. Under certain well-defined and ritualistically determined conditions, the loa may temporarily displace the gros-bon-ange of a living person and become the animating force of that physical body. This we know as "possession". In the terminology of Voudoun, it is said that the loa "mounts" a person, or that a person is "mounted" by the loa. The metaphor is drawn from a horse and his rider and the actions and events which result are the expression of the will of the rider. Since the conscious self of the possessed person is, meanwhile, absent, he cannot and does not remember the events; he is not responsible, either for good or for bad; and he cannot, as a person, himself benefit from that possession. The function and purpose of such divine manifes-tation is the reassurance and the instruction of the community. The complete process can be understood as a closed chain circling life and death.* The power of the loa to become manifest in living matter marks their final mastery of matter. The interlocking mechanism of the links is a system of partial and progressive ambiguities, clearly apparent in the succession of receptacles for the gros-bon-ange, which in part overlap and yet are graduated. The gros-bon-ange may be separated from the body even during the lifetime, and stored in a bottle, as a kind of isolation from malevolent forces. At the *canzo* cere-mony—the ceremony of initiation or spiritual birth**—the gros-bon-ange is placed in a *canari* (clay pot) or *pot-de-tête* (receptacle for the "head", soul or mind) and left in the care of the houngan or some trustworthy person. At death this pot-de-tête is broken, to release the gros-bon-ange to the waters of the abyss; but one year later, this receptacle is replaced, at the moment of reclamation, by the govi, in which the soul, now referred to as an esprit, is lodged once more and which is as a throat, making speech possible. Thus far the graduated pro-gression of receptacles is evident, and each step is achieved with ritual. But the decisive moment, when the ancestral soul, passed down from generation to generation in the govi, emerges finally from this clay shell as loa, is beyond the will of man and the prejudicial power of their prayers. It is as an interlocking of links that takes place beyond the scope of an immediately cognized time and space, as if in the outer reaches of the cosmos. There is no ritual either to make or even to mark this ultimate transfiguration.[5] It is a moment as unknown, as unwitnessed

---

* Campbell's (p. 29) discussion and elaboration of the circular life-death concept in other mythologies and as a universal mythological concept, illuminates the Haitian concept and it is apparent, once more, that, far from being a collection of miscellaneous superstitions, Voudoun is a religion of classic mythological character.

** This ceremony will be described *infra*, pp. 220–2.

as the very origin of the first physical life, and it results in physical life. Unlike the mere ancestral spirit which must be passed down in a govi, the loa are part of the very blood of the race, and are inherited automatically. They can neither be denied nor destroyed. They may also be lodged in a govi or in stones, but these are as secondary residences. Just as a child's physical body inevitably is issue of the physical component of his parents, so his loa are his psychic inheritance* and they carry forward, into his contemporary gros-bon-ange, the moral accumulation of the race.[6]

This automatic inheritance is not at all contradicted by the apparent power of discrimination and selection implied in the phrase "temperament mun, ce temperament loa-li" (the character of a person is the character of his loa). If the original families were each distinguished by certain of the major loa, intermarriage has, by now, introduced all the major loa into all the family lines and all major loa-principles are latent in every-one. The reference to the sympathetic relationship between the character of a person and that of his loa relates to the *maît-tête*, the "master of the head", or the loa which is dominant above all others in the psyche of an individual. It may also refer to the particular aspect of the loa (since these major principles may be manifest in various aspects, i.e., Ogoun as the primal hero archetype or as a more recent warrior, etc.) which is carried in

---

* When the Haitian says "inherits" he does not understand it (as we do in our culture) to be an element distinct from and even opposed to environment. The conditions of family life in Haiti are such that in effect the two ideas are virtually identical. As in all primitive communities, the family is a tightly knit, cohesive and continuous entity, and is the basic unit of the communal structure, rather than the individual. In sheer geographical terms, even the grandfather does not become part of one's past, since one rarely moves away. He is there today as part of one's present. Certainly this is true of one's parents. The transmission of principles, as loa, from parent and even grandparent to child, is not, then, so very mystical as might be understood from the word "inherit". To say that one has inherited the father's Ghede or the mother's Erzulie is to say (if one were to translate the concept into the logic of our culture) that the father has contributed to one's make-up a sense of and concern for the idea of death and resurrection as contained in the Ghede complex, or that from one's mother one has "learned" the importance of love and the dream of beauty which is Erzulie.

the head of a person. In any case, the ambiguity of the phrase is significant. It can imply, for example, that Ogoun, who is the deity of power, confers the favor of his presence and guardian/ ship on a person whose temperament he has found sympathetic; but it can also mean that a person selects, concentrates on, becomes obsessed by and possessed by the deity who personifies his own personal emphasis. Or, finally, it suggests that the two processes may operate simultaneously. In any case, the fact remains that a person who has been possessed by Ogoun is one who emphasizes the principle of power or strength in his own activities.

If this emphasis has been expressed in his life to a remarkable degree, he will be remembered, after death, for this distin/ guishing characteristic. As time passes and he becomes, to the living, that depersonalized abstraction which is an ancestor, he may then be assimilated into the concept Ogoun, and so lose his identity altogether in that of the great loa; or his name may be incorporated in the invocation to Ogoun; or, again, if his way of strength was a very distinctive variation on the traditional pattern, he may even become a deity under his own name, a deity understood to be one of the family of Ogouns. By this process, a potentially infinite number of ancestral spirits become condensed into a feasible number of variations of the principled archetypes.

The immediate descendants of the deceased, who may be subject to vanity or other selfishly personal motivations, can do no more than lay the foundations of ultimate elevation into loa by reclaiming the parental soul from the abyss. Time must pass, the purification by time must take place, and the gradual process of abstraction. There is no loa who can be remembered as human being.[7] Even the gros/bon/ange, or the esprit, as a singular identity, must cease to be. In the final analysis it is not the ancestor who is worshipped; and the final verdict, the last transfiguration and resurrection, the ultimate elevation into divinity, is in the hands of history and the collective.

Deification, therefore, does not consist in the spiritualization of matter; on the contrary, the ceremony of *retirer d'en bas de l'eau*, which is itself the ritualistic reversal of the rites of death, restores the disembodied soul *to* the physical, living universe which was its origin and, in so doing, restores to it a major portion of its original material attributes. The Haitian is an eminently realistic, reasonable man. His loa must share the needs as well as the privileges of life; to have great power is to need great energy. And so the loa, like living, functioning mat' ter, have an unrelenting need for sustenance if their life energies are to be maintained. The physical feasting of the loa is at once the most common and the most important of the obligations of a worshipper.

The entire chain of interlocking links—life, death, deifica' tion, transfiguration, resurrection—churns without rest through the hands of the devout. None of it is ever forgotten: that the god was once human, that he was made god by humans, that he is sustained by humans. Hence the Haitian loa, however revered and honored, do not have that quality of absolutism which, in another culture, might characterize the deity of presumably supernatural origin.* The loa bow to the priest, are hurt by disrespect, weep for neglect. And the worshipper is devout but demanding; he both begs and bargains. If he expects and accepts the constant intervention of the loa in the daily affairs of his life, it is not because he has an easy belief in miracle; it is because he does not regard such intervention as miraculous. The undertone of his devotion is, rather, that it is the duty of the loa to intervene; for the gros'bon'ange, from which it derives, was itself created by life and was reincor' porated into life at the ceremony of the *retirer d'en bas de l'eau.*

---

* It is significant that the loa who were houngans or mambos during their lifetime—in other words, the ancestral divinities who derive from men—are considered to be "stronger" than those which are cosmic forces, of cosmic origin.

4

THE COSMIC MIRROR AND THE CORPSE ON THE
CROSS-ROADS

For the Haitian, the metaphysical world of les Invisibles is not
a vague, mystical notion; it is as a world within a cosmic
mirror, peopled by the immortal reflections of all those who
had ever confronted it. The mirror is the metaphor for the
cosmography of Haitian myth. The loa are addressed as mirror
images and summoned by references to a mirrored surface.
The song for the loa Legba says: *O Creole, Sondé miroir, O Legba*
(O Creole, fathom the mirror, O Legba). Sometimes they
sing that the mirror breaks through rocks,[8] for the mirror is as
an X-ray and its vision penetrates matter. The *vevers*—the
sacred symbols drawn during ceremonies—are frequently
designed in mirrored symmetry to both sides of an horizon. The
loa are invoked as *Loco-Miroir* (the mirror-Loco) and *Loco-De*
(Deux, or Loco-double) or *Agassou-Dos-Miroir* (Agassou of
the back of the mirror).[9] They are served in inverted mirror
terms: "Papa Damballa, Mistress Erzulie, with Miss Aida, I
give you to eat with the left hand. It is with the left hand because
you are the Invisibles."[10] They are greeted in mirror terms: the
infant who is presented to them is carried on the left arm. They
are saluted in mirror terms: the houngan and the loa, face to
face, turning and curtseying in mirrored symmetry.[11] They act
in mirror terms: when they possess a person they greet the
others present with a double handshake, at first with the right
hand, and then with the left, it being with the latter that the
psychic contact is established and that the spirit of the loa
is transmitted into the body of the other, to possess him also. Or
holding still the left hand, the loa may spin the person counter-
clockwise, a spiral journey which crosses the divide and almost
inevitably leads to possession. The ritual dance movements
likewise revolve counter-clockwise around the center-pole.
There are even ritual details in which inversion and reversal

suggest a mirror held up to time. When it is ritualistically necessary for the special guardian loa of a *hounfor* (parish) to be present, and if that loa has not become manifest by possessing some one, his presence may be represented ritually by the *la-place*, one of the high functionaries of the hounfor. To signify this, the la-place emerges *backwards* through the door leading from the sacred altar to the ceremonial area. It is like a motion-picture projected in reverse, a diver shooting back up out of the water on to the spring-board. By this gesture of the la-place, time itself is symbolically run backwards to a time before the death of the man whose gros-bon-ange eventually became this loa. As long as a man lives, his gros-bon-ange is as a reflection on the surface of that cosmic mirror, held to that surface by the existence of the body which it mirrors. But with death, there ceases to exist the flesh, the force which held it buoyant, and it sinks into the depths of the mirror.

The metaphor for the mirror's depth is the cross-roads; the symbol is the cross. For the Haitian this figure is not only symbolic of the totality of the earth's surface as comprehended in the extension of the cardinal points on a horizontal plane. It is, above all, a figure for the intersection of the horizontal plane, which is this mortal world, by the vertical plane, the metaphysical axis, which plunges into the mirror. The cross-roads, then, is the point of access to the world of les Invisibles, which is the soul of the cosmos, the source of life force, the cosmic memory, and the cosmic wisdom. As the daily life of a man depends upon his constant communication with his own gros-bon-ange—his own memory, intelligence, imagina-tion and invention—so the Haitian, individually and collec-tively, would communicate and draw upon the world of les Invisibles. For this reason, the cross-roads is the most important of all ritual figures. Where other cultures might conceive of the physical and the metaphysical as, at best, a parallelism, a necessarily irreconcilable dualism, the Haitian peasant resolves the relationship in the figure of right angles.

The foot of this vertical plane rests in the waters of the abyss, the source of all life. Here is *Guinée*, Africa, the legendary place of racial origin. Here, on the Island Below the Sea, the loa have their permanent residence, their primal location. To it the souls of the dead return, taking marine or insect forms until their reclamation into the world,[12] their rebirth, as if the ancient myth had anticipated the statements of evolutionary science. To address oneself to the earth, then, to rap upon it in ceremonies, to pour libations upon it, to dig into it and there to deposit offerings, to kneel and touch lips or forehead to it—these are gestures addressed not to the earth itself, but to the cosmos which is contained within it.[13] Whether drawn in flour on flat ground, or traced in the air, the sign of the cross-roads is always the juncture of the horizontal with the vertical, where the communication between worlds is established and the traffic of energies and forces between them is set up. It is at this point of intersection that the food for the loa is placed; and here also that they emerge to act upon the material world.

Particularly are trees the great natural highway of such traffic. And the leaves, properly plucked and treated, may therefore carry divine and healing properties. The most ancient of loa are known as *loa racine* (root loa); the songs tell of their "racine sans but" (root without end). The master of the island below the sea, *Grand Bois D'Ilet*, is often represented by a branch.[14] And if one or another tree is particularly consecrated to this loa or that, it is not because the loa is the spirit *of* the tree, it is, rather, in the sense of that tree as a preferred avenue of divine approach. The stylized tree, its branches and roots symmetrically extended to both sides of an horizon, is signaled, over and over, in the vevers. As center-post—*poteau-mitan*—this same vertical avenue, axis of the metaphysical cosmos, is built into the very center of the *peristyle*,[15] the ceremonial enclosure. Around this poteau-mitan revolve the ritual movements and the dance; at its base the offerings are placed; and through it the loa enter the peristyle.

Since this vertical dimension exists at any and all places, one has but to signal intersection. The sign of the cross appears

VEVER FOR GHEDE

everywhere, whenever communication or traffic between the worlds is to be indicated. The vertical dimension comprehends both the abyss below and the heavens above the earth, the dimension of infinity; the horizontal comprehends all men, all space and matter.*

All ceremonials begin with the salute to the guardian of the cross-roads, the loa principle of crossing, of communication with the divine world. Yet the figure of cross-roads can be seen from the perspective of either of the worlds which it straddles. When approached as interlocutor with the loa, keeper of the gate, whose permission gives access to the life source, he is saluted as Legba, and his symbolic color is white. But that world of the Invisibles is also the cosmic cemetery of the souls of all the dead. Hence, if it is to deal with les Invisibles as the residue of the dead, the figure is black, is Ghede, God of the Dead. The rituals conclude with a salutation to him.

Ghede is the dark figure which attends the meeting of the quick and the dead. This is the loa who, repository of all the knowledges of the dead, is wise beyond all the others. And if

* For a more complete statement of this principle, see pp. 97–100, *infra*.

the souls of the dead enter the depths by the passage of which Ghede is guardian, the loa and the life forces emerge from that same depth by the same road. Hence he is Lord of Life as well as of Death. His dance is the dance of copulation; in the chamber dedicated to his worship, the sculptured phallus may lie side by side with the three grave-diggers' tools. He is the protector of children and the greatest of the divine healers. He is the final appeal against death. He is the cosmic corpse which informs man of life. The cross is his symbol, for he is the axis both of the physical cycle of generation and the metaphysical cycle of resurrection. He is the beginning and the end.[16]

5

THE MARASSA—TWO AND TWO EQUALS FIVE

Ghede, loa of life and death, is the corpse of the first man, who, in his original twinned nature, can be thought of as a cosmic totality segmented by the horizontal axis of the mirror divide into identical twins. The worship of the Marassa, the Divine Twins, is a celebration of man's twinned nature: half matter, half metaphysical; half mortal, half immortal; half human, half divine. The concept of the Marassa contains, first, the notion of the segmentation of some original cosmic totality. In Voudoun songs, there still exist vestigial references to the ancient African myths of origin. The word Silibo (and the loa Gran' Silibo) which is sometimes mentioned in songs, is the African Dahomean word for a *tohwiyo*, a founder of an ancient sib; the Dahomean tohwiyos are considered to be the offspring of one human and one supernatural parent.[17] Today the Marassa are said to be the first children of God and their feast has, in some cases, been assimilated to Christmas,[18] itself a celebration of a holy child, offspring of one human and one supernatural parent. The sense of firstness, newness, beginning, innocence—in sum, the sense of the childhood of the race, is preserved in the fact that the Marassa are still conceived of as

. SOULS OF THE DEAD, LODGED IN WHITE-WRAPPED GOVIS. The phoenix, painted on this Voudoun altar, represents one of the patron deities of this hounfor.

2. INITIATE, EMERGING AS NEW-BORN. Rituals of birth, initiation, death and reclamation all involve white coverings. The protective, ritual mask is of palm fringe.

children, and when they possess a person, they play at marbles and other children's games. The food destined for them can later be offered only to children.[19]

Yet, if they are the first humans, they are also the first, the original Dead. The Dead and the Marassa are, indeed, cele⁄brated on the same occasion, All Souls' Night.* The first food offered at death rituals, which are conducted under the loa Ghede, is for Legba, guardian of the cross⁄roads, and for the Marassa; the plate for the latter is then given to children, with the ritual question: "Are you now satisfied?"[20] And if they are the first dead, they are also, by logical extension, the first ancestors, hence the first ancestral loa. As origin of all loa, the Marassa are saluted first, in ceremonies, before the loa. In a certain sense they are considered even stronger than the loa. "Papa Marassa is the one who must be fed before all the gods." Nothing can be accomplished, particularly no magic, without their proper and precedent salutation.[21]

The metaphysical character of the Divine Twins is reflected in the beliefs and practices relating to contemporary twins, who are understood as two parts of a whole, hence sharing one soul just as the *plat⁄Marassa* (the plate for the food offered to the Divine Twins) consists of two clay bowls joined together.[22] Since the twins are, essentially, one, that which affects one part affects the other and whatever disease or accident may beset one twin is understood to threaten the other; and their violent separation may lead to disaster. Every effort is made to have all their important activities, such as marriage, occur simultane⁄ously. Moreover, the concept of the Divine Twins as straddling the great divide, and thus being half in the metaphysical world, is also carried over to contemporary twins, who are considered to be endowed with powers of divination and magic.

But the Marassa, as the first cosmic totality, may also be thought of as intersected on the vertical axis as well as the horizontal one. The intersection on the vertical axis would

* Hallowe'en, in our culture, also relates children with the celebration of the Dead.

yield two halves of which each rests partly in the physical and partly in the metaphysical world. This is the segmentation of the first androgynous cosmic whole which yielded the differentiation: male and female.[23] Thus the Marassa are the parents of the race, and this progenitive function gives them, in fact, their major importance. They are feasted at harvest time[24] (which seems to be a more ancient placing than Christmastide) and the *mangé Marassa*, as their feast is called, is part of a general fertility ritual. They are also especially invoked at childbirth, to aid in making the delivery easy.[25] At the canzo ceremony, which marks the spiritual birth of the initiate, a little boy and girl are called in to baptize and name the one newly born, filling here the rôle of the Marassa as parents.[26] The service of the Marassa does not necessarily refer to any known twins in the history of the family, but as the source of all mankind, they are the ancestors of every family line: "Papa Marassa, who represents the four races."[27]

But the Haitian myth has gone beyond the concept of Marassa of the same sex, as metaphysical reflection, and Marassa of opposite sexes, as progenitive differentiation. The most common ritual service is for the *Marassa-Trois*, a constellation of three, invoked as *Marassa-Dossu-Dossa*. The vever for this service is a figure of three, and the food plate consists of three small earthen bowls joined to a single head. It is a figure which yields, simultaneously, all possible metaphysical variations. It may be seen as the affirmation of the cosmic totality, as the statement that: whether segmented horizontally or vertically, such segmentation does not liberate the parts from their relationship as a totality. In this sense it is the affirmation of cosmic unity as opposed to the dualism which results from the effort to make of segmentation a total separation.[28] But this trinity may also be seen from the opposite direction, so that the third element is understood as the issue of the twins, and in this sense—male, female and issue—it is an affirmation of multiplicity.[29] Here is the statement that generation is the result of the relationship of the segments. Sometimes this figure of three is ritualistically elaborated in various senses simultaneously. The apex of the triangle of the Marassa-Trois is a statement of the androgynous, cosmic whole; the legs of the triangle signify its vertical segmentation into male (Dossu) and female (Dossa); and these legs are each, in turn, horizontally segmented into the physical body and the metaphysical soul.[30]

For the Haitian, then, it is the relationship of segments which is important. The Twins are not to be separated into competitive, conflicting dualism. In Voudoun one *and* one make three; two *and* two make five; for the *and* of the equation is the third and fifth part, respectively, the relationship which makes all the parts meaningful. The figure of five contains man's entire nature: his single origin and his multiple progeny, his mortal matter and his immortal image, his humanity and his divinity. The figure five is as the four of the cross-roads plus the swinging of the door which is the point itself of crossing, the moment of arrival and departure.

In the concept of the Cosmic Totality of the First, single Source, in the Divine Trinity of les Morts, les Mystères et les Marassa, in the Caballa of the Quintessence* of man's life, the Haitian reaffirms the same principle as an indivisible, prime number. It is the dynamic, the energy, the eternal catalyst which first gave meaning and life to the separate elements of the first chaos.

6

THE RITUALS OF DEATH

It is as if the life of a person were a period during which the various universal elements contributed to and coalesced in that singular, unique amalgam, a specific person, composed of a body, a gros-bon-ange, understood as the spiritual double of the body, and the ti-bon-ange or spirit.[31] The rituals of death are designed to restore each successively to its proper province.

* "Quintessence": (1) the fifth or last and highest essence of power in a natural body; (2) the essence of a thing in its most concentrated form.

If stones and govis serve as physical receptacles for loa, and if the loa can even possess the living body of a man, it is because the Haitian does not, and could not, believe in physical resurrection. He is too close to the constant limitations of the flesh, its fatigues and its weaknesses, its vulnerability to disease, its insatiable, harassing need for food, its too frequent mortality. Being so intimately aware of the cycles and processes of nature, of vegetable growth and animal development, he would never propose a special quality to human beings on a physical level. The body is of the province of matter, and while it may be animated by the soul, or possessed by a loa, it is, in itself, only matter and, as such, must, upon death, be restored to matter.

The death rituals relating to the body are, in sum, directed against physical resurrection—against, on the one hand, a false death, and, on the other, a false life. The initial act of those surviving is to determine that the death is real and not a false death brought about by magic. For, if the regular rituals that dissociate the soul from the body should be performed in ignorance of the fact that the death is false, the body would remain as a live but emptied vessel, subject to the direction of any alien psychic force (usually the malevolent one which engineered the magic precisely for such a purpose). The dread zombie,[32] the major figure of terror, is precisely this: the body without a soul, matter without morality.* To avoid this

* The popular notion—outside Haiti—pictures the zombie as an enormously powerful giant who, being soulless and incapable of moral judgement, is inaccessible to reason, entreaty or any other dissuasion if he is directed to a malevolent purpose by his controlling force. This notion reflects a confusion as to the function of a zombie. Actually, the very essence of magic is *psychic* rather than physical force, and it is by such relatively subtle means that a magician would attain his malevolent ends. The choice of physically powerful individuals for zombies is precisely because their major function is not as instruments of malevolence, but as a kind of uncomplaining slave-labor to be used in the fields, the construction of houses, etc. While the Haitian does not welcome any encounter with a zombie, his real dread is that of being made into one himself. This is not because he fears hard work, for he is accustomed to this; besides, the characteristic insensibility of the zombie precludes any pain or suffering for him. The terror is of a moral nature, related to the deep-rooted value which the Haitian attaches to powers of consciousness and the attendant

development, all measures are taken to make certain that the body is truly lifeless and therefore physically useless. It may be killed again, with a knife through the heart; or its burial may be accompanied by any number of ruses to circumvent a possible resurrection.[33] For example, a plant may be placed in the coffin containing so many seeds that anyone coming to raise the body, but being compelled to count the seeds first, could never accomplish his task before daybreak.* Care is taken, as well, that no parts rightfully belonging to the dead matter should remain in circulation in the living world. Such precautions against a false life, which might also be put to magic and malevolent use, are numerous. The water in which the corpse is bathed is carefully poured into a hole. The three drops of fluid believed to be in a dead man's mouth, under-stood somehow as the final secretion, the residue of the body's life, must not spill out. The hair and nails are clipped and buried, with special care, alongside the corpse. Together with

capacity for moral judgement, deliberation and self-control. In the daily life of the Haitian, this value is reflected in his distaste for the confusions and the lack of self-control which may result from drunkenness, and it is extremely rare to see a Haitian in even the least stage of inebriation. The same value is reflected also in his preference for controlled, and even self-consciously formal behaviour, and any departure from such codes of social conduct is censured by the epithet: "Malelevé!" (Ill-mannered! Uncouth!). In the soulless zombie the Haitian sees the ultimate extension of that which he despises in any context: the loss of one's powers of perception, evaluation and self-control. Thus, the Haitian does not share the notion of the cultivated primitivist—that free, naïve and unselfconscious naturalness is a condition of essential goodness and or that the exercise of the human intellect tends to run counter to the good direction of the divine essence in man. On the contrary, the Haitian conceives of goodness or morality as a function of man's consciousness, experience, information, understanding and discipline; and he conceives of ritual as being a means by which men induce the essentially *amoral* forces of the universe towards moral ends. In the final analysis human consciousness, with all its attendant powers and potentials, holds the highest position in Voudoun metaphysics. It is this which the Haitian understands by esprit and which he separates from the matter of the body, rescues from the abyss, leaves as ancestral legacy to his descendants, and upon which, eventually, he confers the status of divinity. A zombie is nothing more than a body deprived of its conscious powers of cerebration; for the Haitian, there is no fate more terrible.

* Magical logic requires the magician to count the seeds he finds.

these precautions go certain efforts to purify the matter before its return to the earth. For the most part, these consist of rituals of cleansing. In the case of persons dying of leprosy and other such maladies, or from a stroke of lightning, however, a special kind of "quarantine" is prescribed, as well as numerous other, comparatively complicated ritualistic measures.

These rites for the body of the deceased are relatively in, significant in comparison to the African traditions related to the non,physical components of the person. Of these com, ponents, the ti,bon,ange requires the least ritual labor. Indeed it is characteristic of the almost anonymous, transcendent, spiritual nature of the ti,bon,ange that it is automatically liberated at the moment of death and hovers over the body for nine days before ascending to heaven. The ti,bon,ange is understood partially as guardian: a Haitian who drinks much, for example, but does not become drunk, is said to have a "ti,bon,ange who drinks for him". But it is also the objective conscience: the ti,bon,ange cannot lie, and, if questioned through the sleep of a person, will always tell the truth. Apart from this, it is not subject to manipulation, although a cere, mony may be performed to fortify it if it is in a weakened condition.[34] It is, in a sense, the objective, impersonal, spiritual component of the individual. In the rites of the dead it plays no rôle.

The major death ritual is the ceremony of *dessounin*, a ritual of "degradation", whose purpose is to detach from the body both the gros,bon,ange—the personal soul or self—and the loa maît,tête—the divine loa which is the "master of the head". Of the various (and sometimes numerous) loa which a man may inherit there is always one which is manifestly dominant. This loa is usually the first to have possessed him and through, out his life it is his most familiar and intimate divinity. It is the maît,tête who is that man's special patron, and who is most concerned as his guardian; and, logically, it is this loa to which he is most indebted, who has the most facile access to his head and body, and who can be the most demanding and exacting.

The maît⁄tête is his special agent in the world of the Mysteres and the other loa in his head are, in a sense, under the super⁄vision of the maît⁄tête. It is understood that with the liberation of the maît⁄tête, the liberation of the other loa is automatically and simultaneously achieved.

In a certain sense, the maît⁄tête is the divine parent of the gros⁄bon⁄ange, the psychic inheritance from the parents. The ceremony of *dessounin* thus accomplishes two separate but related actions: it severs the loa cord of the gros⁄bon⁄ange; and it separates the gros⁄bon⁄ange from its physical parent—the now defunct matter of the body—launching it as an independent spiritual entity into the spiritual universe, where it, in turn, becomes either part of the general spiritual heritage of the descendants of that person, or even, perhaps, the divine parent, the loa maît⁄tête of some subsequent gros⁄bon⁄ange.

The ceremony of *dessounin* is concerned, then, with ful⁄filling the conditions necessary for a proper remission of the divine heritage.[35] It is felt that if it is neglected, the family would suffer greatly and be plagued by the loa, and this emphasis upon the need of liberating the soul has sometimes been under⁄stood as an effort to send the soul to its heavenly abode so that it might there "rest in peace". But such an interpretation, in terms of Christian concepts, could not logically hold for a people whose major preoccupation is, precisely, to re⁄activate the souls of the dead, to consult them for advice, and to demand their constant intervention. On the contrary, if the separation were not achieved, it is the corpse that would not rest in peace, since it would continue to be animated by psychic powers, both the divine loa and the gros⁄bon⁄ange. And both of these would certainly rage against the family who had failed to liberate them from defunct matter, and, in so doing, also broken the chain by which the divine heritage of the race is extended forward.

Once liberated, the loa and the gros⁄bon⁄ange pursue their separate courses. The loa may return to the abysmal waters, since that is the permanent home of the loa. And he may at any time thereafter possess anyone else he chooses. Moreover, he has been already inherited by the children. But the gros⁄bon⁄ange in contrast, must, in a sense, share in the death of the body. If during life it is placed in a receptacle, a canari, or pot⁄de⁄tête, and if that receptacle then is stolen so that magic may be exercised upon the body through the gros⁄bon⁄ange, the person cannot die until the two are reunited.[36] It descends to the abysmal waters and is there confined—unlike the loa—for a year and a day. This period in the abyss is not a purgatory: to be cold and wet is, for the frequently exposed Haitian peasant, a mild discomfort at most. It is a period, rather, of oblivion, a token death from which it must be reclaimed, or reborn, if it is to achieve any degree of immortality.

7

THE RITES OF RECLAMATION—
THE CEREMONY OF RETIRER D'EN BAS DE L'EAU

A year and a day following the death of a person, the family undertakes to reclaim his soul from the waters of the abyss below the earth and to lodge it in a govi where it may hence⁄forth be invoked and consulted in the event of illness or other difficulties and so may participate in all the decisions that normally unite the members of the family in counsel. Thus the aid of his knowledge, the disciplines of his moral authority, and the inspirations of his intelligence are re⁄incorporated as a functioning force in the reality of his family's daily life.

For this ceremony, the family requires the services of a houngan (or *mambo*—priestess), whose studies and ritual ordeals have endowed him with the power to summon les Invisibles* to manifest themselves in the material dimension of

---

* In some regions a mambo is considered of lower rank than a houngan but when referred to in this book, it is as his equal. The word houngan is often used alone, for convenience in referring to priestly activities, but it should be under⁄stood that a mambo might also fulfill such ritual functions.

this world, whether as a voice or through a possession. Since such a ceremony involves the services of the houngan's entire personnel, who must be brought together to assist him, as well as the purchase of various offerings and other accoutrements, it may be relatively costly for a single family. Consequently it is frequently postponed until a year's interval has elapsed for several bereaved families in the neighborhood.

On the appointed evening, the participants assemble gradually in the houngan's peristyle (a section of the place of worship). Those who are not occupied with the preparations in the adjacent hounfor (altar chamber) dance a few rounds while the drummers warm up.* A small, tent-like structure has been extemporized from a white sheet and set up a short distance away in the large courtyard and since there is neither pond nor stream here, a trough of water, through the surface of which the reclaimed souls will emerge, has been placed within. This trough is the local realization of the abyss.[37]

A stretch of straw mats is laid on the ground leading from the door of the hounfor. Led by the houngan, the white-robed *hounsis*** (initiates), carrying the govis, which have been consecrated and wrapped in white, emerge in a processional toward the white tent. They take care that their bare feet do not touch the ground, for les Invisibles could mount through them and lodge themselves in the jars. As they progress, the mats which insulate them against such contact are hurriedly gathered from behind and laid out once more in front. Then a path is extended through the sacred precinct, winding among trees that are each sacred to some deity. At the entrance to the

* The peristyle is a roofed structure, open at the sides, in which most of the ceremonials and dances take place. (See illustration 10, facing p. 167.) The hounfor may mean all the physical area, ritual equipment and personnel under the authority of a single priest; it may also mean specifically the small chamber containing the altar of one or more loa. (See illustration 1, facing p. 38.) When the term hounfor is used in apposition to peristyle, as in the paragraph here, it denotes the altar chamber. When used without any distinguishing contrast, it refers to the totality.

** The hounsis are those who have passed through certain stages of initiation and are therefore qualified to assist in various ritual activities.

tent, the hounsis stretch out upon the mats. The wide, round mouths of the govis, still held on top of their heads, point toward the entrance like so many empty, hungry skulls. White sheets are spread over the bodies of the hounsis, covering them completely. To one side the drummers and the *houngenikon* (the official leader of the singing) are prepared to greet the souls with the appropriate songs, while to the other side stands the la⁄place (the master of ceremonies, major assistant to the houngan), holding a whip with which to fend off any evil or simply trespassing spirits who might invade the jars.

The shadow of the houngan, projected from within the tent by the flickering of the candle, dances and glides over the folds of the cloth as he completes his final preparations. Then the candle is extinguished. But the moon is bright. It picks out, with a sharp brilliance, the round mound of the tent, the regular stretch of the limbs under the white sheets, the easy vigilant stance of the la⁄place in white trousers and shirt, the white dresses and white⁄kerchief bound heads of the partici⁄pants.

And now begins the rhythmic beat and ring of the priest's *asson,** the instrument of his power over the world of les Invisibles. At times it sounds with a harsh, grating insistence, and at times as a gentle, ringing murmur; but never does it for a moment falter. It is as if this antenna of sound, projected into the dark air, had to be uninterruptedly built up, lengthened, spun and sent forward, until it should penetrate into the deepest recesses of the dark regions of the abyss. Over and over, past the patient silence of the seated figures, past the slight stirrings of small animals in the underbrush, the distant howl of a dog, the squeal of a pig somewhere embroiled in the rope

* The *asson*, or sacred rattle, can be owned and used only by one who has passed through the ceremonies that elevate to the rank of priesthood. It is a gourd with a handle⁄like formation on it and it rattles either by virtue of snake⁄bones or other such objects inside, or because of a loose webbed beading woven around the outside. This latter is exclusively a sacred rattle where a simple gourd, filled with small objects, is commonly used as a musical instrument not to be confounded with the sacred rattle.

that holds it, the cry of roosters beginning high in the mountains and passing downward toward the sea, the small conversations of the night travelers carrying their high loads on
their heads along the nearby road to the city market, over and
over, this rhythmic sound insists like a cosmic signal calling
toward the space of another universe.

And over its grating and ringing, the voice of the houngan
adds the first persuasions of his own invocations. His voice is
low with intimacy, conversational in its cadence, the phrasing
at times urgent, at times invocative. He is addressing les
Invisibles. To those outside, who merely overhear, the words
are, for the most part, unintelligible. But it is known that the
prayers include those addressed to Legba, loa of the cross-
roads, and Baron Samedi, or Ghede, loa of the dead.

The white sheet which in this ceremony of the recall of the
dead is stretched over the bodies of the hounsis is as the winding
sheet that covered the corpse. It is simultaneously the swaddling
clothes of the new-born infant—who, shortly following its
birth, is carried to the sacred trees of the familial courtyard and
there introduced to the familial deities. This sheet is also the
white envelope that encloses the initiate during his ordeal by
fire; and it is the white canopy that covers him the following
morning, when he emerges for his second, his spiritual birth,
to be led, like the infant, to the sacred trees.* It is the envelope
of the womb; and now, at this moment of the *retirer d'en bas
de l'eau*, the houngan, functioning as midwife, assists the third
birth, the rebirth of the soul from the abysmal waters.[38]

The tone of his voice changes from that of prayer and invocation to a quality of patient yet persistent urging as the houngan
strains to draw the dead from the land below. He in turn
protests, persuades, verges on exasperation, returns to a tone
of cajoling, or, once more, to a patient effort to persuade.
Occasionally the name of the first person summoned can be
heard.

He calls for Papa Telemach. Faintly, at first, and then

* See illustration 2, facing p. 39.

rapidly growing stronger, a whining quaver is heard by those outside the tent. Telemach is an old, old man. He begins by· complaining that his family has left him in the cold and wet too long. The houngan interrupts to excuse the delay: the family is poor, and, as the old man knows, the ceremony is costly. But Telemach, in the fashion of old men, seems either not to hear or not to wish to listen. There is much discussion. The low, recognizable voice of the houngan breaks in upon the complaints of the high, half-broken voice. At times the two seem to be insisting on their separate points simultaneously. At other times a sound of gurgling water eclipses the old man's protestations and some moments elapse before the conversation is resumed. One is listening to an old man, who has had too much time to brood upon an imagined neglect, being reasoned with by a friend of the family, who would be a mediator. The old fellow demands to know, finally, who, of the family, has undertaken to reclaim him. The houngan restates this question in a louder voice. From somewhere in the darkness, a girl calls, "It is I, Lamerci, papa." This affords the old man an opportunity to recapitulate his complaints, and to make reference to some intimate family disputes and incidents. The daughter apologizes, giggles, is overcome by embarrassment at this public airing of private family affairs. Telemach finally asks concerning the welfare of those who are not present and Lamerci reports that the brother is ill. There is a long exchange, a consultation over the symptoms and as to whether the brother has done this or that. The houngan, feeling that too much time is being spent on this individual, tactfully tries to interrupt, but the old man stubbornly continues until, presently, he prescribes a complex herbal treatment. Again the houngan suggests that it is time, now, for him to enter the govi, but the old soul refuses to surrender his moment of glory. He retorts that, having been kept waiting so long, he will not be rushed. General laughter breaks out and both the priest and the daughter plead with him to be reasonable. He renews his original complaints. He will not be readily consoled. But at last, and reluctantly, he prepares to surrender. He asks for a song of salutation to his guardian loa, his maît/tête. The houngenikon thereupon starts off the song, the drums and the chorus join in and when it is ended the houngan inquires: "Are you satisfied?" The old man agrees. There is a pause in the conversation. The body of one of the hounsis under the white sheet stiffens, contracts, her limbs jerk as if from inner shock. It is understood that the soul has entered the govi on her head.*

During all this time the rattle and bell have not ceased sounding for a moment, and now that communication with the abysmal regions has been established, the other souls follow more readily. One even has the impression that they are crowd/ ing in a line at the far end, that they jostle each other and com/ pete to emerge from the cold, wet regions. Sometimes the houngan seems to argue with two of them at the same time; he pleads for patience, insists on one's seniority over the other, asks their names, labors to expedite the entire procedure as fairly as possible. A girl begins weeping for joy when she hears her mother's voice. Another one excitedly recognizes her father.

And then a certain voice rises higher, more plaintively than the others. This is a man, weeping. The houngan asks for an identification. The answer is unclear. He asks again, but does not recognize the name. Finally he calls out to the assemblage: "Does any one know this man?" There is no answer. "Where are you from?" "Jacmel." It is a town on the opposite end of the island. Someone wisecracks: "Father, you certainly lost your way", and the whole crowd laughs. The voice explodes into a fit of rage. "It is all very well for you to laugh now, but wait until it is your turn, and your good/for/nothing family doesn't trouble to bring you up." Then, just as suddenly, the voice breaks down into a fit of sobbing. His anger and his sorrow have sobered the crowd, and compassion moves them. The

* The exact means by which this transference is achieved is one of the secret knowledges of the priesthood, as is the means by which the voices of the reclaimed souls emerge, apparently from the trough of water.

voice of the houngan, gentle and sad, explains that unfortunately all the govis are already reserved for certain dead.[39] It is
impossible for anyone to receive him now. Perhaps his family
has had some financial reverses and surely, any day now, they
will make the ceremony. Gently, tactfully, the houngan asks
the soul to withdraw, to go back down, to permit the others to
emerge. The sobbing begins to grow fainter, more distant,
finally fades away. In the darkness someone murmurs, "poor
vagabond", and the others nod in compassionate agreement.

Someone begins telling of a similar incident and a general
babble sets up in the court. Angrily the voice of the houngan
shouts out to them. How can he be expected to hear the voices
of the dead when the living are making such a confounded
racket. The chastened crowd falls immediately silent. There is
no sound but the grating and ringing of the asson for several
moments. Then a woman's voice, its timbre somehow characteristic of a market-place vendor, can be heard clearly.

"Business must be pretty good", she says to the houngan, "if
the family can manage to pay your fees." The crowd bursts out
laughing, and the houngan's angry retort is lost in the noise.
"Or perhaps", she says, "little Cocotte, there, has developed a
side line." The niece who has been referred to, turns and flees
while the crowd laughs louder than ever. "It's Marie, all right",
one person says to the other. "It's certainly her", they repeat.
The spectators are very alert, ready for the good show that Marie
would always put on with her off-color comments. "You ought
not to say that", the houngan says. "Cocotte is a good girl, you
know that", and he begins talking rapidly, to avoid any further
embarrassing comments.

Some of the souls arrive in anger and are difficult for the
houngan to handle. One, apparently very powerful, gives him
great trouble, and at a certain moment the houngan's voice
seems to be choked off, as though the spirit were threatening to
possess him. He calls for his la-place to assist him. There is a
confusion within the tent, and it is as though the soul has had
to be forced into the govi, for the hounsi whose jar receives him

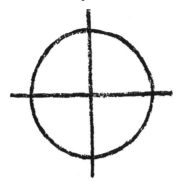

CROSS/ROADS AND CENTER/POST

jumps up violently, as if struck. The la/place and the houn/ genikon rush to her assistance, forcing her to lie down again, and replace the white shroud, which she has disarranged, as rapidly as possible.

Finally the task is completed. It has taken several hours, but the seven souls have all been reclaimed. The sound of the asson stops. The communication is broken. The hounsis rise to carry the govis back to the hounfor, but their walk is now uncertain, as if they were bearing great weights on their heads. Some of the souls are not resting easily, as yet, and their bearers totter from side to side. Within the hounfor the govis are arranged upon the altar, and are left in the custody of the houngan.*

In the adjoining peristyle the drums have begun for the *danse de rejuissance*, the dance of rejoicing, but the work has been long and everyone is tired. The ceremony of *bruler/zin*, a vivifying ritual, which had been scheduled for this evening to "warm" the spirits, is postponed until the following evening. The houngan seems extremely fatigued and withdraws immediately. After a few rounds of drumming the gathering disperses.

* See illustration 1, facing p. 38.

CHAPTER II

Les Serviteurs

I

THE CHRISTIAN INFLUENCE

THE divine heritage to which the *serviteur* Titon was born was not only rich numerically in the number of its gods, but testified to the fact that the family lines on both his father's and his mother's side had served their deities with such consistency and fullness that they had maintained the great ancient *racine loa* in a condition of effective vigor. Some time after his father had died, his mother had contracted an eye disease, and she had subsequently been converted to Protestantism on the grounds that her affliction was punishment by the Christian God for serving Voudoun loa. The fact that the disease did not diminish was interpreted as an inducement for her to convert her children, similarly, and this she had succeeded in doing with her four daughters. Titon alone had refused to abandon the ancestral loa, although, like all other Voudoun serviteurs, he sincerely insisted that he believed in the Christian God and in Jesus, and always made ritual obeisance to these before passing on to the Voudoun service. As a matter of fact, he knew the Catholic litanies so well that he was often called upon to assist the houngan by standing in as the *prêt-savanne*, or bush priest, whose function it is to invoke the benediction of the Christian deity upon the Voudoun ceremony to follow.[1]

Yet it was the African tradition which, in a sense, had prepared this serviteur to acknowledge God as "le gran' maître". In the South Rhodesian myth of origin there is a first god, called Maori, who created the first man, Mwuetsi, and his two wives, Massassi (who bore the entire vegetable kingdom of the earth) and Morongo (who brought forth animals and men).[2] The Ewe-speaking people of Dahomey likewise have a

54

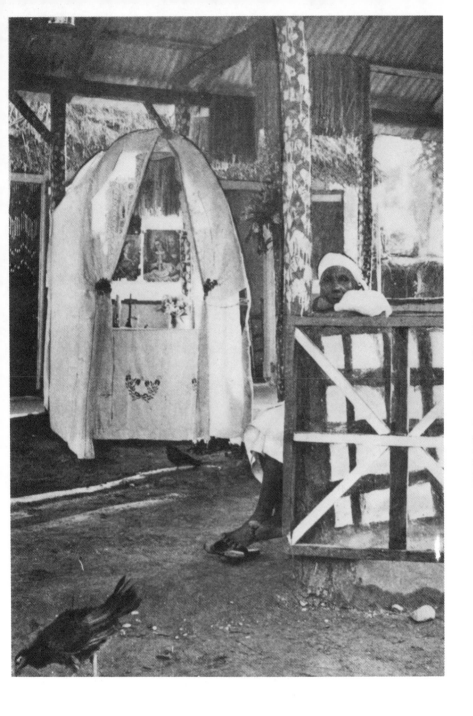

3. NICHE FOR ERZULIE. Voudoun has assimilated compatible objects from non-African cultures, such as the Catholic images and French-inspired embroidery above.

4. INDIAN INFLUENCE. The striped motif of the center-post, the sacred vever drawings, and the three-horned deity are among the many indications of Indian influence.

legend of a first deity, Nanan-bouclou, who was both male and female, and who created the twin children, Mawu-Lisa, from whom sprang all the deities.[3] Throughout Africa this first deity, the source of the universe, was considered too greatly elevated to be concerned with the petty affairs of human beings,[4] and consequently was rarely worshipped. When Christianity taught that such a primal figure was concerned with human affairs, and was to be personally and intimately addressed, this was accepted as a welcome modification of the African tradition. If religious belief can be understood to range from an almost abstract divinity at one pole to the manipulations of magic at the other, then the Christian deity—who was subject to persuasion by prayer, and who might intervene as a supernatural force—was much easier and more comfortable than the usual High God of Africa, whose absolute objectivity placed him beyond the pale of human reference.[5]

Such a comparison reverses the orthodox evaluation of "primitive mentality", which has been characterized as incapable of abstract concepts, bound to material specifics (as in animism), and tending to personalize in precise and immediate terms the general forces of nature. "Primitive mentality", on the contrary, conceives in hierarchical terms. Almost inevitably it proposes a myth of the world's origin from an abstracted source which is not worshipped, just as the scientific mind amply recognizes a first source and evolutionary principle and concerns itself primarily with modifications of the subsequent issue. The "primitive" then places, on a second level, the first creation of God, the original man and woman, who partake of the divine nature in its loftiest sense but are human. The deities governing the affairs of men are then on a third level. These can modify but they cannot create. They can help a garden grow and can bring rain, but they did not create either the seed or the water. In effect, the deities to which the "primitive" addresses himself, for all such modifications, are analogous to the Catholic saints.

Like the saints, the loa are considered to be on a level far below God. According to the Haitian peasant, Agaou (the loa of thunder) says, "If God is willing."[6] Like the saints, the loa were once human and are the immediate guardians of the people. Like the saints, they have special provinces of action. Is it so strange, then, that, failing other images, the Voudoun serviteur today covers his altars with the Catholic pictures of the saints, which he understands as representations of the loa? St. Patrick, in the act of sending the serpents into the sea, is Damballah, the great serpent deity—since there are serpents in the picture. The chromo of Lazarus, in which he is an old man with a staff and attended by dogs, represents old Legba, guardian of the cross-roads, to whom dogs were sacred in Dahomey. St. Ulrique is Agwé, god of the waters, since he holds a fish. St. Isidore, dressed in humble garb and kneeling in the fields, is Azacca, god of agriculture. Nothing could please the serviteur more than the fact that there are, indeed, such inexpensive and colorful ready-made representations of his loa.[7]

Voudoun would not have come into existence, nor would it still be flourishing so vigorously, if it had been governed by men rigidly dedicated to superficial sectarian distinctions. It is, in fact, a monumental testament to the extremely sophisticated ability of the West African to recognize a conceptual principle common to ostensibly disparate practices and to fuse African, American Indian, European and Christian elements dynamically into an integrated working structure.* Where, at first glance, it might seem that Christianity had triumphed over Voudoun, it becomes clear, on closer study, that Voudoun has merely been receptive to compatible elements from a sister faith and has integrated these into its basic structure, subtly transfiguring and adjusting their meaning, where necessary, to the African tradition.** The cross, for example, has been assimilated to the cross-roads. Baptism was already a Negro

* See illustration 3, facing p. 54, and 4, facing p. 55.
** The carnivals on Mardi Gras and especially on Good Friday (the "Rara" Festival, as it is called) scarcely reflect, in tone, the Christian events which they ostensibly celebrate.

tradition. The triple libation for "les Mystères, les Morts et les Marassa" is applied to the Father, Son and Holy Ghost. And the concept of trinity has blended well, on many grounds (Marassa-Trois, and three as a magical number), with African belief. The hierarchical and pantheistic system as a whole is receptive to additional deities, and even to the prêt-savanne as a kind of colleague of the houngan, being able to assimilate them all in its own terms.[8] Against the serviteur who sin-cerely insists that he believes in the trinity, who baptizes his children and his drums, places the saints on his private altar, and makes lavish use of the sign of the cross, the Catholic Church has been, in a sense, helpless. It is in the peculiar position of trying to convert the already converted. A religious system that opposed Catholicism would have been overcome. But in the face of such tolerance, the violent efforts to eradicate Voudoun have remained relatively ineffective.

Protestantism, on the other hand, has been able to insist, more clearly, upon its incompatibility with Voudoun. Indeed, to the Voudoun serviteurs, there is a far greater incompatibility between the two branches of Christianity than there is between the Catholics and themselves.

The Haitian can even pray thus:

"In the name of God the Father, of the spirits, and of my Mystères . . . I, the only living child of my family, I haven't given up Voudoun [an allusion to the anti-Voudoun campaign]. I am asking the Saints, the Dead, the Marassa, you who are my only defense before God, you who are placed for my defense against the infernal enemy, do not stop helping me during my life. . . ."[9]

2

THE AFRICAN HERITAGE

Whether the converted members of Titon's family had dis-missed their loa ritualistically,[10] or merely abandoned them, and whether the familial govis and *pierre-loa* were still in existence somewhere or had been destroyed, is not quite clear. Neither is it all-important, for such objects, which serve to focus or localize the manifestations of the loa, do not confine them. The deities did not belong to Titon's parents, as a property; they infused the parents. And in the very same sense in which the son was the physical issue of his parents, so also, was he their spiritual issue.* His inheritance of his parents' loa, therefore, was automatic.[11]

History had made, of that heritage, a complex affair. The original Negroes had been imported from many African states, predominantly Yoruba, Dahomey, Loango, Ashanti, and Mandingo.[12] They included the Senegalese, who, according to reports of early colonial writers, were "easily dis-ciplined"; the Bambaras, considered "insolent and thieves"; the Aradas, who were "good at agriculture but very proud"; the Congos, who were "prone to desert their masters"; the Mondongos, who were "cannibalistic and cruel"; the Mines, who were "capricious, and despaired of themselves"; the Ibos, who depended much on each other and committed suicide so readily that they became known as "those who hang themselves"; the Loangos, the Mahis, the Fons, the Fulas, and dozens of other tribes.[13] All brought with them their particular traditions, their language, their gods, their rituals, their dances, their drum beats, the memory of their homelands and the names of their towns and rivers.

Inevitably, and even deliberately (for the colonists were con-cerned to minimize the strength of a people who outnumbered them), the tribes were broken up and scattered throughout the island of Haiti. Yet all these West Africans had certain basic beliefs in common: ancestor worship; the use of song, drums and dancing in the religious rituals; the possession of the wor-shipper by the god. Encouraged by the communal need of unity on the economic and political level, and by personal requirements of intermarriage, they integrated, around this core

* For a discussion of loa inheritance, see pp. 31-3 ff, *supra*.

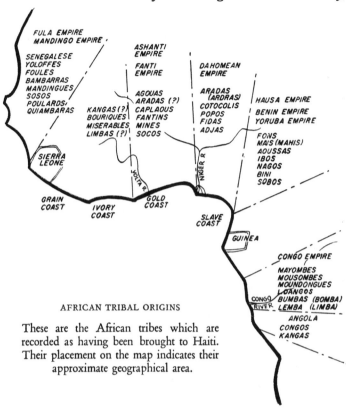

AFRICAN TRIBAL ORIGINS

These are the African tribes which are
recorded as having been brought to Haiti.
Their placement on the map indicates their
approximate geographical area.

of what they had in common, the great diversity of their tribal
systems. Obviously, since each people had a complete religious
system with its own set of major deities, there was much overlapping to be resolved. In some cases, the deity of the numerically dominant group absorbed the similar deities of the others;
or the emphatic character of one tribe, such as the warlike
quality of the Nagos, gave their deity of war, Ogoun, pre-
eminence over all other representatives of that principle. And
yet, because Voudoun was a collective creation, it did not exact
the abandonment of one tribal deity in favor of another. On
the contrary, it seemed rather to delight in as generous an
inclusion as possible. With a conscious tact that seems unique

in religious history, the original identifications were even retained. Hence, today, Voudoun (which is the Fons word for god) includes the loa (the Congo word for the spirits) of many nations; and they are invoked as stemming from their various homes.[14]

The majority of the deities are Dahomean and the rites of these are called Rada, from the town Allada. Yet everyone dances *Yanvalou*, which means "supplication" in the speech of the Whydah, the people of the Dahomean seaport of that name. And they also dance the Nago of the Yoruban people of western Nigeria, for the god of war Shango, or, as the Daho-means would have it, for Ogoun Shango. There is an Ogoun Badagry, named for a sea-coast town in western Nigeria; and an Ogoun Balindjo, after the god of the Ogoun River in western Nigeria.[15] The separate figures have been integrated around a principle, as its modifications, variations, or multiple aspects, just as individual ancestral loa, who share a similar character, become grouped together as personal variations on a principal theme. They are said to "marcher ensemble", to "walk together".[16] The African place-names, tribal indications, or family lineage names have come to serve, meanwhile, not so much as geographical identifications—which could hardly have much meaning for the contemporary serviteur—but as a means for adjectival characterization. When a deity carries, as a sort of second name, the word "Wedo" or "Oueddo", this serves not to inform us of his having been brought to Haiti by the Whydah-speaking people, but to indicate a special quality of benevolence, respected authority, and prestige.*

For it was the Dahomean culture that became dominant, and around which a major portion of the other African deities was integrated. The Rada rites stand, in a sense, therefore, for the basic African tradition. They reflect, furthermore, the emotional tone of their place of origin. For Dahomey was an absolute and well-organized monarchy, based on agriculture,

---

*At the conclusion of this chapter is a chart that attempts to organize some of the loa according to cosmic principle, tribal origin and emotional tone.

with the development of co-operative work systems. It was a well-stabilized, hierarchical nation and, within it, the deities played a protective rôle. They were the guardians of that integration, that stability, against whatever might threaten it, and so were essentially benevolent, paternal and passive, unless a need arose to defend the moral principles that they represented. But the conditions of the new world were not those of Dahomey. The stability, the integration, the traditional, established patterns were disrupted, diffused, broken and violated, often brutally. The traditional defensive, protective attitude could not suffice where there was no longer anything organized or solid to defend. It was a moment of specific and urgent need: the need for action. In the new world there arose a new nation of loa, the loa of the Caribbean: the Petro nation.

3

THE NEW WORLD ANSWER TO NEW WORLD NEEDS

The difference between Rada and Petro is not to be under-stood on a moral plane, as an opposition between good and evil, although its violence and its closeness to magic has given Petro a reputation for malevolence. The Rada deities may punish severely those who fail in their obligations toward them; and the Petro loa, if properly propitiated, will "behave".[17] As the Haitians put it, the Petro are "plus raide": more hard, more tough, more stern; less tolerant and forgiving, more practical and demanding. If the Rada loa represent the protective, guardian powers, the Petro loa are the patrons of aggressive action.

This is apparent in the nervous tension that is the emotional "color" of the Petro rites. Whereas most of the Rada drumming and dancing is on the beat, the Petro drumming and dancing is off-beat. Sometimes the distinction is revealed with great subtlety as when the cross-roads vever for Rada-Legba emphasizes the cardinal points while that for Petro-Kalfu or

Carrefour (his Petro counterpart), emphasizes the points between.[18] Sometimes the distinction is made manifest with overwhelming psychological insight. For example, whereas Erzulie, the Rada Goddess of Love, who is the epitome of the feminine principle, is concerned with love, beauty, flowers, jewelry, femininities and coquetries, liking to dance and to be dressed in fine clothes, weeping in a most feminine fashion for not being loved enough, the figure of Erzulie Ge⁄Rouge, on the Petro side, is awesome in her poignancy. When she possesses a person, her entire body contracts into the terrible paralysis of frustration; every muscle is tense, the knees are drawn up, the fists are clenched so tightly that the fingernails draw blood from the palms. The neck is rigid and the tears stream from the tightly shut eyes, while through the locked jaw and the grinding teeth there issues a sound that is half groan, half scream, the inarticulate song of in⁄turned cosmic rage.

Petro was born out of this rage. It is not evil; it is the rage against the evil fate which the African suffered, the brutality of his displacement and his enslavement. It is the violence that rose out of that rage, to protest against it.* It is the crack of the slave⁄whip sounding constantly, a never⁄to⁄be⁄forgotten ghost,[19] in the Petro rites. It is the raging revolt of the slaves against the Napoleonic forces. And it is the delirium of their triumph. For it was the Petro cult, born in the hills, nurtured in secret, which gave both the moral force and the actual organization to the escaped slaves who plotted and trained, swooped down upon the plantations and led the rest of the slaves in the revolt that, by 1804, had made of Haiti the second free colony in the western hemisphere, following the United States.** Even today the songs of revolt, of "Vive la liberté", occur in Petro ritual as a dominant theme.[20]

---

* It is still true, and extremely significant, that wherever Voudoun has been especially suppressed (at the insistence of the Catholic Church) it is the Petro rites that become dominant. Suppression always destroys first what is gentle and benevolent; it inspires rage and reaction, encourages malevolence and magic, and so creates the very thing which, theoretically, it would destroy.

** Historians of Haiti agree on fixing the beginning of the revolution on a cult

VEVER FOR PETRO

ceremony held on August 14, 1791. They also agree on the details, namely, that it was a ceremony conducted by a houngan named Boukman (he is sometimes called a *bocor*) who had been born in Jamaica. It seems that, in the middle of the ceremony, a great storm arose, and there suddenly appeared an old Negress whose body was trembling violently and who danced a "wild" dance, holding a large knife over her head. As a climax of the dance she sacrificed a black pig. All the participants drank of the blood of the pig, and swore to follow Boukman. A week later the revolution was in swing. This event is cited by Verschueren (Vol. 2, p. 26) and Simpson (II) among others. The description of the ceremony makes it clear that it was a Petro ceremony, since those are distinguished by pig sacrifices. It is quite possible that the woman was the original Marinette, or was possessed by Marinette, the major and violent female of the Petro nation. Simpson also points out that one of the inducements to revolt was the concept, proposed by several of the Petro houngans, that the souls of the dead would return to Africa. He also says that "meetings of slaves were dangerous to colonials because of the possibilities they offered for plots and revolts". Most historians do agree that Voudoun was responsible for the unity that made the revolution possible. Simpson also says that Voudoun took form between 1750 and 1790, but ceremonials must have been occurring since the arrival of the slaves from Africa, otherwise the African forms could not have been preserved. His dating does, however, link the revolution to a "preparatory" period in the development of Voudoun.

For this kind of action the Dahomean traditions had not prepared them; nor were the Rada gods the kind of deities who could inspire an enslaved people to revolt. Whence, then, did the African Negroes draw the inspiration? Where did they discover the technique that resulted in their triumph? The first slave-trade shipment to Haiti was in 1510. The first slave revolt recorded was in 1522, a mere twelve years later. The type of protest known in French as "marronage", running away into the hills, must have begun as early, if not even before. Haiti came under French rule in 1677, but this did not diminish the "marronage". It is recorded that in 1720 alone, a thousand Negroes gained their freedom in this manner; while by 1751 the number had grown to 3,500.[21] Stress has been laid on the fact that, in these circumstances, it was logical that escaped Negroes should fortify their morale by a continuation and growing emphasis upon religious practices. But almost no attention has been paid to the fact that, in those hills, they *must*, during the Spanish period, have encountered the Indians, who, being on home ground, would, no less than the Negroes, have had recourse to such escape from the brutal massacres that characterized the Spanish colonization.* Wherever and

* The emphasis upon the Indian influence, which I have undertaken here, has not been shared, to my knowledge, by other writers on Haiti, who, except for Maximilien, have been content to deal with Petro by briefly indicating that it was of new-world origin. However, I was struck by the great difference between the *ethos* of the Rada and that of the Petro rites. (*Ethos*, according to *Webster's Dictionary*, is the "characteristic spirit, prevalent tone or sentiment of a people or community; the 'genius' of an institution or system".) Gradually I began to suspect that this striking difference in ethos indicated the interpolation of Indian culture and its moral techniques. If this was true, then such an inter-polation, even more than the assimilation of Christian elements, was the monumental testament to the dynamic ability of Voudoun to keep pace with the current needs of the serviteur. It would also throw a new light upon the apparent polarity of Rada and Petro, for a comparison of the two did not really lend itself comfortably to the "good-evil" duality. For this reason I undertook to investigate whether, indeed, the Indian culture did play such a rôle. While the investigation does not presume to be definitive, it yielded such logical answers to several important problems that I have felt justified in at least a tentative assurance that such an assumption would be, in general, correct; and I have in-cluded this material and analysis as a separate Appendix (pp. 271–86, *infra*).

whenever the African and the Indian met in the hills they had two major bases for a common cause: they shared, as human beings, a hatred of the white man, who had dislocated both races and from whose brutality both were fugitives; and they had in common the so-called "primitive mentality", with religious traditions strikingly similar, toward which they both looked for their reply to this catastrophe.

It is doubtful whether any other two peoples, of different racial and continental origins, could have discovered such an astonishing coincidence of religious beliefs, not only in basic pattern but in basic ritualistic and even accessory detail. Both religious traditions had in common a creator deity as first source; myths of the first human pair, or twins; a concept of the abysmal waters as the life source; a pantheon of divinities of the elements, or natural forces; a serpent deity of prime importance; the worship of ancestral spirits; a metaphysical concept of the cardinal directions, of cross-roads, and of trees; a belief in the manifestation of psychic or cosmic forces in the physical world by possession; a belief in the manipulation and control of these forces by human beings who functioned simultaneously on religious (priest), social (king) and physical (doctor) levels. In both systems, the manipulations, on a magical level, involved fetishes that brought to focus meta-physical forces and referred either to ancestral spirits or to elemental forces (such as rain and fertility). The relationship between humans and nature was expressed in a concept of metamorphic power, the ability to change into an animal, for instance. Moreover, the worship of the metaphysical forces was ritualistic, rather than meditative, and involved, for both peoples, the idea that the energy of the metaphysical forces had to be sustained by feeding, or sacrifice, and their benediction maintained by propitiation. Ritualistically, the major faith ordeal of both systems was related to fire; and the service of supplication involved drumming and collective dancing (rather than performances by the specially chosen, as in Bali). Ritualistic accessories included rattles, in both cases. And finally, both religious traditions, being polytheistic, were mutually tolerant rather than absolutistic and exclusive. The overwhelming similarity of these two systems of belief not only precluded any antagonism but must have been a strong incen‑ tive to amalgamation, mutual assimilation and confusion. If one were to consider the material facts alone, ignoring the different emotional colorings of the two systems of rituals, the differing tensions in the attitudes of the body in the dancing and all those other nuances in which ethos is manifest, one could confound them entirely. The historical situation of the African Negro, however, made him welcome precisely the *difference*, and the moral, intellectual and magical techniques that reflected it.

As we have said, the African tradition, particularly of Dahomey, had developed a centralized state; but the more primitive decentralized, shamanistic stage of the Caribbean Indians was eminently suited to the new situation, and could serve as a methodological guide to reorganization on a de‑ centralized, democratized basis. Inevitably, such decentraliza‑ tion would lead to an emphasis on magical rather than on divine and royal authority,* and this stress would involve cabbala‑like elements already present in the Indian system. The emphasis of Indian religious practice was aggressive, imperialis‑ tic and active, assertively dynamic, which met the new‑world need of the Negro in a way that his own Dahomean religion— almost settled and passive with security—could not match. And finally, the American pattern was strongly colored by the severity of the divinities: propitiation had the violent bloody character typical of the Aztecan, Mayan and Incan cultures. Indeed, it is only logical to serve violently those divinities of whom one requires aggressive action. As an outlet for the new‑ world rage of the African, the violent or tense ritual was certainly psychologically most valid. For when divine power is to be put into action by human beings it becomes magic. Whereas the divine principle in itself is primarily natural and

---

* For further comparisons of divine and magical powers, see pp. 76–7, *infra*.

moral, and acts "in general", the magical principle[22] which brings it to focus and directs it to a desired end is deliberate, amoral and specific.

In the hills, then, their common place of refuge, the fugitive slaves of the two races must have met and joined in their common rage. For we find in the Petro—the violent, aggressive, "plus raide" side of Haitian Voudoun—an extremely powerful contribution from the Indian. Indeed, one may say that in contrast to the Rada, which is Africa or Dahomey, Petro is America. The two worlds are joined in Voudoun, yet retain their distinctions to this day: the traditional cults of the old, monarchic homeland, and the revolutionary cults of the new and terrible slaveland. Moreover, just as the broken and various African elements were combined and fused into a new, self-consistent system, so were those of the uprooted Indians— multitudes of whom were carried in slave-ships to Haiti (Hispaniola) from every shore and atoll of the Caribbean.*

One might have imagined that Ogoun, the great warrior and ironsmith on the Rada side, could have represented aggressive action; today he is the divinity most favored as guardian of a hounfor. But Ogoun is, in a sense, the honest, the chivalrous warrior; whereas the situation called less for a heroic champion than for a wily and ruthless one. There were, of course, benevolent, medicinal, therapeutic divinities among the Indians. These were retained in the Petro category—which again indicates that Petro is not so much a polar opposite, an evil cult as opposed to the good Rada, but a total cultural interpolation, with an ethos of a different tone. This fact is again indicated in the manner in which Petro was integrated into the total religious structure. The Haitian, manifesting a keen sensitivity for ethos, and an infallible sense of diplomacy, incorporated the American divinities as a "nation" of loa, a cultural rather than a moral category, just as the various African

---

* Spanish law permitted enslavement in the new world only of cannibals, others became serfs on their own land—Caribs (cannibals) were shipped about, carried by the thousand to Hispaniola.

tribal divinities had been related, in Voudoun, as a congress of divine nations.

The skill of this arrangement (if the word skill can be applied to what actually constituted a collective phenomenon) is made evident by the fact that no conflict was set up between the old world traditions and the new world techniques. Most houn⁄gans and mambos very openly "serve with both hands";[23] it is considered the sensible thing to do. At ceremonies, the Rada loa are served first; they govern initiation and all hierarchical elevation and are still the guardians of the morals and the principles; but a service for Petro often follows, since evil might result if the Petro deities were not served. The Petro are invoked particularly if there is any need for aggressive action. Moreover, the two cults are never confused. Today the cultural distinction is still preserved for Petro, even more scrupulously than for the various nations from Africa. The loa Petro are virtually never worshipped in the same peristyle with the loa Rada, unless economic circumstances absolutely prohibit the construction of a second peristyle. Petro rites are never beaten on Rada drums, whereas under certain circumstances the Congo and Ibo (the other two major nations that have best retained their identity), which properly have their own drums, are sometimes beaten on either Rada or Petro drums.*

Petro seems to have assimilated to a major extent the ritual and deities of the Congos (who had a special reputation for "marronage") as well as certain deities of other nations (Bomba, Limba) whose character was compatible with the Petro ethos; just as Rada had absorbed the Nago's Ogoun, and the loa of other compatible nations. Yet certain Congo divinities remain separate (the African Congo Franc being distinguished from the Congo Mazonne[24]) pointing again to the separateness of Petro as a nation, while Ibo has tended to remain entirely individual.

At the same time even the Rada nation, as if with an eye

---

* Courlander has an excellent discussion of the various drums of the nations and the differences between them.

to the efficacy of its methods, learned from Petro in at least three major ways. Its structure was similarly democratized, so that, whereas in Dahomey the sacred rattle could be conferred only by the king, the apprenticeship, ordeal and ritual resulting in the achievement of this mark of priesthood could now be undertaken in the hounfor of any established houngan. It borrowed various elements of magical and esoteric manipulation or gave greater emphasis to like elements in its own system. The cult of the twins, which in Africa seems to have had a magical position somewhat apart from the religious structure of divinities, was elevated to the primary rôle which it commands in Indian mythology. The fetish stones which, in Africa, were primarily related to thunderbolt deities,[25] now came to incorporate, as the Caribbean Indian Zemi did, any cosmic or ancestral spirit. The vever, as a cabbalalike method of invoking the gods, was included as a primary ceremonial device in Rada. The sacred *langage*, by which the priest communicates with the deities, began to include Indian words. And finally, the Rada deities took over some of the accoutrements of equivalent deities on the Petro side. Damballah, the serpent, is sometimes conceived as the Plumed Serpent of Indian myth.[26] And Azacca, agrarian deity whose name derives from the maize culture of the Indians, has almost completely displaced Dadal, the African deity of vegetables.

At the same time, the Rada serviteurs who began to attend Petro service, carried certain of their divinities with them, and there, those divinities were transfigured. Ogoun GeRouge came into being as a Petro aspect of the warrior. The gentle, feminine Erzulie, became in the Petro context the corn goddess whose propitiatory service in the Indian culture had been extremely violent and bloody.

Above all, America contributed the complex divinity Baron Samedi, at once Lord of the Cemetery, of the crossroads (as brother to Maît' Carrefour, the Petro equivalent of Legba) and of the magic related to both the Dead and the crossroads, whose major, or at least, bestknown expression is the zombie.

Both the word zombie and Samedi are from the Indian Zemi which connotes both the spirit of the dead, the soulless living, and the fetish stone by which magic is accomplished. Ghede, who is a Lord of the Dead of apparently African origin, has been identified with the Baron Samedi complex, although sometimes he is considered a Rada deity, and would seem to be the gentler manifestation of death. Baron Samedi, however, is usually understood as Petro. In any case, the ceremony for the Ghede‑Samedi complex is performed after the Rada rituals (being considered almost as a separate rite), and when Ghede is concerned, is separate from the Petro as well.*

From the Indian Zemi, the magic‑working fetish, comes also another of the major figures of the Voudoun structure, Simbi, patron of the rains (in the maize culture context) and, above all, patron of magicians. Although Damballah and other Rada deities are related to rain, it is Simbi who is considered most powerful in this connection. His magic, therefore, has strong elements of benevolence, as well as of aggression. He is referred to as "straddling" Rada *and* Petro, for like the Samedi‑Ghede complex, Simbi contains elements of each nation in almost equal measure and so stands apart from both.

And so there sprang up a new growth of loa, born in and of the new world and because of the very nature of that new world. A very few, such as Azacca of the maize culture, were incorporated into the African ceremonials, the Rada rites. Some of the new deities, as Ogoun Ge‑Rouge, were created by the transfiguration of an African principle into a new‑world manifestation. Some, like Samedi, emerged as independent, separate figures born of the almost equal fusion of the two cultures (and it is significant that these are now regarded as perhaps the "strongest"). And some, like Dan Petro himself, retained their new‑world identity completely. To his already substantial African heritage, then, the Haitian added these. History shapes men, and men become ancestors, and when

* This extremely complex divinity is discussed more fully in the pantheon chapter that follows, and in the Appendix dealing with Indian influences.

ancestors become loa the history of the race runs in the blood of the race as part of the psychic heritage which is passed on from generation to generation.[27]

4

TRADITION AS A CONTEMPORARY FUNCTION

It is clear that Titon's heritage could not possibly have con-tained *all* of his individual ancestors, on both sides of the family; for the obligations toward such a multitude would have been an intolerable burden for a single individual.[28] The structure of Voudoun provides several means by which such a number, though continually increasing, is, simultaneously, continually subject to condensation. The major "device" is that of historical selectivity: the loa who are to be served individually, as prin-ciples, are distinguished from the mere Dead, who are served as a collective total. A second device is the assimilation of individual ancestral loa into the figures of whatever major and precedent loa seem to exemplify the same character. And finally, since the children of a single family are inevitably different in their development, the family deities are, as it were, divided up between them. One child will be claimed by the mother's Erzulie, another by the father's Ogoun. But the psychic inheritance of the child is a latent religious force. While his physical heritage may show resemblance to one parent or the other, in infancy, his deities, including the maît-tête, become manifest only with maturity and establish their special position.*

* It is clear that the Haitian relates general maturity and adulthood to psychic development. Thus, if a child (even past the age of puberty) should become possessed, that is not understood as a good omen or blessing; on the contrary, it is regarded with consternation and disfavor and every effort is made to avoid the recurrence of such an event. The feeling is that a child is not yet equipped or prepared, as a human being, for relationship with divinity, that he cannot yet "endure" a loa, nor "control" him, and there is even the danger that the loa may harm him by overwhelming him. This reflects, again, the high regard in which the Haitian holds his own individual psychic power, for he does not think in terms of being the helpless subject of his loa, but of a relationship of mutual service and respect.

It was this last process of selectivity which, through the default of Titon's brothers and sisters by conversion, had been denied him. The consequent congruence of deities in his head had created for him not only a numerical complication but certain characterological conflicts that would not have normally occurred. He had become the carrier of deities who would otherwise have lived through other children and were incompatible with his personality. Yet this very diversity gave a scope to his heritage that was impressive, and, to some extent, rare.

Titon had come to number his loa as 21, but it is unlikely that the number was precise. Counting all of the individual ancestral deities, it would easily have numbered more. On the other hand, with all the deities properly grouped under dominant principle loa, it would probably have numbered less. It may be that 7, as a magic number of reasonable amplitude, had been taken as representing the major categories, and that this then had been multiplied by three as a means, again magical, of indicating the variant manifestation of these basic loa. The number 21, therefore, was probably Titon's statement of the degree and intensity of the psychic force with which he was infused.

For the Haitian, it is his heritage that is the source of his life force, it is his history that equips him for his immediate activities, and it is from his ancestral loa that he derives the psychic energy and intelligence upon which he relies to empower and instruct him in his daily life.* It is not difficult, then, to understand why his major preoccupation is with the means by which he may achieve contact with that world of

---

* In this connection, the following statement by Malinowski (pp. 91-2), is very relevant. "Myth, as a statement of primaeval reality which still lives in present-day life and as a justification by precedent, supplies a retrospective pattern of moral values, sociological order and magical belief. . . . It fulfills a function *sui generis* closely connected with the nature of tradition, with the continuity of culture, with the relation between age and youth, and with the human attitude towards the past. . . . Myth is . . . an indispensable ingredient of all culture."

les Invisibles where the life force upon which he is dependent is generated.[29] For the serviteur the cross-roads is more than a metaphysical principle, or one operating only at birth and death. It is at this point of intersection that the abstract and ancestral principles which are the loa—whose location is in an absolute time and an absolute space—become a living organism of this immediate moment and this particular place. As the principle enters reality it not only acts upon that reality but is, of necessity, defined, shaped and modified by it. It is at such intersection that tradition meets contemporary need and faith becomes the *act* of ritual service and divine response. At this intersection the idea lives as action.

In Haiti the idea, the principle, must live, must function, for the conditions of Haitian life are indeed difficult to endure. The morning greeting is: "Et la nuit?" (And how was your night?) and the conventional answer is: "Pas plus mal, merci" (No worse, thank you). Even among the bourgeoisie the answer is: "On se maintient" (One gets along). These are not the theatrical exaggerations of a nation given to complaint. On the contrary, the Haitian has a fine comic sense, and welcomes the opportunity to laugh. These colloquial statements of rock-bottom endurance are merely realistically accurate expressions of things as they are.

The man of such a culture must be, necessarily, a pragmatist. His immediate needs are too insistent, too pressing and too critical, to permit the luxury of idealism or mysticism, and they must be answered rather than escaped from. He has neither time, energy nor means for inconsequential activity. His religious system must do more than give him moral sustenance; it must do more than rationalize his instinct for survival when survival is no longer a "reasonable" activity. It must do more than provide a reason for living; it must provide the *means* for living. It must serve the organism as well as the psyche. It must serve as a practical methodology not as an irrational hope. In consequence, the Haitian thinks of his religion in working terms. To ask him whether he "believes" in Voudoun is to pose a meaningless, irrelevant question.* He answers: "I serve the loa", and, more than likely, he will say, "I serve so-and-so", giving even to general divine power a specialized focus. He speaks of "la science des Mystères" (the *science* of the Mystères); he respects the degree of *connaissance* (knowledge) in a houngan, and his consequent ability to *regler* (govern, control) the loa. And he demands action of his loa. They are required to pre-scribe treatment for illness, to advise on planting and marriage, and on affairs in general.

But needs change and those who serve loa largely because loa serve them well transfigure those divinities according to those needs. Ogoun, ancient loa of thunderbolts, ironsmiths and warriors was, and is still, the principle of power. But, as the Haitian has learned so well, power is political. Thus, in the new world, a new aspect of Ogoun appeared: St. Jacques, whose symbol is the national flag, who is greeted by the national anthem, and is regarded as we might regard an influential man in power politics and economic affairs. No one denies that Ogoun is the greater figure—that beside his noble grandeur St. Jacques seems merely pretentious, almost ridiculous. The serviteurs are awed by the moral stature of the divine hero, and they worship him; but they know that St. Jacques is more useful, and they serve him well. The very nature of "functional" loa is that they are more susceptible than the great loa to the

---

* The Haitian must be, and is, a very realistic person. His idea of the universe is built upon observations and evidence; and he is also reasonable enough to understand that reality extends beyond his immediate capacity and opportunity to experience and observe it. He judges such unseen realities by a pragmatic test: certain observable results indicate the reality of unobservable forces and facts. But these are understood as realities, not as ir-real ideas or "beliefs". It is significant that, in Creole, the word "believe" is never used in our sense of "a belief", but only in the sense of an opinion as in "I believe that he will come before nightfall". A Haitian does not think of himself as "be-lieving in" something; he thinks that it is so. If someone disputes with him about anything in Voudoun, he considers this as he might any dispute about reality, and conflicts about the loa, as conflicts about anything else, are under-stood to result not from any ambivalence in the fact or event itself, but from improper or insufficient observation, understanding, or from some selfish motive for prevarication.

flattery of ceremony and more inclined to barter their services. Thus it may frequently occur, for instance, that a houngan will serve several major loa (such as Damballah, Legba, Agwé and Erzulie) during a single day's ceremony, while, out of concern for his large farm acreage, he will devote an entire day to Azacca, loa of agriculture and a relatively lesser deity in the hierarchy.[30] There is, as a matter of fact, an entire category of *loa travail* (work loa) whose importance lies entirely in their usefulness and their capacity for work. In these times their number and their ritual service seems to be increasing, although there is never any question as to their minor stature relative to the great loa.

For those men who are extremely ambitious, and willing to risk dangerous bargains, there is even a category of deities who can be "bought". These appear to be related not to any cosmic principles but to magical manipulation, and they usually belong to the Petro nation. Such spirits (and they can hardly be called loa) are even further removed from the divine loa than the work deities. As a matter of fact, the real loa may refuse to associate with the bought deities, and may abandon the houngan or serviteur who deals with these latter.* It is this threat of abandonment which has restricted the widespread growth of such otherwise perhaps profitable arrangements. Certainly the great loa will have nothing to do with the *bocor*, the professional magician, who deals in zombies and in *baka* (malevolent spirits contained in the form of various animals). Thus, in their fashion, the great loa still serve men well, for if the serviteur, grown either desperate with need or anxious with ambition, should pursue the logic of ritual service and divine reward to the point where he comes to exploit divine power for personal ends, the loa themselves create a crisis of alternatives.

In the final analysis, religion and magic stand as opposites.

* Another dangerous risk is also involved, namely, that such bought loa may be inherited by the descendants, and, being malevolent in nature, cause them much trouble. It is even possible that an elaborate ceremony might have to be performed in order to restrain them. Herskovits (p. 222) speaks of this possible development, and also of the withdrawal of the familial gods in anger.

Religion presumes that the major forces of the universe (which, after all, created life), are essentially benevolent in nature.* But, like all organic powers, they have various requirements. Their energy, which is constantly expended in the very act of being, must be constantly replenished, and this is one of the obligations of the serviteur. These huge forces are also a little "vague", and may sometimes go awry all of themselves, and so the serviteur, through prayer and proper devotion, endeavors to assure their benevolent disposition and to activate this positively. From time to time, some intimately personal favor may be asked and granted. But the overwhelming emphasis of religious service is directed toward the improvement of the universal condition, which will in turn accrue to the benefit of the individuals within it. Religion, being a collective enterprise, is concerned with directing the cosmic forces toward a collective public good.

The secrecy which characterizes magic, on the other hand, is a clue to its character. Magic is an individual action, undertaken because the cosmos is not believed to be benevolent by nature, or, at least, not benevolent enough to that person. Magic is not based, then, on a confidence in the character of cosmic forces, nor is it concerned with improving their condition in any respect. On the contrary, it is dedicated to the means by which some portion of those forces may be "tapped", channeled and focused to some personal end. The magician, or the one having recourse to magic, sees himself as separate from, in competition with, or even bitterly opposed to the collective and the cosmic good. Where the religious man would pray for rain—knowing it will fall upon his neighbor's field as well as his own—the magician is jubilant and triumphant if he succeeds in controlling and focusing the shower precisely within the limits of his own fence.**

If today, in Haiti, the contemporary serviteur tends to give ceremonial emphasis to the loa whose favor is immediately and

* The Haitian saying is: "God is good."
** For further comparison of religion with magic, see pp. 200–1, *infra*.

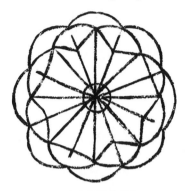

MAGIC PENTACLE

materially useful; if many houngans are proud of "work loa" and some even unashamed to have "bought" a loa; if magic (it is still protective rather than aggressive for the most part)* is becoming widely accepted as a necessary complement to religious activities—these developments are evidence of the fact that the Haitian is less certain than he was that the cosmos is essentially benevolent; and they reflect, moreover, his feeling that the society in which he lives has lost most of that integra⁄ tion, cohesion and homogeneity which marks a collective culture. The Haitian approaches the moment when, as in so many of our "civilized" cultures, man will come to feel himself singular, alone and pitted against a hostile universe.

Meanwhile the great loa fight to arrest this development. They rage against the deterioration of ritual disciplines; they complain of insufficient service, attention, food; they strike at the neglectful serviteur; they repeat their ultimate threat—that they will withdraw. And, indeed, very gradually, their

* One of the functions of the houngan is to protect his people from the malevolent machinations of the bocor. This means that he too must perform magic, and must answer the evil *wanga* (charm) with the protective *garde* (talisman). This has contributed to the great confusion between Voudoun, as a religious practice, and the magical practices, which are actually completely separate and outside the religious system. A man may be strong and powerful because the loa have made him so; but it is the *man* who makes magic, not the loa. Herskovits (p. 220) emphasizes this distinction, as do other observers.

appearances have begun to become rarer, while the minor deities now come often and with great aplomb. The Haitians are not unaware of this. They say: "Little horses cannot carry great riders."

5

THE SERVITEUR AS CONTEMPORARY CITIZEN

One of Titon's distinctions was that the great loa which were his psychic heritage still came frequently. He was proud of this, and cognizant of his responsibility. He took care not to bring them into hounfors where they might either be humiliated by lack of proper reception or possibly exploited by unscrupulous persons. But this heritage had become, in recent times, a mixed blessing. The twenty-one loa were not only a positive power, but one which had to be ritually controlled so that its energies should not spend themselves anarchically. Moreover, the heritage involved proportionate obligations, and demands, which Titon could not always fulfill, and so he was in continual danger of arousing a divine rage.

It is undoubtedly for this reason that Titon had begun, at an early age, to train himself in those knowledges and practices that were designed to control the loa. It was logical that his degree of control should be matched by a degree of service. Consequently, as his mastery increased, the loa increasingly demanded that Titon should dedicate himself completely and become a houngan. Under normal conditions this would have been the natural course for him. For, both in his divine heritage and in his personal talents, he was equipped much better for the priesthood than most houngans. But the contemporary state of affairs in Haiti, and his own situation in particular, had, so far, prevented him from achieving that degree of elevation.

The vocation of the houngan is usually hereditary. Along with the profession itself, the heritage normally includes the parental hounfor, peristyle, drums and other accoutrements of service. In Titon's case, however, the dislocation of his family to the city, when they had given up or sold their land, had left him without even a piece of ground upon which to begin building. Moreover, his family's conversion to Protestantism, and their opposition to Voudoun, had so dislocated Titon himself that he had no place in which to store his pot-de-tête, the canari containing his gros-bon-ange. He had placed it first in one hounfor, then in another, and finally, since he had come to feel that the houngans involved were untrustworthy, he had removed it from their protection altogether. It was at once comical and tragic that he should have had no place worthy of his pot-de-tête, the most intimate of sacred objects, and that he finally should have ended by depositing it in the home of an ethnologist whose disinterested sympathy could be relied on.

With all his talents, it would seem that it should have been possible for Titon to find jobs and to earn the money (a modest sum even by middle-class Haitian standards) to buy the small piece of land, and to build his hounfor, purchase the drums, and pay for the ceremony of his elevation to houngan. Yet, just because these talents were related to his religion, the most obvious opportunities were eliminated. During the period of the Haitian International Exposition, an effort was made to present Voudoun as a folklore attraction for tourists: to stage dances and rituals, and even to simulate possession by the deities. Titon's ability as a dancer and singer made him an obvious choice for this entertainment. Yet from the beginning, his Ghede opposed his participation. Titon himself could not understand the opposition, and in a desperate desire to earn the needed money, accepted the employment. But he appeared for only one performance. From the first moment of his appearance on the stage, his left eye began to close, by the will of Ghede. By the time the evening was over the eye was entirely closed and Titon was negotiating his withdrawal from the "folklorique troop".

In our terms, it may appear obvious that this was a psycho- somatic phenomenon. Yet it is typical of the means by which the Voudoun deities operate, enforcing moral principles even when these are not consciously comprehended. Titon himself had neither the sophistication nor the experience to evaluate the presentation precisely. It was true that it enjoyed official sponsorship, and indicated the ostensibly complimentary popular interest in the religion; and it is true that the costumes were more costly than those that a simple houngan could proffer for the celebration of the loa and that the audience was larger than any that had ever attended a regular ceremony; nevertheless such exploitation as folklore attraction constituted a degradation of the religion. It was the ancient loa who, with divine accuracy, understood this and perceived also the falsification and corruption implicit in the fact that the songs would be sung, the dances danced, and the rituals performed not in the service of the loa, nor in the exercise of obeisance and discipline, but for the purpose of self-exhibition and self- aggrandizement. It was the ancient Ghede whose "roots are without end"—who had been passed down in the family line through countless generations—whose ancient hand reached from the infinitely distant past, to act with such immaculate contemporary judgement.

Titon had hoped, when he had contemplated the employ- ment, to earn at least the money necessary to have a houngan perform the ceremony of "taking the asson", the ceremony of priestly investiture. Now, however, and by the act of his own maît-tête, this way had been closed to him. Meanwhile he was acutely aware of the fact that he was more capable and worthy than many houngans who had had the good fortune to inherit not only their profession, but the material means with which to implement it. And particularly when he had been witness to the relative inadequacy of such priests, he would defiantly, and in desperation, proclaim that there was no houngan great enough to give him the asson. It would be the loa themselves who would confer upon him this sacred instrument of divine power, as soon as he had managed to get the money together to build the hounfor and the peristyle.

To call upon his loa, thus, at this critical moment, was to call upon everything of which he was, himself, the final issue —to call not only upon the generality, the principles of his patrimony, but, beginning with the Marassa, the first men, upon the roll of that ancestral progression which had successively borne that complex forward: the African tribes, the Indian allies, the thousands of individuals whose blood had nourished it and whose diverse personal genius had swelled and elaborated its manifold and various aspects. His invocation was the genealogy of his own divinity, and, condensed into the short-hand of this nomenclature, contained the record of the race, of all that which, flowing like a river forward in time, was to be funneled now into this single individual so that, in his own person, the accumulated force of moral history would be pitted against contemporary circumstance.

NANCHONS: (Nations, Tribes)	RADA RITES (Initiatory, Benevolent Divinities)				
	Dahomey		Nago (Nigeria)	Ghede	Juba Martinique
FAMILY LINES:	Wedo	Dwarf Boar			
PRINCIPLES CROSSROADS Phallic principle; fertility; childbirth, sun-fire, androgeneity, omniscience. Characteristics: tree, cane, hat.	Legba-Sé Attibon-Legba Avradra Agao-Loco Bayé	Alovi	Kadja-Bossu	Obatala Ogoun Panama (hat) Ogoun Bayé	
CHTHONIC, UNDERWORLD Death; phallic principle; fertility; childbirth; night; moon; androgeneity; omniscience; cemeteries; magic; trickery and jokes; island below the sea.			Alovi-Ghede Bossu-Trois-Cornes (?)	Ogoun-Badagris	Ghede-Nimbo Brav Ghede
TELLURIC, EARTH Farming, vegetables, fertility.	Agao-Wedo			(Ogoun-Badagris) Dadal	Ghede-Mazacca	Azacca-Medé Cousin-Zaka
URANIC, HEAVENS Sky; rainbow; life-principle; cosmic egg; serpent; rivers and springs. Also: thunder, wind, lightning.	Damballah and Ayida Wedo Sobo Badé, Badessy Agarou-Tonerre			Ogoun Shango Ogoun Batala	Ghede L'Oraille Ghede Z'Eclai
SEA Wind; thunder, cannon-fire. Also: boats, sea-shells. Also: male consort of female principle.	Agwé Arroyo			Agwé (?)	Immamou
FIRE Power; War; Iron-forging; weapons. Red color.			Bossu-Trois-Cornes (?)	Ogoun Ferei Ogoun Fai St. Jacques	
FEMALE Seduction, feminity; fertility. Protectress.	Erzulie Freda Dahomey La Sirène La Balianne Gran Erzulie				Brigitte
ANCESTRAL Racial origins; androgeneity; priesthood; trees; healing powers; guardian of traditions; parental disciplines.	Nanan-bouclou (androgynous) Silibo-Gweto (androgynous?) Loco-Attiso (male) Agassou (male) Ayizan (female)	Akadja Adja Kadja-Bossu		Loco-Roi-Nago Nago Piman	

INDEPENDANT	AMBIVALENT	PETRO RITES (Magical, Malevolent, Daemons)					
Ibo and Kanga	Quitta Simbi	Congo	Petro				Miscellaneous
(African origin) Ossange (?)	(American origin) Owl	(African origin)	(American origin)	La Flambeau	Ge-Rouge	Crab	
Ianman-Ibo Caplaou (Kanga) Legba-Ibo	Simbi-en-deux-eaux Quitta-Bayé	Legba-Congo	Carrefour (Kalfu) Legba-Petro	Amine-Gatigal-La Flambeau		Bambarra-Taiba	Sousou Pannan Moundongue Limba Zao Pimba
Ibo-Lazile	General-Brisé Baron Piquant Maît-Grand-Bois-D'Ilet		Baron Samedi Baron La Croix Baron Cimitière Azagon La Croix			Ghede	Criminelle
		Congo Zandor Congo Savanne	Marinette				
Damballah Ossange	Simbi	Congo Zandor Congo Savanne	Dan Petro Ti-Jean Petro Saint-Blanc	Damballah La Flambeau	Damballah Ge-Rouge	Simbi	
Ogoun-Ossange	Simbi				Agwé Ge-Rouge		
	Simbi	Congo Zandor Congo Savanne	Petro rites in general related to fire Nanchou	Ogoun-La-Flambeau	Ogoun Ge-Rouge		Ogoun Yemsen
Mai-Louise	Ti-Quitta	Marinette-Congo	Marinette Bras Chêche Pied Chêche Erzulie Mapionne		Erzulie Ge-Rouge		Erzulie Lemba
Ibo-Lele Ibo-Loco	Gran-Simba	Congo-Yamingan	Linglessou			Agassou	

The origin of a number of these loa is somewhat obscure; moreover, observers differ as to whether others should be classified as Rada or Petro. This chart, therefore, cannot be considered definitive. Nevertheless, it serves to illuminate the manner in which the various tribes, family lines and American-Indian divinities have been organized together into a single, compatible system. A complete ceremonial service would include the major principles (Cross-roads, etc.), as expressed in each major category: Rada, Ibo, Quitta, Congo, Petro. As an example of such a ceremony, the loa which might be invoked have been underlined. In a sense, the nanchons, or nations, have come to represent various aspects of those principles, differing according to moral or magical emphasis and particular ethos, so that a principle can be followed through its mani-festations in the benevolent Rada line, to the ambivalent Simbi (who is understood to straddle the Rada-Petro division) to the dangerous and even malevolent Petro. Each of these nanchons include, in addition, a differentiation in family lines which have, in some cases, retained their identity by place-name (Wedo) or ancestral totemic symbol (dwarf, boar, owl, or crab).

It is also clear that each of the eight principles contains elements of all the others: the cross-roads can be understood to include the entire cosmos, below and above earth; the sky, or life-principle, represented by the serpent rainbow reflected in—hence encompassing—the waters, thus comprehends the abyss as well as the sky; the abyss, or underworld, is the actual domicile of the ancestors, etc. The distinction between these major principles is, then, primarily one of emphasis, and these distinctions are not equally marked in all the nanchon lines. Simbi, for example, stands almost as a single figure covering the entire cosmic range, in contrast to the differentiations in the Dahomean line. The absence of any important chthonic or telluric figure in the Dahomean line would indicate that the African Legba, as a cross-roads loa, may have comprehended those provinces; and that Ghede and Azacca, both of whom have strong American elements, were interpolated into the Rada rites in Haiti. On the other hand it is interesting to note that although in the Rada rites, the Nago Ogoun is primarily the warrior, or power principle, there still exist Ogouns who represent all the major differentiated principles, and thus make up a complete Nago cosmic system. The Ghede and the Ibo lines, judging by available data, are less differentiated; in the Ghede line the cross-roads principle would seem to be the position from which the cosmic whole is comprehended, while in the Ibo line, the ancestral principle is the point of cosmic departure. The Congo line has been largely assimilated into the Petro, and this later American nanchon is as strong and full as the African Rada. The text of the Pantheon Chapter which follows and the footnote references contain the data upon which this chart arrangement was based.

It is interesting to note that the ancestral principle, as an educational, initiatory force, is strong on the Rada side and weak in Petro where the underworld, as the basis of magical manipulation, is notably emphasized. Petro also contains the strongest agrarian figure, in Marinette, and is characterized by an emphasis on fire and earth and by an absence of a water loa of any stature unless Simbi is included in the Petro category.

CHAPTER III

The Divine Horsemen

THE NATURE OF THE LOA

J U S T as the physical body of a man is a meaningless, material substance, devoid of judgement, will and morality, unless a soul infuses and animates it, so the universe would be but an amoral mass of organic matter, inevitably evolving on the initial momentum of original creation, were it not for the loa who direct it in paths of order, intelligence and benevolence. The loa are the souls of the cosmos.*

A religion so based on the belief that matter is animated by a non-material "spirit" would ordinarily be classified as animistic. Such religions are said to be characterized by gods of the natural elements and by the belief that trees, stones and other such material objects are rendered animate by spirits. By these standards, Voudoun would seem, at first glance, to be an animistic religion. However, any effort to systematize the Voudoun pantheon in terms of the major elements—earth, air, fire and water—becomes a Procrustean operation which amputates such major divinities as Legba, God of the Cross-roads, Ghede, God of the Dead, Erzulie, Goddess of Love, and makes of Ogoun a loa of fire (which is actually but his characterological symbol) instead of the God of War. More-over, although the loa may reside *in* trees (and, as a matter of fact, in stones, streams, etc.), these serve merely as physical vessels for them; and just as the loa *in* a govi could not at all be properly called the loa *of* the govi, so the loa cannot be under-stood as the spirits *of* the trees or of any physical vessel in which they may be lodged.[1] It becomes apparent, then, that the

* The loa did not create the cosmos; that was the function of the initial creator divinity. For a discussion of the rôle of this first source in Voudoun and the position of the loa relative to it, see pp. 54-6.

86

metaphysical system of Voudoun does not lend itself to the orthodox arrangements of the animistic classification.*

It is also customary to assume that a man of "primitive" culture, lacking an advanced scientific understanding of the physical universe, and lacking actual technological facilities, seeks to control it by devotional appeal to, and magical mani/ pulation of these "mystical" spirits to whose activities he attributes all phenomena.** But the fact is that within the limits of their equipment and needs, the men of such primitive cultures *do* have an excellent pragmatic control of their im/ mediate environment. Explorers have long ago learned to be guided by native techniques (when limited to native

* For a critical discussion of anthropological misinterpretations of the so/ called primitive mentality, see Notes III, 1–4, pp. 296–8.

** In the usual course of events, a primitive culture is first invaded by another culture, so that a series of new problems is abruptly posed. The invaders are usually aggressively bent on exploiting this culture, and, to facilitate this, set out deliberately to destroy its integration. The religion of those invaded—being both unprepared for and disarmed by the new circumstances—is understandably ineffectual and is consequently judged to be a "mystique" divorced from reality. But this was not true of its relationship to the realities of the indigenous context in which it was evolved, and for which it had represented a very satisfactory adjustment. Moreover, in Haiti, for instance, practices which may initially seem to be superstitious often prove, upon greater familiarity with the situation, to be eminently practical in that particular context. The fact that such habits persist even when the individual is removed to a context where they are no longer valid—as with peasants moved to the city—and that they are then observed within this new context, has created a distorted and exaggerated notion of the manner in which a primitive undertakes to cope with reality. As a matter of fact, apart from the very universal tendency of habits to persist, they may serve an important psychological function in such a situation, as a familiar and stabilizing pattern, a comforting echo of the known past in an otherwise confusing and frightening new world.

It is true that occasionally a "taboo" may prevent the most complete adjust/ ment to immediate reality, but this may have been initially reasonable (as was the Jewish prohibition of pork) and such taboos are, in any case, very specialized in application.

As indication of the unfortunate substitution of superstition or magic for science, the examples cited most frequently refer to the treatment of disease. Even here any final conclusion warrants careful consideration. For a discussion of the herbal knowledge of houngans and the prevalence of psychosomatic disturbance for which ritual provides effective therapy, see pp. 162–71.

equipment) for exploiting the available resources; they have been struck by the practical ingenuity demonstrated in the accomplishment of apparently impossible feats; and they have testified to a native familiarity with natural cycles and symptoms which amounts, in effect, to an astonishing ability to predict natural phenomena with great accuracy and to use or avoid them as the case may require.

Instead of regarding primitive religion as a falsification of the true nature of matter, as compensation for and even as antagonistic to a true understanding of the physical universe, it might be useful to assume, as a hypothesis at least, that such religious systems propose ideas which are essentially correct and in harmony with the true nature of the physical universe. Thus, one might reconstruct the origin of Voudoun as follows: that the Haitian—or, more properly, his African ancestor—observed the universe, both nature and man as part of nature, and, in its operation, discerned certain major and recurrent principles; that he distinguished between the principle of the thing and the thing itself and remarked that the material objects or phenomena are transitory or destructible and singular, whereas the principles themselves are persistent and pervasive, or immortal and universal; that he consequently estimated these latter as of an order superior to matter; and, finally, that it is this superior order—these principles to which he himself is subject —which he conceives of as divinity. In a sense, then, he did not so much ascribe divinity to matter as deduce the spirit of matter from its manifestations. Moreover, these principles which have been abstracted from the phenomena in which they are manifest are not less real than the phenomena, but merely non-physical and invisible; and this fact may illuminate the Voudoun concept of les Invisibles as real.[2] The loa are supernatural in the same sense that a principle is super-natural or abstract.

However, since the forces in question—whether understood as principles or as les Invisibles—can be perceived only when manifest in matter, the serviteur addresses himself to material objects and phenomena, particularly in ritual, whose purpose is at least partially instructive; and in this context such material manifestations may be said to serve as exemplary demonstra/ tions.* Moreover, there are certain physical phenomena in which the principle is so dramatically manifest that there has been almost no dissociation between the divinity and the physical manifestation. This is the case with major elemental forces such as the sea, which alone, as a physical phenomenon, adequately expresses its own complex and primordial principle. Yet the distinction remains explicit in Voudoun: it is not the sea that is sacred; it is Agwé, the spirit of the sea, who is divine. *To worship the loa is to celebrate the principle, not the matter in which it may be momentarily or permanently manifest.*

If divinity is understood as a reference to principle (whether of life, death, love or affinity, war or conflict, etc.), the insis/ tence of the primitive that all physical phenomena are animated by divinity, his refusal to conceive of accidental—i.e. un/ principled—phenomena, and his conviction that even the most minor detail is an expression of a major force—these beliefs are consistent extensions of the conviction that the universe is completely integrated and entirely logical, however devious or obscure that logic may sometimes seem. The Voudoun loa do not have a supernatural prerogative of arbitrary decision. An event which, to the serviteur, does not seem logical is not accepted with good grace as the "will of God"; on the con/ trary, the serviteur is aggressive in calling the loa to account and in exacting the explanation to which he feels entitled and which would indicate the corrective procedure he should follow. This belief that all phenomena must contain some logical principle, this concept of a pervasive logical causation is, as a matter of fact, identical with the premise underlying scientific in/ vestigation.[3]

* For a discussion of ritual as a means of disciplinary training and as a palpable demonstration of abstract principles for educational purposes see pp. 194, 198. In effect, this use of ritual constitutes the primitive version of the new theories underlying audio/visual instructional aids and the contemporary appre/ ciation of the efficacy of movies and television as means of concretely conveying the operation of scientific principles and theories.

However, the *perception* of principle—the organization of experience into a meaningful pattern—is a function of the mind of man; the Voudoun expression is precisely "to have loa in the head".* Moreover, while Voudoun recognizes, for example, that both the sea and Agwé, the principle of the sea, are objective realities, it specifies that Agwé—as a figure separate from the actual sea—comes to one's head *not from the sea but from one's parents.* The inheritance of loa, then, refers to the transmission of ideas or principles, or what is, in effect, education. Furthermore, these principles are handed down in the very blood that links one generation to another. Just as blood itself is constantly subject to glandular and dietary variations, so the psychic chemistry of these individual carriers, itself affected both by internal conditions and by external circumstances, in turn affects the principles which it nourishes. *The loa, then, partakes of the nature of the head that bears it. The principle is modified by person.***

This would seem to leave the way open for such limitless variations upon the theme, as it were, that the identity and

* For a discussion of the human mind as a source of divinity see note *infra.*

** For a discussion of "inheritance" as parental influence during the formative years, see pp. 149–50. As the parents play the decisive rôle in a person's psychic development, it is that particular aspect of the loa which has characterized the family line that is inherited. Moreover, it is recognized that the inheritor will, in turn, further modulate (to a very minor degree) that loa in reference to his own character. (See discussion re "baptism" of a new loa, p. 219.)

It should also be noted that the fact that the major principle is modified, modulated and particularized into an aspect by individuals may appear—to those accustomed to the untouchable, abstract absolutism of divinity in non-ancestral religious systems—to affect a reduction in the stature and scope of the original "racine" loa. This impression is encouraged by the frequent smallness of the contemporary "horse", who is consequently mounted by minor aspects of the loa. However, the same process may and does enlarge the scope of the loa and add significant potency to his activities, since they come to encompass contemporary concepts, as was the case when Titon's Ghede acted so strongly in reference to the Folklorique troupe. (See p. 79.) In any case it is a system which democratizes the divinity, and accepts the consequent results, for better or for worse. Certainly such a system is less mystic than those religions which detach divinity from man, and, in so doing, imply that divinity is an attribute *per se* of the cosmos.

continuity of the principle would be almost obliterated by individual particularizations. But in a relatively homogeneous culture too great a diversity of individual attitudes would not occur. Moreover, the attenuated process by which a parent becomes ancestor, and the ancestor in turn becomes archetype, serves to filter out the merely decorative elaboration, the purely subjective modulations of that first principle. Only that variant endures which can remain as significant to a distant descendant as it first appeared to the immediate family. In the course of the evolution into loa there emerges, from the singular person, the general principle which characterized him. Thus, just as principles may be deduced from the objective phenomena in which they are manifest, so they may be discerned in the subjective attitudes of persons. Religion includes an analysis of the physical universe but its function is to propose moral values; it is not concerned exclusively with matter, but equally, even predominantly, with man. The optimistic man perceives reality as a benevolence; the unfortunate man knows intimately its violent faces. *A loa contains both subject and object, both the seer and the thing seen. In Voudoun neither man nor matter is divine. A loa is an intelligence, a relationship of man to matter.*[4]

Such a degree of philosophical and psychological awareness —containing, as it does, such strong similarities with modern relativism—is admittedly unexpected of a so-called primitive culture. Yet it is the only interpretative reconstruction of the Voudoun metaphysical logic which is confirmed by the actual structures, beliefs and practices and in terms of which both the major assertions and the ritual details emerge in meaningful relationship.* It reveals the precedence of the Marassa over the

* A religion such as Voudoun, whose function is to impart to the individuals of the community a system of mental and emotional convictions upon which the very survival of the community is dependent, does not, and *could not* require of them that they perceive and understand its principles on an abstract, metaphysical level in order that they be inspired to participate in it. On the contrary, every possible physical technique—particularly drumming and dancing —is used to involve the individuals in activities in which those metaphysical and moral principles are structurally implicit, so that these are, in a sense,

loa as a statement that men perceive and hence, in a sense, precede principles; it clarifies the function of loa-inheritance as the transmission of values; it explains why maturity is a con-dition for the manifestation of the loa maît-tête, and why this loa dominates the other loa of the person's heritage; it illuminates the apparently ambivalent relationship of a man to his loa as a delicate and dynamic balance between devotion to and mastery of one's principles; possession can be understood, in this light, as a transitory period of exalted and exclusive obsession with a principle; finally it provides a guide for the organization of the loa into the pattern of a meaningful and consistent pantheon.*

unconsciously absorbed by the participant. This is no more, but certainly no less, than a highly developed form of the "learn by doing" educational method, and the techniques employed in Voudoun are further elaborated in the discussion on the function of ritual, in Chapter V. Indeed, it is precisely because these concepts have been unconsciously absorbed and have become the very premises of their subsequent thought-patterns, that the individuals are least aware of them as explicit concepts. When a serviteur speaks of Vou-doun, he speaks, as it were, "after the fact", from a point of view already determined by his participation and one so deeply "natural" to him that he is not aware of it as a particular point of view. If this point of view were to be repeatedly challenged, he might arrive at an articulation of his premises in the course of being obliged to justify them to some opposing point of view. (The most articulated metaphysics belong to those mythologies whose history has exposed them to opposition and the consequent need for exposition and justifi-cation). But Voudoun has tended to adjust and assimilate other ideologies to itself rather than be challenged by them and has not arrived at such self-articulation. It has been, and is still, satisfied to fill its primary function: the creation of serviteurs who live in terms of its metaphysical and moral structure. The metaphysic of Voudoun is not, then, to be arrived at by questioning a series of informants who, baffled by an approach on unfamiliar, abstract grounds, embarrassed by a sense of personal inadequacy and humiliated by the implication that they lack in an understanding of their own practices, would improvise answers according to their respective powers of invention. However, the inadequacy of such confused and conflicting articulations is precisely an inadequacy of articulation and not of the metaphysic itself; and just as the Bible serves as a more reliable source for the Christian metaphysic than the fumbling answers of some chance pedestrian, so it is the ritualistic structure itself of Voudoun which has here served as the source for a study of the meta-physics implicit within it.

* The efforts to systematize the presentation of the pantheon seem consis-tently to have been based on a rejection of the possibility that it expressed a

An arrangement of the Voudoun pantheon which would be accurate in terms of the metaphysical system of which it is a part, must indicate simultaneously, both the cosmic and the human principles of which a loa is compounded; it must, in a sense, locate each loa as point of intersection between the objective and the subjective realities. This is the method which governs both the accompanying chart (pp. 82–5) and the discussion which follows. The cosmic principles are distin' guished in one direction, so to speak;* and at right angles to this plane are the major *nanchons* (nations or tribes) and family lines. The purpose of the tribal identification is not primarily to indicate historical origin, but to designate an

metaphysical logic of even minimal caliber. The loa have been listed in order of ceremonial invocation (Maximilien), without any interpretation of the logic of that order. They have been listed in the order in which they occurred to the mind of informants. (Herskovits has so listed them. He elsewhere remarks that the loa may be divided into categories such as the "great" loa, the ancestral, the personal, etc., but does not arrange the known loa in such categories.) They have been listed alphabetically. (Simpson (II) lists 152 loa in this manner.) They have been classified according to the animistic system (Denis). Most frequently they have been arranged in terms of tribal or national origin. (Cour' lander has devoted great care to such an arrangement, but within the tribal group the loa have, again, been listed alphabetically instead of in order of importance or logical precedence.) Such an arrangement does not account for the link between tribes, does not illuminate what they hold in common and even conveys the impression of presenting a comparative study of separate cultures instead of clarifying the principle by which the various tribes could amalgamate into a single religious system and showing in what manner such an amalgamation affected the original and separate pantheons.

* The order in which these are presented is not the ritualistic order. Legba, who is normally first, being guardian of the gates, is here followed by Ghede, who is usually saluted separately, at the very end of the Rada rite. However, Ghede seems to have absorbed so many of Legba's original functions that it has seemed meaningful, in presenting the pantheon, to place these two loa in immediate proximity and so reveal Ghede as principled complement to Legba. Loco and Ayizan, as patrons of the hounfor and the priesthood, normally follow Legba, since they are understood as the agents of communica' tion with the loa. While this is ritualistically logical, I have preferred to retain the continuity between all the elemental loa, and to put the priesthood principle at the end, since it is essentially a different order of principle and leads one back to the human world after the divine tour. These are the major departures from the conventional ritualistic order.

identifiably characteristic attitude or ethos, which is the meaning such identifications have come to have for the contemporary serviteur. When a Haitian says "Nago", for instance, he may or may not be aware of the original geographical location and the history of the Nago tribes. But he is certain that a Nago loa is characteristically more militant than Rada, although perhaps less cosmic in the primordial sense; more established and powerful than Petro, but less immediately aggressive and forceful; more generally respected than the Ibos, but less intimately authoritative for Ibo families. In short, he intends an identification which contains, for the informed serviteur, a complex characterization relative to the other nations. Within such major tribal designations, he may also make reference to family lineage, either as an indication of personality (as a minor variant of the major character or aspect) or because such designation serves the personal psychological function of proclaiming his own intimate and physical relationship to the divinity.[5] In a sense, he thus describes the family tree from the original racine or root principle, up through the major divisions, to his own family branch.

Where there had previously appeared to be a mass and maze of assorted loa, such an arrangement suddenly reveals a galaxy of unanticipated integrity and dimension. The enormous range of the aspects illuminates the scope and grandeur of the principle; and the principle, in turn, gives meaning and stature to the manifold variations. Indeed, it reveals the truly cosmic nature of the major loa, for each of them contains elements of all the others. Each incorporates, in one way or another, and to varying degrees, life force or fecundity; the protective or paternal; some aspect of both the over- and the under-world or death; some degree of both the positive and the negative aspects of the dominant principle represented; and some measure of both abstraction and magical immediacy. The loa are distinguished, one from the other, not by their limitations, but by their differing emphases, and the emphasis colors the elements which they share. In a sense, *each loa is but an aspect of one central cosmic principle differentiated by the emphases which that central principle manifests according to the varying contexts in which it operates.*

Such an arrangement of the pantheon reveals, as well, a significant facet of the Haitian serviteur. For the characterological details and accessories by which the various manifestations of his loa are identified are not decorative, whimsical accoutrements; they are evidence of his genius for creating a concrete physical expression, not only of the general ideological sense of each loa, but of the subtle emphasis and even nuance by which each aspect is distinguished. As Rada Goddess of Love, Erzulie speaks in diminutive, soprano accents; in her Petro aspect her voice has a primordial, almost beast-like growl.* Such characterological delineation in living actuality stands, in Voudoun, in the place of the literature and art in which most other mythologies portray their divinities.

The intimate relation between loa and serviteur, the dependence, as it were, of the loa upon the very blood of the serviteur for existence and transmission, has been the guarantee of the loa's life. Today the gods complain more and more frequently that they are not served well enough, nor feasted adequately. And, indeed, if their energies are not restored, they may, for want of proper devotion, in turn soon grow too weak to support the devotee. Meanwhile the serviteur, throwing up his hands in an ambivalent gesture at once of helplessness and defiance, says: "Let them do what they wish with me. I can't do any more." Displacement, poverty, instability are effecting a gradual but certain demoralization. The psychic blood of the people is growing thinner; the great gods appear less frequently. The serviteur says, with a nostalgic resignation: "Big loa cannot ride little horses."

When they do appear, many of the major loa weep. Various

---

* Almost every detail is specified for the aspects of the loa, and these serve both to identify him and to guide his ritual service. Postures, voice level, attitudes, epithets, expressions, etc., are formalized for each aspect; and each has specific colors, days of the week, trees, beverages, diets, etc., sacred to him. Such information is given throughout the works of writers on Haiti, and Rigaud has been especially systematic in recording such detail.

explanations are given for this. But the loa presumably have vision and the power of prophecy, and it is possible that, with such divine insight, they sense, already, the first encroaching chill of their own twilight. It is not surprising that this should come. It is more surprising that it has not, already, long since passed into night. Yet the gods have known other twilights, and the long nights, and then the distant but recurrent dawn. And it may be that they weep not for themselves, but for the men who served and will soon cease to serve them.

When this occurs, this pantheon which has been manifest only as living form, will leave behind it little of written record, save what may be subsequently recorded in the light of another world, another era. In this suspended, composed twilight, which neither distorts by dazzling nor yet destroys with darkness, the loa seem to linger a moment, as one might pause on the threshold of departure, to remember, and to be remembered, and to be perhaps recorded in this luminous light.

I

LEGBA—THE OLD MAN AT THE GATE

The myths of all men agree that, first, there was light: the birth of the world and the birth of the sun are one. In Dahomey, this fire of life in which divine creative power was first made manifest, was Legba; and today, in Haiti, the ritual bonfires burn for him.[6] As the sun, then, he was the medium through which that primal energy was funneled to the world, the cord which connects the universe eternally with its divine origin. Thus, of all earth's procreation, Legba is both the parent and the patron.

As principle of life, as the initial procreative whole, Legba was both man and woman and his vever still bears the sign of this totality.[7] As navel of the world, or as its womb, Legba is addressed in prayers at childbirth with the phrase which signals him: "Open the road for me . . . do not let any evil

VEVER FOR LEGBA

spirits bar my path."[8] But Dahomeans knew him mainly as the cosmic phallus, and the statue of Legba, squatting, staring at his own enormous symbol and source of generation, was every-where: in the market-place, the common square and, above all, at the cross-roads, where its blessing of fertility fell upon all those who passed, as the sun shines in all directions and is itself central to all of them.[9]

Whether as cord or phallus, Legba—life—is the link between the visible, mortal world and the invisible, immortal realms. He is the means and avenue of communication between them, the vertical axis of the universe which stretches between the sun door and the tree root. Since he is god of the poles of the axis, of the axis itself, he is God of the Cross-roads,* of the vital intersection between the two worlds. The poteau-mitan, the center-post of the peristyle, through which the loa arrive at the ceremony, is also called the *poteau-Legba*;[10] and whatever other sacred tree may be missing, there can be no

* The significance of the cross-roads in Voudoun metaphysics has been discussed on pp. 36-7 and pp. 72-3, *supra*. Courlander (pp. 22, 25 and 35) elaborates on other aspects of Legba as cross-roads loa.

hounfor without Legba's tree at the gate (there are usually two); for it is not only itself an avenue for Legba, it is the symbol of all avenues as well.*

Since he stands at the cross-roads, he has access to the worlds on either side, as if he were on both sides of the mirror surface which separates them. Therefore it is of Legba that one may inquire: "Papa Legba, we ask you, What do you see there?" "O Creole, learn the secrets, O Legba."[11] And at the same time, "Alegba watches me. We do not see him, he sees us. All those who say the truth, He is there, he hears. All those who speak evil, He is there, he listens. . . ."[12] Indeed, his knowledge comprehends the whole universe, and because he knows, also, the sacred language of Mawu-Lisa,[13] the language of the highest god and the loa, it is through Legba that all prayers and supplications must pass.

Legba, then, is guardian of the sacred gateway, of the *Grand Chemin*, the great road leading from the mortal to the divine world.[14] It is he who grants contact with the loa, and he who must be first saluted if this is to be achieved. "Papa Legba, open the gate, Attibon Legba, open the gates so that we may pass through, Papa; When I will have passed, I will thank the loa. . . ." "Legba, who sits on the gate, Give us the right to pass."[15] Indeed, in Haiti it is now Legba's major function to guard the gates.

As origin of life, the sun was origin of time, too, and of history, and, as origin it contains, as well, conclusions. In Dahomey Legba was called *Fa* (Destiny),[16] for, once initiated, nature and time pursue their logic and follow their inevitable course. The *Grand Chemin* is the celestial arc of the sun's path. Legba, who knows the divine language and through whom one might seek recourse from destiny, is himself the destined answer to the riddle of the Sphinx: he was once the new-born

---

* Offerings to the loa are usually made at the center-post in the peristyle, although they are sometimes made at the trees sacred to the loa. Offerings to Legba are made, usually, at his tree, however, and a *macoutte* (straw sack) filled with food is kept hanging in it for him. Various songs make reference to this macoutte.

infant sun, lived through the fertile prime of his noon, and is now the old sun, walking with a cane—the "third leg" —in the afternoon of life.* The serviteur sings tenderly of this venerable ancient, who was a good man. "Legba, limping along. It is a long time since we have seen you";[17] "Old bones, oh old bones. . . . O Papa Legba, O can't you see I have no bones!"[18] And they would help him, for he is their past: "I will carry Legba's macoutte [straw sack]; Put it on my back."[19] And when he can no longer even walk, they will carry him and his burden: "Try to walk, now, Alegba; We will carry Attibon Legba; We will carry his poteau⁄mitan. . . . When we're tired we'll set it down. This post we carry on our back."[20] Indeed, the Haitians do not know him as the beautiful young man of Dahomey, the patron of sexual urges. They say that he is an old peasant who has worked his fields hard all his life and is now at the end of his powers. When he possesses a person, the limbs are crippled and twisted and terrible to see.[21]

Legba, who was life and its destiny, who was the Sun, itself destined to descend from the noon of each year, from the zenith of its ardent fire, has become an old tattered man shuffling down the road, with his crude twisted cane or crutch, a small fire in his pipe,[22] a little food in his macoutte, and sores on his body, as if the maggots had begun their work already. It is as if in coming westwards, the Africans had left behind the morning and noon of their own destiny, the promise and power of their own history. The God of the Cross⁄roads himself approaches the Cross⁄roads,[23] and already in the dark mirror of the nether regions appear the first dim outlines of his inverted reflection, as the sun, setting into dark waters, might there appear as a new darkly rising moon. Already Legba, who is the tree stretching skywards, carries also the name Grand Bois,[24]

---

* The walking⁄stick upon which the sun leans as it grows old and weak is a classic and universal accoutrement of the sun deity. It is the "third leg in the afternoon" of the Sphinx's riddle, and was especially marked by the Egyptians in a celebration rite for the "nativity of the sun's walking⁄stick" (Frazer, p. 78). In Haiti the twisted, gnarled cane is known as the *baton⁄Legba* (Courlander, p. 109).

master of the island below the waters, of its submerged forests. Already his omniscience, which was the result of his central, supreme position in the center, from which all could be seen, becomes the omniscience of one who, being below earth, is of all parts of it.[25] Already he is linked to Carrefour,[26] whose other hand holds firmly that of Ghede, Lord of the Underworld, God of the Dead.*

. . . AND CARREFOUR—THE YOUNG MAN AT THE CROSSROADS

Yet destiny has an immediate as well as cosmic aspect; the daily death of the sun forebodes the year's end. Legba, SunLord of the Crossroads, of the meeting point of opposites, is twinned by his own opposite. Across from him, on the same gate, sits the Petro Maît' Carrefour (also called Kalfu)[27] and he too commands the traffic through it. If there were no gate, the world would be much less divine; but it would also be

* Basing himself altogether on other mythologies, Campbell has related the sun to the Tree of Life, hence the Sun Door as Navel of the Universe (pp. 41–46), where the opposites which guard it are transcended (p. 89) and which may also be considered the universal Crossroads "through which man ascends and God descends" (p. 260). This same concept is represented in the figure of the Yoruban Edshu, trickster deity of the crossroads, who is characterized by a hat of several colors (one for each direction) and who is beautiful on one side and tattered on the other, as well as by the African Chiriwi, who is a halfman at the crossroads (p. 72). Both of these figures represent Death as well. And the same metaphysical crossroads is personified in the androgynous creator deity as well as in the Chinese Tao; this latter is defined as "road" or "way", as the course of nature, *destiny*, cosmic order, the source of law of being, and is composed of Yang, the light, active, masculine principle, and Yin, the dark, passive, feminine principle, which are represented enclosed in a circle, divided by a serpentine line into black and white (p. 152). Finally, Campbell relates the crossroads with these other elements into a concept of crucifixion as a coincidence of opposites. What is both significant and astonishing is that all of these various elements, culled from various mythologies, are contained in the figure of Legba and precisely in the metaphysical relationship in which Campbell has perceived them. In Legba, however, many of the elements had already been lost, or were preserved only in cryptic, vestigial details. (The Sun motif, for example, has almost vanished.)

more reasonable and more just. For it is Carrefour who may loose upon the world the daemons of ill chance, misfortune and deliberate, unjust destruction. No man, however carefully he may have built up a logical structure of proper and good destiny, is wholly safe from such disruption. Legba is the divinity of the cardinal points; Carrefour is the master of the points between.[28] If Legba commands the divinities of the day, Carrefour commands the daemons of the night. The divinities of the day are fundamentally just, and if they cause a man misfortune, it is for just cause, a punishment that disciplines the recalcitrant serviteur. But the daemons of the night are dangerous, for they can be put to work by the arbitrary will of men and by the manipulations of magicians.[29]

Yet it is Carrefour himself who can protect against these very daemons, and it is in his name that the garde against such harm is fashioned.[30] Thus, he is not, himself, more evil or malevolent than Legba.* If the Haitian has come to serve Carrefour and invoke his protection almost as often as he supplicates Legba, we must infer that he finds the daemons of misfortune active and widespread. His evaluation of the world in which he finds himself is precisely rendered in the figure that Carrefour presents when he manifests himself through the body of a serviteur. This is no ancient, feeble man; Carrefour is huge and straight and vigorous, a man in the prime of his life. His arms are raised strongly in the configuration of a cross. Every muscle of the shoulders and back bulges with strength. No one whispers or smiles in his presence.[31]

Thus, as the cosmic year of the race wanes, and Legba, the sun, droops toward the cosmic horizon which divides the upper regions from the underworld, so even in the daily, immediate round of day and night it is Carrefour, the moon, who has the greater immediate power. Daily, at the hour of midnight, his noon, he is at the zenith of his vigor, and forms, with Grand

---

* This again reflects the concept that, while loa make men powerful, it is the men who make magic, not the loa.

Bois—master of the night earth and night forests—and with Baron Cimitière—sovereign of the cemeteries—the patron trinity of the magicians.[32]

2

GHEDE—CORPSE AND PHALLUS;
KING AND CLOWN

If Legba was the sun, at first young, then growing old, Ghede is the master of that abyss into which the sun descends. If Legba was time, then Ghede is that eternal figure in black, posted at the timeless cross-roads at which all men and even the sun one day arrive. The cross upon a tomb is his symbol. But the sun is each year reborn. If Carrefour is the night death which attends each day, then Ghede is the night sun, the life which is eternally present, even in darkness. The cosmic abyss is both tomb and womb. In a sense, Ghede is the Legba who has crossed the cosmic threshold to the underworld, for Ghede is now everything that Legba once was in the promise and the prime of his life.[33] Indeed, it is to Ghede Nimbo that they now sing: "After God we are in your hands, Ghede Nimbo",[34] as if he were the first and most immediate expression of original creation; they also call him "Rising Sun".[35] Ghede is, today, the phallic deity, also. If Legba was once Lord of Life, Ghede is now Lord of Resurrection;[36] and the difference between them is Death, which is Ghede. It is the knowledge of death that has transfigured Legba, and has given to all that they have in common the particular color and accent which is Ghede.

Life for Ghede is not the exalted creation of primal ardor; it is a destiny—the inevitable and eternal erotic in men. He is lord of that eroticism which, being inevitable, is therefore beyond good and evil and is beyond the elations and despairs of love. Of this he is neither proud nor ashamed; if anything, he is amused by the eternal persistence of the erotic and by man's eternally persistent pretense that it is something else.

He may gently ridicule the sentimental, by singing in childish syllables: "I love, you love, he loves, she loves, What does that make?" (Chorus, drawn out) "L'AMOUR." He may mimic the passionate. Or, again, he may invent variations on the theme of provocation, ranging from suggestive mischief to lascivious aggression. His greatest delight is to discover some one who pretends to piously heroic or refined immunity. He will confront such a one and expose him savagely, imposing upon him the most lascivious gestures and the most extreme obscenities. Thus he introduces men to their own devil, for whoever would consider sex as a sin creates and confronts, in Ghede, his own guilt.* Such incidents amuse him, but they represent no real challenge, for he knows that no one can elude him, who is master of both life and death.

As Death, he is the keeper of the cemetery, guardian of the past, of the history and heritage of the race. The cross of Baron Samedi (as Ghede is sometimes called) is in every cemetery; and the graves that are under the special protection of his female counterpart, Maman Brigitte, are marked by a mound of stones.[37] Just as one must first address Legba for divine counsel, so whoever would seek ancestral counsel or support must first address Ghede: "Ghede Nimbo, behind the cross, Ghede; Before Baron, Ghede; . . . Today I am troubled; Gedevi, call Ghede, . . . I am troubled. . . . Cease to sweep, sprinkle, hoe; I am troubled, Baron Samedi. . . ."[38] He is officially notified of marriages, births, quarrels, troubles, all major projects, for the future stems from the past, and if a man would deny him as his past, Ghede will remind him that he is also his future. Perhaps he will sing him the song of the grave-digger, a jerky, blood-chilling, hypnotic melody. No one who has ever seen Ghede in that death's-head aspect, and heard that

---

* Ghede's unfailing discernment of attitudes toward sexuality accounts, I believe, for the sexual emphasis which visitors have found in Voudoun, for nothing will more quickly provoke Ghede's appearance and his defiant, overt obscenities than the presence of white visitors, particularly those of Puritan tradition. Sexual obscenity and the breaking of taboos is characteristic of the death figure in many mythologies, including that of the American Indians.

hysterical "ke ke ke ke ke" of the grave-digger, could ever forget it.[39]

As Lord of Eroticism, he embarrasses men with his lascivious sensual gestures; but as God of the Grave he terrifies them with the evidence of the absolutely insensate: he will not blink even when the most fiery liquid is sprayed into his eyes, and only Ghede can swallow his own drink—a crude rum steeped in twenty-one of the hottest spices known.* Thus he may alternately remind men that he is their past, their present and their future, that he is master of their compulsive drive to life and of the inevitability of their death; that he is, in fact, their total lord. So accustomed is he to this complete power over men that he does not belabor it as a power, a triumph or a threat. In fact, he prefers not to be bothered with the grimmest of his manifestations. Instead, he achieves the ultimate in disdain by his ostensible negligence of that very power which is of such ultimate importance to men. All men will one day be "swallowed by the grave"; perversely, Ghede poses most frequently as a poor wandering beggar, famished of course, but content with the crudest of food, which he consumes ravenously. His omnipresence, too, he translates into a mockery, as if it were mere chance, or at worst an indiscretion, that he should always show up at the wrong moment.[40] Even the houngans cannot discipline him. He will frequently arrive, unbidden, at a ceremony for another loa, to "spoil" it, as the houngan would say, and he doubles this impertinence with his wandering beggar pose.

One day, for example, a strong houngan was conducting an important ceremony for the loa. Both Damballah and Ogoun had already come in full force. This was cause for rejoicing and everyone was occupied with these deities and the rituals attendant to their presence: the sacrifice of the chickens,

---

* Since it is possible that an insincere serviteur might wish to take erotic advantage by pretending to be mounted by Ghede, any suspect possession is subjected to these two tests. Obviously, only a really possessed person could stand them.

the drawing of vevers at the foot of the trees that Damballah had climbed, the bringing of the saber to Ogoun, and the ritual salutations to both, with the ceremonial flags. Into the midst of this pious activity, dressed in a motley assortment of bits and pieces of garments, one worn over the other, and proudly sporting a peculiar multicolored little cap, strolled a benign and plump Brav Ghede.* At first the houngan was distressed and asked him to leave, since, as he could see, this was not yet the moment for his presence, which would be enthusiastically invoked a little later. Ghede listened with a sympathetic, understanding air. "Oh, I just dropped in", he said, making a self-effacing gesture, "to look around a bit. Don't bother with me. Go right ahead with your ceremony. I'll just stroll around and look things over." The houngan, relieved that Ghede was in such a reasonable mood, thanked him, and turned to attend to his ceremonial. "Oh, by the way," said Ghede, touching his shoulder, "I'm just starved! I'm sure you can spare a couple of cassavas [flat breads] for me to munch on . . . say about nine of them." The houngan still was getting off easily, for these cassava breads only cost a penny apiece, and if that would pacify Brav Ghede, it was well worth it. So he brought nine cassavas from a little wayside booth, presented them to Ghede, and went off about his pressing business.

Ghede immediately started eating two cassavas at a time, one from each hand. With the others tucked under his elbow, he modestly took his place among the spectators at the ceremony, standing there as if he were just "one of the folks" watching the great loa Ogoun and Damballah. Then he put his seven cassavas down on the ground, and, after a bit, wandered off.

The Ogouns and the Damballahs were extremely active that day, and everyone's attention was concentrated on their activities. At the moment of Ghede's departure, all were clustered around another tree, in which Damballah seemed to be on the point of deserting the man whom he had possessed, leaving him his merely human powers to climb down again.

---

* Referred to usually as "Brav", this is one of the "racine" aspects of Ghede.

Since this would be dangerous for the man, the houngan was pleading with Damballah to bring the man down before he left his head, and everyone was concerned with the outcome of the incident. Suddenly a great howl came from Ghede, who was now standing at the first tree.

"There are thieves! . . . thieves! . . . thieves!" he was shouting. "Someone stole my seven cassavas! I left them here, I went off to look over the place, to 'surveille' [to supervise things] and they were stolen! Who is the thief?" On and on he went, causing such a disturbance that everyone moved over to him to try to pacify him. He questioned one after another, he screamed, fussed, made a great circle with his arms to indicate the size of a cassava more enormous than any that had ever been baked, and said that his cassavas had been of that girth; then he caught hold of the poor distracted houngan and repeated the story over and over, stamping his foot, shrieking, weeping, protesting against this terrible treatment. The whole place was in an up⁄roar. Damballah and Ogoun were being neglected. There was nothing for it but to purchase Brav a whole new batch of cassavas, and some biscuits as well this time, to appease him for this great effrontery and hurt which he had suffered.

As he accepted the new offering his face flooded with a smile of such sly triumph that the entire incident, which had been suspect all along, was clarified. As a matter of fact, one young woman who had been sent to fetch something from the hounfor had all along protested that she had observed Ghede surreptitiously taking away one of his original cassavas. But Ghede had quite out⁄screamed her. Now, as the loa turned to walk off with his new food, the houngan, smiling, said to him: "Are you sure that it wasn't a man in a little multicolored cap who stole those cassavas?" Ghede wheeled with enormous eyes of innocence. "A little cap? What man in a little cap?" And as the houngan turned to attend to his other duties and Ghede again started off, presumably to eat in peace this time, someone else called out: "Are you sure that you don't know who stole your cassavas?" Whereupon, looking at us out of the corner of

his eye with a delightful and endearing mischievous expression, Ghede winked once, slowly, and walked away.*
What testifies most to Ghede's importance, however, is the
fact that he can function in a somewhat similar manner even
outside the religious context. It seems that some years ago, under
the régime of President Borno, there suddenly appeared in the
streets of Port-au-Prince a crowd of Ghedes (all of them
houngans possessed by Ghede) wearing the "formal" costume
of the lord: the tall top-hats, long black tail-coats,[41] smoked
glasses, cigarettes or cigars, and canes. An enormous crowd
naturally collected about them, and joined them in their march
to the National Palace. They all took the guards by surprise,
and, singing, swerved through the gates and up the drive and
to the door itself, where they demanded money of the President.
President Borno, who is reputed to have been sympathetic to
Voudoun ritual (secretly so) and yet feared bourgeois opinion,
was in a great dilemma. He finally gave in, ostensibly merely to
quiet the mob, and the Ghedes with their supporters left the
grounds. But Ghede had made his point. Death, who has
consumed so many heroes, bows before no man and will
remind even the most illustrious that one day he too will be
consumed. So Ghede had gotten his money and went off to
gorge himself, singing the song which commemorates the
occasion and which is today one of the most popular songs of
Haiti:

> Papa Ghede bel garcon, [he is a handsome fellow]
> Ghede Nimbo is a handsome fellow,
> He is dressed up all in black,
> He is going to go up to the palace!**

Indeed, wherever and whenever men assemble he may

---

* In this episode the similarity between Edshu, the African cross-roads deity,
and Ghede is striking, not only in trickster personality, but particularly in
regard to the motley cap. Ghede is frequently concerned with hats, and usually
wears a black top-hat.

** This account, which is common knowledge, is purported to be a historical
occurrence and is related by Courlander (p. 86).

choose to appear among them with his nasal voice, his black or purple color, his smoked glasses and his perpetual hunger.[42] As Death consumes the world, so Ghede is the archetypal glutton.* Even in his most elegant manifestations, he eats ravenously, stuffing the food into his mouth with both hands. There is a special Creole word for the way he eats: "baffler". He washes the meals down with his fiery drink, and when his stomach cannot hold any more, puts a cigarette or cigar in his mouth. There are even certain malevolent aspects of Ghede where his need to consume turns in upon itself. As Criminelle, a Petro manifestation, he sinks his teeth into his own arm, and the friends who would protect the man possessed by Criminelle from this voraciousness must work hard and frantically to unclamp the jaws before the flesh is torn.

One time, when Brav seemed in a genial, informative mood, we asked him why he liked to wear smoked sun-glasses. "Well," he explained, "I spend so much time in the dark underground that it makes my eyes sensitive to the sun." "Why", we asked then, "do you remove the right lens so often?" "Well, my dear," he answered, "it's this way: with my left eye, I watch over the whole universe. As for the right, I keep that eye on my food, so that no thief will get it."** And indeed, Ghede does not miss any opportunity to fix his worldly eye on food even when it is not, strictly speaking, within his dominion. As Lord of the Dead, he is, theoretically, concerned with men's souls; his physical gluttony is, presumably, symbolic. As Lord of the Underworld, he should not (theoretically) be concerned with the earth's agrarian surface, except perhaps to participate (symbolically) in fertility rites. But Ghede, who respects no prohibitions at all, is not inclined to recognize the fine distinction between the telluric and the chthonic zone, which is properly his. In his most casually arrogant manner, he has completely invaded the province of Azacca, loa of agriculture, who becomes, in such competitive comparison, a very minor

* See illustration 5, facing p. 150.
** This one-eyed effect suggests Wotan, one-eyed God of the Dead.

VEVER FOR AZACCA

figure. Ghede does not even consider it an impertinence to attend a ceremony for Azacca; he assumes that he is also expected. This is explained by the comment that Ghede and Azacca are brothers.* While Ghede does, in fact, have an indulgent, protective attitude towards him, it is not entirely disinterested, and the privileges of such "brotherhood" are not at all mutual, for Azacca would rarely presume to appear at a ceremony given specifically for Ghede, and their happy relationship is undoubtedly due to the fact that Azacca never tries to use it to his individual advantage and knows his own place.

In some ways Azacca's personality would seem to be modeled after Ghede, as a younger brother might slavishly imitate the elder, but since he is a mere peasant, his efforts fall short constantly. Like Ghede, Azacca has a ravenous appetite; unlike Ghede, however, he is very insecure and when he gets

* It should also be noted that there is a Ghede Mazacca, an obvious statement of relationship between the two loa, and Herskovits (p. 280) identifies Azacca Médé with the River God of the Dahomean Styx.

his food he runs off with it into a dark corner like an animal hiding in its lair. The greedy, slobbering manner in which he consumes that food is a reflection of crude ignorance; he has no notion of the arrogance which Ghede intends by his deliberate vulgarity. The exaggerated sexuality which, in Ghede, reflects his sophisticated defiance is nothing but simple, direct animalism in Azacca. Whereas Ghede speaks in a nasal voice because a properly buried corpse would sound that way, and because, incidentally, it projects perfectly his cynicism, Azacca's vocal stylization consists of the almost unintelligible sounds of a goat. All in all, this inarticulate, gauche peasant Pan* is the sort of person whom the sophisticated, dexterous Ghede would normally ridicule to distraction. However, there is a certain sympathy between Ghede's knowing perceptiveness and Azacca's peasant shrewdness. Moreover, Azacca is a very hard worker, and appreciation of that is shown in the relative frequency with which he is ritually feasted by the grateful farmers. Ghede, in fact, knows a good meal-ticket when he sees it, and he is not above taking advantage of it; or, to put it otherwise, he *is* above any concern with the appearance of dignity.

Perhaps his indulgent kindness, even gentleness, is inspired

---

* In addition to his "hick" peasant aspect, Azacca also appears (more rarely) as a young peasant boy, with all the shy and innocent charm that is part of such a personality. On other occasions he is "Ministre Azacca", Minister of Agriculture, with all the pompous postures of authoritarianism. One of the striking things about the Voudoun pantheon is the lack of an agricultural deity of first magnitude. In the interests of "rounding out" this pantheon, one is tempted to place Azacca Médé in this position. But he is very close to being a work loa, in spite of the fact that he is well served and does have a greater depth and range of personality than most other work loa. However, the idea of fecundity in general is implicit in most of the major loa. Ritualistically, agrarian fertility is covered in the African *ceremony-yam* (pp. 210–12, *infra*) which is still of major importance in Haiti and is not, significantly, under Azacca's patronage. Azacca seems to be an interpolation in Rada ritual from the Indian maize culture and it is in the Petro rites of that culture, that the propitiatory ceremonies which would normally mark a major agrarian deity, take place. (See Appendix B.) Thus Azacca is a minor expression, in Rada ritual, of the principle which is mainly carried by the Petro cult.

by something else as well. For Azacca's simple, honest affection, his natural, even admiring acceptance of this brother, must be a welcome change from the anxiety, fear and ultimate with‑drawal which Ghede senses in all men and which all his clowning and all their laughter can never quite obscure. In‑deed, this ruler of men is, of all loa, probably the most lonely; he is never so touched as by the least sign of genuine affection and to Azacca he must be grateful for the one thing he cannot command. Perhaps it is because of this need that, of all loa, he is the most interested in the trifling, intimate details of men's daily life. With his keen worldly eye he learns all the secrets of the neighborhood: who flirted with whom, and what that brother called his sister. But his need could not go so far as to make him sentimental or respectful, and he will tell all the juiciest morsels in public to the embarrassment and amusement of everyone. Sometimes his omniscience takes the form of a knowingness that makes him at once the most modern and sophisticated of the divinities. For this modulation, his mani‑festation as Mr. Entretoute is the supreme example. If Brav Ghede is a broad trickster, Mr. Entretoute is a subtle wit. Where Ghede would be obscene, Mr. Entretoute is slyly erotic. Whereas Ghede's dance is broadly sexual, Mr. Entretoute moves with an intimate, suggestive subtlety. Whereas Brav is the beggar, wandering afoot, Mr. Entretoute complains about the upkeep of his "Dynaflow". This Mr. Entretoute is the somewhat special Ghede who is in Titon's head, and Titon, be it observed, has never been outside of Haiti. Through Titon's head, nevertheless, Ghede, the cosmic God of the Dead, has become Mr. Entretoute, cosmopolitan *par excellence*. The cosmic eye and the worldly one feed into the same brain.

Although Ghede's vast range of power and information never confuses him, he may delight in using it to confound others. He is both tattered and beautiful. He confounds sex with sex, dressing women as men and men as women.* He is

---

* Though it is rarely explicit, there is frequently a suggestion of Ghede as a hermaphroditic deity, like Legba.

both sensual and insensate. He even confounds life with death. One day, as Mr. Entretoute, he told a hilarious story of how he had gone to a doctor because of pains in his heart. The doctor discovered that he had heart murmurs—"battiment de coeur" —and decided to operate in order to remove the murmurs. But according to this poor Mr. Entretoute, the doctor had made a terrible mistake. He had removed the heart and left the mur/ murs, from which Mr. Entretoute still suffers.

While he would seem to prefer the rôle of the witty clown, Ghede will also use his wisdom in a more serious manner. Since he contains the knowledge of the dead whom he has consumed, it is from him that one may learn whether one's father thinks it best to plant a field with cane or corn, or what mother's prescription is for a nagging headache; or which of two suitors is the more reliable; or whether this woman would make a good wife. And Ghede is generous with his wisdom. He may be playing the clown, but if you will call him aside and humbly ask him, in all seriousness, an important question, he will generally answer you thoughtfully and carefully, and it will usually be the best possible advice. Clown though he be, and trickster, he is also history—the experience from which the living learn—and in this rôle is as deeply responsible and trustworthy as he is bizarre in his other aspects.[43]

Straddling the great divide between the living and the dead, Ghede is, naturally, not only the lord of both, but the lord of their interaction. Therefore, if anyone would make magic, would set invisible forces to work in the visible world, it can be only with Ghede's permission. Whether as Baron Samedi, as Baron Piquant, or as Baron Cimitière,* it is he (with Carrefour, often Grand Bois, and also, often, Simbi) who governs the indispensable, invisible forces of magicians. It is through him that the zombies are brought up from the grave,

---

* Again, it is men who make magic, not the loa. There is much disagree/ ment among authorities as to which Ghede is Rada and which is Petro. Actu/ ally, the Ghedes, as Maximilien suggests, are separate and independent of both, and their rite usually comes after the Rada and before the Petro ceremonies.

and there is even a song in which those who are digging up a corpse ask Baron Samedi to ". . . hold that man. Don't let him go, heavenly judge, hold that man . . ."[44] so that the body will not escape. Here, in this dark phase of his powers, the trickster becomes transformer. Under his sign the malevolent bocor may take the shape of an animal, and men may be transformed into terrible bakas.* But it is Ghede, also, who can protect against such magic. The *paquets* Congo or Petro—the gardes against illness and evil—are bound under his auspices (with Carrefour and Simbi).[45]

Finally, Ghede, who is death and has the power to animate the dead as zombies, to change a man into a beast, is also the greatest of the healers, the last recourse against death. When a houngan conducts a ceremony for Ghede, he brings out the gravely ill who are under his care and commends them especially to Ghede's attention. For Ghede is just, and if it is not yet time for a man to die, and if that man humbly asks him as a defense, he will refuse to dig his grave no matter how much the magicians under Baron Samedi, may insist on it.[46] Thus Ghede is the last recourse, the final judge of a man's life and of the worth of his soul in death.

Particularly, Ghede is known as the guardian[47] of children.** If he has consumed life, he will also give of it when necessary. In one case, the godchild of a mambo was gravely ill. The little girl had been taken to doctors in town, had received injections and treatments, both medical, herbal and ritual, yet continued to waste away and it was clear that she was on the point of death. Consequently, as a last recourse, the mambo undertook a strong ceremony for Ghede. It took place at the replica tomb which was erected in Ghede's honor in the court of her hounfor,*** and was attended not only by her own hounsis, but by several mambos, friends of hers, who had

* See Chapter II, p. 75, *supra*.
** It is interesting that Hallowe'en, "All Souls' Night", which falls on the same date as the Haitian annual Feast of the Dead for Ghede, is celebrated here primarily by children.
*** See illustration 6, facing p. 150.

come to lend their own strength as well. The songs for Ghede were most fervently sung. Several black chickens were given him, and then the large black goat, an exceptionally strong offering, was killed.

With this evidence of devotion, Ghede agreed to intervene. He possessed one of the mambos, and asked that the child be brought out and placed on the tomb. He took the blood of the goat and, undressing the child, anointed her with it. Then, singing fervently, he reached down between his legs and brought forth, in his cupped palm, a handful of fluid with which he washed the child. It was not urine. And though it would seem impossible that this should be so, since it was a female body which he had possessed, it was a seminal ejaculation. Again and again he gave of that life fluid, and bathed the child with it, while the mambos and hounsis sang and wept with gratitude for this ultimate gesture. Of the life which he had in the past consumed, he now gave forth in full measure.* And though there is no reasonable way to account for this, the child lived.[48]

3

DAMBALLAH—THE GOOD SERPENT OF THE SKY...

Damballah Wedo is the ancient, the venerable father; so ancient, so venerable, as of a world before the troubles began; and his children would keep him so: image of the benevolent, paternal

---

* No similar episode has been cited in the literature on Voudoun, possibly because of a sense of discretion on the part of the writers. I have included it here as a definitive example of the life-making aspect of Ghede, an aspect which is often lost sight of inasmuch as his sexuality usually has an emphasis upon obscenity. At dances, indeed, he usually appears in his clown or vulgar aspect. It is only in the important ceremonies that his life-giving and healing attributes have a sober aspect. This particular ceremony was witnessed in the fall of 1948, in the plains about fifteen miles outside of Port-au-Prince. Taken all together, Ghede's character and activities are a perfect realization of the metaphysical principle which he represents—the corpse which informs man of life—as elaborated earlier, pp. 23 and 37.

innocence, the great father of whom one asks nothing save his blessing.* He comes as a snake, plunging at once into the bassin[49] of water which is built for him,** and then writhes, dripping and inarticulate, upon the ground, or mounts a tree, where he lies in the high branches, the primordial source of all life wisdom. He makes his signs, his gestures of benediction; when he speaks, it is a barely intelligible hissing.[50] There is almost no precise communication with him, as if his wisdom were of such major cosmic scope and of such grand innocence that it could not perceive the minor anxieties of his human progeny, nor be transmuted to the petty precisions of human speech.

Yet it is this very detachment which comforts, and which is evidence, once more, of some original and primal vigor that has somehow remained inaccessible to whatever history, whatever immediacy might diminish it. Damballah's very presence, like the simple, even absent-minded caress of a father's hand, brings peace. As *Da*, origin and essence of life,[51] of the dynamic movement of which his own movement is such a graphic demonstration, Damballah is himself unchanged by life, and so is at once the ancient past and the assurance of the future.

He is shown as a snake, arched in the path that the sun travels across the sky;[52] sometimes half the arch is composed of his female counterpart, Ayida, the rainbow.[53] He is patron of the waters of the heaven which he dominates, and of the springs and rivers which the heavenly waters nourish and upon which the race for ever nurses. As it plunges into the sea, the cosmic waters, the rainbow is reflected (or, in the bassin, is painted

* Although the familiar relationship between divinity and devotee is one of the most important and touching aspects of Voudoun, and has been strongly manifest in attitudes toward Legba and Ghede, the serviteur has a rather special, respectful reserve toward Damballah. This is reflected in the songs, which rarely cite incidents but are mainly in general praise of him, saluting him as the great serpent and referring to his affinity with water. Courlander (p. 93) quotes a song in which he is compared to a stone wall for his strength.

** See illustration 11, facing p. 182.

as reflection).* Damballah and Ayida, who together represent the sexual totality, encompass the cosmos as a serpent coiled about the world. The egg, the world egg[54] is the special symbol for them; and an egg is the particular offering to Damballah. He drinks it, crushing the shell with his teeth.[55]

When, in the course of ceremony, the houngenikon opens with the words: "O Wedo, calling Wedo, O Wedo there, it is Damballah Wedo", the drums and the chorus surge forward with such solid sound, such deep fullness, as rarely marks the invocation to any other deity. It expresses a special profound reverence, impressive beyond whatever degree of love or intensity, excitement or tenderness might mark their other invocations. For Damballah is the major benevolence, the mighty protection, the lofty evidence of a just and eternal good.[56]

Associated with Damballah, as members of the Sky Pantheon, are Badessy, the wind, Sobo and Agarou Tonerre, the thunder.[57] It is possible that there was a time when such natural elements were very important in men's lives, and although these divinities still hold their important position in the ritual order, they do not frequently possess the serviteur. They seem to belong to another period of history. Yet, precisely because these divinities are, to a certain extent, vestigial, they give, like Damballah's detachment, a sense of historical extension, of the ancient origin of the race. To invoke them today is to stretch one's hand back to that time and to gather up all history into a solid, contemporary ground beneath one's feet.[58]

. . . SIMBI—THE SNAKE IN THE RIVER . . .

Since, by his very nature, Damballah is a positive force, and encircles the universe, he has no contrasting equivalent, either in the underworld or in the negative, malevolent sense. He does have, however, an equivalent on a plane of more immediate

* Marcelin (p. 56) cites a song which says, "I say: Sky, salute the earth!" an exceptionally poetic reference to the serpent, sun or rainbow bending towards the earth.

action. Simbi, who occupies a rather remarkable position in the pantheon (see chart), shares characteristics and functions not only with Damballah but with all the major deities on both the Rada and Petro sides. In a certain sense, he contains, in his own person, all the primary principles of an entire religion, and in very explicit fashion. He is definitely a cross-roads loa, and his symbol, or vever, is a snake in a field of crosses.[59] In this he is related to Legba, on the one hand, and to Carrefour, Ghede, Baron Cimitière and Baron Samedi, on the other, depending upon whether he is called on the "point" of Rada or of Petro. In Simbi's case, the cross-roads principle is extended to the concept of straddling the Rada-Petro division in one direction (it is said that, while Simbi is primarily Rada, a "hungry" Simbi would be invoked through Petro)[60] while in the other direction, he is known as Simbi-en-deux-eaux and straddles the waters above and the waters below the earth, which are understood either as the heavenly and the abysmal waters, or as the sweet and salt waters. His primary Rada function is as patron of springs and rains, and in this, as well as in the snake symbol, he is related to Damballah, and to the other "white" deities who are guardians of springs. As patron of rains he is understood to be even stronger than these others. This strength is partially due to his other major function, that of patron of the magicians, and it is in this connection that Simbi is most often called.[61] Certainly it is a rôle for which his pivotal position in the cosmos and in the pantheon equips him admirably, for he radiates in every direction from this central location. (He is the only loa, for instance, who overlaps into Agwé's dominion.) All magic is performed under his patronage, whether it be the medicinal, protective paquet, or the less benevolent wanga. Yet, for all his activity, his personality is more obscure than that of many other loa. Songs refer repeatedly to his reluctance to enter the hounfor gate, his loitering outside, like a sociable neighbor newly come to the district, who is still a little shy for all his knowledge and power."

... AND THE PETRO RIDDLE UP A TREE

In some regions Simbi is predominantly associated with Petro, in reference not only to Carrefour and Baron Cimitière, but also to Dan Petro, the father of the Petro tribe of loa.[62] As such, Simbi is the link between Damballah and the major Petro deities who, while they could not be considered as "Petro aspects of Damballah" (in the sense that Legba and Carrefour are twinned opposites), do command an equivalent position in their respective hierarchy and also share other characteristics with Damballah. As a matter of fact, there is a Damballah La Flambeau (the torch) who is understood as a Petro Damballah and La Flambeau is, in turn, understood as synonymous with Saint Blanc or Petro Blanc.[63] Of this latter it has been said: "He is a great chieftain who commands his servants, and these are often evil."[64] In a sense, then, even Dan Petro or Congo Zandor, as he is also known, is not himself malevolent.

The linkage with Damballah is further suggested in the figure of Ti-Jean Petro, son of Dan Petro, who is characterized as having only one foot, or perhaps no feet at all, and, simultaneously, as being extremely agile in climbing trees, which he almost always does as soon as he appears.* If one were to pose a riddle, asking what creature has no feet yet always climbs trees, there could only be one answer: a snake. Such a cryptic formulation is in character with the cabbala-like magic which typifies Petro. It is even possible that Dan, in Dan Petro, does not stand for the Spanish word "Don" but for the snake principle.

Thus the major Petro divinities—Dan and Ti-Jean Petro, Congo Savanne and Congo Zandor—function, like Damballah, as the ancestral reference of the cult, as its life source, guardians, and water patrons. In a sense Damballah, Simbi and Petro are not opposites at all, but are rather like three

* For a comparison of Ti-Jean Petro with the one-legged Aztec God of the Underworld, also patron of cross-roads and magicians, and related to the night sun or moon, see the Appendix on Indian influence.

concentric snake circles encompassing the world. The outermost, Damballah, is at once the most abstract, ancient and benevolent; Simbi has both the power and the ambivalence of his middle position; while the Petros are at once the most stern, hardheaded and forceful. Moreover, they add an element which is lacking in the other two; they are the closest to the earth, and the most concerned with it, the entire Petro cult showing a strong agrarian emphasis.

4

AGWÉ—SOVEREIGN OF THE SEAS

On the day of the ceremony for Agwé,* God of the Sea, the large court of Mambo E—— churned with activity. In one spot hounsis were washing the sacrificial chickens; in another they were ironing their white ceremonial dresses. In addition to the regular outdoor kitchen, charcoal grates had been set up here and there throughout, to accommodate the vast amount of cooking. People arrived constantly with their personal offerings of cake, bottles of *crème de menthe* and other liqueurs, even champagne. The peristyle was being sprinkled and swept, and some of the torn paper decorations were being prepared. In the shade of a large tree, the drummer, surrounded by curious children, was replacing the worn ropes which held tight the drum head. But the two exceptional objects which caught the eye were the sacrificial ram and the *barque d'Agwé.***

The ram had been thoroughly bathed, as was customary with all sacrificial animals, in water steeped with certain purifying leaves. What was extraordinary was his bright blue color, the result of massive amounts of indigo. It was not quite clear whether this was due to an overzealous miscalculation of the amount of bluing necessary to make him a brilliant

* Although it is sometimes written as Agoué or Aguet, the spelling Agwé has been used to make clear that this loa's name is not of Latin derivation.

** See illustration 12, facing p. 182.

white; or whether it was intentional, since blue, as well as white, is a color sacred to Agwé. His electric color, the royal composure with which he permitted the attentions of the three young women who curried and combed him, the graceful postures of their bodies, all these composed into a scene of strangely archaic import, as if one had stumbled upon the fragment of an ancient urn, and was shocked into a sudden understanding of the sacred sacrificial beast.

In the shade of one of the adjacent peristyles, surrounded by those who were momentarily unoccupied with ceremonial preparations, the painter was putting the last touches to the large, square barque which was to hold the offerings. It was made of wood, and was over a foot deep and about six feet square. Extending inward from the rim was a narrow shelf, with round holes cut out at intervals. Into these the bottled offerings would be inserted, and held upright throughout the long rough journey to and on the sea, so that the arrangement would be beautifully intact when the banquet table was set before Agwé.

The barque was blue, and the painter was now completing the symbols and decorations around the outer edge. His technique was naïve, and full of delight in color. Yet the brightness seemed internally weighted with sobriety, so that one felt, without knowing precisely why, that even the most frivolous flower, set, as it was, in a constellation of three, or five, was portentous. Clearly, the planning and painting of this had taken days of labor.

To judge by the symbols, it was Agwé's banquet, with other major divinities of the pantheon as guests, as it were. Agwé, represented by a large sailboat (with the word IMMA⁄MOU upon it), and his wife, La Sirène (the sea⁄aspect of the Goddess of Love, Erzulie), shown as a mermaid to Agwé's left, sat together at the head of the table. Beside her was a white pigeon, or dove, a bird sacred to the major "white" deities and particularly associated with the Goddess.

Along the side to Agwé's right were the Wedos, Damballah

VEVER FOR AGWÉ

and Ayida, supreme family of the pantheon. Their two
serpentine forms wove through a field of nine five-pointed
stars, to confront each other across a central altar which supported their particular symbol, the world egg. The side to the
left of Agwé and La Sirène had, at its center, the checkered
heart which was the major symbol of the Goddess. It represented Erzulie (as "land"-Goddess of Love), whose constant
gentleman companion was known to be Ogoun, the hero God
of War, recently turned diplomat and politician. Ogoun,
himself, had been placed (according to the crossed flags and
saber which were his symbols) to her right, that is, at the immediate left of the head of the table. He was deity of fire; and
legend had it that there was a constant feud between Ogoun
and Agwé, based not only on the antagonistic elements which
they each represented, but upon their competitive relation to
Erzulie, who, both in her own person and as Sirène, was
acknowledged as consort of Agwé even while, simultaneously,
being chronically "en affaire" with Ogoun. To have trustingly

placed Ogoun between La Sirène and La Maîtresse, with the gentle white pigeon or dove of love and peace in immediate proximity, was a conciliatory gesture of generosity, as well as of subtle diplomacy on Agwé's part. To the left of Erzulie, the heart motif was repeated, enclosing, this time, the initial M. This letter, by a most fortunate coincidence, stood both for "Maîtresse", the familiar form of address to Erzulie, and for Mary, with whom she was identified, because they were both the major female divinities in their respective provinces, and shared certain feminine refinements. The inclusion of the M heart balanced, if it did not entirely correct, Erzulie's legendary promiscuity. (It is said that even the venerable Damballah, as well as others, had at times succumbed to her charm.) At the foot of the table, there were a fish and a crab, with the inscrip/ tion "Master of Z'ile Minfort", the island below the surface of the water to which the barque was to be delivered. The crab represented an ancestral houngan, Agassou, who was Agwé's lieutenant, and the fish represented St. Ulrique, who had been identified with Agwé by virtue of the fish he holds in the Catholic chromos. When one compared the sides of the table carefully, one remarked that the side dedicated to Agwé's aides, in the Voudoun and Christian churches, was just a little more modestly set, having only three flowers as a decorative garnish. And this discretion was a most subtle deference to the other more illustrious guests, the Wedos, Ogoun and Erzulie.

The ceremony itself was in honor of Agwé, specifically. But the Lord of the Sea is a man of royal habits, and it was pro/ bably felt that he would prefer to be gracious host at a cele/ bration, rather than to receive, simply, a vast amount of food to be consumed in submarine solitude. To serve a deity well is to make him happy; and reverence lies in a sensitivity for the particular personality of each loa, his attitudes and his tastes.

The preparations continued throughout the afternoon. The coming and going involved an amazing number of people, who, to judge by their expressions, were each of them charged with a responsibility of major importance. And if it could be observed that ten women seemed to be occupied with a task which, with any degree of efficiency, could have been accomplished by any two of them, one had also to recall that any one of them habitually accomplished, in her daily life, a succession of chores and arrangements which would have seemed to require at least three active people.

The sea ceremony for Agwé is, for an inland mambo (or houngan), perhaps one of the most elaborate of all ritual undertakings. She must accumulate the offerings: vegetables, cakes, maize, bananas, pigeons, rams, chickens, etc., etc. She must assemble all the extra equipment, borrow cooking-pots, purchase and properly consecrate the new vessels in which the feast would be served to the deities, arrange for the construction of the barque. She must convene her *société* (or parish), delegate and supervise responsibilities, provide food and lodging for all her helpers and guests, arrange for a truck to transport everything and everybody, rent the sailboat which would carry them all out on to the sea, and remember a million other secular details. Apart from this, the actual organization of the ritual details of the service was itself an enormous responsibility. Because it was both costly and difficult, many houngans and mambos never undertook it at all. The others did so at increasingly rare intervals, during which the promises made to Agwé accumulated substantially. The ceremony thus became a very special occasion and in the end the real problem of the mambo was not how to inspire interest and devotion, but how, diplomatically, to keep the number of eager participants within manageable limits.

By twilight the major tasks had been accomplished and everyone had convened in the large peristyle for the preliminary service. The vevers were traced, the libations poured, and, in their proper order, the invocations followed: to Legba, that he should open the gates; to the Christian Trinity and saints, that they should bless the undertaking; to les Morts, les Mystères, and les Marassa; to the important deities and those which were guardians to the mambo; and finally, and above all, to Agwé and his consort, to "signalé" (inform) him that all this was to be for him, and to ask him to accept it. The day had been building up to this moment, and in these songs the drums and the voices were deeply fervent. And over and above the singing, carrying far into the space of the night, sounded the clarion call of trumpet and conch shell (used as a horn), the particular call for Agwé.

It was close to eleven o'clock, and since everyone had to be up at four o'clock the next morning, there was no dancing following the ceremony. Each one went off to the sleeping-mat in the corner which had been allotted. Excitement had made me sleepless, and I wandered down the road to walk it off. When I returned, a single oil lamp burned in the rafters of the large peristyle, and I was curious to see what might still be going on. I realized then that the ceremony had not, after all, been yet completed. At one end of the peristyle a table had been set up as an altar, covered with a white embroidered table-cloth which reached to the ground. Branches of palm had been bent and bound together to make high, parallel arches, and over these had been stretched another large, white cloth, embroidered and lace-edged, to form a high arched canopy over the table. Ropes of a brilliant pink flowering vine out-lined the arches along with bouquets of fragrant laurel. Two large chromos of St. Ulrique and the Virgin were pinned to the inside of the canopy, and on the table had been placed a sampling of the finest of the offerings, including a bottle of champagne, another of perfume, and again, a vase of flowers.*

On the ground immediately in front of this altar, a huge double bed had been extemporized from layers of thick straw sleeping-mats. It was made up with immaculate linens, and two pillows in embroidered, lace-edged cases, had been placed close together at the head. One corner of the white cover was neatly and properly turned down. And a little below the

---

* See illustration 3, facing p. 54.

pillows, where, I imagine, the hearts of the bodies would be, there lay an exquisite bouquet of roses, and close beside it, a conch shell of the most perfect shape and color. Never had a bed been more tenderly and lovingly prepared. And never, certainly, had it been destined for lovers such as these. Divinity is cosmic in scope; and the cosmic implies real stature. The bed measured at least twelve feet in length and eight in width, and it seemed even more grand than that. It was the nuptial bed of Agwé and Erzulie.

A candle burned at the foot of the center-post, and to one side, seated in a rocker, the mambo was keeping vigil. She had dozed off for a moment, and held her sacred rattle loosely in her lap. Some small night sound must have awakened her. Without opening her eyes, she shook the rattle gently several times and began rocking slowly back and forth, her lips beginning the small movements of silent prayer.

I think that in the heart of most mambos, and of most women serviteurs, Agwé holds a special place, and that who- ever may be their maît-tête (and this might often be one of the male divinities), as women they identify with Erzulie. Though her relationship with Damballah was important, and that with Ogoun most exciting (because of his contemporary power as hero politician, and his fiery aggressive personality), it is Agwé who is, in a sense, the ideal husband and lover, being, as the sea is, both immediate and enduring, both a ready strength and a deep peace.

The first sounds of preparation began at three in the morning. The offerings and all the enormous quantity of paraphernalia were packed in baskets of every shape and size. At four the two large open trucks, of the kind used for carting gravel, arrived, and benches were lined up in them. Then the loading began: the drums and the ram and the barque d'Agwé and a huge seven-tiered white wedding-cake, and the chickens and the pigeons and the baskets of food and the ceremonial flags and much more; and finally, after that, the people, who seemed, by then, to number several hundred, but probably added up to about fifty. Then, with the more agile hanging on to the frame-work, the trucks lumbered off down the road.

The drums set up the initial beats, and the blowers of the trumpet and the conch shell, who were perched on the roof of the cab, picked it up, and the voices lifted into the cold dawn. In every small community clustered along the road, the people ran out and cheered us on. Eventually the trucks left the high-way and turned down a tiny, rutted, mud road which cut directly toward the sea. It was obvious, soon, that the mud would make it impossible to reach the shore by truck. We pulled to a stop and unloaded at a point which turned out to be a good two miles from our destination. The barque, the baskets of food, everything was hoisted up on the heads, and, in single file, safari fashion, we started out for the sea on foot. The sun was rapidly growing hotter, while the mud gave way to a gray, oozing clay in which one sank deeper and deeper with each step. When it no longer seemed humanly possible to go any farther, the screen of trees which we had been ap-proaching thinned out, and there, anchored a good distance from shore (for the ocean floor sloped gradually here), was the sailboat which awaited us, its bright trimmings dancing in the wind. On the shore we gathered once more for ritual, vevers, salutations, songs. And again everything was hoisted to the heads of the people, even the ram had to be carried this time, and the safari waded into the water.*

It was over five feet deep at the boat, but, as they said, the gods were with us, for nothing was lost and everyone managed to clamber in and set about arranging things in the impossibly small space. It was already ten o'clock, and, there being no shade from the sun, the heat was soon unendurable. Those who had no hats wrapped handkerchiefs around their heads, moistening them from time to time. The clothes, initially wet from the wading, were kept wet now by the perspiration which poured from everyone. Those who were responsible for arranging the barque were particularly unfortunate, since they

* See illustration 7, facing p. 151.

worked in the deep open hold of the ship, into which no breeze penetrated.

In the flurry of ritual preparation no one had thought to bring fresh drinking water, and within a short time every face seemed rigid with the effort of endurance. Lips were painfully parched. There was practically no conversation. Those who were concerned with the final arrangement of the barque communicated by gestures. Grouped together, silently passing the things from hand to hand, or indicating placement to one another, they seemed to be dancing a strange, cryptic ballet in slow motion, seen through the shimmering veil of rising heat.

But they sang, and the drums beat and the trumpet and conch shell called, over and over. In the intervals between songs, the grating and ringing of the mambo's rattle and bell was the only sound. She stood near the mast, apparently oblivious of everything, sounding her rattle and from time to time she lifted the two white chickens which she held in one hand, toward the cardinal points, signaling Agwé. They made no protest, and the ram, too, had been stunned into silence by the heat.

Again they chanted—songs on behalf of sailors, and in praise of La Sirène, and, for Agassou, and, above all, in praise of Agwé and the mighty thunder of his cannon, the flash of his lightning strokes. But especially they repeated, several times, the most haunting song of all, a calling kind of melody, which rose and fell in a minor key, and seemed to be borne so swiftly away on the wind that the mind's eye saw, in swift kaleidoscope, the waters of the brilliant Mediterranean, the grey Arctic, the South Pacific, and the never-seen, unknown seas everywhere, wherever they might be—with these voices, borne by this melody, ruffling the waves of each of them, calling the god everywhere, over the vast reaches of his domain.

> Cina, Cina, Cina,
>   Dogwé sang, cina lo-gé
>
> Agwé Arroyo, protect your children,
> Sea-shell in hand, care for your little ones,

Cina, Cina,
Cina dogwé sang
Cina lo⁄gé.

And if one watched the sea, or closed one's eyes against the heat, one might imagine the singers of these divine songs as themselves of divine, ecstatic aspect. But the sounds rose from creatures disheveled with effort, almost "decomposed", as they said, with the heat, the faces grim with endurance, even ugly with irritability. What, in such a context, did it mean when, somewhere, someone would state that belief was comfort, that ritual "released" the "inhibitions"? Here the serviteur was a worker and his every movement, his every aspect, workman⁄ like.

Apparently we were nearing, now, the island beneath the water, although I was never to discover exactly how this was determined. Suddenly a certain haste was made to complete the preparations. The barque was now piled high with every conceivable food and delicacy, arranged to make the finest possible display, and topped with the huge white wedding⁄ cake. The houngan who was assisting her took the chickens from the mambo, killed them with a deft movement, and laid them also on the barque.

At this first offering, two women were almost simultaneously possessed by Agwé. The initial convulsive movement occurred so suddenly that almost no one had remarked it, and now their faces, which had been normally feminine, planed off, im⁄ perceptibly, into a masculine nobility. Water was drawn up from the sea in a pail and poured over them, since normally Agwé, being a water divinity, would have immediately immersed himself in the bassin. Those who were near saluted the arrival of the divinity, and, through each of the women, Agwé spoke a few words of greeting in a voice which gurgled as if with rising air bubbles, and seemed truly to come from the waters. His mood was not displeased, but it was sober. The houngan, conscience⁄stricken, began to explain that he, too, would soon make a ceremony. The two Agwés listened to him, their eyes at once forgiving and somehow detached. One thought: perhaps they forgive because they are detached. And, with the same air of noble, gentle sadness, they looked slowly from person to person, from the barque of food, to the mambo. There was something in their regard which stilled everyone. One had seen it in the faces of those who prepare to leave and wish to remember that to which they will no longer return. They met each other's eyes, and as a way was cleared for them, approached each other, and crouched down in an embrace of mutual consolation, their arms about each other's shoulders, their foreheads lowered, each on the other's shoulder. So mirrored, they wept.

It is said that the gods of the Sky Pantheon all weep. Some say it is because they first came from the waters below the earth and are still, in a sense, wet. Others say that the rains which fall are the tears of the gods; so it is because the gods weep for man out of compassion that life can go on. But I had seen Ogoun weeping also, and neither of these legends would explain his tears.

The people in the boat were accustomed, now, to the fact that their great gods wept, and they accepted it, sometimes saying to them, as one would to a child, that they mustn't weep. Yet, after all, one could not hope to understand all the moods of the gods, and there was work to be done, and the ceremony to be continued. The houngenikon began a song, the drums, trumpet and shell joined in, and the chorus. The preparations gathered speed, and, with everyone moving deftly so as not to disturb or intrude upon the Agwés, the ram was passed forward. One hardly had time to observe it before the animal was lifted to the rail, where it balanced for a moment, and then plunged into the water.

Apparently we were now directly over the sacred "zilet" for the last ritual consecration of the barque was accomplished with almost frantic speed. It was so heavily laden that six men were required to lift it to the rail. A cry of "Attention!" went up, the boom swung widely in the opposite direction, the boat swerved and tilted sharply on its side. In that split second, when the water lay almost level with the rail, the men slid the barque on to the surface of the sea. Our boat lurched and righted itself and there, below us, and already behind, the barque was drifting swiftly away in our backwash. It looked incredibly lovely, the high-piled offerings, crowned with the sparkling white cake, drifting in the deep blue of the sea. As we all watched it silently, it seemed to hesitate to a stop, and then, as if a great hand had reached up from below and grasped it, it disappeared abruptly into the quiet water.

The houngenikon, the drums, the chorus burst forth all at once, into a vivid song of "rejouissance". It was the first song of joyous nature since the beginning of the trip. Beside me stood the painter, his eyes fixed on the spot where his barque had disappeared. He was singing joyously. Everyone had worked hard, and had given, each in his own fashion; but for the painter there must have existed an image of special pride in his mind's eye, as he saw the fabulous submarine palace where the great Papa Agwé, pleased with his servant's labor, was already motioning his illustrious guests toward this banquet table.

I turned from him to the glad faces of the others, and turned away to the sea and wept. It was at this moment that I understood why the gods, who loved these men, would weep.[65]

5

OGOUN—WARRIOR HERO; STATESMAN AND
DIPLOMAT; POLITICIAN AND GANGSTER;
MAGICIAN

The Nigerian Ogoun who crossed the ocean from Africa was a figure in the same classic tradition as the Greek Zeus. He was a sky divinity, Lord of the Thunderbolt,[66] of fire and of might.[67] By logical extension he was patron of warriors and of the iron-smiths, forgers of war-weapons. But the Ogoun whom the

VEVER FOR OGOUN BADAGRIS

houngans so often choose as the guardian deity of their houn⁄
fors today is not altogether this original figure. Ogoun is might,
power, authority, triumph; and the means by which these are
achieved vary with historical circumstance. Today power is
political; and Ogoun is, in fact, often a political figure.

If one were to assemble the various manifestations of Ogoun
and parade them in order, one would have, in fact, a
procession of the hero⁄types of history. The most poignantly
noble would probably be that of the mortally wounded
warrior, whose opening song, sung haltingly and in obvious
pain, announces: "I am wounded, oh, I am wounded." The
wound seems to be in his heart, and, since he is dying and
unable to keep on his feet, he is held upright by someone on
either side. His arms are thrown loosely over the shoulders of
his supporters and the tears begin to roll down his cheeks as he
is half⁄dragged, half⁄carried to a chair. In this moment—with

the side-stretched arms, the drooping head, the profoundly noble expression of the face, the attenuated, fallen posture of the body, and the tenderness of his two supporters, whose bodies are slightly bowed beneath his weight—he becomes the uncannily precise image of Christ being taken down from the cross.* (It is improbable that these people have anywhere seen that Christian image. Yet even if they had, and if this were an unconscious re-creation of it, it would be the ultimate testimonial to their profound perception of the meaning of Christ. And if the image is not derived, but original to Voudoun, that also testifies, in another way, to an equal profundity.)

Although this may, in a certain sense, be the most impressive manifestation, there are many other important Ogouns, just as there are many ways of power, and each Ogoun can strengthen the devotee in his special fashion. As Balindjo or Batala, Ogoun is known as a healer. In this aspect he often shows particular concern for children, and will spend a long time preparing some herbal remedy. As Ogoun Feraille,** he will impart strength to a serviteur by slapping him firmly on the arms, the thighs and the back, as if to infuse that body with a portion of his own power. As Ogoun Badagris (who, like Ghede, is related to fertility, wisdom or prophecy, and magic)[68] he may lift a person into the air and carry him about the peri-style, an indication of his special patronage of that individual. There is even an Ogoun Bayé (barrier, gateway) and an Ogoun Panama (straw hat), who as gate-guardians, recall Legba. Whatever his aspect, an Ogoun always bears that special Nago mark, of power and militancy.[69]

The idea of force, conflict, and power is almost inevitably linked to fire and heat. Ogoun is deity of fire, and red is the color sacred to him. Moreover, he must not be saluted with the usual libation of water. Instead, rum is poured on the ground,

---

* This manifestation occurred in precisely the same way several times, over a five-month period, and was accepted without surprise, as if those present were familiar with it, although it does not seem to be a very common aspect.

** Frequently spelt "Ferei".

and a match is set to it, and he is brought in on that fire. As the flame moves toward its destination, led by a houngan trickling the rum before it, one senses keenly the arrival of a dynamic force. When Ogoun himself is present, he may pour rum on the ground and light it, and the warm aroma which rises and pervades the peristyle seems to be the very breath of power and strength. Those who are present gather the fragrant fumes in their cupped hands, as if it were a liquid, and wash their bodies with it.

Power resides, too, in the saber or machete which is sacred to Ogoun. To indicate that he is its master, he will press the very sharp edge into his arm or his thigh and then reveal that the flesh has not been pierced by it. Sometimes he will go to the extreme of planting the hilt of the saber in the ground, so that the blade is vertical. Then, with his diaphragm resting upon the point, he will slowly lift his feet from the ground, until his body is spread-eagled and its full weight balanced entirely upon the point of the saber. Although the shirt is pierced, Ogoun's flesh is not.*

Another characteristic manner is manifest in St. Jacques, the loa named after the saint with whom Ogoun Feraille has been identified. He is the national hero, the general who is greeted with a military salute and the national anthem, an impressive figure. Obviously authoritarian, a disciplinarian, he paces rapidly back and forth, every gesture and expression conveying a sense of crisis, of urgency, the pressure of battle or of conflict. Intense, ready to fly into a rage, he periodically shouts: "Foutre tonerre!" (By thunder!) which is his special epithet, or announces: "Grains moin fret!" (My testicles are cold)—his particular way of demanding a drink of rum. Often he will spurt this rum through his teeth in a fine spray, a gesture special to the Ogouns.[70]

It is this same revolutionary hero who is representative, too, of the political Ogoun, for a political figure does not lend itself

* I witnessed two Ogouns in this incredible posture simultaneously, at a hounfor near Carrefour (just south of Port-au-Prince) in September 1949.

to an archetypal statement in the grand style. The politician's craft is primarily verbal in its overt expressions. Moreover, as the Haitian well understands, it is not even this overt verbalism which is the real source of expression of a politician's power. The actual battle is conducted in secrecy and intrigue, and these are not the materials out of which a grand figure can be externalized as personality. Therefore Ogoun continues to appear as the military general which he became during the struggle for independence. Nevertheless, if a man is influential, politically or economically, if he can ease the way for the required permit to conduct a ceremony, if he can "arrange" for a cheaper price for the new tin roof, if he seems prosperous or prospering, if he moves in official or authoritative circles, then it is almost assumed that Ogoun is his patron, perhaps even his maît'tête, although the man may have nothing of martial mien about him.

Sometimes, in minor aspects of Ogoun, the politician will emerge more clearly. There is a deity Jaco (derived from St. Jacques) who is definitely of the Petro cult and whose charac' teristic activity is the sly creation of disorder, ill'temper and misunderstandings between people. Unless he is rapidly con' trolled or sent away, the ceremonial or dance soon dis' integrates.[71]

It is also significant that most of the houngans who claim the patronage of Ogoun belong to the Masonic Order.[72] It is a logical association. As ironsmith, upon whose craftsman' ship much depends, as moral authority, as the respected "influential" citizen much involved in civic affairs and welfare, as a natural leader and organizer of men, and certainly as a believer in ritual, initiations, hierarchy, etc., Ogoun might very well have been a leading member of a local Masonic lodge. Moreover, since Voudoun is not a centralized religion, the Masonic order has come to serve, curiously enough, as a kind of unifying meeting ground for the houngans, even to the point where the Masonic handshake has become a standard part of the ritual Voudoun salutation between houngans. It is possible

that other Masonic symbols have been introduced into Voudoun ceremonial, but it would require an advanced member of
the Order to recognize the actual degree to which this is so.
It might be expected that the warrior divinity would be
strongly represented in the Petro ritual, but Ogoun's essential
nature, in spite of all the modifications which history has
imposed upon it, is an honest heroism, at variance with the
spirit of Petro. Neither the African Ogoun, nor St. Jacques,
the military general, could have initiated the revolution of
independence. It was not a movement of massed troops led by
a hero on a white horse; it was, at least in its beginning, a
conflict of another kind, in which secret plotting, sudden raids
and guerrilla tactics were in order. And so the Petro cult, with
its "guerrilla" organization, its individualistic emotional
intensities, its emphasis on magical means, supplanted Ogoun
in the rôle that, theoretically, he might have played. Moreover,
since the Petro loa altogether are stern, violent, or even
malevolent, and work with fire, a Petro Ogoun would simply
duplicate functions already fulfilled. Ogoun Yemsen and
Ogoun Ge-Rouge,[73] who are among the few Petro Ogouns,
are not as important as are Dan Petro, Ti-Jean Petro, and
Congo Zandor, of the Rada side.

Although Ogoun, as a divine warrior, has largely given way
to the figure of authoritarian force, and this, in turn, is beginning to give way to the even lesser figure of political skill,
the original hero, in all his divine dignity, has not been entirely
consumed by history. He still exists, and has even been given
a more profound dimension in the Christ-like image of the
martyred hero. If this great figure is finally eclipsed, it may not
be by the soldier, or the guerrilla, or even by the politician
ward-healer; it would probably be by the figure of some
Haitian equivalent of our "Captain of Industry", or, what is
worse, an archetypal opportunist or careerist.

At the moment, Mounanchou[74] is admittedly a minor deity,
a work deity of a mambo, and for the moment he would seem
to represent nothing more ominous than the principle by which

an individual might function well—a sense for organization, for the executive attitude, for the creation of an air of respectability. When he possesses the mambo who is his special devotee, (and who devotes a full day to his service), he keeps people waiting a long time while he prepares for his appearance. Then, dressed in a good business suit, he arrives with a processional pomp greater than that of any other loa. He may be angry if things are not done well; he has been very much annoyed when his "reception" banquet table did not seem ostentatious and elaborate enough. Apart from this, his overt actions reveal nothing of a malevolent character.

Yet, if one begins to track down certain details in his ritual, one discovers that Mounanchou has some very strange and suspect connections in the criminal underworld of the Mystères. For example, the vever which is his symbol, is a man with three horns.* This immediately and unmistakably relates him to Bossu of the Three Horns. The Bossu family is quite large and presumably contains some good Bossus. Yet its malevolent Petro emphasis is unmistakable. Bossu is referred to as a "diobolo",[75] a "soldier of Maît' Carrefour",[76] and is altogether related to malevolent magic and the fearful bakas (malevolent spirits who frequently take animal form). Thus, underlying the apparent innocence, and even, in certain respects, pompous absurdity of Mounanchou, there exists an entire network of underworld connections. This leads, in the end, to a story which is both instructive, and, in its way, ominous; for Bossu appears to be related to Kadja Bossu, and

* Rites relating to loa whose function is primarily magical are far less "open" than other rites. Preparatory details are accomplished in secrecy, the public rite is often performed with a haste which prevents careful observation, there is an absence of the customary casual, knowing remarks which might be informative, and the attitude of the officiants prohibits the kind of inquiry which is normally welcomed. It is even probable that some of the public details serve, deliberately, to dissemble and conceal the important and significant actions, so that no observer could learn the magic formula. Since all this was characteristic of the rites relating to Mounanchou, it was impossible to definitely ascertain his rôle and relationship to Bossu, and this relationship is suggested here as a strong probability, based on a series of significant details.

thus, perhaps, to Akadja, who—legend has it—was an ancient king of Dahomey. "In his kingdom there was no Vodu; women bore goats and goats gave birth to men, and everywhere could be seen men coupling with she-goats and he-goats with women. A woman . . . came from Adja . . . and was very bewildered by the sights she saw (and she explained to the king that in her country) the women bore human children and goats bore kids . . . because they had Vodu there. Akadja requested her to bring the Vodu from Adja. . . ."[77] It would seem, however, that although Voudoun was brought to that kingdom, there still exists, ready to be regenerated at the ambitious and propitious moment, the animal-men from the times before the loa were introduced, and the archetypal careerists then will defeat the divine hero.

6

ERZULIE—GODDESS; THE TRAGIC MISTRESS

It is typical of the naturalistic, almost scientific metaphysic of Voudoun that it relates fecundity to such essentially andro-gynous figures as Legba and Ghede, to coupled totalities such as the Marassa and Damballah-Ayida, and (although fecun-dity is not regarded as one of the major meanings of the sea) even provides La Sirène[78] as female counterpart to Agwé. The female principle thus participates in all of the major cosmic forces (with the exception of the distinctly masculine forces personified in Ogoun) and Voudoun does not idealize woman, *per se*, as the principle of fecundity. Neither does it give pre-ferential emphasis to the maternal womb over the phallic principle, either as cosmic origin, or in the prevalent psychology as reflected in ritual. Because of this explicit insistence that generation is the responsibility of male and female equally, the female principle enjoys less singular and specific importance here than in several other major mythologies.*

* In European and other mythologies, the female fecundity principle appears as the agrarian principle, and, as Frazer makes clear throughout *The Golden*

But if Voudoun denies woman this distinctive rôle as a separate cosmic element, it proposes an alternative one which shem ight well find even preferable; for while the elemental cosmic principles which are personified in the other loa apply equally to all levels and forms of life, Voudoun has given woman, in the figure of Erzulie, exclusive title to that which distinguishes humans from all other forms: their capacity to conceive beyond reality, to desire beyond adequacy, to create beyond need. In Erzulie, Voudoun salutes woman as the divinity of the dream, the Goddess of Love, the muse of beauty. It has denied her emphasis as mother of life and of men in order to regard her (like Mary, with whom Erzulie is identified)[79] as mother of man's myth of life—its meaning. In a sense, she is that very principle by which man conceives and creates divinity. Thus, to man himself, she is as mistress.

It is significant that, to the Haitian, she is as important as the loa of the elemental cosmic forces and even more beloved. For the Haitian is not at all a simple, elemental man. Even though (or perhaps precisely because) it is so difficult for him to acquire even those things which are requisite for daily life, he is almost obsessed with the vision of a life which would transcend these, a dream of luxury in which even the essentials of life are refined to appear as indulgences. The lady of that sublime luxury is Erzulie. In her character is reflected all the *élan*, all the excessive pitch with which the dreams of men soar, when, momentarily, they can shake loose the flat weight, the dreary, reiterative demands of necessity; and the details with which the serviteur has surrounded her image reflect the poignant, fantastic misconceptions of luxury which a man who has only known poverty would cherish.

Bough, is the corn mother, the wheat mother, or, as we know her, mother earth. This aspect is incorporated in the Petro rites as Marinette, wife to Ti-Jean Petro, and these rites reflect the American Indian maize culture, as well as the charac-teristic elements of Indian propitiatory rites—violence, fire and bloody sacrifice. Ceremonies for Marinette have been described by Denis-Rigaud and by Maximilien, while Courlander (pp. 42 and 44) lists a number of Marinettes, such as Bras Chêche, Pied Chêche and Marinette Congo.

He conceives of Erzulie as fabulously rich, and he neither inquires into nor explains the sources of this limitless wealth, as if by such disinterest he becomes himself freed from concern with sources and means. He shares her impatience with economies, with calculation, even with careful evaluation. Erzulie moves in an atmosphere of infinite luxury, a perfume of refinement, which, from the first moment of her arrival, pervades the very air of the peristyle, and becomes a general expansiveness in which all anxieties, all urgencies vanish. The tempo of movements becomes more leisurely, tensions dis-solve and the voices soften, losing whatever aggressive or strident tones they may have had. One has the impression that a fresh, cooling breeze has sprung up somewhere and that the heat has become less intense, less oppressive.[80]

Her first act is to perform an elaborate toilette[81] for which the equipment is always kept in readiness in the hounfor or the private chapel; and it is always the very best that the houngan or serviteur can afford. The enamel basin in which she washes is neither chipped nor discolored; the soap is new, still in its wrapper; there are several towels, probably embroidered; and a special comb, mirror and even tooth-brush have been con-secrated to her. She is provided with a fresh white or rose silk handkerchief which she arranges carefully around her hair. Perfume is imperative, and there may be powder as well. A white or rose dress of delicate cloth, with lace or embroidery, has been kept in readiness for her. And, finally, she is brought not one necklace, but several, of gold and pearls, along with ear-rings and bracelets and her three wedding-bands.

It is the elaborate formalism of her every gesture which transforms this toilette from a simple functional activity to a ritual statement. The cleansing with which it begins (and which, as such, would hardly be necessary for the serviteur already at his best for a ceremony) is a ritual of purification.*

---

* Basil leaves, which are understood as a purifying agent, are especially associated with Erzulie and are steeped or rubbed in the water for her bath. Her demand for absolute cleanliness is another of her special traits.

The careful, unhurried accumulation of costume is an act which, step by step, rejects the primitive, the "natural condition", and, step by careful step, instructs the fortunate attendants in the idea of beauty, the sense of form, and, above all, the cumulative painstaking process by which a work of man—be it art or myth—is created. The Goddess examines each article minutely; where alternative choice exists, her considered selection, her indecision are very pointed; each effect is critically scrutinized, often rejected and rearranged. The very process of this creative transformation becomes so significant that whether it is a large audience or a small family who await her, or how long they may have to wait, ceases to be of any consequence. What is of consequence is the act itself, and the demonstration of the fact that such an act can transfigure the female into the feminine.

Thus attired, powdered and perfumed, she goes out into the peristyle escorted by several of the more handsome men, her favorites.[82] There she may make the rounds, greeting the men guests effusively, but extending only the little fingers of each hand to those women who are not special devotees.[83] Her voice is a delicate soprano; her every gesture, movement of eyes, and smile, is a masterpiece of beguiling coquetry; with her, human relationship becomes itself significant rather than merely a means to an end.[84] She may visit her altar chamber and be pleased that the flowers are fresh, for flowers are her passion. She may ask for a favorite song, for she loves to dance and is the most graceful of all loa; or she may simply give audience to her admirers, and by her postures and attitudes transform the crude chair in which she sits into a throne. If she is being feasted that day, she eats delicately, of a cuisine that is more exacting than that of any other loa—a just-so blending of seasonings and sauces. Above all, she favors desserts, decorated cakes and confections of all kinds. Or, if she has arrived on an impromptu visit, she may be content with a sip of the *crême de menthe* or the champagne which, theoretically, should always be ready for her appearance.*

Admittedly, requirements such as champagne seem an exaggeration in the face of the general poverty. She has even been known to say—when there was no water to sprinkle on the earthern floor to settle the dust and cool the room— "Sprinkle perfume instead!"[85] And if one indulges even such exaggerations, it is, in part, because of the overwhelming innocence with which she proposes them. She is not so much indifferent to the difficulties her requests create for the serviteur, as ignorant of the existence of difficulties; for there are none for her, and she is herself as bounteous as demanding. As Lady of Luxury, she gives gifts constantly:[86] her own perfume, the handkerchief she wears, the food and money which she conscripts from the houngan and distributes generously. She particularly rewards those who are handsome, or who dance well, or whose personality pleases her. She never neglects one who is devoted to her.

As Lady of Luxury she is, above all, Goddess of Love, that human luxury of the heart which is not essential to the purely physical generation of the body. She is as lavish with that love as she is generous with her gifts. She treats men with such overflowing, such demonstrative affection that it might seem, at times, embarrassing. She will embrace them, and kiss them, caress them, sit with an arm around those to both sides of her. Nothing is meted out or budgeted, there is more than enough; this is her way of loving, this is the divine fecundity of the heart. A heart is, indeed, her symbol, most often the pierced heart identified with Mary.[87]

It is a fecundity which minor men would call promiscuity. But her several lovers among the loa, who are major men, and the serviteurs, who have learned to see her through their eyes,

* Her sense of form extends to a rather strict sense of decorum. She will not countenance any boisterousness or disorder. She punishes those whom she finds unkempt. She will not tolerate the drinking of hard liquor in her presence, and her special devotees respect this prohibition on the days sacred to her, whether she is present or not.

have never called it that. Her past includes them all—Damballah, Agwé and Ogoun. It is for these three that she wears
three wedding-bands simultaneously. There has been, also, a
flirtation with the lesser Azacca; a dismissal of the love-struck
Ghede because he was too coarse; and any devotee who might
especially please her may be taken for her lover.[88] Yet it has
never been suggested that she betrays any of them, nor are the
loa exasperated with what might seem frivolous indecision.
Ogoun may battle with Agwé for her,[89] but in a curious way
this battle seems of purely masculine significance, a pattern
which the male ego must follow; and one senses that each of
them seeks rather to retain her favor than to exclude the other.
Indeed, it is as if, from the limitless wealth of her heart, she
could love many, and each in ample and full measure. Her
generosity is so natural that one is caught up in her exuberant
innocence, believing, with her, that all is good, is simple, is
full-blown. It is in order to feel this that the serviteur indulges
her extravagant demands, for if what is so difficult for him is
so normal for her, that very fact confirms the existence of a
world in which his difficulties do not occur.

Yet this moment, the achievement of which has strained his
every resource, is, for her, a mere beginning, the promise of a
possible perfection; no sooner is she pleased with such promise
than she moves toward that perfection. In the midst of the
gaiety she will inexplicably recall, as women sometimes do, some
old, minor disappointment. She will remark the one inadequate detail here among the dozen major achievements. Suddenly it is apparent that imperceptibly she has crossed an
invisible threshold where even the most willing reason and the
most ready reality cannot follow; and, in another moment, she,
who seemed so very close, so real, so warm, is suddenly of
another world, beyond this reality, this reason. It is as if below
the gaiety a pool had been lying, silently swelling, since the
very first moment; and now its dark despair surfaces and engulfs
her beyond succor. She who has been loved by all the major
loa (and it is not they who were promiscuous) is convinced,

by some curious inversion, that they have each betrayed her. She reiterates this complaint, even against the reminder that Ogoun still presses his court and that Agwé still takes care of her in her illnesses. She, who is the wealthiest of the loa, the most frequently gifted with luxurious accoutrement, suffers for not being "served" enough. She, who is the most complimented, most beloved, most often wedded in the sacred marriage of devotee and divinity[90]—she who is Goddess of Love—protests that she is not loved enough.[91]

Inevitably then—and this is a classic stage of Erzulie's possession—she begins to weep. Tenderly they would comfort her, bringing forward still another cake, another jewel, pledging still another promise. But it would seem that nothing in this world would ever, *could ever*, answer those tears. It is because of these tears that the women, who might otherwise resent her, are so gentle. In their real, reasonable world there is no grief like this.

There are times when this sense of all things gone wrong is projected in that combined rage and despair which is Erzulie Ge-Rouge.[92] With her knees drawn up, the fists clenched, the jaw rigid and the tears streaming from her tight-shut eyes, she is the cosmic tantrum—the tantrum not of a spoiled child, but of some cosmic innocence which cannot understand—and *will* not understand—why accident should ever befall what is cherished, or why death should ever come to the beloved. But whether the raging tears of Erzulie Ge-Rouge, or the despairing sobs of Erzulie Maîtresse, this weeping is so inaccessible to reason that one thinks, inevitably, of a child's innocence of reason. It is this sense of innocence which emanates from her that makes her identification with the Virgin Mary somehow seem truer than her promiscuity, than even the fact that the devotion of prostitutes makes of her almost their patron saint.[93]

It is possible, even, that there is no conflict between these several truths, for the concept of Erzulie as virgin is not intended as a physical analysis. To call her virgin is to say that she is of another world, another reality, and that her heart, like the secret insulated heart of Mary Magdalene, is innocent of the flesh, is inaccessible to its delights and its corruptions.* To say she is virgin is to say that she is Goddess of the Heart, not of the body: the loa of things as they *could* be, not as they are, or even as they normally should be. She is the divinity of the dream, and it is in the very nature of dream to begin where reality ends and to spin it and to send it forward in space, as the spider spins and sends forward its own thread. For the loa of cosmic forces, there is an end to labor in the achievement of some natural cosmic balance. But the labor of Erzulie is as endless as the capacity of man to dream and, in the very act of accomplishing that dream, to have already dreamed again. It is upon this diminutive feminine figure that man has placed the burden of the most divine paradox. He has conceived her without satisfactions, without balance, to insure an over-whelming balance against his own satisfactions. This is the meaning of the merciless muse, the most unhappy Medusa. Erzulie is the loa of the impossible perfection which must remain unattainable. Man demands that she demand of him beyond his capacity. The condition of her divinity is his failure; he crowns her with his own betrayals. Hence she must weep;[94] it could not be otherwise.

So, Maîtresse Erzulie, weeping, comes to that moment which has been called her paralysis. Just as the hurt of a child mounts and transcends both its own cause and solution, reaching a plateau where it exists as a pure pain, so her articulate com-plaints cease, even the sobbing; and the body, as if no longer able to endure, abandons the heart to its own infinite grief. Her limbs, her neck, her back go limp. Her arms, stretching across the shoulders of the men who support her on either side, her head tilting, the cheeks wet from tears, the lids closing over eyes turned inward toward some infinite darkness, she presents, as Ogoun did, the precise attitude of the Crucifixion. So she is carried from the stilled, saddened public to some adjacent

* It is this which places her love affairs at the extreme opposite end of the emotional scale from the sexuality and obscenity of Ghede.

private chamber. Stretched on the bed, her arms still outflung, she falls asleep as a child might, exhausted by too great a grief. Those who brought her in, and others, who, unreasonably, would still wish to do something for her, stand about quietly, speaking in whispers. They are glad to see that sleep has come, and with it, respite; for they sense that her pain is not only great but perhaps even eternal. The wound of Ogoun was a defeat which might, perhaps, not have occurred or might, conceiv-ably, be healed. The wound of Erzulie is perpetual: she is the dream impaled eternally upon the cosmic cross-roads where the world of men and the world of divinity meet, and it is through her pierced heart that "man ascends and the gods descend".*

7

LOCO AND AYIZAN—THE PRIESTLY PARENTS

Physically, man is a descendant of the sea, and in his blood he still carries its chemistry; psychically, he is descended from the divine essence beyond the sun-door; and just as the sea had to be concentrated into his veins by gradual stages, so that divine essence is funneled by stages into the microcosm of his individual consciousness. Through the sun-door it was first introduced into the general world and the major forces distinguished by elemental function; but these forces, as such, are not the loa which have just been described. To speak of loa is to recognize a second door, a second gateway, through which

* The possession described here is that of Erzulie Freda Dahomey (also known as Maîtresse), recognized as the major Erzulie and consistently characterized by her "tristesse". La Sirène resembles this Erzulie in most of the feminine details, except that blue is her color and her voice contains a hiss, as though the sea were in it. Gran Erzulie also makes relatively frequent appear-ances. She is very old, and so crippled with arthritis that she cannot walk, but goes along on her knees and with a cane. (Herskovits also has made note of this [p. 174]). Although, as grandmother, she is the most maternal and protective of the Erzulies, she retains essentially the same character as the young one, even to greeting women only with the little fingers of her hands.

the forces have once more been funneled, specifically to the race of man, here becoming divinity—a relationship of man's consciousness to cosmic force. In line with Legba, as if on a place concentric to him, stand Loco and Ayizan, the first priest and the first priestess, who are pre-eminent among the ancestral loa.[95] In them the major themes of Legba are restated as if in a minor key, changed in emphasis by their closer position to man.

In Loco, who is known as "chief of Legba's escort",[96] the theme of the sun returns again, in songs, in the walking-stick[97] which he carries, and in the often reiterated title of King. In songs he is called "Sun" Dahomey, or King, or Nago King,[98] and like the Dahomean king (and Damballah as well), he must not be seen eating, lest his sacred soul escape from his mouth or lest an evil spirit seize the opportunity to enter.[99] Ayizan too is related to Legba. She salutes him in song, as a mambo would greet a loa; and sometimes she is referred to as his wife.[100] Here, in Ayizan, are the last echoes of the andro-gynous divinity. In some regions she is referred to as "he";[101] and in songs she is related to the ancient androgynous founders of the race: Silibo-Gweto and Nanan-bouclou, said to have preceded even Mawu-Lisa,* from whom the deities originated.[102]

But Loco and Ayizan are much closer to the human race than Legba, and this is apparent in their heterosexual division of labor. The functions of the phallus and of the womb or umbilical cord are not blended as in Legba, nor is the dis-tinction minimized, as in the other cosmic male-female couples. Legba's major symbol, the tree, is recapitulated by Loco Attiso, "he of the trees",[103] and as houngan, Loco also controls Legba's center-post, the poteau-mitan. Thus Loco governs the major highways of the loa; as houngan, he is, so to speak, in charge of the divine traffic. Again, like Legba, he is understood to have access to both sides of the mirror and hence

---

* In this connection, it is significant to recall the androgynous aspect of the Marassa and the fact that these preceded man.

VEVER FOR AYIZAN

to be capable of cosmic knowledge and prophecy.[104] And just as Legba was the means by which life and time began in the world, so Loco, as the first priest, must have given the first ritual recognition to death. There is a song which commemor, ates the first *retirer d'en bas de l'eau*, and the first spirit so reclaimed was Ghede himself.[105] If one would invoke the loa, then, it is imperative to have the accord of Loco, no less than that of Legba.

In the heterosexual, human world, the concept of the vertical axis of the universe—the tree or center, post which serves as channel for the divine life forces and is governed by Loco—is differentiated from the point where it intersects the plane of this world and, it may be said, the channel empties itself; the public square and the market, place (which the African Legba included in his dominion along with the road itself and the sun, door as source and origin) is here under the protection of Ayizan, Loco's spouse and female counter, part.[106] Moreover, she is patron, as well, of the ritual stages of initiation which culminate, finally, in the canzo ceremony of spiritual birth. It is her palm leaf which purifies and protects when shredded into a fringe; it is worn as a sort of mask by the

initiate on the occasion of his first emergence into the world.*
Thus she is the loa of the psychic womb of the race and she is
guardian of the place of spiritual birth, the hounfor. In the
absence of the houngan or mambo, the sacred objects and
drums are consigned to her, as well as to Loco, for protection.[107]
But just as Loco is more than gate-guardian, so Ayizan is
more than womb. These are the moral parents of the race, not
only in the sense of source or origin, but even more emphati-
cally, in the sense of guardians. In them the rôle of the priest is
defined, for unlike the cosmic loa, they neither represent the
cosmic forces nor create them; rather, they represent the
ultimate in *awareness* of those principles, and their function and
responsibility as priests, and as parents, is to intervene on behalf
of their parish or progeny. In Voudoun the priest serves the loa
in order to serve man. It is upon the priest that man depends for
the means of controlling these cosmic forces, of correcting their
errors and failures. Loco and Ayizan, accordingly, are the
major healers of the pantheon. The invisible forces which come
by way of the trees may bring either good fortune or bad.
Significantly, it was Loco who discovered how to draw their
properties from the trees and to make the best herbal charms
against disease;[108] and while Loco thus functions as the doctor
who heals and repairs the body in an almost scientific sense,
Ayizan protects against malevolent magic, and is the psychic
security which is power and health.[109] To cure and to protect
against magic, both imply the dual function of the houngan or
mambo: on the one hand such work restores, to its sound and
natural state of health, the cosmic body, and on the other hand,
it restores the human being as well. It is a rôle which proposes
neither the superiority of the divinity nor that of the human
being, but is concerned with the adjustment between them.
Loco and Ayizan, then, are not mere interlocutors between the
loa and the serviteur, they are mediators, and their prejudice is
on behalf of the welfare of man.[110]
    None of the other cosmic loa are much concerned with

* See illustration 2, facing p. 39.

instruction; but Loco and Ayizan, who have known mortality, know that the future of the race depends upon imparting to their progeny the *connaissances*, the knowledges, by which such control and such adjustment are achieved. They know that their protective power, their control of the cosmic forces, derives from those knowledges and from themselves as dis‑ciplined, self‑controlled beings. It is this control, in turn, which they would convey to their progeny and apprentices. They not only heal, but they teach the curative prescription; they watch over the ritual discipline, lose temper with and punish the negligent houngan.* The gradual elevation of the serviteur marks his growing knowledge of the nature of the loa, the cosmic principles, and signifies his increasing mastery of those principles. It is often pointed out that the loa who were once houngans are stronger than the others, for those who control the cosmic forces are, in a sense, stronger than those forces. Loco and Ayizan represent the belief that such control is the function and privilege of spiritual maturity. Whoever understands the sun‑door and the underworld, the life forces of sky and sea, the powers of war and of love, can control them, and so can himself become the moral spirit, the soul of his cosmos. The labor of the priest is concerned with men, with the transmission and the development of divinity in man. To salute Loco and Ayizan after Legba but before the other loa is to salute first the divine miracle which is life as a physical force and then to salute the divine miracle which is man as a psychic force; it is to say that when Loco first reclaimed Ghede from the waters of the abyss, that was the first meeting of the quick and the dead which was the point of departure for man's consciousness of life, his myth and his metaphysics; and it is to say also that the dark room of the neophyte's solitary meditation is the soul‑bearing womb of Ayizan. To salute Loco and

---

* Loco is known for the violence of his anger whenever he finds that ritual disciplines are breaking down. He tends to break things and strike out in fury. Simpson (II) describes Linglessou (a loa known to eat glass) in terms which would seem to suggest that he is a Petro aspect of Loco.

Ayizan as guardians of the priesthood and the rites is to salute that in man which knows and serves divinity; it is to say that if a man should ever deny this in himself, neglect its develop, ment, corrupt or suspend its activity in the service of the loa, then there would be no loa, his cosmos would be without soul, man would cease to be man and, only as an animal, along with the other merely animal forms of life, would be, come once more part of an amoral mass of organic matter, part of the purposeless inevitabilities moving on the purposeless momentum of original creation.

5 and 6. GOD OF THE DEAD AS GLUTTON. Since death constantly consumes the universe, Ghede is known to be always hungry. Above: having "mounted" one of his devotees, Ghede eats sugar cane and keeps a covetous eye on his ritual feast. Below: Ghede's symbol, a square cross on a tomb, and a black goat, destied as offering to him.

7. CEREMONY FOR AGWE, SOVEREIGN OF THE SEAS.

CHAPTER IV

Houngan, Hierarchy and Hounfor

I

THE BEGINNINGS OF A HOUNGAN

ISNARD's father had been a houngan. In the later years of his life, however, he had devoted himself more to the cultivation of his lands, which were considerable, and less to the practice of priesthood, although personally he remained very devout. Isnard himself had been sent to stay with relatives in Port-au-Prince so that he might attend school, and, as he put it later, he considered himself a resident of the city. Even when his father died and he theoretically inherited the hounganship from him, he regarded the country property as farm land, and proposed to remain in the city as a shopkeeper or small-business man. Of course he retained his ancestral loa; but he never intended to carry out his heritage as houngan, and, as he says, he even felt a certain detachment from the entire religious structure. From time to time, however, the loa began to declare, either in his own dreams or through possessing another person, that his abandonment of the inherited profession was wrong. At first he ignored them, but their insistence became more stubborn. They began to inflict punishment upon him: he would become ill, or various of his undertakings would begin to turn out badly. The pressure increased and accumulated. One day, he says, he knew that the loa's claim upon him was so imperative that he could not deny it. Brusquely he wound up everything in the city and returned to the country. He had been unable to evade his heritage.*

* It is possible to summarize the Haitian concept of heredity, as follows. There has been no need for the Haitian to distinguish between the heredity and the environment of a child, since in a primitive culture the child is consistently subject to the parents' influence. The character of the parents—their value structure, emotional emphasis, ideology—does, in fact, become transferred to the

151

Being claimed, selected, or called by the loa is, in fact, the decisive moment.[1] Even if Isnard had never left his father's side, and, as the eldest son, had expected to follow in his footsteps, the loa would have had to confirm (or perhaps not confirm) his inheritance of the profession upon his father's death. For the Haitian, inheritance does not exist unless it is manifest. The soul of the deceased, for instance, must be heard as a voice in a govi, and the govi in which the voice sounds is passed down from generation to generation. Likewise, the elevation of this soul to the rank of loa, while it takes place invisibly, is recog-nized as having occurred only at the moment when (having become a principled archetype) it possesses a serviteur. Even the inheritance of the established parental loa is merely an invisible potential until, with maturity, the maît-tête and the other loa indicate their real, active existence in the living individual.* So also here, the inheritance of the priesthood could be ignored until, in the individual himself, that principle proved to be a dominant, dynamic and compelling force.

Inheritance, then, is a potential which may or may not be realized in the course of a person's development to a stage of decisive maturity. While it is not an autocratic imposition upon the individual, neither is it a system of autocratic

children as much as their physical characteristics. The break-up of the family unit has not required a revision of this concept for reasons, which, in fact, would be best advanced by scientific psychology: namely, that the definitive period of character formation is in very early infancy. Consequently, even an early separa-tion—as in Isnard's case—would not undo the initial influence of the parents. As a matter of fact, psychoanalysis seems to place that formative period so far back in infancy that even in our own culture the distinction between heredity and environment is rapidly becoming as irrelevant to an analysis of psychological sources as it is alien to a Haitian's concept of psychic formation. It is significant, for instance, that in addition to inheriting loa from one's real parents, one may have a loa placed in one's head by a houngan, a spiritual parent with no physical affinity. Maximilien (p. 267) refers to the inheritance of the profession of houngan.

* The phrase: "The character of a person is the character of his loa", implies the mature development of human character as a condition for determining which loa infuse him.

exclusion. The loa had claimed Titon for houngan,* although his father had not been one, and he had been prevented from becoming one by purely secular circumstances. If the inheritance of loa refers to the transmission of principles, the inheritance of priesthood can be understood as the transmission of professional responsibility and devotion to those principles. These qualities, in the final analysis, must be manifest as active principles in the individual's own character; they could not be imposed simply by the circumstances of birth.

This inheritance, moreover, had not only to be confirmed by the son's characterological development; it had also to be implemented by his own efforts. Although Isnard was relatively fortunate in having inherited the basic physical accoutrements of priestcraft—the land and buildings which would serve as his hounfor—he had neither learned priestcraft from his father nor passed through even the initial stages of such elevation. Like Titon, therefore, he had to begin at the beginning by attaching himself to some houngan of his choice and there serving his apprenticeship. He had, in a sense, to find a further parent, one who would father him as a spiritual being.

In calling both the priest and the loa "papa" (or "maman"), as is the common practice, the serviteur simultaneously indicates two basic concepts: first, that he expects of both the divinity and the priest the protective prejudice which a child assumes of its parent; and second, that the parent commands an authority and respect similar to that which is accorded the priest and the loa. When the loa are worshipped in private family ceremonies it is, indeed, the father who plays the rôle of priest, and it is perhaps the father's or mother's great-grandfather who is manifest as loa. This interchangeable relationship reflects the universal tendency of children to regard their parents as gods and priests. In accepting this rôle, the Haitian parent does not simply take advantage of a human need, nor does the priest automatically benefit from childlike trust. The parent accepts the responsibility of bringing divine power to his

* cf. *supra*, pp. 78–9.

protective function,* and the priest accepts the responsibility of living up to that trust in the services he renders his "children". For the priest, who does not have the benefit of his "children's" sentimental prejudice (as does the parent), the preparation for such a rôle is arduous.

2

THE LEVELS OF HIERARCHY

As spiritual parent, who would instruct him and guide him in such preparation, Isnard chose Houngan Joe, a strong and renowned houngan who had been a close friend to his father. In so doing, he began by becoming a member of the *société*,** the communal group which at once serves and is served by its houngan—a relationship similar to that of family and father— and his initial rank in the *société* was as a bossale, which means wild or untaught, and applies to one who has minimal control over his loa.[2] The hounsi bossale and the hounsi canzo together act as chorus and do most of the dancing in the ceremonies, but otherwise the distance between them is

* In the interests of preventing a child's fixation upon the parent, the prevalent practice in our culture is to minimize the authority and stature of the parent; but it is a question as to whether this does not rather benefit the parent, who is thereby absolved of the responsibilities of godhead—absolute justice, rightness, control, etc.—while it denies the child a model image which might serve as incentive for emulation. A Haitian child is rarely made weak and dependent by the dominant authority of his parents; on the contrary, it seems very eager to develop to the point of parenthood and mature stature and authority itself.

** This term refers to all the people connected with a specific hounfor and defines them as a communal entity. While the hounfor itself is referred to in the name of the houngan, it is understood as being under the sponsorship of the *société*, which has a separate name. The *société* may even include members who live in town and attend only the most important ceremonies, but upon whose assistance the priest can rely should he need to raise money for an expensive ceremony, to arrange transportation, to be advised on building, etc. As a collective unit at the basis of the religious structure, the *société* is represented by two heavily embroidered ceremonial flags. Carried by two flag bearers, these banners are used to salute the loa and as a mark of respect to any distinguished guest at ceremonies. When one arrives at a ceremony, the accepted greeting is: "*Bonjour, la société.*"

considerable.* The hounsi canzo is one who has gone through the education for and the trial by fire, and conse-quently is understood to have relative mastery over the loa. In view of their long apprenticeship, the canzos are also familiar with much of the ceremonial organization and detail. While the hounsis bossales are charged with largely menial tasks, the hounsis canzos can be entrusted—in both a practical and a moral sense—with many of the more important duties. Al-though Isnard could not have been called a hounsi (by definition a woman) his apprenticeship included sharing their activities, at least sufficiently for him to be able one day to direct the work of the hounsis of his own hounfor. And he must have served also as houngenikon, at least when the

* The hounsis, both bossale and canzo, are usually women. As a matter of fact, the word means "serviteur-wife" (Courlander p. 9), and, in terms of the family structure of which the religious organization is an extension, the hounsis are, theoretically, as wives to the houngan (which means "chief of spirits"). The original reference, undoubtedly, in a polygamous culture, was to the several wives of the chief who was usually both priest and king. Today the relationship between the hounsis (they may sometimes number fifty in a hounfor) and the houngan is, at its most intimate, rather that of father and daughters. Most of these women, who are usually living in common-law marriage with other men, come to the hounfor only when their services are explicitly required for cere-monies, and they call the houngan "Papa". According to Courlander (p. 10) "placage" bears a relationship to the hounsi status. "Placage" is a term designat-ing a recognized form of relationship between a man and a woman. Simpson (IV) has listed four such recognized forms of relationship: "femme caille", or the woman of the house (which would be a common-law wife); "mamans petits", who, as mother of a man's children outside his home, has certain rights and privileges; "femme placée", a woman who is taken to live with a man but is not the mother of his children; and "bien avec", who might be a man's mistress. The formal recognition of relationships other than those of civil, church, or common-law marriage should not be interpreted as promiscuity, with the derogatory moral connotation which it has in our culture. The willingness and even eagerness of Haitian women to bear children, and the fact that no effort is made to conceal an "illegitimate" child, merely results in evidence of relationships which birth control conceals in other cultures. Separation between man and common-law wife does not occur more frequently there than divorce does here and infidelity even less so, since the accessible privacy of cities provides conditions more favorable for promiscuity than does a small community, where all are con-stantly aware of everyone's comings and goings and a jealous woman would scream out the story from the cross-roads for all to hear.

woman who held this position for many years needed relief from her arduous task. In due course of time, he had become the la-place.

The houngenikon and the la-place are the immediate assistants to the priest. They have both passed through the canzo initiation and are usually preparing to "take the asson", as the ceremony of priesthood is called. In general, the duties of the houngenikon are to launch the songs in the proper hierarchical order; to recognize the arrival of a loa and to initiate the song of salutation to him; to judge approximately how long one song should be continued, and, conversely, to exercise the discretion of terminating it if a loa threatens to arrive at an inopportune moment for the officiating houngan. In the absence of the houngan and the la-place, it is the houn-genikon who is primarily responsible for the ceremony. The la-place is, in a sense, master of ceremonies for the houngan. While the houngan may be occupied with leading the prayers, it will be the la-place who prepares the sacrificial goat, checks to see whether the offerings have been assembled and brought to the center-post, notes whether the dish of food for the loa contains the proper ingredients, and adds chairs to accommo-date the late arrivals. It is often the la-place who draws the vever, sets up any improvised outdoor shrine or altar, and kills the sacrificial animal, unless a loa or a houngan himself has particular reason to do so. Should the houngan be mounted by a loa, as is often the case, the smooth conduct of the cere-mony and even the withdrawal of the loa from the houngan's head fall to the la-place.[3]

The special position of authority which both the houn-genikon and the la-place occupy cannot be an expression of some favoritism on the houngan's part. It is dependent upon, and presumes an advanced degree of *connaissance*, a con-siderable knowledge of "la science des Mysteres". The entire hierarchy, in fact, is no more than a statement of the gradations of that knowledge. The ceremonies of elevation are like the final tests and recognition of a graduation from level to level of *connaissance*. In a sense, this formal religious elevation is an extension of the spiritual education which begins in the family; or, to put it another way, it is concerned with teaching the child (and even an adult is a spiritual child until he knows enough) the means by which he may master and implement the heritage which infuses him; and he must be taught an under-standing of those forces if he is to control them rather than be victimized by them.* The training one receives in the hounfor is more stringent than that which the individual may have experienced in the intimate family context, and it does, in fact, create a spiritually stronger individual. Such mastery consists not only of a knowledge of ritual procedures and of their meaning, but includes a training in discipline *per se*.

Within this context obedience serves several purposes. First of all, it is a means of character training. But it is also a reference to the development of the individual relative to the *connais-sances*. The Haitian does not believe that any man of any age can understand all things. He believes that our ability to understand increases with our experience and maturity. If the houngan seems sometimes reluctant to explain something, yet insists that it is to be done as an act of obedience, this is not necessarily because he wishes to conceal the reason as a personal power secret. It is rather because he questions the neophyte's ability to understand the explanation even if given. As a matter of fact, the major portions of many rituals are visible to the public gaze; neither the ritual nor the meaning of it is kept secret. However, the true significance of what occurs can be comprehended only by those who have gone through the training and ordeals and have reached the necessary degree of *connaissance* which clarifies it. The hounsi bossale and the houngan both participate in the same ritual and in many of the same activities in respect to it. The difference is not in what they do or see but in how much they understand of what both

---

* It must be emphasized that neither mastery nor control implies a simply negative action, in the sense of restraint. Both mean an ability to channel and focus the loa-energy to the best possible end.

of them do and see. This is why it would be absolutely useless
for a neophyte to memorize and imitate the gestures of the
priest, and why the sacred rattle, however powerful in a
houngan's hands, becomes powerless in any other's. It is in
this respect, also, that religion differs sharply from magic, for
the sorcerer's apprentice has only to learn the proper words and
their proper order to achieve the desired result. The magic
ritual is made mysterious because the magician conceals his
means from the eyes of the observers; the religious ritual *seems*
mysterious because the observer cannot yet grasp the meaning
of what he sees. In a sense, religious training develops the
psychic perception and power of the individual; magic
apprenticeship provides informations as to the means of mani-
pulating the world.*[4]

In sum, then, the hierarchy is a recognition of the degrees
of understanding achieved with spiritual maturity, and an
individual who has passed through all the ordeals and stages
of elevation and has become houngan has undergone a personal
characterological development of considerable scope; he is
consequently a distinguished figure in the community.

3

THE HOUNGAN AS COMMUNAL FATHER

The "strong" houngan enjoys a quality and degree of respect
which the Haitian extends to no one else. This is not only a
tribute to his religious authority; it is a recognition of the fact
that the problems which confront a houngan are far more
complex than those which other men face. One who succeeds
in resolving them deserves that respect.

One inherits one's loa, and their divine authority is automatic. One "inherits" and is dependent upon one's parents,
and their immediate authority is consequently also relatively

* For a discussion of other aspects of the secrecy of magic, see pp. 76–7,
supra.

VEVER FOR AGASSOU

automatic. By due process of law and force, one becomes subject to a civil authority. But one neither inherits a specific houngan, nor is dependent upon him, nor does there exist any centralized religious authority which might designate him as local authority, to be automatically accepted by the community. It is the individual members of that community, acting upon their free initiative, who may adopt a man as father, priest and "king",[5] and this adoption is neither absolute nor permanent. If he should fail to fulfill his manifold responsibilities, he can be abandoned. He retains his sacred rattle; but no one comes.

To be a father, he must be wise. He must show, both in the management of his own personal affairs and in the advice which he gives others, that he "knows" about life. And this know/ledge covers all provinces of the secular and includes the economic and political spheres. The houngan is expected to know how to do things, many things, all the things, in fact, which a full life experience would have taught a father: how the gate should be repaired; where the bridge should cross the river if it is built; which cow is likely to give good milk; why it is best to plant peanuts this season (because there will be a shortage and the price will rise); what percentage of real cement should be mixed with the sand so that a wall will not soon crumble; where to buy what, and least expensively; how to write (for his largely illiterate parish). And he must know these things not only for his own purposes, but because his parish turns to him for such advice and assistance, assuming, as they would of a parent, both the rightness of his knowledge and their right to it.

His political knowledge and prestige are also of enormous importance. For one thing, he cannot hold ceremonies without permission from the police. He must, therefore, be on cordial terms with such officials. It is preferable that he be also on good terms with politically influential persons who will "facilitate" matters.* This means that he must know certain sophisticated proprieties and manners: how to organize an "ovation" when the cortege of the president passes through his district; how to receive visitors; how to serve them refreshments; how to con∕ duct himself in town. He must know, in a sense, the ways of a world from which the peasant is distant.

Part of his civic∕political rôle is to intercede on behalf of any member of his parish, perhaps for a job on the new road being built through the area. If a young priest whom he has just launched after apprenticeship should have difficulty getting permission for ceremonies, he should be able to exert influence on his behalf. If someone is in legal trouble, or has been accused of stealing, the houngan will often be called upon, informally, to clarify relationships, to comment upon his character in general, to indicate whether he is, on the whole, honest, or whether there have been "incidents", so that the

---

* The hounfor is the only organized center outside of the large cities. For the peasant it serves not only as a religious center, but also as social center. This fact, plus the prestige of the houngan, makes it a center, as well, of political dissemination, and though the peasant vote rarely plays an important part in the country's politics, it is, nevertheless, a potential power. For this reason, even though Voudoun is outlawed, it is still in the interest of politicians to "facili∕ tate" matters for the houngans, and to insure themselves of their support. Such favors seem even more valuable and heroic for being "extra∕legal".

community has come to suspect that person. Often he must play the rôle of a Solomon in the disputes between his own parishioners, between husbands and wives. Informally, he raises the prestige of a person he favors, or inflicts social "punishment" by neglecting and ignoring someone who is chronically disagreeable. In any case, his position requires of him that he be extremely perceptive in his relationships, sensitive to psychological subtlety, and that he develop a degree of social grace and personal charm.

It goes without saying that his knowledge of the mass of complex ritual detail is thorough; but as among several houngans whose knowledge is equal, special respect will be shown to that one whose execution of ritual is marked by personal excellencies. This may include a kind of artistry, a feeling for arrangement, a love of the decorative celebration of ritual acts. The very appearance of the hounfor, for instance, may reveal that he has trained himself in the service of Erzulie, because of the particular attention paid to the arrangement of flowers, the disposition of objects on an altar, the play of colors, the drawing of vevers, and the preparation of food "fit for the gods". His special quality may be a power of personal projection, or magnetism, so that, under his direction, the chorus will answer with more meticulous timing, the drummers function at a level higher than adequacy, and, altogether, the ceremony move with dispatch and intensity, perhaps even with an element of personal style.

4

THE HOUNGAN AS HEALER

But the houngan's major rôle is medical. It is a rôle which has been exceedingly misunderstood and much maligned. He has been considered as the primary antagonist to modern medicine. This is not, in fact, so. A person who becomes ill begins, as is normal, by attempting to treat himself. In primitive communities this is often as valid as in the modern culture of patented medicines, for the race could not have survived without a widespread knowledge of herbalism. It is true that that knowledge may have been arrived at by trial and error; and it is true that the form in which the drug is administered —most frequently the brewing of a tea from leaves or roots— is relatively crude. But it is also true that the average Haitian peasant knows which leaves to brew for indigestion, which for a headache, which for a cold. If he wakes up without a voice, he chews on a strong parsley root and this restores it rapidly. If someone is suffering from shock, the Haitians soak coarse salt in a small jigger of rum and let the person drink it. If someone is bleeding badly, they apply a spider's web to the wound and the blood coagulates immediately. If a certain parasite enters under the skin, they know exactly where to insert a pin point and draw it out whole. If a wound is infected, they rub it with garlic, and the sulphur is an effective antiseptic. The peasant midwife is extremely efficient, especially if one considers the very primitive conditions in which she must often function. Basil-leaf water soothes and cools; peppermint leaves are steeped for nausea, etc. They are proud of such knowledges and the remedies are passed down in the family.

If the illness or discomfort does not pass, they consult a houngan. And his first task is to decide whether it is a really physical disease or one of "supernatural" origin. If it is physical, he may attempt to treat it with the more extended knowledge of herbalism to which he has access by summoning his loa in the govi.[6] Like the simpler remedies of the peasants themselves, the houngan's treatment is often chemically sound, though crude. But if he sees that the illness is beyond his resources, he will himself recommend that the person get professional medical attention, for it would never be to his credit to fail in a cure. He will even lend the bus fare money for the visit to the dentist or doctor. He himself gets professional medical and dental treatment.

Some of the ailments, such as skin disorders, are the result of malnutrition. If he undertakes merely to relieve these, it is because he knows (as unfortunately many of the health planners do not) that the primary need of the Haitian peasant (particularly in districts such as the vicinity of Port-au-Prince, where the land is drained to feed the city) is more and better food. It is also true that the Haitian peasant is reluctant to get professional medical attention. But it is not the priest who is the greedy antagonist. The resistance of the Haitian peasant is less against the medicines, which he accepts readily from the houngan or from known friends, than it is against the doctor, as a total stranger. The Haitians prefer their houngan because they trust him. And they trust him not only for religious reasons, but as a human being whom they have known all their lives, whom they have observed under all sorts of conditions, whose personality and character is hence familiar and predictable. They know the percentage of success and failure in his cures. Above all, he lives in their community and is subject to their control: to their approving patronage or the censure of their withdrawal.

But the professional doctor in the city (and their experiences with the city have not always been pleasant) is a man whom the peasants do not know very well. His dress, his speech, his every gesture emphasizes the distance between their world and his. His professional objectivity contributes to their impression of his human detachment, and they see in this a potential irresponsibility toward them. Small wonder that they are reluctant to surrender themselves to his ministrations.

The free clinic is not as psychologically persuasive as might be imagined. The hard life of the peasant community does not prepare a man for the idea of getting something for nothing. His relationship with his neighbors is based on mutual support and assistance, an exchange of favors. When he pays the houngan, he not only gives money, but also buys a control, a right to demand and expect that he will "get his money's worth". With the free clinic there is no "fair exchange", either social, religious, or financial. He feels he has no control over the doctor, no power to demand results. Conversely, he does not really expect responsibility and efficacy. He does not trust the doctor as a human being, nor does he believe him bound to a fair exchange of responsibility. These attitudes are not metaphysical; they are profoundly logical from the normally human point of view. And no modern doctor would dispute the real importance of a patient's trust.

If the medical profession is to accomplish anything in Haiti, it must begin by abandoning the ancient prejudice against the houngan and relinquishing the melodramatic images of "witch doctors". For one thing, since the recommendations of the houngan are so readily accepted by the people, it might be possible to use him as intermediary for the dispensation of medications. But it is even more important to re-examine his methods and really to understand exactly how he functions within the context with which he is so much more familiar than persons who received their training in the peaceful marble halls of distant universities. It is necessary to remember that his clientele is extremely demanding of actual results and not inclined to grant that professional immunity from the implica-tion of error and failure which is the peculiar code and privilege of doctors in more "sophisticated cultures". And it is especially important to appreciate the real sense of the houngan's dis-tinction between "natural" and "unnatural" disease. One has simply to read "psychosomatic" for the latter term.

No one who has lived long among the peasants could have failed to remark their peculiar conviction of their own frailty. They regard themselves as particularly susceptible to "grippe" and "fievre", and they are especially convinced that if a twilight dew which they call "la sirène" moistens their head, it will certainly cause at least the "grippe" if not some more disastrous ailment. I myself have never been able to remark any percep-tible amount of dew at that moment of the day. Yet it is not uncommon for even the strongest men, the same who might beat drums all night, to cover the tops of their heads with a ridiculous little handkerchief against this dampness. One never encounters anything like the contempt for caution which one associates with persons who assume good health as a natural condition. The Haitians seem, on the contrary, to accept the idea that they may easily fall ill, and they are constantly concerned with a variety of precautions. This constant fear is not at all justified by the physical circumstances to which they relate it. And the precautions are such that they could hardly suffice if that threat were really as grave as they say. Actually, it is no more than a projection, on to the physical plane, of the profound insecurity and despair with which they live from childhood until death.

For real reasons, which are too numerous to elaborate here, the material situation of most Haitian peasants is, indeed, hopeless. For the time being, at least, the majority of them are doomed to a life without one moment's relief from the most desperate, nerveracking struggle to eke out daily sustenance. So rarely does an individual achieve some measure of economic gain that the concealment and disguise of such good fortune is the general practice.

Coyote and La Merci, who had for many years been together as commonlaw man and wife, had long dreamed of being able to afford a regular marriage ceremony, a church ceremony, to be followed by the little "reception", as they called it, for their friends. They had served me loyally and well as domestics, and I had become very fond of them as people. Shortly before I was to leave, I proposed to them that I should pay for such a ceremony, for the new suit and dress, and the reception, as a farewell gift. They were ecstatic. But several days later they approached me shyly, uncertain whether they could make themselves clear. There was nothing they would rather have, they said. But, on the other hand, after my departure, they would return to the country to live in their neighborhood, which, as I knew, was extremely poor. They were afraid, they said, that their neighbors would too much envy their good fortune. And they would overestimate it, thinking that any such advancement actually meant unlimited resources. Things would be stolen from them, because people would feel that they had ample funds to replace such articles. They would be plagued for loans of money, and their refusals would be greatly resented. Prices of food would be raised for them specifically, they insisted, because everyone would think they could afford it. They would become altogether suspect. And so, they said, they felt that, in the end, it would give them more trouble than pleasure.

I asked them, then, whether I should use this money to set them up in a little business, to stock a little country store from which they could get started. This, they said, would have similar disadvantages. But cash, I pointed out, would just get used up without anything really to show for it. They nodded and went away. Two days later they appeared with the solution. If I would buy them a cow they said, they could leave it with Coyote's brother, who lived quite far away in another direction. His brother's neighbors would know it did not belong to his brother. And Coyote's neighbors would not know that he had one. And that was, according to them, the real answer.

If the Haitian peasant has some good luck he permits himself only a minimal display, until he is in a position to move up a whole step in the economic scale. Sometimes this concept and practice is even carried to the extent of deliberately scarring a child so that it should not, by its beauty, inspire the evil eye of envy.[7]

The concept of frailty which the Haitian expresses in so many different ways is only his manner of recognizing that his life is spent in a state of precarious balance on the edge of an abyss of despair. (The common "fever" is perhaps ten per cent recurrent malaria. For the rest it might be more properly called the fever of despair.) Consequently, even the most minor shock or threat immediately sets in motion a system of defenses which, in a more stable and secure people, would be reserved for only the most critical challenges.

Coyote was a drummer whom I had come to know well from the ceremonies in the Plains district, where he was much

8. A CONTEMPORARY VOUDOUN PRIEST, HOUNGAN ISNARD.

9. MAMBO LEADING CEREMONIAL INVOCATION. The ritual dress of a Voudoun priestess is frequently of satin, or may be elaborately embroidered.

10. CEREMONIAL PERISTYLE. On the back wall are painted the "coats of arms" of the powers which support the hounfor: the patron deity, the *société,* and the houngan.

in demand. When I returned for a second visit to Haiti, I found a small house in the hills north of Petionville, and pro-posed to Coyote that he come to "take charge" of my house. I asked him, also, whether he knew of a woman who could do the cooking, and learned, then, for the first time, that he was "married" to La Merci. (The Haitian is so extremely discreet or undemonstrative in public that it would be impossible to guess, at a ceremony, which man was related to which woman.)

As drummer, Coyote had "been around", in the general neighborhood of Port-au-Prince. But for La Merci this employment represented her first real dislocation, as I later found out. In the first days everything seemed to be going very well, and both of them began to make friends in the new neighborhood.

About a week later I noticed that Coyote often brought the coffee, or laid the table (a task usually filled by the woman) and that there seemed to be a good deal of brewing of leaf-teas going on in the little back court. La Merci, it seemed, was not feeling well. She was having pains in her abdomen. But that would shortly be straightened out with these teas. Two days later La Merci was virtually unable to carry out her duties. I suggested consulting a doctor, but this was refused. Instead, an old woman of the neighborhood, who was renowned for her medications, appeared with a bundle of herbs and roots and set about mixing her remedies. These seemed to give La Merci some relief, but it proved to be temporary. That night I heard in their little hut, such moaning and weeping, that I deter-mined to intervene, for the Haitians do not easily express physical hurt. She was in extreme pain and it seemed to me precisely localized at the appendix. On my own initiative I immediately called a physician who arrived and diagnosed it as an acute appendicitis. She was to leave immediately for the hospital, as soon as she had been dressed (for even in her pain she insisted that she wear her very best dress), and the doctor left to prepare for the operation.

In spite of the urgency, La Merci's preparations took a long time, and I could hear a good deal of discussion in the little hut. Finally she emerged, completely dressed, even to her hat, but with the announcement that she would not go to the hospital. "Those who go to the hospital die", she announced. (As a matter of fact, statistically she was correct, since by the time the peasants finally decide to go to the hospital their condition is such that little can be done to save them.) "Besides", she said, "it was a loa who 'cambiꞏli' [had grabbed her].[8] It is not for the hospital." Convinced that this was a case where primitive superstition would result in death, I pleaded with her, cajoled, threatened, discharged her, promised rewards, all to no avail. Feeling, finally, that all this excitement would even accelerate the disaster, I permitted her to withdraw to her hut, and I was fully prepared to be summoned to her deathꞏbed during the night.

The next morning she was still alive, and even, it would seem, a little better. I was resigned to my helplessness and let the matter take its course. That evening, while Coyote and I were discussing the situation, the child from next door interꞏrupted to tell us that a loa had mounted the head of his grandꞏmother, and had a special message for Coyote regarding La Merci. We both went next door immediately and saluted the loa. It was an Ogoun. La Merci was not, he said, "naturally" sick. The loa had gripped her because she had not properly carried out her last obeisances, upon leaving her ancestral land, where the *cailles Mystères* of her family stood. Specifically, she had thrown water and "signaled" in only two directions, and the loa were extremely angry over this negligent leaveꞏtaking. La Merci, Ogoun said, must return and must ask forgiveness and must propitiate the deities by offering them a chicken. Ogoun then concerned himself with matters pertaining to the other family, and Coyote and I left.

Coyote had been essentially in agreement with me as to the physical nature of the illness. But, as he pointed out, it was impossible to convince La Merci of this, and so it might be well to do as the loa suggested. The loa, he said, would probably accept a cheap chicken this time, if they were promised a better feast upon her final homecoming.

Accordingly, the following morning, La Merci, looking much better already, was given the money for the fare, and for the chicken, along with an extra amount, so that she might bring some small gifts to her neighbors. It was a long trip. When she returned the following afternoon she was in high spirits, full of energy, and the stomach-ache was completely gone. She had reaffirmed her ties with her ancestral loa; she did not feel lost any more. And her relationship with everyone was no longer marked by the subtle anxiety which had at first been present.

If a loa had not intervened as diagnostician, a case of such severity would probably have involved the consultation of a houngan, who would have called up his own loa in the govi, and discussed the case with him.[9] Having ascertained the reason for her loa's anger, he would also have been instructed about (or would have decided for himself) the curative measures. In cases where the psychosomatic projection may have been carried to the point of organic disturbance, he might have simultaneously given the patient both a herbal treatment, to relieve these effects, and a ritual treatment, to make peace with the loa. It is, in fact, because he often combines the two elements that his treatments have been so misunderstood, for the ritualistic measures are interpreted as directed at the physical ailment, or as an unnecessary embellishment of the herbal cure.

Our general tendency is to regard the psychosomatic act of transferring a difficulty from the psychic to the physical system as "bad". This evaluation reflects, more than would be admitted, a moral dislike of "dishonesty" and a scientific rejection of "untruth". But an organism cares little for such abstract criteria. It is concerned with self-preservation. When a man is threatened by a blow, his instinctive gesture is to raise his arm over his head and face, to protect the most fragile portion of his anatomy, the brain. To receive the blows "honestly" on the head, would soon make him punch-drunk. When a situation is temporarily or permanently and irremediably brutal, the organism behaves like a clever boxer: it shields the mind from the blows which would only destroy it, and absorbs the shock in the muscular and durable flesh. If the Haitian peasant were forced to "face" his hopeless situation, it would be moral suicide for him.* What possible moral justification can there be for making a man stare into the jaws of his own death? And where is the medical wisdom of telling a patient that his indigestion, or worse, is due to his own insecurity, or the world situation, and thus brutally destroying the flimsy veil of tolerable discomfort by which the man sought to conceal from himself his intolerable despair?

The methods of the houngan not only respect the essential wisdom of the psychosomatic mechanism, but—and this is the most remarkable feature—use it therapeutically. The diagnosis of "unnatural" or "unphysical" illness is not simply a negative judgement, as it seems to those who conceive only in terms of physical causes. On the contrary, the houngan's main job is to discover the non-physical or unnatural cause. This may be either an act of aggressive evil magic against the person or a punishment for his failure to serve his loa properly. In either

---

* Obviously, there has been some disagreement as to whether or not the situation is hopeless. Simpson (II) implies that it is not hopeless, since he speaks of Voudoun as releasing aggressive impulses and deduces that this release prevents the peasant "from utilizing other types of action to solve problems". He says, further: "Voudoun ceremonies and magical acts perform a mental hygiene function for the individual and thereby contribute to preserving the status quo." It is impossible to define objectively a degree of hopelessness, and, indeed, a stranger would be inclined, at first glance, to think that much could be done by the people to ameliorate their condition. Gradually, however, as one becomes more familiar with the hidden complexity of the political system —both on an international scale (the lack of Haitian capital forces a dependence upon American capital, which is not above exploiting the situation) and on a national scale (the entrenched, traditional methods of politics, the illiteracy of the majority of the population and their ignorance, almost deliberately created, of political manœuvres, the education by the French clergy, which exchanges its support for that of whichever government insures its standing, the shrewd technique of "buying out" any incipient peasant leader)—all of these accumulate into a complexity which should not be righteously minimized. Moreover, Voudoun is most often opposed and suppressed by the government as a threat to the status quo.

case there exists the possibility of a resolution through action of some sort. Instead of the hopeless finality of absolute, abstract despair, the man is immediately involved in the idea of promis, ing action. The very fact that an answering action is inherently indicated, is the first therapeutic device which is set into motion. Thus psychosomatic projection serves not as an evasion but as a means of making the moral problem accessible on a level of real action. And it is an accepted fact that activity, hopeful activity, is the only thing which can prevent demorali, zation and can rehabilitate after shock.

The second therapeutic manipulation consists in the requirement that the action shall not be executed by the priest but *must be carried out, in major portion, by the patient himself,* under guidance of the priest. The patient must himself straighten out his difficulties with the loa. In other words, the patient treats himself, and this is another boost to his morale.*

Finally, the nature of the action is almost inevitably disciplinarian. It exercises the will, tightens one's forces, focuses the personality into an integration. The salutary effect of the exercise of self-discipline is admittedly remarkable. Instead of accepting an objective destiny with indulgent despair, the Haitian assumes a subjective failure which is accessible to correction. Thus, in the final analysis, the loa and the houngan treat psychic shock through the physical channel and propose the only moral therapy which exists: action and discipline.[10]

5

IN BALANCE BETWEEN WORLDS

Medical treatment is only one of the ways in which the houngan may mediate between the loa and the people. He is expected to represent the people, as well as the loa. If, in the

---

* Almost inevitably, no matter how ill the person is, he must take part in the rituals relating to his treatment.

course of a ceremony, the loa should make an unreasonable demand for someone's shirt, or ring, or money, the houngan will intercede on behalf of the person. If the loa is so violent that his "horse" might be injured, or the clothes torn, the priest will work hard to pacify the loa or send him away altogether.

At one ceremony Ghede had the unusual luck of having been given a dollar bill. He immediately made for the little food-stand to buy something to eat. But the seller had no change. At the same time, she was a very poor woman and could not afford to make Ghede a gift of any of her breads. Ghede became enraged at being unable to buy something to eat. Moreover, he interpreted it as a lack of respect, and threatened her with various misfortunes. In desperation, the seller called upon the houngan. He pulled Ghede aside, and talking quietly, as if man to man, explained the situation to him. In the end he contributed five cents so that Ghede was able to eat, the woman was paid, and the entire incident was smoothly resolved. On another occasion, when Loco arrived and was particularly violent and destructive, it was pointed out that if the houngan had been called immediately (he was else-where, attending to details of the ceremony) he would have brought Loco under control.[11]

Just as the father is physically closest to the ancestor, so the houngan, as spiritual father, is closest to the loa. The houngan is reverent and respectful toward his loa; but he also knows how to "restrain" them in the knot of a handkerchief and how to bury a troublesome loa.[12] The loa is dependent upon the houngan both for his energy—for the houngan feeds him—and for his opportunity to "live" in the world. Thus the relation-ship between houngan and loa is an interdependence which fluctuates in its nuance. The houngan is the means by which the great cosmic forces are made manifest. And when the loa comes, his first act is to salute the priest.

It is significant that La Merci's treatment took place within the family circle, without the intervention of a houngan, although if Ogoun had not mounted the head of the old neighbor, a houngan might have been eventually consulted. It is difficult to say what proportion of the people serve their loa within the private family context, with the father com‑ manding the position of houngan. Such family services may range from the fairly elaborate, in cases where there is even a *caille Mystères*, of which the hounfor is essentially a develop‑ ment, to extremely simple services conducted in the one‑room hut which is the family dwelling.

One such service was conducted by an old woman on behalf of her son and it was directed primarily toward Ogoun and Ghede. The small hut could not have measured more than ten feet square and the bed, which served as the sole seating facility, had been pushed against one wall. A little table, covered with a white cloth, served as an altar upon which the offerings were placed, and a candle burned on the dirt floor at its base, where the vevers were drawn. A relative, who apparently had the best mastery of the songs, served as houngenikon, and the mother (the father was dead) conducted the ritual in the capacity of mambo.

For the greater part of the time she was mounted, first by Ogoun, and then by Ghede, and although her loa carried out the major tasks of the ritual, such as sacrificing the chicken, her brother concerned himself with such details as contributed to the smooth running of the ceremony. A neighbor, who was known to have a strong Ghede in her head, had been parti‑ cularly urged to participate and to lend her divine "charge" to reinforce the ceremony. In every respect the service was extremely modest, for the woman could not afford anything elaborate. There were no drums, but it is not certain whether this was due to her inability to get drums and pay the drummers the customary fee, or whether it was because the loa, in setting a date for the ceremony, had specified one which came during the course of the week, rather than on the Saturday and Sunday upon which ceremonies were permitted. It was probably the latter reason, since all the activity was confined to the interior.

The singing was spirited, and the loa came in gratifying numbers to the heads of the participants. As the noise within the hut increased, the "petit jazz", the little three-piece orchestra stationed just outside the door, played and sang its meringues* and rhumbas louder and louder to cover and disguise the sounds of the ceremony within. The door had to be left open to provide some ventilation, and sitting at the entrance, one was aware of a fugue in which the suggestive, frivolous, sometimes vulgar rhumbas which were officially approved made astonish- ing counterpoint to the splendid songs and the divine invoca- tions which were "illegal".[13]

For all its modesty, this service had an intensity comparable to the most elaborate services of a houngan. Intimacy even lent it a quality of more genuine profundity. As the Haitians put it, these persons and these loa were all in the family, and really concerned with each other. There was no showing-off. Above all, since the woman, in the capacity of mambo, was also the same who paid for the ceremony, there could not be, as might be the case with a houngan, any overcharging.

There are many Haitians who serve the loa entirely within their family. They point out that a real father is more trust- worthy than a houngan. They tell of an ambitious houngan who bought a Bossu, and how his own family deities, the good *racine* ones, deserted him in protest. They told of another who charged fees which went as much for decorating his hounfor and making elegant display as for the real task at hand.**

* The popular "ballroom" dance of Haiti.
** Such hounfors, criticized for placing too much emphasis upon "gangance", are none the less to be completely distinguished from those few hounfors in Port-au-Prince that put on ceremonies for tourists, and these, in turn, are distinct from "dances" in honor of a loa which a houngan may give when provided with the money to do so. Since ceremonies are a costly affair, a houngan may solicit a contribution for a real ceremony which he "owes" to some loa, from someone who has been a frequent visitor to his hounfor and who has enjoyed the houngan's hospitality in matters of food, drink and general comfort. The same holds good for less costly dances, which, none the less, require a certain minimum expenditure; this is more or less comparable to giving a party for the

There were other hounfors where no sensible man would leave his pot-de-tête, for the houngan might try to reinforce his own powers by stealing the gros-bon-ange. The woman with a strong Ghede in her head insisted that she would never bring her loa into a hounfor where a houngan could exploit his power.

Yet, in the very act of stating these criticisms, they were also enumerating the very restraints which would make it impossible for a houngan to carry any villainy very far, for he is aware that he is in "competition" with this recourse which all people have to private worship. If he is to build up his clientele, he must "prove" himself, in the most pragmatic way. He must win the respect which is automatically accorded the father or mother. And if the parent is, in a sense, god to the child, the houngan must demonstrate that he has even greater access to divine power. And even if it is granted that the houngan is

hounfor, on the basis of friendship for the houngan and the *société*. Both such cases are entirely acceptable and are to be distinguished from false "ceremonies" —deliberately incorrect in detail and in general—whose main purpose is to make money from the tourist. It is curious that travelers who, in their own country, are extremely meticulous about "returning" dinner and party invitations, Christmas gifts and New Year's cards, who would be embarrassed to make a poor showing in the collection plate, and whose contributions maintain the elaborate organization of the Catholic Church, are often disoriented in a country such as Haiti, and the anticipation of reciprocity there is condescendingly regarded as a kind of commercialism, particularly suspect when it is related to Voudoun as a religion. Actually, it is most unreasonable to imagine that a houngan, whose parishioners are virtually penniless, has any less need for contributions than the minister or priest of any American community. Moreover, it must not be forgotten that the hounfor is the *private* property of the houngan, that the ceremonies and dances are the *private* functions of the *société*, and that a visitor, arrived either by chance or invitation, is in every sense a privileged guest. A failure to reciprocate appropriately is not only bad manners, but a humiliating effrontery to the Haitians as people and to their religion. It is, however, an equal effrontery to reward the houngan elaborately and overtly, as if he were a night-club master of ceremonies who had successfully assembled a good show for his patrons. The conditions of communal life make actual privacy virtually impossible, in lieu of this, the Haitian has developed a high degree of formalism and discretion, and he is justifiably contemptuous of the frequent lack of these social sophistications in visitors who presume to represent "advanced" cultures.

generally stronger, in this sense, than the father, there is no imposed hierarchy among houngans. Each one is, in a sense, in competition with all the others.[14]

His every failure to cure or to resolve the difficulties of his parishioners either with their loa or in their daily affairs, reflects upon the houngan's degree of control, his "standing" with the divine powers. If such incidents accumulate, his parish turns to someone else. The personal sacred object, which the individual has left in his trust, may be removed. Religious commitments may be revoked. And should the houngan want to punish a deserter by sending after him the curse of illness or misfortune, the serviteur would rely upon his new and stronger houngan to protect him and to invalidate the curse.*

The houngan, then, is the pivotal figure in a hierarchical structure, yet is subject to democratic controls. He is dependent upon the continuity of a circular, or rather spiral process, by which his control over the loa gives him access to greater divine power; this he must in turn properly serve in order to control it, and he must constantly demonstrate his achievement.[15] If his major advantage over the father as "houngan" is his greater *connaissance* and control, gained by his apprenticeship and the ritual ordeals which mark his gradual elevation in the hierarchy, he never enjoys the father's absolute security in the personal loyalty of his "family", which would at once make them more tolerant of the parent's failures and place him above competitive comparison.

The houngan is a man on a tightrope. This is reflected even in the way he walks, with a certain awareness of the act of balance. He is intelligent, perceptive and efficient beyond the average man, for the requirements of his position are such that the natural process of selection eliminates the merely average. He lives in a state of tension, which gives his personality a curious ambivalence. At times, he is peculiarly distant and

---

* There have even been cases where a young houngan abandoned his spiritual father—that is, the houngan who trained him for the priesthood and gave him his asson; but such cases are quite rare.

detached, and, at others, most keenly alert. He may be alternately generous and expansive, or "touchy" and overly
sensitive. On some occasions he displays his superior position
in a pose of almost aristocratic indolence; at others one has a
sudden glimpse of the nature of his hard apprenticeship and
training, as when he executes the most menial ritualistic tasks
with great skill and dispatch.

And his position is finally complicated by the fact that
although he can never enjoy the absolute security of a father—
in the heart and loyalty of his children—his entire hounfor is
structured around the family principle of the education of the
young. It is he who instructs his sons and daughters and elevates them, eventually, to a spiritual adulthood, to the priesthood, where they stand in equal and competitive relation to
himself.

The delicate balance of the houngan is most explicitly
symbolized in a certain ritual detail which occurs in the early
part of virtually every ceremony. The laplace, representing (as
distinguished from being possessed by) the loa who is master
of that hounfor, comes out carrying a sword and flanked by
two hounsis carrying the ceremonial flags representing the
société. The three of them salute first the four cardinal points,
then the poteaumitan, then the drums, and finally the houngan.
This last salute frequently involves a dramatic elaboration. For
the houngan, holding his asson, and the laplace, holding his
sword and flanked by the flags, seem to engage in some strange,
mock battle. While they do not make actual contact, the
sword causes the asson to retreat, and then is suddenly pressed
into retreat itself. Back and forth they go, the sword threatening
and shaking and the asson rattling and ringing. There is no
question but that it is a competition, reenacted, to be sure,
between the power of the loa and the *société*, together, against
that of the houngan. The resolution of this battle is most
illuminating. The laplace, or the loa which he represents, along
with the two flag bearers, representing the *société*, bows and
kisses the earth at the houngan's feet as a mark of respect. But

the houngan, simultaneously, kisses the hilt of the sword and the top of the two flags. Thus, although the control of the houngan over the loa and the people is acknowledged, he is, in turn, held responsible to them, to the principle of the *société* or community as well as to the principle of divinity.[16]

6

THE HOUNFOR

Hounfor is a term which designates the sacred precincts in which all the religious activities take place, and comprehends the sacred trees, the various structures—individual altar chambers, peristyle, small huts for accommodating those being treated for illness—all of the sacred and ritual objects, equipment and accessories as well as all the parish and personnel. However, it may also designate, specifically and exclusively, the small chamber (also called *ghuevo*) which contains an altar (called a *pé* and sometimes a *sobagui*) to a loa.[17] In such usage it distinguishes that chamber from the adjoining peristyle and from the rest of the precincts. The altar room is devoted exclusively to religious acts and objects whereas secular life and activities inevitably take place throughout the entire court, including the peristyle, when there is no ceremony in progress. In order to avoid confusion, the simple term hounfor, in these pages, will refer to the precincts, their sacred contents and the personnel; when the reference is to an altar room, that will be indicated by specifying the name of the loa to which the room is sacred, e.g. Damballah's hounfor.*

* It must be remembered that, in translating Voudoun terms into English terms which are, in turn, associated with the objects and practices of Christian religions, there occurs an inevitable distortion of meaning. The word sobagui, for instance, is the name of an object or structure which is only generally comparable to what we know as an altar but has an appearance and a function specifically related to Voudoun and these, in many respects, are entirely unrelated to those of an altar.

The physical aspect of a hounfor varies enormously from city to country, and from district to district. In the city there may be virtually no courtyard at all, but simply a small structure divided into one, two, or three altar chambers, and, adjoining it, a peristyle for ceremonial action and dance. The walls of the peristyle may be relatively high, for purposes of privacy, or they may even entirely enclose the area, so that it becomes a large hall. In the country the hounfor of a relatively successful houngan may be laid out somewhat in the manner of an estate, with many structures, and even several peristyles, devoted to the Rada, Petro, Ibo and Congo cults respectively. In some districts a hounfor is immediately recognizable, not only by the planning and placement of the structures, but by a high degree of decorative and symbolic embellishment. In other districts, any such visible arrangement or display is completely lacking. Even the altar room may be extremely and deceptively plain, small in size, with unpainted walls and containing only a crude, waist-high cement block which serves as altar. It would be almost impossible to identify such simple rooms as sacred hounfors.

The difference between such extremes is only partially explained by differences in wealth, decorative taste, and local or family traditions. It would seem to reflect, primarily, the varying status of the religion in diverse districts. The legal status of Voudoun is extremely ambiguous, and, in the final analysis, is really determined by the personal prejudice of the particular chief of police of the district. In the region of Jeremie for instance, the official opposition to Voudoun is so absolute that one may spend months in the region without hearing a single drum beat. Ceremonies and dances do take place, of course, but in remote corners of the valleys and under conditions of extreme secrecy. The natives are even afraid to acknowledge a recognition of the mere word "Voudoun" when spoken by a stranger, and it would seem that they had been forbidden, under threat of some extreme penalty, to permit any visitor even to suspect the existence of such religious rituals. In view of such rigid intolerance on the part of the Jeremian police and church, it was indeed instructive to be invited to accompany a medical doctor on a professional visit which involved a three-hour muleback trip into the deep recesses of the mountains, here to discover that he had been summoned by an old houngan who was suffering from some kidney disturbance and wished to have the advantage of the most modern medication. The houngan's attitude toward the doctor was both respectful and dignified and he obviously understood that the medical code protected him from betrayal, just as his own code would have prevented his betraying any of his parish to the police. It is obvious that in such districts every effort would be made to conceal the practice of Voudoun and to avoid the easily identifiable and conspicuous structure or object. In such regions, then, hounfors are virtually non-existent in the sense of physical structures and equipments. Ceremonial ritual, drumming and dancing are also on a lower plane of formal realization and expertness than elsewhere, since there is relatively little opportunity for the people to practice and develop these forms, or even to preserve the most basic ones.*

In the region of Port-au-Prince, for political reasons too complex to elaborate here, the practice of Voudoun is more or less accepted, within limits. In this relative security the religion has been able to create and evolve its logical extensions into physical expression in its architecture and ritual equipment. The hounfors here are not typical of Haiti; they are, in fact, typical in the degree of their elaboration. But they are perhaps atypical, in general, of what a hounfor would be under normally accommodating circumstances.

---

* Among those observers whose personal cultural traditions involve a religion of abstract and ascetic inclination—such as Protestantism—there has been a tendency to imply to such forcedly "ascetic" regions of Voudoun some specially pure, profound or genuine quality, and to regard as a little suspect and frivolous those hounfors, in other districts, where a delight in decorative elaboration is proudly displayed. Yet the notion that beauty and sensory pleasure are sinful is peculiarly Puritan; in Voudoun, as in most religious traditions, these qualities are among the special delights of divinity.

The first impression of a hounfor is of grounds well planned and expertly maintained. It definitely conveys the sense of a formal architectural and landscaped unit, an integrity brought into focus by a distinct entrance to the grounds. Such an entrance has a formal significance which is not in the least diminished by the fact that the grounds are not fenced in, or are marked by a token fence at most, and that therefore one may come and go by many paths apart from the main entrance. Immediately inside the formal entrance there are usually two trees sacred to Legba, as patron of gates, entrances and cross-roads, and trees sacred to one or another divinity are profusely scattered throughout the grounds. Such trees, since they are sacred, have escaped the fate of being cut down for firewood (a need which has resulted in the critical deforestation of large parts of Haiti), and they give a hounfor a distinctively cool, shaded and pleasant quality. The bases of these sacred trees—called *reposoirs*—are usually encircled by clay or cement blocks or troughs. The grounds are inevitably well-swept and often have flower-beds in informal but colorful arrange-ment.

Another delightful aspect is the profusion of white doves, pigeons, chickens, beautifully marked guinea-hens, and other fowl, which roam the grounds and rise to roost in the trees at twilight. Since the hounfor is usually part of the houngan's plantation, it is often "walled in" by groves of banana-trees, whose gigantic leaves throw an almost total shade and create perspectives of deep green corridors, while their slow move-ments increase the cool sense of a submarine vista. Almost all the structures are brilliantly whitewashed, unless, in honor of a certain loa, his special hounfor has been painted a pale pink or blue; and these structures are almost all thatched, although this extremely cool roofing is being somewhat snobbishly replaced by corrugated tin roofs, which, on the contrary, absorb the heat of the sun and project it into the interior of the peri-style.

There may be several peristyles, but the one dedicated to the

Rada deities is visibly larger and more elaborate than the rest.* It is enclosed by a wall approximately three feet high, with an entrance on each of the three sides. Where the lines from these entrances would intersect (not necessarily at the exact center of the rectangular peristyle) there is the poteau-mitan, which is the dominant architectural and ceremonial element of the peristyle. It is usually brightly painted in a spiral movement, and the smaller posts around the edge of the peristyle are also decorated. Around the foot of this poteau-mitan there is a circular cement step, about a foot high, which serves as an altar and upon which offerings are placed during the course of the ceremony. Along one end of the peristyle is a structure which may con- sist of a single, long room but is usually divided into three chambers, and these are consecrated to specific divinities. They open out into the peristyle, and in addition to the doors (which are sometimes left open during ceremonies), they may have door-curtains of colored bamboo sections strung on cord, in the manner of beaded curtains. These permit the free passage of air into the chamber, while veiling its interior and lending a bright note of color to the whitewashed walls. This same major wall may be decorated with the "nom vaillant" (battle- name)[18] of the houngan, with the symbol of the loa which is master of that hounfor, and with the coat of arms of the *société*.

Within the individual altar chambers the arrangement of both the altar and the objects is determined by the loa to whom that particular chamber is dedicated. Thus, in the one for Damballah (which is shared by Ayida, and usually by Agwé and La Sirène) there is the bassin of water[19] with the repre- sentation of these loa painted mural fashion on the walls over it and the altar. Upon this latter are arranged various objects, the pierre-loa,[20] the Catholic chromos of the saints which are identified with these loa, as well as offerings consecrated to them,

---

* See illustration 10, facing p. 167. I should like to stress that the description that follows is based on observations in the district of Port-au-Prince, Leogone, and Jeremie, but is not intended as typical of *all* hounfors.

11. BASSIN DAMBALLAH. When filled, this pool will be used by Damballah and Agwé (represented by the fish and boat) when they possess a devotee.

12. BARQUE D'AGWÉ. This elaborately decorated raft is loaded with offerings and put adrift to sink and carry the feast to Agwé, god of the seas.

13. PETRO DRUMS BEING COVERED. Goat-hide is used for these hand-beaten drums.

14. DANCE OF CELEBRATION. In addition to ceremonies, most houngans occasionally sponsor religious dances which abide by ritual traditions but are primarily festive.

and any accoutrements such as handkerchiefs,* walking-sticks, sabers and other objects which are used by these loa when they manifest themselves. A dish, containing a burning wick floating in oil, usually stands in the center. In a hounfor of any size, a special chamber is generally consecrated to Erzulie and is notable for the glamour and luxury of its appurtenances. There lie her jewelry, mirror, comb and brush, a cake of soap, several bottles of cologne and perfume, perhaps the dress consecrated to her; and the whole is decorated with such a profusion of painted, artificial and real flowers that the total effect is incomparably feminine.

A special chamber is usually dedicated to the loa master of the hounfor. If it is Ogoun, it is dominated by the saber which is thrust into the earth, directly in front of the altar. The flags of the *société* would be in this chamber, and the govi in which the houngan would summon him, as well as the pots-de-tête of those who have been initiated under his patronage (on his "point"). It is probably here that the houngan would keep his asson, and if it were his custom to retain custody of the ceremonial beads of the initiates, these too might be found in this chamber.** The pictures of St. Jacques and other saints identified with one or another aspect of Ogoun would be pasted to the wall and on the altar there would be several red handkerchiefs and bottles of rum awaiting his arrival.

If a deity such as Azacca had particular importance for the houngan, he might also be given a chamber. Here there would be the large peasant straw hats and several of the large knapsack-like straw bags which peasants habitually carry. In some of these there would be a little food and a bit of clairin for Azacca.

* Each loa has such handkerchiefs, according to the color sacred to him, and these are used during ceremonies both for decoration and by the loa himself for wiping the perspiration which inevitably appears during ceremonies and dances.

** These beads consist of two long strands, a single "male" strand and a double "female" strand, whose double rows are joined together into every seventh bead. The beads are worn so as to cross over the chest, and the two strands are tied together where they cross in back and in front. (Note these beads on the Initiate in illustration 2, facing p. 39).

Undoubtedly there would also be the yoked peasant blouse of denim, with its elaborate embroidery of white stitching, and Azacca would be dressed in this the moment he arrived.

Occasionally, but quite rarely, there may be a chamber for Ghede, containing a fascinating assortment of objects. There would be a balancing scale for weighing the soul, three picks, three shovels, and three hoes; various kinds of skulls; one or several phallic objects; and a *tabour maringué* which is his special and favorite instrument.* Every hounfor, however, has the regular symbol of Ghede in some corner of its grounds. This is generally a tomb-like mound of earth, or it may be a cement tomb, or a tombstone surmounted by a cross. Here and there about the grounds there may be other sacred objects and structures: a large cross for Simbi; a huge outdoor pool for Damballah, Ayida and Agwé;** the traditional whip hanging in the Petro peristyle and other such ritual objects.

The drums usually hang from a rafter in the peristyle. A hounfor which has separate peristyles for Rada, Petro and Congo rites will also have an appropriate set of drums hanging in each one. Of all the sacred equipment of a hounfor, the drums—the Rada drums particularly—are perhaps the most important. Certainly they are the objects to which the greatest degree of independent divine power is attributed. The asson, for example, is useless in strange hands; the houngan, on the other hand, is not powerless without it, but merely seriously hampered. But the drummer has no position whatsoever in the religious hierarchy; it is the drums themselves which are the sacred voice of address to the loa and they are, at the same time, the voice of the loa as well. The ceremonial order of salutation places the drums following the cardinal points and the center-post, but preceding the houngan.***

* This drum is also known as a children's toy.
** See illustration 11, facing p. 182.
*** Drums are fully discussed in Chapter VI, which deals specifically with music and dance.

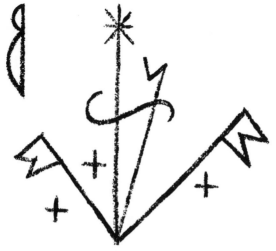

VEVER FOR OGOUN ST. JACQUES

7

THE DOORS TO THE DIVINE WORLD

None of all this vast and complex equipment would have the least religious value if it were not all properly consecrated. The loa must have been "introduced" into the precincts as a whole, and again must have been specifically "introduced" into the peristyle, and finally, ritually installed in the individual chambers. All of the objects related to any part of the ritual must be properly baptized. The major objects, such as the drums, are individually baptized in the name of the loa to which they are especially dedicated. Miscellaneous equipment may be collectively baptized under the name of the master of the hounfor, or under all the major divinities of the pantheon together. It is hardly surprising, then, that baptism should be the ceremony which occurs most frequently. Its function is to infuse the object with divine essence, and the ritual is more or less elaborate according to the importance of the object. For the baptism of handkerchiefs and other minor objects, only a token offering is made to the loa. The baptism of the drums or the asson, on the other hand, is often part of a larger ceremony in which a substantial amount of food has been given the loa, in order to encourage their good will and power. It may sometimes happen that the loa themselves will come to baptize the object personally, and this is the "strongest" baptism possible. Once an object has been baptized, its use is specifically limited to sacred purposes. To make other use of it is a profanation which the loa may punish severely. For example, a girl who had a handkerchief which had been consecrated to Ghede "borrowed" it from him one day to carry into town, since she had no other. The following morning she had a very severe headache, which persisted for several days, until finally Ghede was invoked and explained the reason for his displeasure and punishment. The distinction between the things which belong to oneself, personally, and those which belong to one's loa, is very clearly observed. This does not mean, however, that the sacred object is completely detached from its human owner. The accidental loss of the same sacred handkerchief, whose secular use resulted in rather severe punishment, would not bring commensurate power (or any power at all) into the hands of the finder. Moreover, it is a very simple matter for the owner to remove the divine spirit from an object. Even the drums may be so "degraded", for one has but to light a candle and simply announce to the spirits in the drums that one wishes to remove them—in order to sell the drums, or for whatever reason one might have. Thus, while baptism is essential to all ritual endeavor, it is also the most simple of ceremonies in itself.

If one pieces together all these separate details regarding the baptism of objects, it becomes apparent that baptism does not so much confer divinity upon the object *per se* as it makes of that object a "door" by which divine energy may be drawn into this world by those who possess the key, which is the name to be called.* The owner of the object, then, possesses an

* It has been pointed out earlier (Chapter II, p. 56) that Voudoun baptism is not a borrowing from Christianity but a simple continuation of ancient

access to divine power, but he does not possess the divine power itself, nor does he have absolute control over that energy in action. To think of the baptized object as a "door" illumi-nates, also, the fact that this object is not sacred in itself but only when it functions as an access to divine power, and it is this latter which is sacred. Thus the baptized object is sacred only in action; and since an act is transitory in time, Voudoun has, indeed, a quality which can only be described as a con-stant "disappearingness"; for when its function is fulfilled, the object ceases to be sacred.

The peristyle, which, during the evening's ceremony, was a holy temple place—vibrant with a sense of divine power—becomes, the morning afterward, once more a meaningless area in which chickens and dogs wander about, women sit gossiping, and children sleep. The vever which was drawn with such elaborate care is destroyed by the offerings placed upon it, by the dancing feet, and is finally swept away with the debris of the ceremony. The loa, whose every demand was fearfully or eagerly met, leaves the head of a man to whom one may then casually refuse even a cigarette or a piece of bread. Nothing is accomplished for ever; it must always be done again. Moreover, an invocation to Legba, sung by a radio per-former, is simply a song. On the other hand, the hounsis of the chorus command no particular respect or recognition. Neither the song nor the singer is sacred; the sacred moment is the sing-ing of the song for the sacred purpose of summoning Legba. Divinity is an energy, an act. The serviteur does not say, "I believe." He says: "I serve." And it is the act of service—the ritual—which infuses both man and matter with divine power.

African traditions. The concept that the *name* is virtually the same thing as the identity to which it refers, and that therefore a knowledge of the name and its proper pronunciation gives the power to invoke the spirit so identified, appears in some form in virtually all religions, mythologies and folklore. One of the most obvious examples is the "Open Sesame" story; but the widespread practice of naming war aircraft after some "goddess" of stage or screen (with the implied intention of so invoking her protective patronage) is also a varia-tion—however diluted and imprecise—of this same universally persistent practice.

CHAPTER V

The Rites

I

THE RITES AS COLLECTIVE DISCIPLINE

WHENEVER modern industrial techniques are introduced into a primitive culture, the ritualistic practices rapidly decline and disappear. It has therefore been deduced that the purpose of ritual is the magical control of environmental forces, a function more effectively fulfilled by modern techniques, which it is argued, have therefore come to replace the rituals. However, only a small percentage of religious ritual (as distinct from magic rites) is concerned with such material phenomena. And on the other hand, machines have not so much given man control over natural disasters such as drought, flood and epidemic disease, as made possible compensatory, remedial and rescue measures. Moreover, the machine and the culture it has produced make for disasters unknown to primitive man: automobile, train and airplane accidents, nervous disorders, sexual crimes, and the unprecedented enormity of war's destruction. Certainly it cannot be claimed, therefore, that ritualistic appeal against catastrophe can have been eliminated because modern industrial man is more secure physically or morally than man in a primitive culture. If one were to compare such cultures in terms of the proportion of negative to positive factors within their respective contexts, it is extremely doubtful whether, relatively, the modern culture would show the greater positive weight.

At the same time, the dazzling nature of modern technology has so obscured the very existence of primitive technology (which, in its context, is skilled enough to maintain a positive balance of forces) that ritual and technology have been presumed to stand in principled and mutual antagonism.

Nevertheless, in Haiti it is precisely the loa and the ancestors who are consulted for technical and practical advice in reference to planting, buildings and, certainly, medicinal remedies. All mythology contains legends in which divinity instructs man in some practical technique for survival; God's directives to Noah concerning the ark constitute a perfect example of such an occasion. And just as such instruction signified Noah's favored position in the eyes of God, so a man of primitive culture is inclined to interpret any special technical or practical "know-how", not as the beginning of a separation from, or an opposition to divinity, but as an indication of divine benevo-lence and favor. Moreover, if technological advance does not provide greater cosmic control than ritual appeal, nor stand in opposition to rites as a means of adjustment to the immediate environment, neither does the new mass of creature comforts and the dime-store jewelry which it brings with it serve as a simple alternative seduction away from ritual. The concept of comfort is, in primitive cultures, often associated with divinity, and, in the hieratic royal courts, may attain even to luxurious realization. In Haiti, Ghede has adopted modern sun-glasses and Erzulie delights in modern jewelry and sanitation. The loa are not at all opposed to modern improvements on the material level.

In the final analysis, modern technological and primitive ritual are not competitive in terms of man's relationship to the cosmos or to matter; their apparent opposition stems from the fact that they have to do with different orders of the relationship of man to man. A tractor, which does not replace the need for water or good soil, *does* replace the ten neighbors upon whom a farmer once relied in times of planting, plague and harvest. Running water in the house brings to an end the groups of women who gathered at the stream to do their laundry, and who, together, agreed not to pollute its source and to parcel out and share its meagre trickle in times of dryness. The importation of ready-made cloth replaces no ritual; but it does eliminate the complex system of intimately personal relationships which were involved in the barter of raw materials, dyes, looms, etc. In effect, the machine creates a society in which men are no longer dependent upon men, but, instead, upon machines and upon the anonymous, unknown, distant creatures behind the machines, who, like the machines, are impersonally regarded as productive forces. Just as the machine has neither beliefs, convictions nor morals, so it has become a matter of principle to consider the religious, social and political convictions of the operator of the machine, as equally irrelevant. The relationship and interdependence between men shifts from an intimate, moral basis to impersonal, material grounds; all human diver⁄ sity is reconciled in the spoon, the dress, the refrigerator. Indeed, the measure of such a machine culture is the degree of tolerance it has for individual heterogeneity, diversity and disagreement. Socially, this principle is expressed in the high value placed upon individual privacy, the opportunity to withdraw or isolate oneself from potential and actual disagreements with other men rather than be forced to resolve them. Economically, men are shifted from a co⁄operative to a competitive relation⁄ ship. And politically, a system is created in which the public policy is the statistical sum of private opinions; the singular, subjective persuasions and prejudices of individuals become by quantitative accumulation, the plurality, the objective reality of communal order.

Only the legal system reflects the existence of a man's public self, that is, his person as part of a collective whole, and the consideration that the interests of this public self may be different from and even in conflict with the interests of his private self. The minimum limit of the collective's tolerance for individual variation and aggression is known as the public welfare, and is legally defined in predominantly negative terms: protective limitations such as food and drug acts, the restriction of criminal aggression, the control of public noise and nuisance, etc. The law, which might be said to codify collective morality in the public context, is actually not so much concerned with exacting a positive contribution from the individual on behalf of the common good (taxation and military service are the only exactments of this kind) as it is with preventing any infringements upon individual welfare.

It is significant that, just as in most primitive cultures, the rôles of king and priest were originally combined, so the protection and preservation of the collective welfare—which, in an industrial culture, is the specialized concern of the legal code— is, in a primitive community, the primary function of the religion. In effect, it could not be otherwise, for here a man is so much more continuously and organically involved with the rest of the community in interdependent relationship that it would be impossible to codify legally all the occasions and circumstances in which he must respect the collective welfare. In such a community it becomes imperative that the individual be imbued with the *principle* of collective action and that this serve not only to restrain him from anti-social actions, but also to induce him toward positive contribution. Since the very life of the tribe stands or falls according to the degree to which this principle pervades the individuals, the collective rituals— whose function is to reaffirm this principle constantly and to integrate the morality—play a dominant rôle.* As modern individualistic independence replaces collective interdependence, this communal religion of collective public rituals is

* This accounts for the formality that is markedly noticeable in all but the most intimate relationships. Yet it does not subjugate the individual as a personality in non-ritual contexts. On the contrary, since one's public behavior is virtually guaranteed and prescribed, one's individual idiosyncrasies of personality as a private individual are not understood to threaten the public welfare. There is, in fact, virtually no social inhibition upon private personality and, as a consequence, a group of Haitians is far more "colorful" and diverse than an equivalent group of individuals in our culture; for, among us, personal persuasion is directly projected as public policy—there is no distinction between the self in private context and the self in public context, and the integrity of the culture therefore becomes dependent upon a certain standardization on the personal and private level. In a democratic culture there is a tendency to believe that if someone dresses in a non-conservative style of clothes, he may also be a threat to the institutions of society; in a culture in which the personal and the public contexts are recognized as being quite distinct, on the other hand, the individual is actually freer in the personal context, since there is no feeling that this idiosyncrasy may be read over into public contexts.

replaced, on the one hand, by the legal system, which governs the public self of a man, and on the other, by a religion of private contemplation, where the subjective conscience (reflecting the individual background and the personal powers, whether crude or developed, for the perception of truth and good) is a man's final moral authority in his largely private life.

The public rituals of the hounfor are, in a sense, an extension of the principles which govern a family, where the co-operative participation of all the members—including the children—is necessary for survival. Here, for example, it would not be reasonable if the sheer statistical majority of children gave them authority over the parents in determining the rules governing the labors of the farm and household, or behavior in general. Nor would it be feasible to depend upon the child's ability to understand analytically the reasons why certain things should be done, and how. Similarly, it is obvious that all individuals are not capable of equal perception and moral intensity; that even a single individual may be more acute in one context than in another, may "feel" more conscientious one day and less another. And just as the legal code recognizes that the collective welfare cannot be dependent upon such variability, so the religion imposes forms of conduct (understood as traditions) which guarantee that the collective level shall transcend such individual variability. The individual is obliged to respect the loa in a defined fashion, to celebrate them by joining in the dancing and the singing, to observe obeisances and altogether to participate in the collective confirmation of those principles and disciplines which are essential to the collective welfare. In maintaining this collective level, religion, like the legal code, is first concerned with men's acts, not with their feelings. The use of the phrase "I serve", rather than "I believe", reflects this emphasis upon the objective fact of function rather than the subjective condition.*

---

* This disciplinary function of ritual is contrary to the notions held by two apparently opposite schools of thought: the primitivists, who understand ritual

It is true that in time, and under certain circumstances, such an authoritarian religion, with its secondary regard for individual desires, may develop into an autocracy; that is, the authorities (priests, kings, etc.) may become primarily concerned with the personal benefits of their position and may attempt to preserve such traditions even when these cease to serve the collective welfare, or even begin to conflict with it. But in Haiti, a serviteur is still the final judge of the houngan's efficacy and honesty. He has recourse to other houngans, and even has final recourse to worship within the family group. Moreover, while a legal code is supported by civil punitive powers, and a punitive power also supports, to some degree, the parental disciplines, the religion cannot resort to such enforcements directly. In the very act of proposing a certain tradition, and exacting obedience by such moral pressures as are at its disposal, it must simultaneously *convince* the serviteur that the principles which it proposes are good and proper, just

and dance as the spontaneous expression of unfettered spirits; and the psychoanalysts, who regard these as release valves, permitting a socially accepted form for the realization of repressed desires and the resolution of private trauma. The primitivist ignores the fact that a primitive community must require conformism of its individuals when they function in a collective context and that if public rituals served as an arena for the public display of individual impulses, this would exactly contradict the purpose of those rituals, which is to reaffirm the unity of the community. The psychoanalyst, on the other hand, bases himself entirely upon a society in which the whole—whether political, social or economic—is understood as the sum, the plurality of its individual parts, so that there exists no differentiation between a man as a public unit and a man as a private individual. For the individuals in such a society, public disciplines are confounded with and become private inhibitions, and compulsions of private and personal origin are expressed and resolved in public and social activities. The man of a primitive, collective community, however, distinguishes sharply between these two areas. He regards the collective disciplines as objective realities and accepts (or occasionally rebels against) them on that level. Having committed himself to the public conduct required by the collective as such, he proceeds to deal with his personal life in his private terms. This private life, in so far as it is private, is thus free of those inhibitions which, in our culture, originate in social and public attitudes and requirements. For this reason, and also because the religious ritual is part of the public context and is performed by the "public self" of the man, so to speak, it is incorrect to conceive of them as the arena of individual, private expression.

as good parents are primarily concerned with educating their children toward their own adulthood, and reserve their punitive power as a last recourse. The religious rituals, in the very act of proposing formal disciplines, serve, simultaneously, as exemplary demonstrations of the reasons for these forms. If the serviteur does not show the resistances and defiances which might be expected as a reaction to discipline, it is not because he is docile by nature; it is because he has begun, already, to agree rather than merely to obey. And this early understanding is possible because the means by which he is instructed, or is made to understand, are not an abstract process of analysis, requiring intellectual maturity, but a system of graphic demonstrations. The serviteur learns love and beauty in the presence and person of Erzulie, experiences the ways of power in the diverse aspects of Ogoun, becomes familiar with the implications of death in the attitudes of Ghede. He sings in the chorus, and feels in his own person that surge of security which is harmonious collective action. He witnesses the wisdom of ancestral and divine counsel, and learns the advantages of accepting such counsel, with its history and experience, for his own guidance in action. In effect, he understands the principles because he sees them function.

This major educational service of rituals would be vitiated if they were symbolic in nature. In effect, nothing is more meaningless or perplexing to the Haitian than to be asked what some ritual action "represents", "stands for", or "symbolizes". When food is put down for the loa, the Haitian understands precisely that fact: the loa are being given food; and all ritual action is understood with the same immediacy. The real, visible action of a ritual is not the symbolic statement of some idea; on the contrary, it would be the verbal statement, the metaphysical concept, or the abstract idea which would be understood as a symbol, at one remove from the reality of the act or fact.* Moreover, if the act were symbolic—if its meaning

---

* The current insistence upon understanding all activity as representative of another activity, the refusal to recognize the directness of the statement, may lead

and value were dependent upon historical or metaphysical reference—it would have become, long ago, the religion of an intellectual *élite*, both able and willing to devote themselves to the necessary research; and it would be dependent upon an accuracy which had no tolerance for the diversity and fallibility of human intellect. Furthermore, if the particular action stood in a precisely symbolic relationship to the principle, it could not change to become a statement in contemporary terms. For instance, today, the regular ceremonial costume for the Rada rites consists of a white handkerchief bound around the head, and a white dress; for the men, white trousers and shirt. Every⁄one is bare⁄footed. Long sleeves are expected, unless extreme poverty prohibits this, as well as a high⁄closed neck, and a skirt as long and full as can be made from the amount of material that the person has been able to buy. This is certainly not the African costume, which must have included many immediately symbolic and local references. But just as that was the "best" dress, so this is, now, in the contemporary context, the "best" dress, and it is this fact which is evidence of religious

to certain absurdities. Even Maximilien, who in general is exceedingly percep⁄tive about Voudoun, writes: "She also passes them [the chickens] over the bodies of the hounsis, which is called 'ventailler', a symbolic way of establishing the contact between the humans and the animals" (p. 107). But as he himself describes the action, *it is an actual contact which is being effected,* not a symbol of a contact.

As a matter of fact, the effort to make an action or an image a specific symbol of something may deprive it of the very richness of connotations and ramifica⁄tions which make it meaningful. Damballah, as serpent, is cosmic precisely because of the richness of the ramifications. His sinuosity connotes the dynamic of life; his water habits relate him to water, which is a source of life in several senses. But the sun also is a source of life, and so Damballah is represented as a serpent stretched across the sky in the arc of the sun's path (which is also as a rainbow), and this arc, reflected in the sea, describes a circle which embraces the cosmos, or is comparable to an egg containing the cosmos; and indeed the snake does lay eggs. Moreover, trees, rising from below, with their roots in water, cut through the earth, toward the sun, and so move as an avenue of divine inter⁄section, which, as a matter of fact, the snake—as tree⁄climber—travels. Thus the serpent, when taken as a connotative image, comprehends a whole complex of cosmic principles and this richness would be lost if it were taken as a symbol of any one specific and precise idea.

dedication. *The material detail has changed in order that the moral principle may remain constant.*

This constant principled function transcends not only historical changes, but all the local variations in ritual due to the special history of the community, practical expediency, or stylistic development. At the same time, these variations con-tain, each in its own fashion, an affirmation of the major concepts of the religion. Such variations have sometimes been construed as evidence that the religion has degenerated from some pinnacle of archaic purity; but it would seem, on the contrary, that when a principle can be proposed in terms that vary over time and according to place, this testifies to its truly universal scope. In fact, the meaning of various ritualistic activities may seem secretive or obscure precisely because there is a certain tendency, on the part of the interpreter, to seek out some original symbology which might, in the final analysis, be irrelevant, while the principled and generalized function is ignored. For example, one of the elements of ritual is langage, a kind of sacred language, which is understood to be the means of direct communication with the loa and more persuasive to them than address in Creole. Langage seems to be the vestige of African speech,*[1] and if this is so, then it was originally used to address the loa in words understood by everyone as being such an address. Today, it is doubtful if even the houngan knows what the words mean, any more than the hounsis who sing the songs in which they occur. Yet, today, the sense of direct address to the loa is even intensified, for now *only* the loa are assumed to understand this language, and it is thus even more pointedly an exclusive, sacred language, accessible only to the most spiritually developed, than it was when it was the common speech. This sense and function of langage would not be in the least illuminated by an exhaustive tracing of the words themselves.

* This theory has been discussed *supra*, p. 69.

2

THE RITES AS INDIVIDUAL DEVELOPMENT

The principle of participation, which is at the very core of collective religions, does more than insure that everyone shall witness such exemplary demonstrations of moral principle in action. The rites not only educate from the outside, as it were, but, even more importantly, function in a manner of which the participant may not be consciously aware and which certainly is imperceptible to the detached observer. A devout serviteur, such as Titon, would never neglect to make the libation of water, coffee or rum as a salute to les Morts, les Marassa, et les Mystères before himself drinking. At times he would walk to the threshold of the house and pour the libation directly upon the earth. At other times, however, he would merely dribble it on the cement floor, where it would lie in a pool, be walked in, and eventually dry up. In ceremonies, and on important occasions, he would carry out the ritual in the way that con-formed to its original intention, which was that the liquid should penetrate the earth; yet the abbreviated gesture which he made at other times was not, in a real sense, a complete corruption or deterioration of the original. If Titon had been chastised, he would have smiled, and, as if politely obliging a sense of form, would have gone to the door to spill a second offering on the earth. But in either case the obeisance that he made served its larger function: while this libation to the Dead, the Divine Twins and the loa might or might not influence them, it certainly affirmed in Titon's mind a sense of the history of which he was the issue and an awareness of his relation-ship to a collective. It was one of those rites—and these are dominant in the religion—whose function is not immediate. Designed as a form of discipline, frequently exacting and tedious, these rites do not necessarily yield to the devotee any personal, self-expressive pleasure. Nor do they function directly toward the desired end. If one were to ask, "Does his ritual cause that thing to happen?" the answer would be in the affirmative. But causation, in religious terms, is not causation as defined in scientific terms. The world of a religious man is governed by moral reason, not by material reason. The Haitian does not mean, for example, that health will *result* from a certain ritual action; he means that health will be a *reward* for his performance of it. And if one were to press him to examine the implications of this idea more pro⁄ foundly, one would discover that the value of the ritual would not be negated by some error of ignorance of ritual detail; on the contrary, the serviteur would be rewarded for the devout intention of his effort. In other words, he would be morally correct even though technically wrong, and *this* fact is the religious reality; the material errors are relatively unimportant.

The central link of such a causal chain is, then, an invisible rewarding force, which the serviteur understands as super⁄ natural intervention. But if one substitutes, in this position, the psyche of the serviteur himself, it becomes clear why such rituals do, actually, work so often, for the primary effect of such ritual action is upon the doer. That action reaffirms first principles—destiny, strength, love, life, death; it recapitulates a man's relationship to his ancestors, his history, as well as his relationship to the contemporary community; it exercises and formalizes his own integrity and personality, tightens his dis⁄ ciplines, confirms his morale. In sum, he emerges with a strengthened and refreshed sense of his relationship to cosmic, social and personal elements. A man so integrated is likely to function more effectively than one whose adjustment has begun to disintegrate, and this will be reflected in the relative success of his undertakings. *The miracle is, in a sense, interior. It is the doer who is changed by the ritual, and for him, therefore, the world changes accordingly.*

It is this subjective function of ritual which is perhaps even more important than its objective functions: the disciplines which it imposes by virtue of certain moral threats, and the demonstration of principle by which it supports those

15. RITUAL PRAYERS. A major portion of ceremonials is devoted to solemn prayer. The heavily spangled flags in the foreground represent the *société*.

16. SACRIFICE OF A BULL. Note the vever drawing of a bull and, in the background, the sacrificial bull, draped in a colorful cloth.

disciplines.* For in the final analysis, what is important is not only what the serviteur does (which might conceivably be the right thing for the wrong reasons) nor what he consciously understands (which would vary according to his intellectual capacity) but *what he has become* as a result of his participation in those ceremonials. The intensive and extended rituals of

* This is precisely contrary to the orthodox psychoanalytical interpretation of the function of ritual activity, that is, the release of inhibitions, the realization of repressed desires, and the resolution of private trauma. It is necessary to stress that in a primitive culture there is virtually no privacy, and hence the primary condition for the creation of a trauma or a neurosis does not exist. If an accident has occurred, which might conceivably have become a trauma, the person of such a society does not need a specialist to make him remember, nor a ritual to sublimate, for all the people in the community will readily volunteer his "history". They will say, and repeatedly, that his mother used to beat him, and that she did so because his father left her; or they will say: "Are you going to fall down every time you see a dog, just because you did the first time?" The communal memory is complete, and even if one's intimate friends would censor some unpleasant memory, there are always enemies who will recall it. In a sense, the man of a primitive community has a relatively meager unconscious, in the sense of secreted traumas which are to be searched out as motivations for behavior. Neither can the person of such a society harbor an unresolved relationship—as in our culture—which some professional psychoanalyst must then make him confront; for it would be only very rarely that he could escape it geographically, since no such ready separation of children and parents takes place as in our culture. And if he does not escape it, but is forced to confront it daily, he must resolve it, or at least find some viable adjustment.

Psychoanalysis has based itself on cultures in which concealments, self-censorship, and the Christian idea of original sin (which, it must be remembered, is not shared by most primitive cultures) obtain, and is inclined to suspect human behavior as a mask for some reality which the individual feels compelled to conceal. It has, accordingly, set up a system of symbolic interpretation, in terms designed to illuminate a diseased organism, but which would not be valid for one that was healthy. Even where the symbolic interpretation would be correct, as in certain cases of sexual symbolism, the symbols would hardly have the same emotional value or "charge" for a native who felt no guilt or inhibitions about sexual activity, as for the citizen of a Christian culture in which sexual activity is regarded in a vastly different and more complex light. *The images of primitive myth, and of most myths, are images of resolution, not of disease.* Even in our culture, sexual symbolism may occur in art and various other expressions, not because the artist unconsciously intends any personal sexual reference but because he has consciously chosen, as a means of analogous communication, the one experience which he could safely insist was common to all human beings.

initiatory gradation are devoted entirely to such a creation and development of a "soul".

In this respect the critical distinction between magic and religion becomes evident, for there are no such rites, designed to develop the person, in magic. A magician's apprenticeship consists of exchanging his services for secreted, concealed information, whereas the religious neophyte, by virtue of experience and ordeals, matures spiritually to an understanding of things which have been frankly evident in public ritual all along. Magic refers to power, which is amoral in nature; the primary emphasis of religion is moral discipline and develop-ment. Magic rituals are performed with the intention of pro-ducing a direct result upon the world and their ritual details are immediately linked to the object; in religious ritual the physical act is frequently quite disconnected from the desired reward. In effect, *in religion the serviteur is changed; in magic the world is changed.*

It is of major importance, also, that the principles governing this subjective development in religion derive from the collective context. The individual who functions in interdependent terms with the community cannot forge ahead too far, since this would alienate him from the very forces upon which he is dependent. The impulse and incentive behind the magician, on the other hand, has always been an individualistic triumph, whether for good or for evil. Yet he too has been restrained somewhat by his dependence upon the collective community. Indeed, the best condition for magical action is not the primi-tive community with its collective emphasis, but the modern community, with its individualistic emphasis, and it is here that one may experience the pre-eminent spectacle of the magician at work. He conceives his plans in almost solitary secrecy, or with a few cohorts; he is feverishly protective of the exclusive right to exploit the power of his discovery or invention; he is frequently concerned with an almost occult effort to divine that special twist of public taste which makes for a hit or a best-seller; he is devoted to the idea of a magic combination of words in a certain just-so order, which is a catchy slogan; he labors to create a skillfully obsessive image of material or sexual seduction, and is not above accomplishing this with a maximum of artifice and connotative sleight of hand; he is involved in a complex and formal series of cabbala-like manipulations involving "contacts", publicity incantations, and even what might be accurately termed the cocktail libation. Moreover, this is all pursued in the interests of his own personal aggrandizement and entirely irrespective, in a profound sense, of the public welfare. The hexes, elixirs and fetishes of primitive magicians are paltry achievements compared to the vast powers of such modern magicians.*

Magic on such a scale could not, in fact, exist in an inter-dependent culture in which, on the one hand, projects of any scope could not be undertaken without the knowledge of others, and on the other hand, the collective could not and would not tolerate such an individualistic offensive upon its integrity. So firmly imbued is the man of such a culture with the collective principle, that he assumes any technique to be public property, available for the use of the collective. The innocent, unabashed readiness of "natives" to imitate or adopt some new aspect of dress or manner or method which may strike their fancy is but one manifestation of their complete ignorance of the notion of originality in the possessive, "copy-right" sense. In his mind any technique, and especially any improved technique, is a dispensation of divinity and therefore comprehends the moral purpose of collective benefit. It is this idea that made primitive cultures such easy prey to invaders with superior mechanical equipment. The history of the Spanish conquest of the Americas begins, in each isolated district, not with native resistance but with native welcome. They wel-comed the superior "things" which, they assumed, would, like all other techniques, accrue to the improved welfare of their community; and they welcomed the men who brought them,

---

* For other discussions of the contrast between religion and magic, see pp. 65-6, 75-7, *supra*.

as beings upon whom the gods had chosen to confer such exceptional talent and power. By the time the native priests grasped the immoral function of the equipment of their guests, it was too late to marshal their amazed and demoralized forces effectively. The failure of the priests was a failure to recognize the new face of their most ancient antagonist, the magician. But even if they had recognized it, or could have recognized it today, their battle would nevertheless have been lost. For an industrial culture, while liberating individuals from the interdependence which requires and guarantees a homogeneous morality, is also characterized by an emphasis upon technological achievement *per se*: the invention of means and the development of methods. Such separation of means from ends, of techniques from morals, marks the era of the magician. Against an entire era, the priests of collective ritual religions, proposing their metaphysic of collective morality, are virtually helpless.

3

THE INITIAL RITUAL ACTS

The initial ritual movements of any ceremony are an effort to establish contact with the loa, with the universal, cosmic forces. When everyone has assembled in the peristyle,* the houngan

* The fact that many of the ceremonies and almost all the dances take place at night has been given a sensational and romantic interpretation by many visitors. The reasons are very practical. For one thing, the personnel of the hounfor is usually busy with various labors and chores during the day. For another thing, the heat of a tropical climate between the hours of eleven and five in the afternoon is almost unbearable. The daytime is usually spent in preparations: cooking, decorating, etc. The actual ceremony, and certainly the dancing, is postponed until late afternoon or the coolness of the evening. It should also be pointed out that whereas the visitor may find the night an unfamiliar and mysterious landscape, most of those who participate in the ceremonies are not accustomed to electrical illumination and have long ago become adjusted to the dark. Moreover, they have come to know every last corner of their community so well that they could easily find their way about blindfolded. The night is not mysterious for them and holds nothing of the atmospheric excitement which it does for the visitor.

(or the person on whose behalf the ceremony is being con-ducted) takes a jug of water, and, lifting it successively toward the four cardinal points, signals the Mysteres. He may address an audible plea to them; sometimes it is a cursory signal, an almost familiar gesture; at other times, as he is poised there, with the jug of water lifted overhead and his eyes fixed into that space, one has a sense, suddenly, that the distant air is peopled with invisible hosts whose attention he would command, and whose presences he would draw from all corners of the universe to this particular moment and this particular place. Thus the very opening gesture of the ritual immediately gives it vast and cosmic scope.[2]

This initial salutation is, in a sense, comprehensive. It includes Legba, without whose permission no contact could be made with any of the Invisibles. It is also addressed to the two trinities: the Christian Father, Son and Holy Ghost, and the Voudoun Mystères, Morts and Marassa. The salutation may include, in addition, any particular deity with whom the houngan or serviteur may be especially concerned, such as his maît-tête or the maît-hounfor, or the loa on whose behalf this particular ceremony is being conducted.

Having so signaled them, he pours three libations at the entrance to the peristyle. This is a mark of respect, a first offering; it is also a gesture of the hand, inviting the gods: "Here, if you please." Often, beginning at the entrance, he trickles a thin line of water across the peristyle to the poteau-mitan. Then he draws another line of water (for the loa are led in on water) from the second and third entrances, and so creates three rivers which converge at the poteau-mitan, making it the cosmic axis of the world.[3]

In proper hierarchical order, the jug is passed on to the distinguished visitors and members of the *société*, who repeat the libations (although, for expediency, and because the houngan's invitation was the major statement, they do not necessarily draw the line of water). Throughout the ceremony many of the ritual acts are thus repeated, in less elaborate form, by the participants. The sense is not so much that their actions add any real persuasion, but rather that they can thereby share the relationship with the loa which the houngan has initiated. It is also a matter of pride to the houngan when distinguished visitors participate in such salutations to the loa of his hounfor. In the meantime, the houngan or the la⁄place has lit a candle and prepared to draw the first vevers. The plate of flour or ashes (the material used depends upon which vevers are to be drawn) is oriented, as was the water. (Almost everything used during a ceremony, and all the offerings, are first signaled toward the cardinal points.) The chorus might have begun to sing the song: "Fait un vever pou moin" ("Draw a vever for me"), and if it is not Saturday or Sunday, when drumming is permitted, they will be clapping time with their hands.

The drawing of vevers requires real technical skill. A small amount of flour is picked up between the thumb and fore⁄finger and let sift on to the ground while the hand moves in the line of the form which the vever is to take. The first thing drawn is a circle around the base of the poteau⁄mitan.[4] From this center the vevers radiate. Sometimes, when the service is for a specific loa, the vever may be drawn at the entrance to his particular chamber. When the service is being conducted at his sacred tree in the court, it is drawn there. Each loa has his special symbol, or vever. The basic form, and certain details, are traditionally fixed. The cross⁄roads is the sign for Legba; the heart is for Erzulie: a boat represents Agwé; serpents are for Damballah and Ayida, etc. But even with these fixed forms, there is great scope for personal variations of style.

The vever consecrates to the loa which it represents the area which it covers. Sometimes it is an elaborate, painstaking tracery, made even more lace⁄like by the granular ruffling of the lines, and even more fragile by the impression that the slightest breeze would blow away the light ridge of flour. But this fragile aspect is, at the same time, balanced by the strong contrast of the white lines against the very dark ground, so that it seems a coat of arms, an emblazoned shield. When especially elaborate, it projects the sense of a celebration of its loa, a public feat displayed in his honor. In such cases, however, the com/ pliment to the loa would seem to rest chiefly in the labor of the making and the disciplinary ordeal of dedication; for all this elaborate design is bit by bit destroyed by the grains of maize, peanuts and other food placed upon it, smudged by the death throes of the sacrificed chicken laid upon it, and, in the end, the god having eaten, and the vever's function being thus fulfilled, it is walked on, danced on, and finally its remnants are swept away. At other hounfors the vevers may consist of no more than a few strokes, accomplished with that sense of intimate ease which comes from assurance and cer/ tainty. Here one feels that the houngan long ago successfully completed his "courtship" of the loa and that it remains for him, now, simply to signal his presence—as a long/married man might simply rap on the door of his wife's chamber, as a mere gesture, and enter without even waiting for her response. At other times, some quality of the vever's very form will suddenly illuminate the fact that it does, indeed, create a door in the earth, which leads to the loa living in the abysmal waters below; so that whatever is placed upon it does not rest on the surface but seeps down an invisible funnel.[5]

If the ceremony is one in which several loa are to be fed together, in the beginning, thus requiring the drawing of several vevers around the poteau/mitan, these may have been made even before the official opening of the ceremony. In any case, after the first libations, the two hounsis, carrying the ceremonial flags representing the *société*, and the la/place, carry/ ing the saber and representing the loa maît/hounfor, emerge ritualistically from the chamber of the maît/hounfor. They come out backward and revolve in one direction, then in reverse, until they attain the center of the peristyle. Thereupon, they proceed, successively, in the directions of the four cardinal points and at each edge of the peristyle perform the ritual salutation: a full turn to the right, then to the left, then to the right again, each turn punctuated by a sort of curtsey, and the whole concluded by kneeling, and kissing the ground three times. They then perform the same salutation before the poteau-mitan, and, if the drums are being used, next address this salute to the drums. The formation now salutes the houngan, with that mock competition between asson and saber which has been already described.[6] And after the houngan they salute any visiting houngans or mambos in the same manner, the older and "stronger" houngans having precedence. Also they salute the houngenikon, and, finally, any distinguished visitors. These salutations, which are meticulously repeated, detail for detail, in reference to a large number of people, may sometimes take a long while to complete, and foreign visitors, anticipating ritual as an intense, dramatic experience, find this portion (and other similar portions) most tedious. Even the members of the *société* are merely patient. Yet in what better manner could all these single individuals be deliberately and personally involved and integrated into the ceremony from the very beginning? To be approached and confronted by this trio—delegatès of the loa and the *société*—to be obliged to rise, move in formation with them, give attention to the proper order of movements and gestures, signal in the cardinal directions—to do all this is to become irrevocably involved and committed to the ritual. One arrived in the peristyle as a secular individual; after such salutations the person who resumes his seat is no longer that at all. From this moment on, his gestures, movements, attitudes take on metaphysical reference. To wander away, to neglect the ritual obligations, would now be a deliberate blasphemy; to participate properly is to engage divine benevolence.

In the meantime, the houngan of the hounfor and the visiting houngans and mambos will have been exchanging their formal salutations, and the manner in which these are carried out constitutes a statement of relative authority. If, for example, the houngan's "father" is present, he does not execute the turns: the younger houngan turns in front of him, although the two curtsey together at the conclusion of each turn: and the "father" remains standing while the younger man kisses the ground at his feet. Then, taking his hand, he raises the younger houngan, who repeats the three turns. Their hands are joined and held high during the entire salute, which is concluded by a double handshake. A stronger houngan may, however, "raise" the standing of someone who salutes him by preventing him from kissing the ground at his feet, and by going directly into the second phase, the salutation with the hands joined. This mark of respect is usually conferred upon visitors who do not hold a rank in the hierarchy and also are not subject to the honoring houngan's authority; that is to say, are not of his hounfor personnel. When two houngans of equal standing salute each other, they mirror each other and neither of them kisses the ground; they perform the second phase of the salute with hands joined and turning together. Two houngenikons salute each other as equals, but kiss the ground together.[7] There are many subtle gradations of salutation and these indicate the relative authority of the persons involved.

This pattern of graduated salutations reflects the effort to resolve the circumstance that a single community may have several "competing" hounfors. Just as the father of a family remains the highest authority in any situation which involves even a full-grown son, so the spiritual father of a houngan remains the major authority even in the hounfor of his son; and just as, in communal life, the children of one family have deference for the heads of other families, and these relate to each other in terms of equality or of recognized communal prestige, so the same general principles hold for the religious communal adjustment. This prevents an atmosphere of anarchic competitiveness and resentment from developing between the hounfors, and stabilizes a situation which might otherwise have destroyed the religion altogether by splitting the community into warring loyalties. In other words, the salutations serve to inter-adjust and integrate the collective.

When all the relationships of the participants have been established, and their salutations made to the loa of the hounfor and to the flags of the *société*, the acts of mutual respect having been accomplished, there follow the *action de grâce* and the Catholic litanies. These vary in elaborateness. In a ten-day *ceremony-caille*, an entire afternoon may be dedicated to the *action de grâce*.[8] In a briefer ceremony this may be limited to one or two litanies, three Paters and three Aves, and followed by the *prière Guinée*. This prayer is almost entirely in langage; almost all the loa are called by name, including not only the major loa of the pantheon but all the personal ancestral loa as well. The order of this invocation is determined by various elements. Although such a loa as Legba always retains his first position, the maît-hounfor and various personal loa may take precedence even over such great loa as Ogoun.[9]

The *prière Guinée* is perhaps the most impressively sober and devout portion of the entire ceremony. The heat of the late afternoon muffles the peristyle and seems almost to be the weight which bows all the white-bound heads in prayer and stills every-one to motionlessness. The hounsis are seated along benches and in the clear center area, near the poteau-mitan, the houngan (perhaps with several of the visiting mambos and houngans) sits on the small chair which permits him easily to touch the earth and lift his hand to his lips in a token kissing of the ground, or to press a pinch of earth to his chest, at the mention of those loa for whom he would show particular respect. On such occasions he will also shake his rattle in special salutation. From time to time one hounsi or another will drop to the ground to kiss it, signifying a loa of markedly personal importance to her. But apart from such small movements, there is so little overt emotion that the endless incantation, the regular alternation between the voice of the priest, whose bent head sends the words inward upon himself, and the answering chorus, in the oppressive heat, gives to the whole a sense of endurance rather than of celebration or even invocation. It becomes an ordeal of discipline, not an offering of ecstasy but the more demanding offering of almost unbearable ennui. Finally, with a prolonged sounding of the asson the *priere Guinée* is concluded. Then, together, the drums, the hounsis clapping their hands, and the assons striking the ground or close to it—all in unison—begin the *battérie maconnique*. Their rhythm is one⁄two⁄three pause, one⁄two⁄three pause: an unhurried, deliberate beating, a pounding on the door of the loa world. Fourteen times this triple beat is repeated and then the phrase is ended, to be punctuated, however, by a sustained beating—almost, one might imagine, a rattling of the knob; whereupon, again, the deliberate *battérie* is resumed. The number of times is a matter of ritualistic decision; but the impact of this code beaten upon the door is overwhelming.[10] It is impossible to conceive how this culminating collective effort to establish contact with the world of les Invisibles could possibly fail.

4

FEEDING THE LOA[11]

The loa, whose function is to direct the enormous primal mass of the material universe into patterns of intelligence and benevolence, are involved in a great and endless labor. It is their moral energy which animates this huge hulk of matter, and so, since that energy is constantly expended, it must be constantly replenished. And this is man's duty: to feed the loa, to insure the constant flow of the psychic energy, to assure the moral movement of the universe. Thus, the feasting of the loa is the ceremonial most frequently performed in Haiti. In addition to the general drain on the loa's energy, it is also tapped by the specific, individual demands of men. Thus there are general feasts, for all the pantheon; special feasts for loa of whom one has asked a great deal; annual feasts for the Marassa and the Dead; and certainly, any ceremony whose purpose is to ask something of the loa, begins with an offering of food.

Since the essence of the food is consumed by the loa, it may be scattered for them in all directions, or buried for them, or left standing at the cross⁄roads. It may also be consumed by them directly, when they possess a person; for although the food enters the body of the person, it is the loa who are nourished by its essence: this is made evident by the fact that after the period of possession, when the person is himself again, he will not feel that he has eaten and may be ravenously hungry. When food is left overnight at the altar, again it is the essence which is consumed by the loa; for although the material substance, which remains, will subsequently be divided among the participants, the people have no sense of being greatly nourished by it. In fact, it is never the people who feast at a feast for the loa.[12]

The kind of food, its preparation, the manner of serving it and the selection and quantity of the portions, depend upon which loa is being fed, and vary according to the particular occasion, the local traditions, and factors of immediate expediency. A poor man, for example, may apologetically request of three loa that they share a single chicken. A sense of ritual precision governs all offerings; such precision is equally characteristic of the simple *mangé sec* (the offering of grains, fruits and vegetables which precede a very minor ceremony such as the baptism of minor ritual objects) and of the elaborate feasts which a houngan may sponsor annually on behalf of his hounfor—involving the sacrifice of many chickens, several goats, even a bull, and pigs (for the Petro), which may take up to ten days to accomplish completely.[13]

Such an elaborate ceremony, if it happens to be performed in the general period of the harvest, may begin with a *ceremonyyam*. Theoretically, this ceremony, which is the only important agrarian ritual among the Rada rites, is an offering of the first fruits of the field to the loa, so that they may again bless the earth in the coming season.[14] After the vevers for the major deities (including Azacca, loa of agriculture) have been traced, the litanies and the prayers are recited. Then the hounsis, carrying on their heads baskets piled high with yams and dried fish, form a processional which winds many times around the centerpost before the offering is deposited at its base. There the yams and fish are consecrated and the houngan, holding a candle in one hand, points the saber, which he holds in the other, toward the cardinal points. He then kneels and chops one yam in half, and passes the knife, or machete, to the next person in hierarchical order, who does the same with another yam. One by one every participant at the ceremony slices a yam, and when this has been accomplished, all the pieces are gathered once more into the baskets, covered with leaves of mombin, consecrated with the sign of the cross, and carried in processional to the major Rada altar, where they are *coucher* (laid away), as it is called, for the night.

The overnight *coucher* or sleep, whether of yams, or, on occasion, of drums, or of the initiate, is a rite at once of purification and of strengthening. Perhaps because of the word *coucher*, or because of the blanket of leaves spread as carefully as a coverlet, or because of the complete silence of the windowless altar chamber with its thick clay walls and the single, small illumination of the sacred light—a wick floating in a bowl of oil—or perhaps because of all of these together, the scene is one of profound repose, which is in contrasting yet harmonious counterpoint to the lively dance of celebration which is usually taking place that very evening in the adjoining peristyle. To pass from one to the other is to experience, within the single moment, the entire range of Voudoun: the meditative, introverted sobriety which characterizes the prayers and the solitary withdrawal of the initiate ordeal, the impressive dynamism of ceremonials in which drums, song, danceritual movements, sacred invocation, the designs of vevers, the play of colors sacred to the loa, the decorative genius manifest on the walls of hounfors, the lace of shrines, and the arrangements of objects on the altars all play their part—fuse to create an overwhelming brilliance in which every sense participates in the celebration of the divine powers. On the morning following the *coucher*, the yams are brought out into the peristyle for the ceremony proper. They are once more placed at the altar base of the poteaumitan. Prayers are said; the yams and fish are blessed and consecrated, and since this is an important ceremony, a goat may be sacrificed, and some of its blood sprinkled upon the yams. Finally they are cooked, and a portion scattered in all directions. A certain amount may be ritually buried for the loa, and the remainder is shared by the partiʹcipants.[15]

In many cases the *mangé yam* is the first meal, so to speak, in a feasting of the gods which may last eight to ten days, and which a houngan undertakes every year, or every two years, to propitiate the loa and to invoke their good will toward his hounfor for the coming period. In such a case the ceremonial organization might be as follows: Sunday: *Action de Grâce*; Monday: Service for les Marassa and les Morts; in the evenʹing, the *coucher yam*; Tuesday: morning, *ceremonyʹyam*, late afternoon and evening, feasting of Legba, Loco, Ayizan, Damʹballah, Ayida, Erzulie and Agwé and their escorts (these loa are considered to be on very close terms and amenable to being served together); Wednesday: Ogoun, with a dance in the evening in his honor; Thursday: Azacca, or Erzulie, or perhaps one of the other loa especially important to the hounfor; Friday: Ghede; Saturday, the Petro loa; Sunday: often a *baptême*, followed by a reception; Monday: a personal loa, perhaps a work loa such as Mounanchou. If possible each loa is served on the day of the week sacred to him. The procedure is, usually, to perform the individual ceremony either in the midʹmorning or in the late afternoon, while the rest of the day is devoted to the preparation of food, and other details; and in the evening there is generally a *danse de rejuissance* in honor of the loa feasted that day. In a ceremony offered by an inʹdividual, even when it is conducted in a hounfor, the *coucher yam* is omitted and the entire ceremony is condensed, so that, with short rest intervals, it is concluded in two days.

5

TRANSFUSING LIFE TO THE LOA

In a major feasting of the loa, the *mangé sec,* or *mangé Guinée* is but the "hors d'œuvre", so to speak, of the offering. This does not mean that it is less meticulously prepared, for although the food is, by and large, similar for all the loa, there are differences in detail of composition and preparation and manner of serving which must be observed if the loa are to be pleased rather than angered. In the sacrifice of the animals there are differences not only in the composition of the bath which cleanses and purifies the chicken, goat, or bull, but also in the manner in which the animal is killed, in the cooking of the meat, and in the selection of the portions which are put aside for the loa.

Neither the idea nor the reality of animal sacrifice carries any emotional charge or repugnance for the Haitian. For one thing, his own food is so difficult to come by, and he has so many dependants, both infant and aged, that the feeding of a pet animal strikes him as either ludicrous or actually immoral, and he has never developed any sentimentality toward animals. There are many dogs about, to be sure, and a man may become genuinely attached to these, or to his donkey or horse, but such an individual attachment is not generalized into any feeling about animals *per se.* Furthermore, all poultry, most pigs and young goats are sold alive on the market (there being no facilities for keeping meat from spoiling) and they are kept alive about the courtyard until they are killed to be eaten. A Haitian is, therefore, accustomed to killing animals. This does not mean that the sacrificial animal is killed in "cold blood". On the contrary, in the course of being ritualistically prepared the animal enjoys more tenderness and care than one destined for purely secular purposes. While this could not be understood to "console" the animal, it does make evident to one who has observed it, the fact that the Haitian is completely innocent of any brutal emotion or intention toward it. Chickens and goats are selected according to sex and to the color sacred to the loa for which they are destined.[16] In many cases certain foods are taboo for the animal, since he must be kept pure, yet he must also be reasonably well fed, for a very thin chicken would not please the loa. On the day of the sacrifice the animal is cleansed with a purifying bath. Goats' horns are "dressed" with ribbons of the appropriate color, and a large silk handkerchief is draped over them. A bull may wear a very ornate and elegant robe. The chicken, however, is by far the most common sacrifice.

When the proper time for this act arrives, the chicken is first oriented, and then the houngan, or the loa, holding the chicken by its legs, begins the rounds of the participants in the peristyle. Each one in turn removes his hat and kneels while the houngan passes the chicken over the head and shoulders, or even the entire body, of the serviteur, as if it were a large feather cloth with which he would wipe away any impurity or evil.[17] When everyone has been so cleansed, the chicken is "ventailler", that is, swung in the air, or aired, after which it is held to the food which lies on the vever.[18] When it eats of that food, it becomes identified with the loa, and this is a signal that it may now be sacrificed and will be accepted by that loa. Sometimes the wings and legs are skillfully broken, in order that, with the burden of impurities which have been accumulated from the participants, it may not (either in body or in spirit) fly free and loose these once more upon the world. Immediately following this, it is killed in the manner prescribed by the loa for whom it is destined.[19] For Legba, the neck is twisted; for Loco the throat is cut and the bird is bled.[20] When the sacrifice is performed at the tree sacred to Legba, or at the cross sacred to Ghede, a few feathers are plucked from the chicken, wetted in the blood, and stuck to the tree or the cross. The blood may also be used to anoint the sacred objects, such as the jar of water for the libations, or even the forehead of the person for whom the ceremony is performed.[21] If anyone is ill in the hounfor, a special point is made of anointing the patient with the blood of Ghede's chicken. Then the bird (or birds, if several have been offered) is laid upon the vever and a cross of maize or other flour sprinkled upon it. Bits of the various dry foods, libations of water, coffee and syrup are dropped upon it, and the entire meal is represented in this final offering. A plate is then placed on the body to receive the money, which is given either for the cooks, or as a special offering to the loa. Those who make such contributions (which are used to buy things for the loa) kneel and kiss the ground beside the chicken and when this *adora-tion* has been concluded, the chicken is gathered up and taken to be cleaned and cooked. The prescribed morsels are put in a special plate destined for the loa, the plate is oriented, a small portion is scattered toward the cardinal points, and the dish is set in the appropriate niche before the altar.

Essentially the same pattern is followed for the goat, which is never offered alone, but always in addition to one or more chickens. It is "aired" and oriented by two men who lift it by the legs and swing it toward the cardinal points, and the ritual leaves are offered it to eat by the person primarily involved in the ceremony. Just before it is killed, it is skillfully castrated and its beard is cut off. Then the throat is cut, the blood is gathered into a half-gourd containing coarse salt and deposited on the vever. Both before and after the animal is sacrificed bits of the other foods and libations of the various liquids are poured upon it, and this sacrifice, like that of the chicken, is concluded with an *adoration*.

The detail which distinguishes the sacrifice of the bull is the manner in which it is "aired". After all the consecrations and libations have been made upon it, the la-place, leading it by the rope around its neck, runs it at full speed throughout the entire courtyard, with all the hounsis and other participants in full pursuit. The whole chase is carried out with much laughter, noise and excitement, which seems a veritable explosion after the long, workmanlike intensity of the prayers, the chicken and goat sacrifice. The chase ends at a given tree in the courtyard, where the bull is killed with a single swift stroke of the machete.

The sacrifice of the bull is the ultimate in the feasting of the loa, and it is followed by a dance of great rejoicing; for this is the offering which, as sheer nourishment, will most invigorate the loa. The sense is almost that of a transfusion, and has the same organic intent. The attitude of the Haitian toward the death and blood of these sacrificial beasts is never morbid. The intent and emphasis of sacrifice is not upon the death of the animal, it is upon the transfusion of its life to the loa; for the understanding is that flesh and blood are of the essence of life and vigor, and these will restore the divine energy of the god. The excitement and the rejoicing have nothing to do with death; they project the sympathetic surge of the new vigor and new life with which the loa is now infused.[22]

In addition to feasting, there are many other ceremonies relating to the loa. They are baptized when new to a person,[23] they are installed into a new peristyle, they can be restrained, and even buried, they can be summoned in a govi, and, from time to time, they must be warmed, or activated. This may be accomplished, in a minor way, by the burning of rum during a ceremony, and on important occasions, such as when the spirits are going down into the cold abysmal waters for a year and a day, or when they have been brought back up, there may be a ceremony of *bruler-zin* to re-animate their life. This ceremony, however, is most closely linked to the climactic moment of the initiatory rites, and will be described in that connection.

6

CEREMONIES FOR THE SERVITEUR

If men are so concerned with feasting the loa, it is because the divine energy into which the nourishment is transformed can accomplish things which the greatest physical strength of man could not. Thus, the men upon whom the loa are dependent

VEVER DRAWING OF A BULL

for their strength are, in turn, dependent upon the loa. It is true that the man who serves the loa well evokes, by that very fact, their answering benevolence. Many persons find, indeed, that this exchange is entirely satisfactory, and throughout their life time they may serve the loa privately, in their family circle.

But there may come a moment when a man may say: "I have fed my loa; I have respected their authority and their rules; I have done everything that a man might do. But still I suffer one misfortune after another. My crops are not as good as my neighbor's. My child has been ill for three years and does not seem to get any better. My cow gave birth, but the calf died. Twice I have paid a bocor for a magic charm to protect me from some evil, but the next misfortune always finds a new place to strike. My brothers and sisters are scattered, and we cannot join forces to make a truly important ceremony for the loa. Perhaps I should go to speak to André. He is a good man, and a strong houngan. Perhaps it would help to join his hounfor. Perhaps I should become canzo."

The ceremonies which mark the step by step elevation of a man in the ranks of the hounfor are both the means and the evidence of the adjustment of his relationship to the loa. To his personal knowledge of religious doctrine is gradually added the advanced and professional knowledge which the houngan calls "la science des Mystères", the science of the mysteries. The psychic strength of which the man has been subjectively and privately aware is increased and collectively confirmed by objective ordeal and public recognition. And where his service of the loa had formerly been confined and limited by his personal means, it is now incorporated into the collective effort and so gains dimension.

The rank of canzo, which is only one grade lower than the profession of houngan, marks both spiritual adulthood and participation as a fully-fledged member in the spiritual community. Relatively no importance is attached to the physical development of a person; neither puberty nor marriage is marked by an important ceremony. Only birth and death are attended by rituals. Voudoun is concerned with spiritual maturity and this is considered to be independent of physical development. Elevation in a hounfor does not necessarily mean that the person elevated is more sincerely devout than one who serves only within the family context; it means that he has a greater control over the psychic cosmic forces. He can activate them to a greater degree, and he can better direct that energy. In sum, he has greater mastery, and so, greater spiritual force.

The advantages of membership in a *société* are many. A man is enabled to participate in ceremonies for which, individually, he would have neither the physical means nor the ritual knowledge. His service of the loa is more regular and consistent, for in his lean times he shares in the ceremonies of the hounfor, and he makes his own contribution when his fortunes have improved. Even from the secular point of view he gains a certain security, for there is a social bond between the members of a *société*, a fraternity which can be relied on in times of critical need and even in problems of daily life.

The person who has finally achieved the rank of canzo has passed through a number of ceremonies, and some of these may have been performed even prior to his membership in the *société*. The baptism of the loa maît-tête was probably per-formed quite early, for such an adjustment of relationship between a loa and the "horse" is necessary if the latter is not to be entirely at the mercy of the former. Someone whose possessions begin and end with a certain difficulty and violence, who becomes possessed at inopportune moments, that is, in the midst of some activity which requires his conscious attention, or when he is attending a dance at a hounfor which may not be worthy of his loa, or which he does not know well—such a person is said to need a *laver tête* ceremony.[24] This ceremony, also, may be performed for one by a houngan before one has joined a hounfor. Such ceremonies give a person a certain restraining control over the loa, but they do not give him any positive power over the psychic forces.

Psychic power begins only with one's entry into a *société*, and the initial step consists of a short ceremony whose major element is the taking of a simple pledge of loyalty and respect toward the hounfor and the authority of its hierarchy. In other words, the individual's positive control begins with his deliberate integration into the collective. With this ceremony he becomes a bossale. In all of these ceremonies, which are prerequisite to the canzo grade, the two major elements—purification and mastery—are already dominant.[25]

The canzo ceremony is one of the most elaborate which an individual undertakes, and it may be some time, even several years, before the bossale is able to accumulate the necessary funds and accoutrements. But it would be impossible, in any case, to proceed immediately to canzo, for it is while a person participates as bossale in the numerous and diverse ceremonies of the hounfor that he observes and learns the ritual procedure, memorizes the prayers and songs, trains himself in the dis-ciplines, and becomes altogether familiar with the physical details, as well as psychologically prepared for the responsibilities, which, as canzo, he must assume. It is a development which only experience can provide.

7

INITIATION: THE BIRTH OF A MAN

All in all, from the moment when the candidate withdraws from the world as bossale to the moment when he is led out as canzo, the ceremony of initiation is a process of death and resurrection, a re-creation of spiritual genesis. The first phase is one of purification, both physical and spiritual. It begins with a confession at the Catholic church, and another to the houn-gan, who conveys it to the loa who is master of the hounfor. The candidate then withdraws from the world for several days, and this solitude is devoted to an intensification of the purifi-cation. He meditates and bathes repeatedly. Both the body and the spirit are cleansed of the past, and he is innocent once more.

As an innocent, then, he goes back to the beginning, and this pure, vulnerable state is under the patronage of Ayizan, the loa who is exorcizer of evil and who purifies. She is the loa, too, who represents elements of both Legba and Loco in female principle. She is the loa of the psychic womb, entrance to the world; she is the spiritual mother principle, and the rites of spiritual birth are under her patronage. The ceremony which is performed at this point in her honor, to win her patronage, includes the ritual of *chirer Ayizan*. A branch of the palm, the tree sacred to her, is cut, and the hounsis, singing in her honor, split each thin leaf into the finest possible strips, so that when they have finished, the branch is like a huge plume of finest fringe. Bearing it in a processional that rotates to the right, to the left, and turns, revolving in a dance movement, they deposit it in the chamber where the candidate is secluded. There a purifying bath has been prepared, and after this final cleansing, the candidate is completely enclosed in a white sheet, as if in the shroud of a corpse. He stretches out upon a bed made of leaves of mombin, emblem of ancestral Africa, and of the palm branch of Ayizan which has just been prepared. This is a state in which that person's past has died, has been completely annihilated. In this condition of ultimate purity, and here, upon this bed where the leaves of the original world of the race lie with the leaves of the original womb, the new being is gradually conceived. For four days the body is anointed with oil at noon, when the sun is highest. And in this nascent state the nourishment of the spiritual embryo is entirely liquid: a broth of corn/flour, calalous and mushrooms, and leaves of lal/buinin. The neophytes may not communicate with each other, should there be several in the same room, but they may pray, and beside them is a bell for calling the houngan's assistant to tend to their needs. Outside the door, each day, the other hounsis come and sing, invoking the loa and their blessing upon those within.

And now occurs the ceremony of the first spiritual differentia/ tion, as if, within the embryo, the first definitions now took place. First the loa guardian, the divine force which primarily infuses this being, is determined. This will be the maît/tête. Just as grains of maize are placed on vevers, which are portals of divinity, so now grains are placed on the head and up/ turned palms of the recumbent person; for it is from the depths of the abyss, into and through the person, that the loa will come. The sacrificial chicken, in the color sacred to the loa, must eat of these grains to indicate that the loa accepts this offering. To one side stands the consecrated earthen pot which will be the pot/de/tête, and into it are placed the beak, feathers and blood of this first sacrifice, together with a sampling of the hair and nails of the neophyte. Thus the soul, the gros/bon/ ange, is created. It is a mixture of the cosmic loa and the immediate life essence of the person, defined as a singular amalgam contained in this pot/de/tête. Around it the ritual beads are placed, as a person might wear them,[26] and, in token of the fact that it is part of the spiritual collective, the pot⁄de⁄ tête is not taken home as a private, personal possession, but is entrusted to the care of the hounfor.[27]

This newly⁄created soul is baptized, now, by two children, as if, once again, the original Marassa, the first creations of God, gave name to their first offspring, and so originated the spiritual race of man. The name is a secret name, as a new⁄born child has a sacred name, which is the essence of the self and must therefore be guarded.[28] Then the maît⁄tête is summoned to the head of this newly⁄created soul, and, having arrived, it is fed of the same chicken which had been passed over the person's body and whose beak, feathers and blood had gone into the creation of his soul. With this act, the creation of the soul is complete. It is compounded of both the cosmic force of the loa and the life essence of the individual human being. These have been integrated into an identity which has been baptized and named, and the guardian loa has been fed its initial meal.[29]

Yet this soul, this creation, would be as nothing were it not touched by fire. Fire, and the ceremony of *bruler⁄zin*, which is the ultimate rite of fire or heat, are many things at once. They are the fire of life, and so the ceremony is performed at the moment when the soul of the newly deceased is about to descend to the abysmal waters for a year and a day, and again, at the end of this token death, when it is reborn into the world. At any ceremony rum may be poured upon the ground and a match set to it, so that the fire may "heat up" the loa. Whether in this latter form—a minor, improvised statement—or in the elaborate rite of *bruler⁄zin*, fire is used whenever there is need to animate, to "recharge" the life spirit. It is most natural, then, that at the virtual birth of the soul this ceremony should be performed in its most elaborate form. In fact, canzo means one who is at once master of fire and infused by it.[30]

The ceremony of *bruler⁄zin* is both lengthy and complex in detail, but its essential elements are the three *zins*—or pots— which are filled with oil and set over small separate fires in the peristyle. The zin for Ogoun is of iron; the others, for the Dead and the loa maît⁄tête of the initiate, are of clay. While the oil is heating, the chickens are sacrificed, rapidly plucked, and, along with ground maize and other ritual ingredients, put into these pots. At this point the initiate, escorted by the houngan, the la⁄place and the flag bearers, is brought out of the chamber. Sometimes he (or she) crawls on all fours, like an infant, or sometimes he walks upright, but carefully and tenderly sup⁄ ported by hounsis. He may be completely draped in a white sheet, or the sheet may be carried, like a white cave, around him, but in any case it covers him completely from view. He is led around the zins three times and then kneels before them. The white sheet is extended to cover both the zin and the fire, and, while the initiate is so breathing fire, the houngan plunges his hand into the boiling zin to bring out a fistful of the mealy dough which has been cooking in the oil. He kneads it in his own hand, and then taking the hand of the initiate, which has been rubbed with oil, closes it over the fiercely hot dough. Sometimes there is a cry of pain, but that is rare. This piece of dough, moulded by the hand of the initiate, is returned to the zin. His feet are passed over the flame, and the entire procedure is repeated at each zin. Then the initiate is led back into the chamber. In the peristyle the zins continue to burn, while the gods are sung, one after another. Eventually the clay zins crack, or are taken down from the three long iron nails which sup⁄ ported them over the flame, and broken into pieces. These pieces, along with the food, which is folded in a napkin, are buried in a hole that has been lined with leaves of the mombin. The hole is refilled and every one joins in stamping down the ground over it. The ceremony ends with the salutations to Ghede.[31]

On the morning following, the new initiate emerges into the world. Dressed in white, wearing a large straw hat (like Legba) and the fringed palm leaf of Ayizan, like a protective mask over the face, he is led forward under a white sheet carried like a canopy over his head. He is still weak, and is

repeatedly supported and aided by the hounsis, as the processional, led by the houngan, visits each sacred tree in turn,
where, like a new-born child, the initiate, this new-born soul,
is ritually presented and introduced to the loa. This accomplished, the state of canzo has been completely achieved. In
the afternoon, there may be a "reception" in the peristyle, and,
in the evening, a dance in honor of the new member of the
spiritual community.[32]

ANDROGYNOUS TOTALITY

CHAPTER VI

Drums and Dance

I

THE SACRED FORMS

To think of art is usually to think of beauty; to think, for instance, that dance is an accumulation of grace. If a visitor to Haiti were to spend most of his time on a country roadside, he would have the sense of being spectator at some theater-in-the-round, where a lyric dance drama of prodigious grace and infinite variety is in continuous performance. One could say that the beginning is an overture in the pre-dawn dark, when small groups of "voyageurs", making their way market-ward from the distant mountains, pass unseen along the road, trailing a melodic line—the onomatopoetic rhythms and cadenced phrasing of Creole, which, being an unwritten language, lives still primarily as a sound to be understood rather than as a symbol of meaning. Dawn, like stage lights being slowly raised, reveals a spectacle of diverse elegance. The bodies of the market-bound women are like fine dark stalks, at once supple and steady, bearing tremendous blooms of egg-plant purple, tomato red, carrot orange, greens of all shades, on their heads. Along the side of the road sways a long file of donkeys. The percussion of their hooves is transmitted to the women riders and flows up their straight backs like a rhythmic wave, spending itself finally in the gentle undulation of the large brims of the straw hats. Whether here, or in the men walking toward the fields, the grace of the bodies' bearing is so manifest that it imparts elegance to even the most poorly cut dress and the most patched and baggy overalls. In the backyard, the women cooking, tending the children, carrying water, forever doing laundry or braiding each other's hair, possess, also, this same grace of the body, which, since so much is demanded of it, has discovered how to achieve by balance what might otherwise require muscular force. Indeed, every posture, every movement is in balance. Even the groups of people—resting and talking in the high heat of mid-afternoon—seem to be "composed" in a painter's sense, reflecting, in this easy, automatic integration of physical arrangement, the fact that here is no mere gathering together of individuals but rather that these people live together, relate to one another. All this the body carries even into its sleep. The "voyageurs" from distant places, when accorded the traditional hospitality extended to travelers, settle into the corner of the unfamiliar room with such delicate adjustment that they cease to seem strangers at all.

It is even as if this way of moving, which the visitor's eyes drink in so constantly, were accumulating in his own limbs and muscles; so that even the total stranger may, one day, discover with surprise, in his own posture, this very stylization. It is a natural grace, in that it is a necessary grace for the Haitian way of living; but it is natural also in the sense that the infant spectator, riding its mother's shoulder or hip continually, and even often cradled to the beats of the ceremonial drum,* could not but learn this as the way of the body's movement, could not but come to know the drums' beat as its own, blood-familiar pulse.

It might seem that it would suffice merely to give this pervasive grace a narrative or symbolic sequence, a planned acceleration to a climax, and the spacing of several stylized exaggerations, in order to have what, in our culture, would be known as a dance. Indeed, to a large extent, the ritual dances have been explained as precisely such extensions of natural grace into religious context. But the quality of movement in the ritual dance is not such an extension. Even the walk of a man participating in a ritual salutation is somehow essentially

---

* While it is doubtful whether Negroes are born with a greater sense of rhythm than other peoples, their cultures are such that, even in a modern city, the child learns rhythm from a very early age. In Haiti it is not unusual to see a mother carrying her child while dancing ritual dances, or bringing her children to the ceremonial peristyle.

different from the equally graceful way he walks to the fields, and from the no less formal manner in which he might approach and salute a partner at a ball. The walk of salutation and the ritual dance, like all sacred works or arts (whether music, painting or sculpture) and whatever the national mode (drum beat or clavicord), are distinguished and distinguishable from the secular by a special ethos. It is a quality of form which informs us that the painting before us is a Madonna and not a woman with a shawl. And whoever has experienced this in one context would need but brief familiarity with the local idiom to recognize, elsewhere, one archaic statuette as that of a warrior and another as that of the God of War; or to distinguish the sound of ceremonial drums from those which beat for labor in the fields or for the simple secular dance.

This quality of the sacred form is independent of subjectmatter, symbolic knowledge, and even degree of skill. To some extent, the quality resides in a sense of ulterior reference. For example, it is clear, in the very manner in which it is done, that the purpose of a libation is not that of watering the ground. Yet an ulterior reference might characterize the symbolic movement in a secular context. In the sacred movement, the reference is not only ulterior but metaphysical. Moreover, it is a statement addressed not to men but to divinity. The form of an act derives not only from the purpose of the act, but from the attitude of the one who performs it. Even in daily, purposive movements we can tell that one man is resentful of what he is doing, while another is enjoying his activity. In art, where fictional purpose is substituted for real purpose, the attitude, the manner of the movement, is increasingly important. And in sacred works, where the acts will not, in themselves, result in anything, but may be rewarded if they please the divinity to whom they are addressed—where, therefore, there can be said to be no direct material purpose—the form is the total statement; and its distinctive quality is that reverent dedication which man brings only to divinity. *The sense of the dedicated act is to serve, not oneself, but the object of one's dedication,* and it is therefore characterized by a quality of selflessness, discipline and even of depersonalization.* The performer becomes as if anonymous. It is from this that one derives a sense of the abstract.

2

THE COLLECTIVE AS CREATIVE ARTIST

In principle, a statement of such anonymity would depend upon an intense degree of dedication, devotion. In technical terms, to create a physical statement (whether a painting or a drum beat) which would effectively project such a metaphysical reference, would require an individual at once saint and artistic genius. But if such was the condition of the origin of traditional movements, their subsequent function, in a collec‑ tive religion, provides for precisely the opposite contingency. A collective religion cannot depend upon the vagaries of individual aptitude and persuasion; on the contrary, it must stabilize these vagaries and protect the participants against their own weaknesses, failures and inadequacies. It must provide the generally uncreative, often distracted individual with a prescribed movement and attitude, the very performance of which gradually involves and perhaps inspires him. It must provide the drummer with a beat which will properly unite and pace the proceedings, whether or not, as an individual, he might ever have been capable of inventing that beat. The tradition must support the individuals, give them security beyond personal indecision, lift them beyond their own individual creative powers. Thus the collective functions at a level superior to the creative capacities of the individuals which make it up. It does not rise from their grace, their power, their knowledge. It confers these upon them. In this sense, it blesses them. It brings out the best in them, and serves as a floor below which the collective cannot drop; just as ritual masks achieve

* This is contrary to the common idea that primitive dance is "spontaneous, uninhibited, self‑expression".

a projection that does not depend upon the variable facial expressions of individual actors. The individual participates in the accumulated genius of the collective, and by such partici' pation becomes himself part of that genius—something more than himself. *His exaltation results from his participation,* it does not precede and compel it.

In so elevating the individual, the collective action of religious ritual offers to him qualitative support, as well as security of a numerical, quantitative nature. This, which is a major function of ritual, is something to be experienced only in participation. Thus, while the tradition elevates, it must do so by means accessible to the diverse capacities of the individuals. And this is, perhaps, the most astonishing achievement of the forms of Voudoun, both in song and in dance. The steps of the dances, for example, require no special training other than that of gradual familiarity; they can be performed by children of ten and women of sixty; they are so designed that they can be maintained for six or eight hours by persons of normal energy.* Yet they engage and elevate both the individuals for whom all this represents an effort and those who might, otherwise, be capable of much more. There are many who, in secular dance, display a prodigious virtuosity, excel in inventiveness, energy and sheer acrobatic skill. Yet such achievement never induces in them the exaltation which they know in the performance of the simple, anonymous move' ments of the ritual dance. For the exaltation of ritual dance derives from a sense of dedication, the denial of that very self which is the source of all virtuosity and whose pride is the pleasure of unique achievement. To be a virtuoso is to assert the self, and this would contradict the sense of dedication. By definition, then, a man could not be a virtuoso and remain within the context of the ritual.

* It should be obvious that a "Haitian dance" which strains a trained, professional dancer and leaves him or her winded after a ten'minute performance could not be as "authentic" as the program notes for such theatrical presentations of "ethnic dance" would lead one to believe.

3

THE DIVINE VIRTUOSI

If, in the chorus, one hears, suddenly, a single voice emerging with special tone and insistence, or if, in the crowded peristyle, one remarks, among all these bodies which move with such homogeneity, one whose movements exceed this generality, become spectacular—this is a sign that a loa arrives. For if the mark of man's dedication to the loa is selfless anonymity, the mark of a loa's devotion to man is his most elaborated, realized manifestation. Therefore, virtuosity is the province of divinity. Only the loa are virtuosi.*

A loa is, indeed, capable of putting its horse through paces which that individual, in a normal state, could never achieve. There are times when the loa, as virtuoso, must be restrained by the houngan lest the after-effects upon the merely human body be disastrous. The ancient, partially crippled woman possessed by a young Erzulie, doing the young, lively dance, will break no bones nor suffer any ill while she is mounted by

* Since theatrical performance, in our culture, is necessarily a statement of virtuosity addressed to an audience, ethnic dances (which are predicated on collective participation, presume a common agreement and knowledge among the participants, and are addressed to divinity) can only be greatly and funda-mentally distorted in theatrical presentation. In ritual dances the inevitable personalization of movements remains minimal and subtle in the extreme, since there is no audience to provoke their development and exaggeration. Courlander, in his notes to an album of Haitian recordings, states: "While Haitian dancing is packed with the elements of drama, probably the most important thing about it is that it is primarily participative. Where there may be an audience, that audience is secondary, usually composed of resting partici-pants, the aged and the sick, and others who for one reason or another are unable to join in. What I mean to say is that there is no sophisticated con-ception of a singing or dancing performance as such. There is no tradition of famous dancers, famous singers or famous drummers. . . . Good dancing and good singing are recognized and applauded, but these, like the audience, are a by-product, not the ultimate objective. The prime reason for the dance is participation." For a full discussion of the difference between theatrical and ethnic dance see "Ritual and Social Dances of Haiti", by the present author, *Dance Magazine*, New York, June, 1949.

17. YANVALOU DOS-BAS. These two men, dancing the low-back yanvalou, are apprentice priests and ritually entitled to use the miniature sacred rattles.

18. CONGO DANCE. The Congo is one of the few dances sometimes performed in partner relationship.

19. DRUMMERS AND CHORUS OF HOUNSIS. The three drums constitute the Rada batterie.

the Goddess; in fact, the knee that had been locked stiff by arthritis for the past five years is for that moment as limber as that of a young girl. But when the loa leaves, the body collapses in a heap and the old woman may be in a critical condition for days after. However, possessions which may have such disastrous consequences are rare. The priest intercedes on behalf of his serviteur. And the loa are considerate. Besides, Erzulie, for instance, as Goddess of Beauty, is naturally vain. As Titon has put it, if Erzulie wishes to appear, to become manifest, to dance, will she not rather choose among those at the ceremony the young, beautiful body in which she can dance beautifully? Would she not logically wish to appear in the best manifestation possible? And if one wishes to be so favored—to be the carrier for the Goddess—should not one then prepare one's dancing, one's costume, one's entire appearance to induce her to select oneself as her horse?

Not all the loa are interested in dancing and singing. Damballah, Agwé and Loco might, or might not, dance and sing, might or might not do so with special excellence. But Erzulie, Ghede and Azacca, among others, love to dance and sing and to have a good time. Whenever these come, space is cleared for them. And should Ghede or Azacca or another create some of the boisterous "disorder" which a party spirit so often brings, the people smilingly say: "Quitté yo jouir" (Let them have their fun), with the same indulgent tenderness that one might bring to the occasional excesses of children.

4

THE ANONYMOUS INVENTORS

While virtuosity is thus restricted to divinity, it would not be to the advantage of any tradition to cut off the sources which refurbish and revitalize it, to impose a ceiling which denied the contributions of such individual talents as might be capable of functioning above and beyond the line of duty. Thus, although the songs are traditional, and their order as well, it is possible for special talent to be manifest. One could say that Titon, for instance, was one of the best houngenikons in the area. This did not imply that he was an individualistic virtuoso. His talent was neither in conflict nor in competition with the traditions. He did not discard or abandon the traditional methods; rather, he amplified and developed them, and extended his execution past the level of performance of which the ordinary serviteur was capable. The *recitatives* with which he, as houngenikon, launched the songs, were of an intensity which restored the invocative sense to phrases and words grown too familiar, and they magnetized one's attention. He sang the solo portions with such compelling projection that the chorus answered with an ardor that transcended the merely proper.

His degree of mastery, indeed, went to such a point that it made possible even that peculiar, subtle detachment which is professionalism in its best sense. Sometimes when he sang, his eyes wandered about the peristyle with the casual, transitory regard of an habitué. If he noticed something that required his authority—such as the sending of someone to bring a chair for a guest—he would shout out his instructions in the interval when the chorus was answering, and then take up the solo on the next beat. The voice carried a strong, harsh conviction which was hard to associate with the detachment of his expression and attitude. He seemed scarcely aware of his own singing, yet the syllables and sounds continued to come forward in cadences timed so perfectly that one would have been tempted to say he was inspired. Nevertheless, watching him, one knew that this moment did not have for him such an exceptional quality. But there was nothing of sacrilege in this detachment. On the contrary, it was as if the ritual so far surpassed him that it had not even the need of his exaltation.

Those who were familiar with other houngenikons could recognize, also, Titon's personal inventions—a way of raising the voice after the word was completed, which anticipated and drew in the chorus, and other similar techniques. But these were never manifest as improvisations compelled by an excess of ardency, nor was one ever aware of his creative effort. His dedication would not be proven by such moments of personal-ization. On the contrary, the real proof of his dedication lay in the fact that, already, he could bring to his own invention a detachment which seemed to render it anonymous; that through labor he had so perfected the technique that it became independent of personal ardency, and already part of the collective. Yet even this funneling of individual talent into the tradition was not left to the discretion, the religious devotion or collective sense of such an individual, who might conceivably be inclined to use such special talent as an independent assertion. For, since the ritual statement is not addressed to men but to divinity, the judgement of men is relatively irrelevant. The principle of complete participation eliminates an audience; moreover, the attachment of a serviteur to one hounfor or another would never be determined by the fact that in one he *felt* more like singing, since sing he must in any case. For Titon, as houngenikon, there was nothing of any consequence to be gained by being more or less excellent, except praise. There was nothing for him to do with his talent except to funnel it into the tradition; and the tradition, in turn, rewarded him by stabilizing it and incorporating it into the collective.

5

THE SACRED ORATORY OF THE DRUM

In Haiti, of all the individuals related to ritual activity, it is the drummer whose rôle would seem most analogous to that of an individual virtuoso. Yet this, again, is not to say that he is unconfined by tradition; on the contrary, Haitian ritual drumming requires more explicit *craft* training and practice than any of the other ritual activities.* The organization of

* It should not be imagined that everyone in Haiti can drum, or that it is

Rada ceremonial, for instance, could be compared to a congress of tribes and cults, each with its characteristic drum beat and dance movement, so that in the progress of such a ceremonial* it is as if a loa were saluted first by the Dahomeans, with the Yanvalou beat and dance, then by the Mahi tribe, with its national beat and dance, and then by the Nago, with the Nago beat and movement. There are at least a dozen such distinct and specific beats, each of which has a specific movement and is related also to a song.** The drummer must not only learn each of the beats, but must be familiar with a vast literature of songs, so that when the houngenikon launches into a recitative (and it is usually the houngenikon who determines and initiates the song for the divinity), the drummer must immediately know to which nation it belongs and which beat must therefore accompany it. He must, in addition, be able to beat Petro, since Petro rites frequently follow Rada rites, and at dances of celebration it is customary to conclude the evening with Petro dances. When Azacca arrives, he frequently asks for a Martinique or a Juba dance, and it is necessary for the drummer to be able to satisfy this request. Or it may happen that at least a round or more of songs for the Ibo divinities should be included in a feasting of the loa; the Congo, the Quitta Mouillé, and others may also be necessary at one point or another. Since the drummer is, in a sense, hired for his expertness, it is to his own interest to be familiar with as many of these different beats as possible.

merely a matter of "picking it up". Men go to considerable trouble and even expense to be instructed and become practised as drummers.

* There is a distinct difference between a ceremonial—in which a specific ritual is to be accomplished—and a "dance"—which is a celebration of the loa. A ceremonial may take place without being followed by a dance, although it usually culminates in at least a few rounds; but dances frequently take place without rituals. The order in which the loa are saluted, however, is the same in ceremonies and in dances, unless the ceremony is directed toward a specific loa, who then takes precedence.

** In *Haiti Singing*, Harold Courlander has shown outstanding scholarship and appreciation in listing songs, drum beats and dances and in describing dance movements. I have not attempted to duplicate his detailed and elaborate accomplishment here.

VEVER FOR DRUMS AND OGAN

Moreover, most of these beats are polyrhythmic. In the Rada rites three drums are involved: the *petit*, the *seconde* and the *maman*, and these are pitched at specified intervals relative to each other. In addition to the drums, an *ogan*—a piece of iron —is beaten. Not only does each of the three drums have a specific, designated beat which is different for Nago, Mahi, Congo, etc., but all three must combine their separate rhythms in very specific manners in order that the resultant ensembles shall maintain the Nago, Mahi, or Congo beats. If any of the three drummers, because of fatigue, inattention, sheer ignor⁄ance, or, in rare cases, possession, loses his beat for even a fraction of a second, the entire ensemble is thrown off and the total beat disintegrates. The same thing would result, obviously, if any drummer ever sought to improvise individualistically.

To say that the beat disintegrates by virtue of such a depar⁄ture, is not to say that the Haitians are any less capable of im⁄provising together than are American jazz bands. Drummers may sometimes have such sessions for pure amusement, and the entire cultural emphasis upon collective action gives them a great facility for such ensemble adjustment. But a jazz band has no commitments outside of its own musicianship. The Haitian drums on the contrary, are only one of the elements of a vast ritual structure, and they are committed irrevocably to it.

It is, in fact, upon the drumming that the burden falls of integrating the participants into a homogeneous collective. It is the drumming which fuses the fifty or more individuals into a single body, making them move as one, as if all of these singular bodies had become linked on the thread of a single pulse—a pulse which beats, now with the rounded roll of

Yanvalou, sending the body into a slow serpentine undulation which begins in the shoulders; now with the imperious drive of Nago Chaud, which stiffens the spine into the tensions of pride while the muscles of the shoulders and back flex rapidly in the manner of man announcing his strength. It may beat the deceptive Mahi, which brings the legs into play as if gaily, at first, but then, by mere persistence, compels every inch of fatigued, sweating flesh into the tensions of sheer endurance; or again, with the slow massive pound of the Nago Grand Coup, an unequivocal reference to the majestic progress of a warrior of heroic stature, whose great shoulders roll with each gigantic stride of irrevocable triumph. Or finally, it may beat with the special tension of Petro, where, instead of supporting the dancer, the beat seems to drive him before it.* It is im-possible, in mere words, to convey the extraordinary achieve-ment which such beats represent from the musical point of view. Even if a drummer were not ritualistically committed to their execution, it would be a foolish man indeed who would dare propose some personal invention to stand comparison beside such an accomplished tradition. Above all, it is when one records, uninterruptedly, an hour or more of ceremonial, as I have done, that the integrating rôle of the drumming becomes apparent. The microphone, fixed at the center-pole, has faith-fully captured all coming and going. The houngenikon's voice is strong at times, but at other times fades away completely, when in the course of ceremonial procedure, he may have been obliged to move to the other end of the peristyle in order to assist the houngan with ritual details. At other times he is

* The impression that primitive drumming and dance are almost without variation is due to improper theatrical presentation, and the commercial emphasis upon pelvic movement. Actually, the movements of each dance differ very much from the others, and the drumming conveys, in each case, a distinct impression. In addition to what has been said above, I should like to point out that the Ibo drumming is impressively intellectual in its suggestion, and one senses almost an erudite mentality behind it; the Congo has a quality of gradual mesmerization, in contrast to the emotional expressiveness of Rada and the tensions of Petro; while the Ghede beat seems to be the musical crystallization of attitudes of sexual impertinence without the weight of obscenity.

obviously struggling to ward off being mounted by a loa, since this would leave the chorus without conductor; here his voice breaks, and his solo has gaps of silence. The chorus also fluc⁄ tuates in strength and intensity as its attention is transferred to some ceremonial activity, or as a number of the hounsis, becoming preoccupied with one among them who is being possessed, cease to sing altogether, for a brief period. Sometimes the good houngenikon is apparently replaced, for a brief rest period, by someone else, whose leading of songs is far less dynamic. At other times the priest, who happens to have a very poor voice, leads the songs to a loa who has particular personal relevance for him. One hears, intermittently, the cackling of the chickens which are to be sacrificed, the crowing of a rooster. Some dispute about ritual procedure between two people who are assisting can be heard. And suddenly there intrudes the nasal voice of Ghede, telling some joke, and an answering roar of laughter. In the brief silences between songs one is aware of conversations. In addition to the audible record of all this divergency, I can recall that, if there is a wind, the lantern which lights the peristyle frequently goes out and must be relit. Some hounsi is undoubtedly looking for the clean white hand⁄ kerchief which she put down on the bench two minutes ago and which has disappeared. Guests arrive a little late and there is much shifting of seating and standing arrangements to permit such honored visitors a primary place. The houngan has run out of candles, or rum, or something else, and has sent someone off to buy more. Through this multitude of miscellaneous activity, digression, intrusion—which I cannot imagine as making for anything less than complete disorder and confusion in any other context—runs the solid mass of the drum's beating, at once compellingly dynamic and yet of a reliability, a stability, which transcends all miscellany, comprehends it, swallows it, holds steady with such unshakeable persistence that it serves as a magnetic core to which all temporary deviation returns. Listening, one knows that that center is there and will be there; that one may leave but that one *must* return; that, sooner or later, it will have gathered everything to it, and will have fused all divergence into one transcendent whole.*

It is significant that, in the order of ritual salutation, it is the drums which are saluted after the center-post and before anything else; that if one feels that the loa who is being invoked might possess one, and that such a possession is, for some reason, inappropriate at the moment, one may win leave from such possession by ritually saluting the drums at such times; that often the loa themselves salute the drums in the same spirit in which they may salute the houngan—an obeisance to that which makes it possible for them to become manifest.

Indeed, if the center-post is, as it were, the inorganic, static axis of the cosmos, the geographically fixed avenue by which the loa enter and the core around which the *material* facts of ceremonial—the architecture of the peristyle, the vevers, and many of the ritual acts—are organized, then this core of drumming is as the organic axis of the spiritual cosmos, around which all the *temporal* elements of ritual are centered. It is upon these pulsations that, for the most part, the loa are brought forward; and, as they can be led in on water, or on rum, or on the fire of burning rum, so, innerly, it is as if they were brought in on the stream of the blood, pulsed not by the individual personal heart, but by some older, deeper, cosmic heart—the drums.

If I have referred to the drummer as virtuoso, it is not so much in the sense of a deliberate or conscious individualistic departure from tradition, but rather because, in spite of every traditional prescription and standardization, and in spite, also, of an almost metronomic accuracy (so that the beats are always played within a fraction of a second of the same tempo), the drummer, as the man who initiates and paces the beating of that heart, is in a position of especial influence. His slightest personal modulation—whether a negative lack of vigor, which is sensed as a near-lag in the beat, or some positive excellency in

---

* A copy of a portion of these recordings is in the Caribbean Collection, the School of Inter-American Studies, at the University of Florida.

the "break" of the *maman*—is as if amplified by the entire resonance of the drums and inevitably conveyed to all the individuals who, dancing, live by that pulse. As in the case of a houngenikon, a better than average drummer lends to the ceremonial or dance a sharper color and a brighter tone. But apart from this, there are certain elements over which he has a control which cannot be regulated or seconded by anyone else. I doubt that even a profoundly informed musicologist could explain how it can be that, without any change in beat, tempo, pacing, tone or volume, it is possible for the drumming to become more or less intense, although this fluctuation is unanimously recognized and can be consciously controlled by the drummer. He may observe that a loa threatens to overcome the houngan who must execute some complex ritual detail, and he can relieve the situation by making the drumming less intense. On another occasion he may, by simply maintaining that intensity, make futile a serviteur's resistance to possession. Above all, it is in his "breaks" that he has most control.[1] In a "break" the *maman* (and this is the only drum which "breaks") ceases to beat with the other two drums in the fixed rhythm and works at a highly syncopated, broken counterpoint to them for a short period, only to slide back and resume the pattern again. This "break" is related to the cumulative tension which the dancers inevitably experience from constantly repeating a single small movement. Some movements, being by nature tense and tiring, accumulate such tension rapidly. Moreover, it is logical that such an accumulation should be more frequent toward the end of a ceremony than toward its beginning, and also that it should have a good deal to do with the subtle fluctuation of the intensity of the drumming itself, since the muscular ardor of the dancers derives from this.

6

DANCE AS THE MEDITATION OF THE BODY

Yet these dance movements should not be understood in purely physical terms, as if they were secular pleasure dances. At dances for the divinities, which may occur quite indepen, dently of any ceremonial or feasting, there is, to be sure, no ritual choreography apart from the general counterclockwise direction of the floor, movement around the center, post; yet it would not be at all accurate to consider the introduction of rhythmic dance movement in addition to this, as a decorative device designed to make the ritual sensually more impressive or palatable. It is not only the attitude of reverent dedication, characteristic of all ritual action, which distinguishes ritual dance from secular dance; for just as the ritual does not symbo, lize a principle but is an exemplary demonstration of that principle in action, so the actual dance is, itself, principled. Our culture, having no "moral" or "principled" dance, contains nothing which is an accurate analogy, but I hope that the sense of the distinction which I wish to communicate here may be somewhat indicated by considering the variety of ethos in our own social dances. The sheer performance of a waltz movement (providing one is really dancing and not convers, ing) induces in the performer what might be termed a "waltz frame of mind"—an emotional tone which is somewhat sentimental, attitudes of romantic elegance, a strong awareness of coquetry as the feminine projection and courtship as the masculine rôle. By contrast, the sheer performance of the rhumba creates a mood far less romantic and more immediate, compels the woman to attitudes of provocation instead of coquetry, and in the man a stance of conquest rather than of courtship. The square dance, the blues, the boogie, woogie—each has its dis, tinctive ethos, which it imposes upon the performer. In ritual dance, whose very *raison d'être* is the intent to affect the partici, pant, the means by which the physical act creates a specific psychic state are refined and developed beyond the obvious machinery which so crudely distinguishes the rhumba from the waltz. It would, in fact, surprise me if the techniques designed to project from the physique to the psyche, which are in actual operation in the dance movements of Voudoun, were less complex and evolved than the drum beats, whose structure is admittedly of such refinement that it surpasses our own systems of musical analysis; for it would only be logical to assume that the evolution of the drumming and the dancing moved together.

In a sense, then, such dance might be understood as a meditation of the body, so that the entire organism is made to concentrate on a concept as definite and real as the "waltz frame of mind", but more complex and less accessible to verbal articulation.* It is to the concentration of this physical-psychic meditation that the "break" of the *maman* drum is directed.

When the *maman* "breaks", the dancers "break" with it; that is, they interrupt the small, tight repetitive movement and take long, relaxed steps, in time to the "breaking". Since the conditions of accumulating tension are so variable, the *maman* drummer, who has been watching the dancers, is the sole

* Compare the following statements: "To dance was at once to worship and to pray . . . the gods themselves danced, as the stars dance in the sky . . . and to dance is therefore to imitate the gods, to work with them, perhaps to persuade them to work in the direction of our own desire. . . . To dance is to take part in the cosmic control of the world. Every sacred Dionysian dance is an imitation of the divine dance" (Havelock Ellis, *Dance of Life*).

"The ultimate goal of the mystic is a oneness with God, but the paths towards this goal are divergent . . . we Mevlevi believe that soul and body are alike divine—that the soul grows, like a flower, on the body's stem. We accept material beauty as the true mirror of divine beauty. And we seek this divine beauty, this ineffable harmony, in which all things become as one, through the most nearly perfect of sensuous forms—the rhythm of music and the dance." (T. Shawn, p. 13, quoting from an interview by W. B. Seabrook with the head of the Mevlevi sect of Syrian Tripoli).

"With regard to the dance-instinct Lombroso gave the physiological explanation that the auditory nerve stands in so close connection with the spinal cord that we may say 'dancing is a sort of reflective motion caused by music'." (Wallaschek, p. 259, quoting Lombroso, Cesare, *Klinische Beiträge zur Psychiatrie*.)

arbiter of when to give the dancers such a respite. But since this cumulative tension is also the cumulative concentration which brings the loa into the head, the drummer then becomes, to some degree, arbiter of the loa's arrival; for by withholding the respite of the "break", which interrupts this concentration, he can "bring in the loa" to the head of a serviteur. When the drummer is particularly gifted and acute, he can also use the "break" in precisely the inverse fashion. He can permit the tension to build to just the level where the "break" serves not to release the tension but to climax it in a galvanizing shock—the first enormous blow of the "break"—which abruptly empties the head and leaves one without any center around which to stabilize. This is a state of helpless vulnerability. Instead of being able to move in the long, balanced strides of relaxation, the defenceless person is buffeted by each great stroke, as the drummer sets out to "beat the loa into his head". The person cringes with each large beat, as if the drum mallet descended upon his very skull; he ricochets about the peristyle, clutching blindly at the arms which are extended to support him, pirouettes wildly on one leg, recaptures balance for a brief moment, only to be hurtled forward again by another great blow on the drum. The drummer, apparently impervious to the embattled anguish of the person, persists relentlessly; until, suddenly, the violence ceases, the head of the person lifts, and one recognizes the strangely abstracted eyes of a being who seems to see beyond whatever he looks at, as if into or from another world. The loa which the song had been invoking, has arrived.*

* This is not the only means by which possession occurs. It would seem that this rôle of the *maman* drummer in bringing the loa would invalidate much of what has been said previously (namely, that the religion rests on the traditions and on the anonymous generality of the collective) and that, on the contrary, the personal genius, subjective inspiration and particular craftsmanship of this individual was of primary importance. It must be reiterated, however, that the drummer's personal inventiveness, like that of the houngenikon, is not a statement of independence from, or revolt against the collective and the tradi- tions; it is valid only insofar as it is sufficiently in line with these to become a part of them. Indeed, the drummer would never be hired again if his activities

Sometimes the drummer is obliged to return to the beat and set the dance back in motion before the loa is entirely "installed". In such cases, the return to the beat may bring the person back as well, but frequently he is, as it were, abandoned by the drum, having neither mortal nor divine identity, and only the houngan can help. Shaking the asson with as much insistence and projection as possible, the houngan may then also use langage, speaking sometimes with tight, intimate intensity, and at other times virtually screaming, but in any case completely concentrated upon projecting those sacred sounds through the person into the void, to establish contact there either with his proper gros-bon-ange or with the loa. I have seen the sweat stream from a houngan's face and his voice grow hoarse as he labored to make some contact with a spiritual identity which he might bring forward into the body of the person.

disrupted the ritual integrity. Musically speaking, it must be pointed out that, since all improvisation is inevitably based on what the improvisator knows, the habits which he acquires in the process of his training will be reflected in all his performances, even when he is theoretically "free" of those explicit disciplines. In this sense there is no such thing as a completely free improvisation; particularly is this true of the Voudoun drummer, whose cultural and musical background have been so strongly disciplined that even when he sometimes improvises for idle amusement (privately) his beats tend, by sheer muscular habit, to resemble the sacred beats. When he improvises a "break" he is theoretically free of the prescribed beat; but the continuity of the *seconde* and the *petit* (whose beats continue unaltered throughout) and his own rhythmic habits give his free improvisation a firmly disciplined and traditional form.

The degree to which this is so is evident in the fact that, although these "breaks" give him an opportunity to display his virtuosity, their traditional and even standardized quality is immediately apparent when contrasted to those rare occasions when a drummer is possessed by the Hountor, the loa of the drums. Once more it is apparent that only the loa are the real virtuosi, for the drumming of the Hountor is one of the most astonishing musical experiences possible. Significantly enough, since the Hountor drums for himself, his drumming does not bring other loa. On the contrary, these tend to depart, if present; the drummers of the *seconde* and *petit* abandon any effort to accompany this divine virtuosity, and since the drumming has ceased to serve the function of integrating the ritual proceedings, these, also, tend to fall apart. This disruptive effect of the Hountor is no doubt the reason why his presence is not generally encouraged and rarely occurs.

7

THE DRUMMER AS MECHANISM

As between the drummer and the houngan, it frequently seems that the former has command of the superior technique; for it is much more readily effective and may overpower even the houngan himself, whereas drummers are very rarely possessed and seem, at times, to be the persons most in control during a ritual.[2] It would seem logical to expect, then, that the drummer would command a high position in the religious hierarchy. Yet the opposite is, in fact, true. The drummer, as such, has no position whatsoever in the hounfor, although, as a serviteur, he may belong to one hounfor or another. In any case, it has been my experience that rarely, if indeed ever, is the drummer canzo. He takes a professional craft attitude toward his work and may drum at the ceremonies of various and even competitive hounfors of the same region, whereas no member of one *société* participates officially at the ceremonies of another *société*, apart from the houngan, and perhaps the la‚place, who may assist in an honorary capacity. It has been my observation, also, that drummers, on the whole, may frequently neglect to make ritual salutation at the altar of the *maît‚caille*—the patron of the hounfor—where they may be drumming; whereas such an obeisance is required of all members of the *société* and is expected of visitors, whose neglect of such salutation would be regarded as extremely indiscreet and even insulting. During prayers, the drummer may frequently wander away from the peristyle, and is the only individual to do so. This dis‚association from the authority and structure of the hounfor, and psychic detachment from the ritual, place him outside the control of the houngan; except that one who is persistently indiscreet in forcing the loa upon the houngan at inappropriate moments, or who otherwise takes his important responsibilities too lightly, may not be hired again.

Not only is the drummer outside the organization of the

hounfor, but he is systematically distinguished from the drums. It is the drums[3] which are sacred, and it is understood that salutations addressed towards the drums do not include the men who happen to be beating them. The degree to which the drums are understood as independent spirits, almost as loa, is revealed in many of the ceremonies which attach to them. All the sacred objects are consecrated by being baptized in the name of a chosen loa, but the drums are the only objects which are "dressed" for their baptism, as a child is dressed. They are also the only objects which are literally fed with food and put to sleep overnight, a ritual designed to strengthen them. Very special attention is given to putting a "guard" over them should the houngan plan to leave for a trip. They are also conceived as having a will of their own, which can even oppose the will of the drummer, in that they may refuse to speak for him under certain conditions.[4]

In effect, the inanimate object is sacred, although it cannot function at all without the drummer, and he, although in technical control of the presence of the loa, is at the same time without moral commitment or authority in the religion. At first glance, such an arrangement seems very odd. Yet it eliminates a potential which would be infinitely dangerous to the religious structure. The ability to drum is considered, and properly so, as a purely technical achievement, accessible to all human beings of normal rhythmic perception and muscular coordination, who may achieve unusual excellency by dint of practice, or, possibly, by some special rhythmic talent. As such, it constitutes a purely physical or material equipment, and is completely unrelated to moral equipment or development. Just as vocal range and power could never confer upon an individual the hierarchical moral status of houngenikon, which is accessible only through initiatory procedure, so the drummer does not command any moral authority by virtue of his craft mastery, however admired and sought-after he may be. To conceive otherwise would be to place the entire moral organiza-tion of the collective in the hands of men who happened to be endowed with fortunate rhythmic and muscular talent. It is the drums and the drum beats, *per se*, which are the sacred sound, and although one man may articulate the drum's voice more fluently, brilliantly and invocatively than another, he is but a minor part of the mechanism of that speech. If he beats anything except the sacred beats, his most brilliant virtuosity produces not one loa. But the loa will come to a merely adequate rendition of the sacred beats, and to the call of the asson; to just the voices lifted in song or invocation; in answer to ritual gesture; and even, on their own initiative, in answer to silent need.

It is as if the drums were understood as the moral *organism*, whereas the drummer was a *mechanism*, a necessary material accessory to their activity. The loa, themselves non-physical, are not linked to mere matter, as such. They are a moral essence; they answer to moral movement, to moral sound, to moral matter.

20 and 21. POSSESSION. Characteristic postures of the "horse" while the loa is in the process of mounting it: pitching forward on one leg, and inability to maintain balance. Note the casual, habituated expression of other people, including the man whose arm has been grasped (above); also the agony on the face of the girl being mounted (below).

22 and 23. GHEDE. These two photographs, taken six months apart and in different hounfor show that possession is not a period of "self-expression". On the contrary, the individual psyche is displaced by that of the loa, whose character is constant and independent of that of the person in whose body he becomes manifest.

CHAPTER VII

The White Darkness

I HAVE left possession until the end, for it is the center toward which all the roads of Voudoun converge. It is the point toward which one travels by the most visible, the most physical means, yet, for the traveler, it is itself invisible. One might speak of it as the area of a circle whose circumference can be accurately described; yet this circumference is not, itself, the circle which it defines. To know this area, one must, finally, enter.

Upon such a threshold to the unknown, it is inevitable that one should pause to glance backward to survey the area accomplished, to ascertain whether the step is without alterna⁄ tive or whether, perhaps, the devious configurations of this diverse terrain may not conceal some twist, some crevice referring out of this landscape. Surely there was an egress which had escaped attention; for the structure of the terrain had, at times, been so receptive, so tolerant, its contours so undulant and apparently acquiescent, as to seem almost malleable, and frequently to lack those confinements and constrictions by which one has learned to define form. Yet, in such a survey, the impact results from the contrary discovery. From no previous vantage point had this geography so clearly revealed its immaculate geometry.

From this central point surges the lavish arterial river of ancestral blood which bears all racial history forward into the contemporary moment and funnels its vast accumulations into the denim⁄dressed serviteur. The entire collective over time, from the demiurgic Marassa to the proverbial wisdoms or the sharp, crafty angers of the grandfather, dead but a year and a day, here is comprehended, here becomes intimate and feeds and comforts. Yet up through this same center emerge also the monumental archetypes, the loa as pillars of the moral cosmos, each of them multi-faceted yet homogeneous, each one a marvel of diversity without digression, and these may simply parade their transcendent perfection briefly, and then leave without intimate contact. Often the loa do nothing, say nothing of any immediate consequence. Yet their very remoteness, evidence of areas invulnerable to immediate anxieties and defeats, assures the serviteur of an essential order and stability. Here it is not nearness but the *distance* between a man and his god which comforts, which assures that the good endures and will endure; for it is to such distance that man removes his divinity to isolate him from the ravages and diminution of human inadequacy, just as, in times of violence, one might secrete one's most ultimate and cherished treasure.

To be made aware, once more, that man is of divine origin and is the issue of and heir to an uncounted multitude of hearts and minds; that at the root of the universe the great imperturbable principles of cosmic good endure; and that even under his torn shirt, his hunger, the failures of his wit and the errors of his heart, his very blood harbors these monumental loa—is to experience the major blessing with which possession rewards men's dedicated service. This major reward comprehends all minor needs, and, with its very generality, soothes all the diversity of singular fears, personal losses and private anxieties. Whatever other benefits the loa may bring—advices, prescriptions, disciplines—these are but secondary.[1]

Demur, if you will, that all this is merely a reference to a man's intellectual powers. Explain that it is the "imagination" which makes him capable of conceiving beyond the reality which he knows, and that this is compounded of memories. Speak of "idealism" as source of his willingness to undergo ordeal on behalf of creative, non-material achievement. Insist that in foregoing immediate reward he seeks historical position. Add, even, that such values are engendered by the influence of father, the love of mother, the praise of men. List all those intellectual and moral qualities—vision, inspiration, imagination—which most distinguish the poet, the philosopher, the scientist; catalogue them, name them, count and differentiate and "explain" their origins, their operation, mechanisms and motivations. The Haitian will not dispute you. When you have finished, he might shrug his shoulders, saying simply, in Creole: "All that, we call 'to have loa'."

If the major value of the loa is their very transcendence, they cannot be, simultaneously, identified with man. To survey the structure of Voudoun is to encounter everywhere this distance, this divide which no man can straddle. It is evident in the final limitations of a houngan's control over the loa who may even subjugate him, and are free to be manifest outside his province;[2] it is defined in the feasts which nourish no man, in the accoutrements which no man may wear; it is implied in all the calling sounds—song, drum beat, asson and langage—which are like lines thrown out, to become the cables of the bridge upon which man would cross that chasm; it is present, as physical fact, in the amnesia which makes even the sense of the loa inaccessible to the very "horse" which bore him. *To understand that the self must leave if the loa is to enter, is to understand that one cannot be man and god at once.*[3]

Thus the possessed benefits least of all men from his own possession. He may even suffer for it in material loss, in the sometimes painful, always exhausted physical aftermath. And to the degree that his consciousness persists into its first moments or becomes aware of the very end, he experiences an overwhelming fear. Never have I seen the face of such anguish, ordeal and blind terror as at the moment when the loa comes. All this no man would ordinarily accept. But since the collective consists of ordinary men with a normal interest in their personal welfare, it is dependent upon its ability to induce in them a moment of extra-ordinary dedication if it is to have access to the revitalizing forces that flow from the center. It is toward the achievement of this—toward the forcing open of the door to the source—that the entire structure of Voudoun is directed. The serviteur must be induced to surrender his ego, that the archetpye become manifest. In the growing control accomplished by the ordeals and instructions of initiation, and in the protective vigilance of houngan and *société*, he is reassured that the personal price need not be unpredictable or excessive.[4] In the principle of collective participation is the guarantee that the burden shall, in turn, be distributed and shared. And finally, the structure has evolved—drum beat by drum beat, movement by movement—a force which compels a man forward, and which, in even the most dedicated, must triumph against that final terror which attends the loss of self, that last convulsive recoil from the dark sense of death.[5] It is in the ceremonial peristyle that all this is brought to a focus and that the momentum is set in motion with the first songs for Legba, Loco, Ayizan.

I can remember an evening when it was as if, with those initial salutations, the drums flung the enormous snare of their sound into the night, across the still landscape, and from every direction drew captives across the threshold into the peristyle. I was among these latecomers. The singing, which might have been desultory at first, became warmer as the stream of arrivals gradually filled the benches, the space near the walls, flooded into the corners and finally overflowed into the court. A neighboring houngan, Joe, arrives, and a chair is placed beside me for him. I compliment him on his last ceremony, which, indeed, was conducted in a very eloquent fashion, and remark that he seems to be recovered from the illness which had troubled him for some time. "Oh, I was finally able to settle my difficulties with Loco", he answers, and since he knows that I am interested in such matters, proceeds to tell me the details of his involvement. I am so concentrated on this recital that I am not aware of the songs or the drumming until Titon, who is houngenikon, shouts in anger at the crowd which has, by now, solidly blocked off the entrance to the peristyle, and I realize that they are now beating and singing the song of salutation for the flags of the *société* and the la-place. A path is finally cleared and this trio enters the peristyle. They salute the center-post, the drums, and Houngan Joe suspends his recital, for in a matter of moments they will address themselves to him. As always, I enjoy watching him, for the authority and grace of his bearing. He returns to his seat and the trio balances in place before me, stepping side to side in rhythm with the drums. As I rise in answer, a sense of nervous self-consciousness over-whelms me, although I have done this many times. (I am not at all alone in this; I have seen the lips of even mambos and houngans quiver nervously in such moments.) Curtsey, turn left, two, three; curtsey, back right, two, three; curtsey, now left, two, three—mirroring the trio before me. I walk west, crossing between the la-place and the flags, as they walk east. I turn, curtsey, then left, curtsey, right, then back; then north; then south. We approach each other and suddenly I cannot remember what I am supposed to do, but no one can perceive this, for the la-place kneels, holding the hilt of the saber high. I touch it with my lips, the two flags cross over it, and I salute these also. Then, with an enormous feeling of relief at having accomplished this act properly, I return to my chair. It seems now as if the drums and the singing were louder, sharper, and I can hardly hear Joe's recital, which he has resumed.

The drums pause, finally, and I am grateful for that, although the heat of the crowded peristyle seems more intense in the silence. The people converse casually, fanning themselves with their straw hats. Suddenly, like a sharp knife plunging into the soft heat and the soft chatter, Titon's imperious voice launches the invocation to Damballah. Over the demanding, compelling rush of its syllables, the tight staccato Yanvalou beat of the *petit* sets in; now the rounder tone, the more rolling rhythm of the *seconde* slides in under it; and then one feels a vibration beneath one's feet even before one hears the beat of the *maman*, which rises as if from some unfathomable depth, as if the very earth were a drum being pounded. Hardly has hearing plunged to encompass this dark dimension, than the high clang of the iron *ogan* sets in, its wind-filled resonance abruptly flinging open all the upper regions of sound, and the very air vibrates as if with tones above and beyond the reaches of the ear's intelligence. For a brief moment this towering architecture of sound, stretching solidly from the abyss below to the heavens above hearing, seems to advance without movement, like a tidal wave so vast that no marker exists to scale its progress for the eye. Then the chorus of voices, having, it would seem, accumulated its force in the trough concealed behind the towering crest, hurls forward over that crest, and the whole structure crashes like a cosmic surf over one's head. I find myself standing bolt upright, singing, or perhaps even scream/ ing the song. Others about me, who had also been seated are now also standing. Most of them move forward to dance, but it is as if the shock of that inundation had completely winded me and I sink back into my seat.

Now it is the dance which suggests water. Before me the bodies of the dancers undulate with a wave/like motion, which begins at the shoulders, divides itself to run separately along the arms and down the spine, is once more unified where the palms rest upon the bent knees, and finally flows down the legs into the earth, while already the shoulders have initiated the wave which follows. The eyes are fixed on the ground, and although the head is steady, the circular movement of the shoulders seems to send it forward, to draw the body after it, over and over; and as the bodies, which began in a posture almost erect, bend toward the earth, the undulation becomes more and more horizontal, until all figures blend into a slow flowing serpentine stream circling the center/post with a fluency that belies the difficulty of the movement. What have they all found there, on that central ground, that their limbs should move with such ease and such perfection while, on the exiled outskirts, my own limbs are burdened with muscles, must ponder and delay my every will to motion? What secret source of power flows to them, rocks them and revolves them, as on a roundabout the bright steeds prance and pursue, eternally absolved of fatigue, failure and fall? I have but to rise, to step forward, become part of this glorious movement, flow/ ing with it, its motion becoming mine, as the roll of the sea might become the undulation of my own body. At such moments one does not move *to* the sound, one *is* the movement of the sound, created and borne by it; hence, nothing is difficult.

The drums cease; I return to my seat and only at that moment realize that I am perspiring profusely. La Merci, my domestic, is carrying my large handkerchief, and I scan the line of hounsis several times before I distinguish her face, which is ordinarily so expressive of her distinct, lively temperament, but now seems to have been planed down into a mask of anony׳ mity blending and losing itself among the other white׳ kerchiefed heads. I try to attract her attention, but fail, and so rise to go toward her. I take two steps and my left leg suddenly roots, numbly, to the ground, pitching me forward. Someone's hand grasps my arm, supports me firmly, while, stunned, I freeze momentarily in this posture, seek to regain center and balance, and finally straighten out. The man who happened to have been standing there, relaxes his support. I smile my thanks and return to my seat, still shaken by this abrupt blow. Someone is sent to get the handkerchief for me. There is an unpleasant lightness in my head, as if the many parts of the brain were being gently disengaged, its solidity, its integrity being somehow imperceptibly dispersed, as a fog might be gently dispersed by a light, inconstant breeze; and as these separations occur, there are little spaces of emptiness.

Foolish to disregard the leg momentarily caught, or this strange, subtle thinning out of consciousness. These are the warning auras of possession. One knows oneself vulnerable.[6] I begin to repeat to myself: "Hold together, hold, hold." As the drums start up again, I feel I must get away if I am to hold and I press through the crowd toward the exit, smiling, so that no one may suspect my predicament, which is as a weakness, as something I should, by now, have been able to master and regulate. At the moment I pass the short wall which marks the edge of the peristyle the sounds abruptly become fainter. The night is cool and luminous. I light a cigarette, cross the familiar court, and wander up the road slowly. How distant the voices and the drums seem, although they are quite clear. I can hear that the round for Damballah has finished. My head is tightening, integrating, becoming solid once more. Yet this cool, quiet, private dark, where nothing demands or insists, is a gentle peace, where I would linger, where I would com-pose and recompose myself once more, while, in the peristyle, the processional advances, celebrating now Agassou, Agwé and Badé.

I hear, then, the first beats of the salute to Ogoun. Now I must return, for this is the guardian of the hounfor and I cannot offend the house by being absent at his salutation. I start back toward the peristyle, hurrying now, for I had wandered farther than I thought. By the time I arrive, the loa has already mounted Isnard. He is barefoot, the legs of the trousers are rolled up, so that the abrupt movements of the feet do not catch in them and trip him, and he wears a bright red handkerchief. He is pacing up and down, in a kind of anger. It is impressive. Isnard is, to begin with, tall and powerful in body; now that sense of stature is enormously reinforced by the psychic projection of the heroic loa which has infused that body. The loa walks to the drums, and, laying his hand on the skin of the *maman*, orders them silenced. He stands and waits. Titon approaches, turns in ritual salutation, kisses the earth at his feet and would with-draw, but Ogoun extends his hand in ritual greeting. I see Titon stiffen, as one might prepare to endure an onslaught. They shake right hands, and the Ogoun extends the left, the loa hand. For a moment Titon hesitates, then he meets it with his left. He staggers a moment, but regains balance and rights himself, holds his ground until his hand is released, and walks away.[7] Now houngan Joe is greeting the loa head-of-the house. I find Titon standing beside me. He looks at me, who must go forward next, and says "Attention! Attention!" He takes my hand suddenly and digs his nail into my palm. The sharp, sudden pain restores me. He had recognized, although I had not even been aware of it, that, once more, I had become vulnerable. As I step forward for my salutation I concentrate upon the memory of that pain, almost as one might finger an amulet at moments of crisis. It serves me well. The contact of the left hand with the loa produces only a momentary shock, which passes rapidly, like an electric current, and I, too, return to my place. Others step forward to make the ritual salutation; Titon launches a song for Ogoun, and the drumming and dance begin again.

I am troubled by this persistent vulnerability, and, pretending to see something in the court outside, I turn my back on the dancers and the drums, a gesture and means of withdrawal. The drum beat of the *maman* "breaks" and at that very moment, a man standing on the sidelines a few yards from me, keels over backward, as if stunned by a blow. The loa can come like this, without warning, as a wind. The fall has been broken by several persons standing beside the man, and they are support/ ing him, bracing the still dead weight of his body, so that he remains on his feet. Then his body jerks violently out of its stillness, and with a mighty wrench which knocks one of his supporters to the ground, he frees himself and hurtles forward into the dance area of the peristyle. Now the drum has caught him up, catapults him from side to side. A woman who has accidently been jarred by the violent *débâtment*, freezes on one leg—as if this contact had been a contagion—lurches for/ ward, is also caught up in the drums. I do not wish to watch this, and I turn my back to the peristyle. It troubles me the more, in that, with Isnard himself mounted, there is no one there now who can help these agonized creatures, no one who, with the asson, could arbitrate between the loa and the human self, which wrangle violently over possession of the bodies, as two hands might fiercely compete for a single glove.

I recall how they would sometimes cling to Isnard, how, with the sound of asson and syllables, he would gradually subdue the last ravaging tremors. It is this that must be learned, above all, I say to myself slowly: not only the power of divine invocation, but also the tender mercy of worldly restoration; so that, to the body which must walk the earth, is returned the self that is appropriate to such dimension.

Still looking out, I say to myself, also, "This is the moment when you must make your decision." For I now know that, today, the drums, the singing, the movements—these may catch me also. I do not wish that. There is both fear and embarrassment in the idea. I know that I can leave now, that I can push out through the crowded exit, and cross the smooth, trampled court, turn up the rutted road, walk down its cool length—the sound growing more and more distant—until, in the small hut, with its thick clay walls, I might lie down, not hearing the drums at all, except for brief moments when the faint, fitful breeze would turn in that direction. Yet to do this would be to read myself out of it altogether, in a large sense. Not that I would be subsequently excluded; not at all. Yet, in my heart, I know that somehow, it is not fair to stay only when it is easy, or pleasurable, or exalting and to withdraw in the face of discomfort. This is as much a part of it, as if, in accepting the rewards, one had contracted to endure the ordeals. There is a sense of pride, too. To run away would be a cowardice. I could resist; but I must not escape. And I can resist best, I think to myself, if I put aside the fears and nervous-ness; if, instead of suspecting my vulnerability, I set myself in brazen competition with all this which would compel me to its authority. With this decision I feel a resurgence of strength, of the certainty of self, and of my proper identity.

I turn back toward the dancers, and join them. I sing, con-verse with Ogoun. Nothing is shaken within me. After many songs Ogoun announces that he is content with the dance, and that now he will leave. He stands there a moment, then a great spasm shakes the body, jerking it off balance. But already there are several to catch Isnard as he falls, to drag his limp body to a chair where, in a moment, he slowly raises his head, looks about him with the puzzled concentration of one who wakes in a room not yet habitual and familiar, and would orient himself.

His hand rubs the arm of the chair with an almost imperceptible movement, as if he would reassure himself of its solid
reality. Then, as the concentration fades from his features,
fatigue sweeps over them. He rises wearily and makes for his
private chamber, where, I know, he will lie down to rest for a
short while before resuming his duties.

Everyone stops to rest, as if some critical moment had been
passed. The drummers stroll into the courtyard to buy soda pop,
grillots, biscuits. Those people who arrived late use this opportunity to exchange personal greetings with the hounsis. We
all wander about, chatting. Then the drummers return to their
seats and I hear Titon urging the hounsis back into the peristyle to take up their formation. Some people have already left,
but the peristyle is still crowded. The next song is for Erzulie.
Once more the drums and the chorus, skillfully, rapidly, in a
matter of moments, construct the vast tidal wave of sound and
crash its surf forward. And once more the dancers ride forward
on that surf, on that sound, the rise and fall of its waves, all of
them once more part of the flow of the Yanvalou together,
circling the center-post with a slow undulation as of a single
serpentine body.

Watching, one senses that if these are united, it is not at all
because they refer to each other. They are separate, as bodies
and as beings; the ground-fixed eyes and the deep crouch
accentuate this sense of each of them in-turned, in-listening,
moving in common to a shared sound, heard by each of them
singly. When, following a "break" and having resumed the
erect posture which would slowly sink earthward again, they
may face each other and briefly mirror each other's movements,
even then the pairs seem less to duplicate each other than to be,
both, mirrors which, face to face, doubly reflect some invisible
figure who dances between and who knows reality only in
such mirrors. It is this which draws one in, for one rises to
commit oneself neither to the dancers nor to the drummers, but
to some pulse whose authority transcends all these creatures and
so unites them. The total is not the sum of its parts: we do not

serve each other; but rather, together, one serves a common which comprehends all.

The drums pause; then, almost immediately, begin again, accumulating, this time, into a Mahi. This has a gay quality and is a dance step which I particularly delight in, although it rapidly tires the muscles of calves and thighs. At first the drummer is considerate and "breaks" often enough to permit the limbs to relax and rest. But as the dance goes on, these "breaks" become more rare and the sense of fun gives way to a sense of great effort. The air seems heavy and wet, and, gasping, I feel that it brings no refreshment into my laboring lungs. My heart pounds in the pulse at my temple. My legs are heavy beyond belief, the muscles contracted into an enormous ache which digs deeper with every movement. My entire being focuses on one single thought: that I must endure.

I cannot say, now, why I did not stop; except that, beneath all this is always a sense of contract: whether, in the end, one be victor or victim, it is to be in the terms one has accepted. One cannot default. So focused was I, at that time, upon the effort to endure, that I did not even mark the moment when this ceased to be difficult and I cannot say whether it was sudden or gradual but only that my awareness of it was a sudden thing, as if the pace which had seemed unbearably demanding had slipped down a notch into a slow-motion, so that my mind had time, now, to wander, to observe at leisure, what a splendid thing it was, indeed, to hear the drums, to move like this, to be able to do all this so easily, to do even more, if it pleased one, to elaborate, to extend this movement of the arms toward greater elegance, or to counterpoint that rhythm of the heel or even to make this movement to the side, this time.

As sometimes in dreams, so here I can observe myself, can note with pleasure how the full hem of my white skirt plays with the rhythms, can watch, as if in a mirror, how the smile begins with a softening of the lips, spreads imperceptibly into a radiance which, surely, is lovelier than any I have ever seen. It is when I turn, as if to a neighbor, to say, "Look! See how lovely that is!" and see that the others are removed to a distance, withdrawn to a circle which is already watching, that I realize, like a shaft of terror struck through me, that it is no longer myself whom I watch. Yet it *is* myself, for as that terror strikes, we two are made one again, joined by and upon the point of the left leg which is as if rooted to the earth. Now there is only terror. "This is it!" Resting upon that leg I feel a strange numbness enter it from the earth itself and mount, within the very marrow of the bone, as slowly and richly as sap might mount the trunk of a tree. I say numbness, but that is in- accurate. To be precise, I must say what, even to me, is pure recollection, but not otherwise conceivable: I must call it a white darkness, its whiteness a glory and its darkness, terror. It is the terror which has the greater force, and with a supreme effort I wrench the leg loose—I must keep moving! must keep moving! —and pick up the dancing rhythm of the drums as something to grasp at, something to keep my feet from resting upon the dangerous earth. No sooner do I settle into the succor of this support than my sense of self doubles again, as in a mirror, separates to both sides of an invisible threshold, except that now the vision of the one who watches flickers, the lids flutter, the gaps between moments of sight growing greater, wider. I see the dancing one here, and next in a different place, facing another direction, and whatever lay between these moments is lost, utterly lost. I feel that the gaps will spread and widen and that I will, myself, be altogether lost in that dead space and that dead time. With a great blow the drum unites us once more upon the point of the left leg. The white darkness starts to shoot up; I wrench my foot free but the effort catapults me across what seems a vast, vast distance, and I come to rest upon a firmness of arms and bodies which would hold me up. But these have voices—great, insistent, singing voices—whose sound would smother me. With every muscle I pull loose and again plunge across a vast space and once more am no sooner poised in balance than my leg roots. So it goes: the leg fixed, then wrenched loose, the long fall across space, the rooting of the

leg again—for how long, how many times I cannot know. My
skull is a drum; each great beat drives that leg, like the point
of a stake, into the ground. The singing is at my very ear,
inside my head. This sound will drown me! "Why don't they
stop! Why don't they stop!" I cannot wrench the leg free. I am
caught in this cylinder, this well of sound. There is nothing
anywhere except this. There is no way out. The white darkness
moves up the veins of my leg like a swift tide rising, rising; is a
great force which I cannot sustain or contain, which, surely,
will burst my skin. It is too much, too bright, too white for
me; this is its darkness. "Mercy!" I scream within me. I hear
it echoed by the voices, shrill and unearthly: *"Erzulie!"* The
bright darkness floods up through my body, reaches my head,
engulfs me. I am sucked down and exploded upward at once.
That is all.[8]

*   *   *

If the earth is a sphere, then the abyss below the earth is also its
heavens; and the difference between them is no more than time, the time
of the earth's turning. If the earth is a vast horizontal surface reflecting,
invisibly, even for each man his own proper soul, then again, the abyss
below the earth is also its heavens, and the difference between them is
time, the time of an eye lifting and dropping. The sun-door and the tree-
root are the same thing in the same place, seen now from below and now
from above and named, by the seer, for the moment of seeing.

*   *   *

How could memory reach back beyond the first thing which
might be remembered? How could I know a void as void,
who had not yet learned substance, or darkness, who did not
know light? My memory begins with sound heard distantly,
addressed to me, and this I know: this is the sound of light. It
is a heard light, a beam invisible but bright, scanning the void

VEVER FOR ERZULIE

for substance to fix upon; and to become upon that substance light. Around the sharp directness and direction of that sound the darkness shapes itself and now it is as if I lay at the far distant end of an infinitely deep-down, sunken well. Each cell of body and brain anguishes upward and yet I cannot lift myself by my own motion; but, like some still unborn, unliving thing, am drawn up, slowly at first, by the sound's power. Slowly still, borne on its lightless beam, as one might rise up from the bottom of the sea, so I rise up, the body growing lighter with each second, am up-borne stronger, drawn up faster, uprising swifter, mounting still higher, higher still, faster, the sound grown still stronger, its draw tighter, still swifter, become loud, loud and louder, the thundering rattle, clangoring bell, unbearable, then suddenly: surface; suddenly: air; suddenly: sound is light, dazzling white.

How clear the world looks in this first total light. How purely form it is, without, for the moment, the shadow of meaning. I see everything all at once, without the delays of succession, and each detail is equal and equally lucid, before the sense of relative importance imposes the emphasis of eyes, the obscurity of nostril which is a face. Yet, even as I look, as if to remember forever this pristine world, already the forms become modulated into meanings, cease to be forms, become the night, the peristyle, the people. The white dresses and shirts, the asson's beaded mesh, still quivering from its labor, these blend, for a moment, with a fleeting memory of a white tent in the dark night and a trough of water. As the souls of the dead did, so have I, too, come back. I have returned. But the journey around is long and hard, alike for the strong horse, alike for the great rider.

APPENDIX A

NOTES ON TWO MARRIAGES WITH VOUDOUN LOA

by Odette Mennesson Rigaud

JUST as in many other religions, so in Voudoun there exists the mystic marriage between divinity and devotee. Such marriages may be requested, and even required, by the Spirits. If a young man has served Mistress Erzulie assiduously, she usually demands such a marriage, particularly if this man wishes to marry a mortal woman, and the mystic marriage with Erzulie serves to reaffirm and reinforce the bonds between the *vodouisant* and his loa. The human partner, on the one hand, receives the benefit of the loa's guardianship, protection, and the blessing of good fortune in all his undertakings; in return, however, he is bound by strict commit/ ments to the loa with whom he has contracted this marriage. Mistress Erzulie, in all her various aspects and aliases, is the divinity who most fre/ quently—more than any of the other loa—requires such a marriage with the men who serve her. Women, on the other hand, may wear a wedding/ ring for Dan/Ba/Lah, Ogou, Guédé (Damballah, Ogoun, Ghede), etc.

It may often happen that a *vodouisant* hesitates so to commit himself, for fear of the jealousies and tyrannies of the loa with whom he would enter into contract; but the loa may make it impossible for him to evade this union: his business affairs may be jeopardized, illness may descend upon him, or he may be threatened with even graver dangers. If he is faced with nothing more than the loa's expressed desire for such a union, he can turn to a houngan and seek, through his intervention, to arrive at some compromises: long/dated pledges, guarantees to regard that loa as pre/eminent, etc. If there is no immediate prospect of a mortal marriage, it is possible to evade in this way the mystic marriage. But if the contrary is true, it is rare that the *vodouisant* can evade it without seriously endanger/ ing the welfare and the very life of his mortal marriage. Warnings, reminders, commands will follow one after another, and then, finally, sanctions will be imposed. Nor will the loa accept as spouse for its "horse" just anybody at all; it will *choose* the one who is to marry or be "placed" with the "horse", and in this way it seeks to act in the best spiritual interests of the *vodouisant*.

Sometimes, however, a marriage with a powerful loa is sought by an ambitious person, who would like to achieve certain definite ends (whether financial, social or political). Here the marriage takes on the quality of a pact, and its conditions are imperious. In such cases celibacy is frequently obligatory. This is no longer a religious union of mystic love, but a magic pact.

Marriage with a loa, as it is usually practiced, is rather costly. It is necessary to prepare a room, hung with appropriate draperies, in which the loa will be received. According to the loa's character, everything which would please her (or him) must be assembled: a complete outfit, in fine silk and according to the taste and colors of the loa. For Erzulie, one must add cosmetics, perfumes and jewels, and wedding-rings or gold are obligatory. Erzulie (or the woman who is marrying a male loa) must own a complete bridal outfit, with a veil and white shoes. There must be a large reception, including cakes, liquors, refreshments of all kinds; and champagne, or other drinks favored by the loa, must not be overlooked. An orchestra may be engaged. To all this must be added the expenses of the ceremony: the fees of the *père savane* and the houngan.

The two mystic marriages which are here described took place in Haiti, near Port-au-Prince. The first one was with Erzulie.

A young man, by the name of Sebastien, wished to marry and have a family. However, he was a devout serviteur of Mistress Erzulie and she, very jealous, wished to retain her privileged position. After several broken engagements, he finally decided to dare marriage with a woman who also served the *Mystères Vodou* (the Voudoun spirits) and with whom he had lived, in common-law marriage, for some time. Erzulie favored this woman, since she lavished much attention on the loa and also knew that on the days sacred to Erzulie (and which belonged to no one else) the room must be adorned and decorated with flowers and basil. Mistress Erzulie did not seem to be opposed to the projected marriage, but demanded a preliminary marriage with herself, which was a usual requirement. It took place on a Thursday, a day sacred to Erzulie, and the mortal marriage was to follow on Saturday. The mystic marriage was to take place in the hounfor where Sebastien served his loa, and the ceremony was to begin at four o'clock in the afternoon. Sebastien, freshly shaven and his hair newly cut, wore a white suit and a beautiful silk shirt. All his costume was new and of good quality cloth. The evening before, he had purified himself, bathing in the water of basil, and he was now perfumed. His fiancée wore her best Sunday dress. The bridal gown was ready in an adjoining room—called "Erzulie's room"—which was hung in light-blue fabrics and filled with bouquets of roses, jasmin and basil. Laid out upon an embroidered cloth on the dressing-table was all that Maîtresse might desire for her coquetry: face-powder, cosmetics and perfumes.

A beautiful *niche* had been set up in the peristyle. It was a sort of tent, made up of embroidered sheets and silk cloths stretched over an armature of flexible bamboo and open in front. Inside was a table covered with a white cloth and bearing candlesticks, a missal, a crucifix, bouquets of flowers, holy water, and, in the background, chromo-lithographs of Erzulie and of some of the other guardian loa. In front of the niche were placed two armchairs for the bridal couple, and one of them was covered with light-blue and sea-green fabric. Behind these were two chairs for the god-father and god-mother. A short distance away stood a long table, overflowing with candy, sweets, liquors and fine wines, arranged about a beautiful wedding-cake which was flanked by bottles of champagne. In front of the niche a fine corn-flour vever had been drawn, representing a heart, the symbol for Erzulie, and, to one side, was the vever of Ogou (Ogoun), who, in the terms of this mythology, was her husband. These vevers were consecrated in the usual ritual fashion by the houngan. Sebastien and his fiancée took their places in the chairs reserved for them, in front of the god-parents and the witnesses. Many guests, dressed in their holiday best, were present. The père savane stood in front of the niche where large candles had been lit. He was a small, thin, dried up old man with a white tuft on the chin, a white mustache, and large eye-glasses perched on the end of his small, round nose; he wore a black jacket and vest and old-fashioned white trousers. His attitude was authoritarian, strongly imbued with a sense of his own importance, and, as he bent over his large Latin book, he brought to mind a dark-skinned rabbi. He began the prayers of the *action de grâce* and the audience answered devoutly; then, following the litanies, he began the canticles. Finally he stepped aside and the houngan took over, following with the canticle, after having greeted "all the saints in heaven"—that is to say, the loa— naming them at great length. The Virgin Mary was, naturally, cele- brated more than the other saints, and then followed the Voudoun songs in customary ritual order, with Erzulie being invoked with especial fervor. However, she did not seem to be ready to manifest herself. Every- one became a little impatient, and the houngan shook his asson and bell, and perfumed the guests. They had hoped that Mistress Erzulie would mount the mortal bride, but she seemed to decline this "horse" that day. Then, one of the women who was to be witness began to sway, at first imperceptibly and then with a more exaggerated movement. Her eyes closed, she fell backward, was held up on her feet, and, here, Erzulie appeared.

The transfiguration was complete. Out of an insignificant young woman, the loa had created an irresistible coquette, who leaned languorously on the shoulders of two young men summoned to support her and to lead her to the room reserved for her use. There Erzulie performed her meticulous toilette with the finest soap, put powder and make-up on, combed her hair endlessly before arranging the golden combs and flowers in her black tresses under the veil of tulle which was held with a blue satin bow. Finally she appeared in her bridal dress, perfumed, shining with golden jewelry, a bouquet of flowers on one arm and a light-blue handkerchief in her hand, her long skirt often lifted to reveal the pink taffeta petticoat, and smiling in recognition of the flattering whispers: "Oh, what a beautiful lady is Mistress Erzulie!" Her eyes shone, her full, moist lips were parted slightly. All men belonged to her and she honored them all.

Erzulie was led to the chair which was covered in her colors and her feet rested upon a soft carpet. The père savane returned to perform the wedding ceremony, which took place very solemnly. The wedding rings, as well as a golden ring set with a blue stone, were passed through the smoke of the incense, blessed, then slipped on to the fingers of the bridal couple. Sebastien was to wear this ring under his own wedding band. In answer to the ritual question: "Do you take this man. . . :" came the statement: "Yes, I, Erzulie Fréda Dahomé. . . ." The marriage contract was written out by the père savane in his best handwriting and was an accurate transcription of the official marriage document, except that here, Erzulie Fréda Dahomé pledged to protect her husband, Mr. Sebastien, and to bring him good fortune and prosperity, and he, in return, was to fulfill all the obligations which he had assumed toward her. Then the newlyweds, the god-parents, and the witnesses, signed the contract ceremoniously and it was placed on the altar in front of the picture of Erzulie Fréda Dahomé in the hounfor.

Mistress Erzulie was surrounded by the guests, congratulated and complimented. Graciously she strolled about on the arm of her husband and then turned to the reception table to cut the wedding-cake, slices of which were offered to the guests with glasses of champagne. Then the dances began, but Erzulie did not remain long. She left as quietly as she arrived, and the young woman, returned to herself, looked with astonishment at the bridal gown which she still wore. The drums continued to resound throughout the whole night for the Voudoun dances. The civil and Catholic wedding of Sebastien and his mortal bride took place the following Saturday. New wedding rings were used.

The tone of such mystic marriages depends greatly upon the character of the loa involved. The ceremony, which, in the case of Erzulie, would be ostentatious would be marked by a solemn gravity and a far more complex ritual procedure in the case of O-Dan or Dan-Ba-Lah (Damballah), while one which involves Guédé (Ghede) always has a humorous and even grotesque aspect. The one which is here described is a marriage ceremony between Guédé Mazaca and a mambo.

One day a young hounsi, Ramise, made fun of the Papa Guédé who danced in the head of one of her woman friends. Papa Guédé was displeased by this, and, in order to punish her, mounted her and declared that at some later date she must marry him. Since that time, this Guédé, having adopted her as his "horse", often mounted her, and Ramise, who became a mambo, finally accepted this with good grace. However, there came a time when he refused to appear, even when he was invoked, and Ramise ascribed the various troubles which beset her to his determination to hurt her. Therefore she went to the person in whose family line this particular Guédé had been inherited and made her invoke him in order to question him. In this way she discovered that Mazaca had decided that the moment had come for the marriage which he had asked for. He refused to compromise on this point and had an answer for every objection. He demanded that the marriage take place and Ramise finally had to agree, since she feared the displeasure of the loa who had previously brought her many advantages. The ceremony was scheduled for the following Sunday, in the late afternoon.

There was a big crowd in the peristyle that day because all the hounsis were present, as well as many guests, including many houngans and mambos. The people wore their very best clothes, silk dresses, satin handkerchiefs, rustling skirts, all in vivid and shining colors. Strips of multicolored, cut-out paper adorned the walls and crossed under the ceiling, fluttering in the lightest breeze. The Voudoun dances had begun several hours earlier, since the Guédés are at the very end in the hierarchical order of the loas and it was necessary, therefore, first to salute all of them in turn, after asking Legba to open the sacred gate. The center-post and the three Rada drums were ritually saluted with a libation of water, which had first been oriented to the cardinal points, as well as with the sacred address in *Guinin langage*. The flags were brought out of the altar chamber, according to the usual ceremonial procedure, being conducted by the saber of the laplace, and were leaned against the center-post. Large bouquets of flowers hung from the rafters and were pinned to the white sheets which formed the niche in a corner of the peristyle. Under these draperies there stood a sort of altar covered with a white tablecloth, embroideries, laces, and, upon it, candles, a crucifix, a basin of holy water and a vase of flowers. Religious pictures decorated the background, while in front of the niche there had been placed two chairs for the bride and groom, and two others for the god-parents. Then the père savane, a tall, thin gentleman, with an imposing mustache which almost concealed his dark face, arrived. His gold-rimmed glasses and tight black jacket gave him the appearance of a professor. First he checked to see that nothing would be missing for the ceremony, and then the Guédés were invoked. The houngenikon launched the songs in their honor, beginning with several yanvalous, and followed by their favorite dances, the crabiniers and bandas. A houngan traced the vever of Mazaca on the soil in front of the niche and then consecrated it. But wherever there is a party going on, the Guédés are only too glad to come, and already many of them had mounted their "horses" and had even had time to put on their special costumes. There was a Brave Guédé Nibo, dressed from head to foot in mauve, and full of high manner and sophistication, his droll tone containing a touch of *précieuse ridicule*, which, however, did not hinder him from dancing the disorderly bandas with a Guédé Nouvavou who wore a most serious, solemn expression under an incredible hat draped with funeral crêpe. The indispensable dark glasses lent their macabre touch to these faces shining with perspiration or drenched with white powder. The faces were rigid, but the bodies whirled in frenzied pirouettes, spasms of shaking, waddling, and bewildered gyration, to the rhythm of the drums. Both Ramise and the woman who served this Guédé Mazaca by family heritage had gone to dress. The latter was not yet mounted, but already seemed to be staggering and losing her balance repeatedly. After a moment she reappeared, wearing a pretty dress of dark-grey silk, printed with small, white and black bouquets. In her hand she held a black scarf embroidered with the name of the loa. She was a lady of reserved character, amiable, small and plump, about fifty years old, with a pleasant brown face under her carefully arranged *coiffure*. She had hardly taken a few steps into the peristyle when she was immediately overcome by Papa Guédé, who definitely mounted her. He had the same serious, dignified character as his "horse", but this did not prevent him from dancing the most suggestive bandas from time to time, without this activity at all affecting his demeanor, however. He raised the satin skirt so high over his short, chubby legs that others were obliged to intervene and lower the satin underskirt, while remonstrating with him. He hardly spoke, his eyes were half closed, and his dark face conveyed a strangely hermetic expression.

Then Ramise entered, in a splendid, white satin dress. Her black skin glowed strangely in this bridal outfit, and a small bouquet of white flowers was set in the very center of her tiny, glistening braids. She seemed more enormous than ever in her tight skirt, which seemed about to burst its seams at her hips and outlined one full curve of her body after another. Brooches, necklaces, earrings, bracelets and rings decorated her as if she were a reliquary. Her jovial nature made her laugh at everything, while Papa Guédé took everything much more seriously. A cortège was formed, the godparents leading the future married couple to their chairs. As they sat in front of the improvised niche, the engaged couple listened seriously to the regular Catholic prayers. Many different Guédés had arrived among the hounsis and the guests, and many of them were already wearing their costumes: jackets, frock-coats, ragged clothes topped by bowler hats and dented top-hats. They crowded behind the bridal couple, singing the litanies and cantiques in voices which were at once nasal—as is true of all the Guédés—and thunderously loud.

Meanwhile the père savane continued with the service in an off-hand tone of voice: "Does Mr. Guédé Mazaca take Madame Ramise, mambo, alias 'Après Dieu', for his lawful wedded wife?" The answer came out loud and clear. The wedding-rings were blessed, then put on the fingers of the bridal couple. In addition to these, the mambo later wore another ring set with a large, black stone. The wedding was over. The contract was signed on a small table arranged for this purpose, having been dictated by Ramise and prepared in advance by the père savane. As usual, the loa pledged to use every possible means to protect his spouse and she pledged herself to fulfill the obligations of a wife. The cortège was formed once again, and proceeded to the hounfor, there to deposit the contract. The flag bearers turned and danced under the direction of the laplace, whose sword was held high. There were two sets of flags, one pair more profusely spangled than the other, embroidered on dark-red and black velvet grounds. Each movement of the flag bearers, who pirouetted at the slightest directive of the agile young laplace, sent the multicolored reflections of the spangles over the peristyle.

The drums rolled and beat louder and louder. This time the bride gave her arm to her husband, Guédé Mazaca, who, with a severe and pompous expression, pulled himself up to the entire height of the stubby figure of his "horse". People rose to congratulate the newlyweds, to kiss Ramise and wish her happiness and prosperity. When the couple returned to the peristyle, the flag bearers and the laplace made ritual salutation to them, and all the hounsis twirled before them, in proper hierarchical order. Then enormous slices of the wedding-cake and other refreshments were served to the guests. It was really a wonderful reception! The songs and dances started up again, better than ever, and, naturally, in honor of the Guédés, who were in their gayest and maddest mood.

The drums beat an imperious salute, which Ramise and then Papa Guédé were to answer by lightly marking time, to salute the drums, and finally placing some money between the lips of each drummer. (This expensive honor is paid to important persons by the drummers.) But alas, Ramise staggered, righted herself, lost her balance again. The hounsis hurried forward to support her and take off the beautiful white dress because Papa Guédé had just mounted her. He escaped from their hold, but they caught him again, and put a black frock-coat over his white satin skirt. He grabbed a pair of dark glasses in passing, and, with a pirouette, joined the dancers in an impudent crabinier. The dancing continued for many hours more.

(These notes have been extracted from Mme Rigaud's work on Haitian Voudoun. The orthography of Voudoun terms which she has adopted for that total work has here been retained.)

APPENDIX B

SOME ELEMENTS OF ARAWAKAN, CARIB AND OTHER INDIAN CULTURES IN HAITIAN VOUDOUN

Unless otherwise indicated, the parenthetical page references are to volume XI of THE MYTHOLOGY OF ALL RACES, Latin-American *by Hartley Burr Alexander, Marshall Jones Company, Boston, 1920.*

HISTORIANS have been content to remark that the Petro cult is probably traceable to a Spanish houngan, Dom Pedro. Herskovits (p. 150) specifies "a Spanish *Negro*", a specification that I have not heard else-where, and one which is not very logical. If this Dom Pedro was the illegitimate child of a Negro woman by a Spaniard, this would hardly be unusual or significant enough to warrant the special classification of Spanish. But a pure Spaniard would have been a white Catholic, not a houngan. The specification "Spanish" was probably introduced into the legend as a means of indicating that this man was not an African, i.e. a Negro. Apart from that of the Negroes, the only other non-Catholic religion which could have existed there at that time, would have been Indian, and if there had been an intermingling of African and Indian religions, the priests of the Indian cults might easily have come to be called houngans. As a matter of fact, it is far from irrelevant that the Spanish word *petreo* means stony and that the traditional phrase used to characterize the Petro loa in Creole is "raide" (stiff, hard). Consequently it is entirely possible that Petro is not a corruption of the proper Spanish name Pedro, but a characterization, in simplified Spanish, which became attached to or even adopted (most proper names have originated in this manner) by a non-Spanish person. Another important clue lies in the fact that a majority of the Petro words are Spanish. This indicates their origin in a period of Spanish domination, a period in which the Indians as well as the Negroes were used as slaves. Spanish was the language that the Indians learned, and it was the linguistic meeting ground with the imported Africans. But whereas the majority of Africans were subsequently (after 1677) imported by the French, and began translating their religious terms into the Creole which began to evolve, Spanish would have become set as the "sacred" or "ritual" language of the religious practices contributed by the Indians, who were almost extinct by the time the French period opens.

It is also inconceivable that the Indians, who were on home ground, should have been any less disposed to run away into their familiar hills than the newly-arrived Africans. And finally, in spite of all efforts to the contrary, certain dances and names are admitted (reluctantly) to be of Indian origin. This proves that culture-contact *was* made. In view of this fact, and the facts cited above, it is difficult to understand why this direction of investigation has been pursued only, and merely to some small degree, by Maximilien.

It may be due partially to the fact that the Haitian intellectual has taken pride in aligning himself with French culture, and, in racial terms, has been particularly self-conscious about his Negroid origin. Conversation with a Haitian intellectual leads one unconsciously to conceive of the island as having been discovered by the French and to ignore completely the Spanish period, which lasted 185 years, and during which the Indian culture must have made its mark before being completely exterminated. For the French historian, the Spanish-Indian period was apparently unimportant. He assumed that whatever he found in Haiti was African.

Another explanation may lie in the fact that the ethnologists who have worked in Haiti were either African authorities (Herskovits), or men especially interested in African elements (Courlander), so that if they were able to find in some African context a possible origin for a Haitian phenomenon, they were satisfied.

Yet certain major Voudoun deities, such as Baron Samedi and the Simbi family, could not be traced to Africa at all; other tracings, such as for Ghede and Azacca, were extremely tenuous. Even where specific artifacts, legends, or concepts could be traced to Africa, they could be so referred only on very mechanical grounds, and without regard for the sharp difference in ethos between definitely African concepts and attitudes (whether of the Dahomeans, the Nagos, the Ibos, etc.) and those present in the Petro ritual, as well as in certain elements of Rada ritual, as, for example, in the vever as a form of symbol.

The Arawakan Taino, who seem to have been the earlier settlers of Haiti and the Antilles, and the Caribs who conquered them, as far north as to Puerto Rico (pp. 16–17), themselves had originated from the tropical forests of the Orinoco and Guiana, and using the Antilles as stepping-stones, had brought the elements of the mainland culture with them: they are of the same linguistic stock (p. 255): as a sea-faring people, moreover, they had made contact with Central America, leaving their imprint in the same region which bore signs of the Aztec world in the Nahua tribes, which had penetrated that far south (p. 43). It was at this juncture of the continent, stretching toward the Greater Antilles and commanding the passage between the Gulf of Mexico and the Carib-bean Sea (p. 43), that the Mayan civilization had been dominant—although it was the Quiche and Cakchiquel, as well as other groups of Guatemala, "whose mountain valleys drain towards the Gulf and the Caribbean" (p. 156), who had preserved the most significant records of the Maya; and it is in those valleys that the ruins of the monumental cities lie. Moreover, in the same Central American zone, the Chibchan dominated the Isthmus of Panama (p. 43), and these (whose center was in the plateau of Bogota), along with the neighboring Quechua (Aymara and Diaguite-Calchaqui tribes), had been conquered by the Inca civilization. Their use of ceremonial objects points to Bolivia, to the Venezuelan coast, and even to the Antilles; which would seem to indicate a remote unity of the whole region from Haiti to Ecuador and from Venezuela to Nicaragua. The central body of Andean myth is that of the Incas (pp. 189–90). At the same time, Oviedo's description of the tribes about the Gulf of Nicoya, where the civilizations of the two Americas meet, indicates a religion of the Mexican type (p. 190).

The Caribs, who were known as extremely aggressive marauders, and from whose practices the word "cannibal" derives, had contact with elements of the great Aztec, Inca and Mayan cultures, as well as with the native myths of the tribes who had fallen under the domination of these three great civilizations, and among whom the practice had frequently been the canny one of not destroying the deities of the subjugated tribes, but putting them into a kind of jail. Students of Indian culture point out that in the new world there was a "oneness of race nowhere else to be found over so great an area"; and that this "unity is best represented neither by physical appearance nor material achievement, but by a conservation of ideas and of the symbolic language of myth which is at bottom one" (p. 343). Thus, the Arawaks and the Caribs, with which the escaped African made contact in the hills, were carrying elements which were either historically derived from cultures as advanced as the Inca, Mayan and Aztec or prehistorically derived from a source common to them all and to all South American Indian culture.

The Africans and the Indians have in common the very basis of religious belief—belief in a deity as first source, ancestor worship, and other elements—and it is inevitable that, starting from the same premise, there would be similarities which developed simultaneously in both continents. Thus, while it would be difficult to distinguish, in every case, the origin of those beliefs, ritual practices and magical works, yet there are many elements in Voudoun today which are either not traceable to Africa or hold a position in Haiti much more dominant than in Africa. When these elements are found in the Indian culture, the latter can at least be considered as a possible source. Most of the elements which point to such a linkage are elements of magical manipulation.

The asson, which is today the sacred rattle of the priest, is dominant in Taino myth. It appears as the calabash filled with bones, in which the bones became fish, and from which "ran so much water . . . as overflowed all the country . . . and from which the sea had its origin" (p. 29). The Orinoco, the immediate forefathers of the Caribs and the Arawaks, tell of the "sacred rattle" of the *peaiman*—the priest; while the Tupinambi of the Amazon were understood to hold sacred a calabash rattle, called *tammaraka* (obviously the instrument we know now as *maracas*), with which they danced and whose sound the priests could interpret (p. 296). Maximilien (pp. 140–1) gives an African source for the asson, but acknowledges that the decoration is Indian. Moreover, in Africa it was (if his source is correct) a musical instrument. Herskovits (p. 269) also mentions the rattle as being West African, but also in the nature of a musical instrument. In Haiti it is a sacred instrument, precisely like that of the Indians.

Yet the most revealing legend in this connection is the tale of the Orinocan Orehu, who are water sprites, or mermaids, and who may drag a man to the depths of their aquatic haunts. This is a very recurrent myth in Haiti. They are not altogether evil; for it is said that in ancient times an Arawak, walking beside the water and brooding over the sad condition of his people, beheld an Orehu rise from the stream, bearing a branch which he planted as she bade him, its fruit being the calabash, till then unknown. Again she appeared, bringing small white pebbles, which she instructed him to enclose in the gourd, thus making the magic-working rattle. She instructed him in its use and in the mysteries of the *semecihi*, who are the medicine men of the Arawak corresponding to the Carib *peaimen*, though the word seems related to the Taino *zemi*. Orehu is no other than the mainland equivalent of the Haitian (Taino) woman of the sea, Guabonite, who taught the medicine hero, Guagugiana, the use of amulets of white stones and gold (p. 261).

This legend is precisely comparable to the stories in Voudoun mythology that are told of the Water People, whom Herskovits (p. 244) classifies as baka, spirits of the Petro group, which are sometimes good but sometimes drag or entice the victim to the bottom of the water. In Voudoun today there is langage, a sacred speech for communicating with the gods, which occurs in the songs and litanies and which the priest alone understands. It has been explained as of ancient African origin. However, there was the use of "words none of our people understand" by the Arawak priests when they were possessed by the spirits (p. 22). Many of the words which are currently Voudoun langage cannot be traced, others are sometimes attributed to ancient Spanish (Courlander, pp. 21, 96) and these sound very much like Indian words. The words written out by Courlander (p. 21) as *ke le manyan* could well be either *peaiman* (Orinoco for "priest", p. 260) or *kenaima* (a deathdealing or vengeful spirit, p. 267). The langage of a song for Ghede is transcribed as *noumonnouce* (Courlander, p. 89), but is quite as likely *guamaonocon*, the name of the supreme deity of the Taino. The langage in a song to Agwé, *cina, cina*, is possibly the Arawak word *cinaci*, meaning "our father", or perhaps *ciba*, the white shells of Orehu. The dance Crabinier (variously pronounced and transcribed as "Crabignien", "Carabiner", and even "Gabienne") which frequently closes the ceremonial dances, is referred to as Indian by Courlander (p. 122) and the name is clearly derived from the word "Carib". The Creole word for intoxicating drink is *tafia* and the same drink is called in the Orinoco tongue *tapana* (p. 262). There are many such examples.

The *paquets* Congo which are bound as magical safeguards and whose efficacy depends on the technique of careful wrapping (the idea being to enclose the soul well, so as to keep it from evil) are suspiciously like the "peculiar type of Antillean cultusimage" mentioned by Peter Martyr, among others, made of "plaited cotton, tightly stuffed inside".

There is a deity, little known but presumably of ancient origin, in the region of Petit Goave, which is known as "CinqJourMalheureux" (Rigaud, p. 53). He is very old, and bent, and much like an older version of Legba, who is the sun as well as the crossroads. "CinqJourMalheureux" is obviously a calendrical figure, referring to the five empty and unlucky days, or the five nameless days, which is what both the Aztecs (p. 99) and the Mayans (p. 147) called the last days of their year —those left over because of the discrepancy between the lunar and solar years. In this period the Sun was old and had to be reborn. It is interesting, moreover, that in the region of Leogone, there is a ceremony of great bonfires during the days between Christmas and New Year, which carries out the principle of heating up and restoring life to the dying sun that has been reported for many cultures (Frazer, p. 359). Such calen-drical concerns are not typical of African culture—unless one can relate them to Egyptian belief.

Perhaps the most striking element in Voudoun rites, yet one that has not been identified as derived from Africa, is the vever, a design made by dropping flour or ash (this is called *farine Guinée*) to form a symbolic figure upon the ground. Each deity has his own symbol, which serves to consecrate the ground for him during ceremonies, the offering being placed upon the drawing. The cabbala-like character and function of the drawings does not suggest any African tradition, but is similar to the intricate drawings of the Aztecs and Indians. (Maximilien, p. 45, has also commented on this linkage.) In the Codex Ferjervary-Mayer, the first sheet is devoted to the figure of a cross pattee combined with a St. Andrew's cross, which is supposed to represent the basic principles of Aztec belief: the five regions of the world, the nine lords of the night, the four trees supporting the four quarters of heaven, etc. (p. 55). The center is the *pou-sto*, "the Mother, the Father of the Gods, who dwells in the navel of the earth". It is this figure which constantly recurs in Voudoun vevers for the cross-roads divinity, Legba, who is also the loa of the poteau-mitan, the center-post, through which all the loa enter the peristyle. Moreover, the Bororo of Brazil have a dance rite called the *bakororo* a semi-secular festival, described as being full of pandemonium, which is held on the eve of a hunting expedition and includes the following action: "They cleared a space . . . and formed animals in relief with ashes . . . especially the figure of the tapir, which they were going to hunt" (p. 291). This kind of sympathetic magic might well be used to invoke a deity. Ashes also refer, undoubtedly, to the ashes of the sacrificial victim, and the universal custom of scattering these upon the fields to insure their fertility. The *bakororo* might also throw light on the Haitian secular "Rara" festival, whose purpose is pandemonium. The Indian sand-paintings of North America are in a tradition similar to that of the vever, and Maximilien (pp. 42-3) has traced a similar rite in Mexico. Certainly the geometric drawings bear more affinity with the Indian cultures than with the African, as do likewise their cabbalistic qualities. (Courlander, p. 22, remarks on the special character of various motifs recurrent in the vevers.)

The Dahomean serpent deity Damballah has his counterpart in Indian myth. The first Carib came from a serpent (p. 272); the Orinoco called him the serpent of the sky and had a legend regarding the cosmic eggs which he nurtured (p. 232). Among the Andean tribes he was associated with the rainbow (pp. 200–1), and in the Mexican-Aztecan legends he is the plumed serpent (p. 100), also represented as a double serpent (p. 100) or a double-headed serpent (p. 72). This strongly suggests the serpent images in Voudoun, where the double snake represents Dam-ballah and Ayida (his female counterpart, whose symbol is the rainbow) and is frequently shown in conjunction with an egg. This represents either an extraordinary coincidence between the Indian and African cultures, or indicates an assimilation of the Indian into the African in the Caribbean. It is particularly significant that both Damballah and (more frequently) Legba are referred to as *Grand Chemin,* which may be a reference, in French, to road and cross-road, or may be the Carib word *emin* or *chemin,* used to designate the great spirit or sky god, a designation signifying "major importance".

The most important parallelism between the two cultures, and conse-quently the area in which ritualistic influences would be most readily absorbed, is in the beliefs concerning the ancestral dead. Among the Arawaks and the Caribs, the dead were understood to return to a vale in their own country (p. 278), which would be in the Orinoco Guiana homeland, and settle to the bottom of the waters of a lake (p. 279). This resembles the Voudoun belief, even to the expression *nan Guinée,* which should be reconsidered in terms of its possible geographical reference, particularly since the Haitians distinguish between *loa Dahomey* and *loa Guinée.* The Indian belief also contained, rather imprecisely, the notion of the center of the earth, as noted in Andean belief (pp. 180, 198). (This distinction between Dahomey and Rada on the one hand, and Guinée, Petro, and Creole on the other, is suggested in various contexts. Marcelin records conflict between Creoles and hounsis canzo (p. 33) and between Creoles, Agaza, and Loco (pp. 42–3); Courlander notes such conflict between Papa Dahomey and the Creoles (pp. 121–2); and Herskovits associates Guinée with Petro in distinguishing the latter from Rada (p. 270). It may well be that the Guinée references in Voudoun songs and litanies are references to the South American continent in certain contexts, instead of the African, which has always been the assumption. The citations above are also interesting in that they indicate a certain period of adjustment in the meeting of African and Indian traditions.)

Moreover, the Taino made a special distinction in reference to their "caciques" or priests, who were not permitted to die natural deaths but were strangled (p. 27). The notion of killing the king (who is frequently also the head priest in a primitive culture) so that his powers, which reflect the powers of the tribe, may never wane, is very widespread. Among the Taino, it serves to distinguish between the general ancestors and the particularly sacred souls of the priestly dead. The bones of the dead, especially those of the caciques and great men, were kept either in baskets or in the plaited cotton fetishes (p. 27); and these dead were also represented by *zemi*—fetish-objects either of stone or of wood. In Voudoun, the placement of such symbolic remains in baskets has been noted repeatedly, and we have spoken above of the *paquets* Congo. As for the cult of *zemiism*, this was dominant among the Arawaks and Caribs about Haiti and has become the name of the aboriginal cult of this area. Each cacique or priest had his particular *zemi*, which was kept in a separate house, or in the case of lay-individuals was given a separate room. The custom is precisely analogous to the special hounfors of the houngan and the *cailles Mystères* of the Voudoun serviteurs. The *zemi* (the word is understood by some authorities to mean "animal" and by others as a corruption of *guami*, "ruler") could be made of wood, stone, or roots, according to the dictates of the vision or the "divine accident" of the particular individual. When the *zemi* were stones, they had a particular nature: "as if they sweated" (p. 29). This is precisely the condition which determines the sacred stones of Voudoun—stones which sweat (Courlander, p. 35)—and these, like the *zemi*, may represent various loa and ancestors, whereas the sacred stones of African tradition are related exclusively to the thunderbolt divinities (Courlander, p. 28).

The *zemi*, which was considered to be the receptacle of the spirit of the ancestral dead and an intermediary between the living and the divine (holding the same position as the loa in Voudoun) was also frequently made, we are told, of wood hollowed inside in some fashion, and connected to speaking tubes leading from a concealed area. The *zemi* would be addressed by the name of the father or other ancestral dead (pp. 22-3) and would speak out advice and oracles, precisely in the manner in which the souls of the dead are addressed and reply in the Voudoun *govi*. (The "speaking tubes", by the way, may well be the figments of the white man's devaluating imagination; for no such quackery is necessary in Haiti today.)

The most important *zemi* (or *cemis*) of the tribe are variously reported as consisting of two or three large stones which sweat, or as two statues of wood, which were kept in a grotto or cave to which the Indians made annual pilgrimage. They were the twinned deities of rain and sun (in the case of three, they were understood to help the corn to grow, the rain to fall, and to aid in the delivery of children), and were represented in the twin-hero myth which runs so persistently through all Indian culture. The power ascribed to these *zemi*—fertility, rainfall and childbirth—are precisely those ascribed to the Haitian Marassa. According to Her-skovits (p. 201), the twin cult is very strong in Africa, and he adds, concerning the Haitians, that some "families worship twins because a houngan has divined that their unknown ancestors in 'Guinée' had included them". Courlander (p. 38) defines Marassa Creole as being twins of the same sex and Marassa Guinée as twins of different sex. If Guinée may be taken to represent the new-world culture (i.e., Petro), Herskovits' reference to Guinée would be to the new world; whereas Courlander's references would be either to the new *and* the old world (if Guinée is Africa), or to a difference between what was the old world for the Indians (Guinée of South America) and the newer world of the Antilles. The fact that there is a definite distinction made indicates, in any case, a coming together of two different traditions. The word *Marassa* itself recalls the Spanish word *marras* (long ago) as well as *Maorocon*, Father Sky (p. 24), and *Marocael*, Watchman of the Caves (p. 28), of the Indian myths, and has not been definitely traced to Africa.

In the Andean culture there is repeated and important reference not only to twins but to a spirit which either has three heads on one body (p. 198) or represents three persons sharing one heart (p. 180). This is precisely the sense of the "plat-Marassa-Trois", and of the belief that twins share a common soul (Herskovits, p. 204).

Like the Marassa, the Indian twin-heroes are considered to have been the first creation of God, and many legends are concerned with the adventures of these demiurgic beings. According to Taino myth, the first two tribes of Indians, Cacibagiagua and Amaiauva, emerged from two caves in Hispaniola (Haiti). And there is a legend of quadruplets, the four Caracarols, which implies that each of the two original *zemi* was itself actually twins. This is similar to the Voudoun elaboration of the Marassa—the invocation to whom also refers to the "four races" (Rigaud, p. 17), which is simultaneously a reference to the cardinal points.

Among the Indian stories referring to the divine hero pair there is told repeatedly a tale of their ball/playing (the characteristic activity of the Marassa is to play at marbles or at ball), which is a symbolic reference to the solar and lunar orbs (p. 173). Time and again, their major power is that of trickster/transformers, or magicians, and the tales of their magical escapades are innumerable. The Marassa are particularly important for the working of magic.

There is an Arawakan tale that tells of Guaguguiana, a hero of the first people who emerged from the caves. He was a trickster/transformer. And he lost his comrade, his twin. In grieving for his comrade, he resolved to go forth from the cave, but in doing so, let out the women and children. He abandoned the women on the island of Matenino (possible source of the Spanish legend of the Caribbean Amazons) and the children beside a brook or an ocean. The children, starving, were crying for milk, calling "toa, toa", and they were transformed into little creatures like dwarfs (pp. 310–32), who are called *tona*. In Haitian Voudoun, there is at least one song to Agwé Woyo in which he is referred to as "Toni Agwé" (Rigaud, p. 15), and the fact that his name suggests Spanish rather than French (Woyo is also pronounced as *arroyo*, which in Spanish means fearless, or fling, hurl, or burn [*arrojar*]) may point to a connection with the Spanish/Indian period of Voudoun development. In Mexican myth there is a comparable synonymy between children and dwarfs, who are considered to be the servants of "rain" (p. 72), and the image is extended to include hunchbacks, who, in one case at least (p. 81), were instru/mental in fashioning the first human pair. In Voudoun, one of the important deities is a hunchback, Bossu, while several deities are repre/sented as dwarfs—particularly Alovi, who is known as mischievous, in the manner of the trickster/transformer demiurgic twins.

In other words, the beliefs concerning the Marassa duplicate in so many particulars the beliefs of the Indians concerning the relationship of twins to rain, fertility, corn and magic, as well as to the origin of the race, that the concordance is too precise to be coincidental.

The Voudoun god of agriculture, Azacca (as well as deities related to him, such as Aza), has never been satisfactorily traced to Africa. He is known as a Juba (Martinique) deity, a group not acknowledged as of African provenience. His name may derive from an Indian word for corn, *zara*, or from some related word, such as *azada*, or *azadon*—referring to hoeing and plantation digging—or from one of the *maza*/structured words from which our own word maize is evolved. This would be an agrarian reference in Indian/Spanish terms, such as should be expected from the history of Haitian agriculture. The Haitian assimilation of Indian agrarian rites is, however, most apparent in Petro, as we shall presently see.

The aboriginal cult of *zemiism* links not only to the Marassa, but, even more surely, to the cult of the Ghedes, to Baron Samedi, guardian of the dead and the cemetery, and to the zombie, the figure of the soulless dead. In many cases Ghede is completely identified with Baron Samedi, at other times there seems to be a slight, insignificant distinction. Herʼ skovits, on the other hand, distinguishes the two sharply, stating that Ghede is just, and will not bury a person even if Baron Samedi wishes him to do so (p. 247). Yet, in another connection, Herskovits asserts that the Rada gods leave when Ghede comes (which is not the experience of other writers) and that there are a number of names compounded with Ghede, which raises the question as to whether Ghede might not be a generic term. "All those loa who bear the same name," he writes (p. 318), "such as all Ogun or Bosu or Simbi deities, are brothers; but who the parents of these groups may have been is not known." Herskovits suggests Gedeonsu, as the name of a Dahomean totem (p. 267), upon whose significance, however, he has not commented; neither has he indicated any special connection of this totem with the dead. Surely the preʼ eminent position which Ghede has come to command in many areas as Lord of the Dead can hardly have been derived from a mere totem.

However, another connection which has been suggested for Africa is the cult of death and resurrection of a secret society of the lower Congo, which was called Ndembo (Frazer, p. 697): Ghede is frequently called Ghede Nimbo. It is possible that both the Dahomean Ghede and the Congo Ndembo were blended into a single grouping which owes its preʼ eminent position and ritualistic practices to Baron Samedi, acknowledged as chief of the Ghede grouping.

In every other respect, however, Ghede and his cult have been treated as standing apart from African Voudoun. In some areas (Herskovits, p. 318) Ghede is not even considered to be a loa in the African tradition, but an evil spirit. And ceremonially he seems always to be treated apart. Likewise, zombieʼism is not considered Voudoun (Courlander, p. 88). On the other hand, various Arawakan beliefs concerning *zemis* are precisely those of the *zombie*—the relation of the words is obvious; as it is equally obvious for *zemi* and *Samedi*. It is interesting, and significant, to note that the archaic Spanishʼ American word for a mixture of Indian and mulatto was *zambo* (this is related to *zambobo*, which means a "rustic clown" and possibly to the American Negro folk character, Sambo; while the *zambapalo*—"ancient Indian dance"—is undoubtedly the source of the contemporary ball-room dance, the Samba). Moreover, if *zemi* and *guamiare* are linguistically linked (see p. 278, *supra*), the word *Ghede* may belong to this context. Or perhaps it is related to *Giadru-vava* (*vava* is a common Arawakan suffix; it is still heard in Voudoun litanies as *vavou*), who was the twin (the dead brother) of that trickster, Guagu-guiana, who led the women and children from the cave. Guaguguiana mourned for Giadruvava when he was turned into a night-singing bird. A Ghede *Novavou* is a well-known loa (Maximilien, p. 101 and Rigaud, Appendix A of this book); the langage phrase "aima sa foula" which occurs in a Ghede song is reminiscent of the Indian *ken aima*; while Baron la Croix, who is also Baron Cimitière (brother to Ghede and Samedi), is also known as Azagon la Croix, *azadon* or *azagon* being the Spanish word for spade, digger, etc.

Zemis, the souls of persons, could be stolen; the practice was recorded among the Indians (p. 22) and is what creates a zombie in Haitian belief (Courlander, pp. 26–7; Metraux, pp. 86–7). Furthermore, among the Indians, people whose souls had fled or been stolen had no navel (the sign of life, the lack of which signified a dead being): it is through the navel that the Haitian houngan liberates the gros-bon-ange and the maît-tête at death. The Indian living dead could also be recognized by the fact that the pupils of their eyes did not reflect: in Haiti, Ghede wears sun-glasses and the test of a real possession by Ghede is the ability of the possessed person to receive a sharp, burning liquid in the eyes without blinking. (Perhaps cognate with the sun-glasses of Ghede is the circum-stance of the Aztec god of the underworld, who is blindfolded, yet sees all [p. 62].) The living dead of the Caribbean Indians were known to walk about at night, and they particularly liked tobacco: a cigar or cigarette is one of the essential accoutrements of Ghede. In addition, Ghede is related to digging tools by the Indian words *mazacca* and *azadon* (cf., p. 280, *supra* and fn. 48, Ch. III). The Caribs had a term *kenaima* (which may be the origin of the Voudoun word *Khensou*; cf. p. 275, *supra*), which meant a class of death-bringing powers, and was the insular equivalent of the continental *maboya*, the great and first snake deity; *ma* meaning great, and *boii* meaning snakes (but also used as the word for "priests" by the islanders). The range of this term (which is linked to *zemiism*), from the sphere of primary divinity to that of the exercise of malevolent magic (as in zombies), is the same as that covered by the Voudoun concept of Ghede. There is, also, a rite recorded among the Ucatan, which is called *em~ku*, or *renascor* (Spanish: *renazco*, "I am reborn"), which is concerned with resurrection: the word *ronsor* occurs repeatedly in Voudoun litanies, in connection both with Agwé (the comrade of Ghede) and with Ghede himself.

(These verbal analogies are hardly more remote than many of the African "sources" that have been found by the authorities. They are presented here, not as philologically definitive, but as clues to congruent spheres of concept and sound, shared by the Indians and Voudoun. The extermination of the aborigines of the Caribbean area before any precise record could be made of their religious and linguistic heritage leaves us with little to go on; but this does not reduce the likelihood of Indian influence on Voudoun. The myths and rites of the Indian world here being noted are certainly closer to certain aspects of Voudoun than anything yet indicated for those aspects in Africa: it is not unlikely that verbal echoes also resound.)

One of the traits peculiar to Ghede is his special appetite for cassava, an Indian bread. In the Arawak legend of origin, when the four Cara~ carol were born, they ate of the fish in the calabash and upset it, which resulted in the inundation of the land and the origin of the sea. The four brothers being hungry, one of them begged for cassava bread, but was refused and struck on the shoulder with a sheaf of tobacco: the shoulder swelled and when it was opened a live female tortoise issued forth, with which the brothers mated, and she conceived. The hermaphroditic brother, who had begged for the cassava and became the mother of the mother~tortoise, seems to have become the Haitian~Arawak god of the underworld (p. 29)—like Ghede. The phrase "o la bel caraco" occurs in a song to Ghede, an obvious reference to the Caracarol.

A third, and perhaps the most important, linkage of Indian and African elements in Voudoun appears in connection with the Petro deities. It has been generally agreed that Dan or Dom Petro, first of the Petro deities, came into existence in the new world. *Dan* may not stand for the Spanish *don*, but may be an African word, *dan*, meaning snake (the snake was worshipped as primary deity both in America and in Africa), while *Petro* may derive from *petreo* (see p. 271, *supra*). The association with the snake would be further born out by the fact that Ti~Jean Petro, the son of Dan Petro, is characterized as having one foot, or no feet at all, and yet is famous for going up trees. Dan Petro himself commonly appears in animal forms, and his son, Ti-Jean, is obviously a snake (Herskovits, p. 191: Courlander, pp. 45 and 132).

Among the Yoruba of Nigeria, when the king was to be killed before the total degeneration of his powers, the custom was to inform him of the moment by sending him the foot of his son (Frazer, p. 274). This may have some connection with the one-footed son of Dan Petro. But the Aztec god of the underworld, Tezcatlipuca Iztli, who was the patron of cross-roads and magicians, and was blindfolded, had one stump of a leg. (The foot was often replaced by a mirror—for divination?—and he was also related to the image of a smoking mirror, which suggests the moon as the reflection of a burned-out sun. Ghede's magical rites take place during the new moon.) Indeed, the idea of the lame god or maimed king, lame goat, or other animal or human, is widespread throughout the world. (Robert Graves has made a good deal of the idea in his *The White Goddess* and in *King Jesus*.) Frazer associates it with the idea of the cut corn (Frazer, p. 455). The Petro cult and rites are especially associated both with agrarian concerns and with magic.

Congo Zandor is known as a man-eater who grinds the sacrificial victim in a mortar, as one would crush maize (Courlander, p. 43). Now, while human sacrifice to the corn deity is a world-wide practice, the special image of grinding the person to death occurs in the Mexican "meeting of the stones" ceremony, where two carefully balanced rocks were allowed to fall together on the victim, grinding him (Frazer, p. 444). This is the kind of concept that the Caribs, themselves given to bloody sacrifice, could easily have picked up from their contacts with Central America. The Congo Mazonne dance (the name, apparently, is a combination of African and Indian words) is understood to be for Congo Zandor (also called Congo Savanne) and is known not only in Haiti but throughout the islands, perhaps because of its derivation from an Indian maize dance (Courlander, p. 157). The word *Zandor* itself may derive from any number of possible sources: Spanish *sangrar*, "to bleed, to be bled"; *mazonear* (an old word, replaced by *apisonar*), which means "to ram, to stamp, to crush". *Savanne*, which is the alternate name for Zandor, suggests not only plains, but also Spanish *savia*, "sap", and therewith, blood.

Yet it is not so much in possible words as in the general tone and in numerous details of the cult that the really striking analogies occur. The characteristic appellation of the Petro deities is Ge-Rouge, red eyes: the Caribs are described (p. 37) as painting themselves with strange devices, particularly staining their eyes and eyebrows to give a terrifying appearance. The Carib women were distinguished for wearing leg-bands fastened just below the knee: the Petro deities tie a band or handkerchief in the same place on the leg, as well as on the upper arm. The Caribs, it will be recalled, were cannibalistic; their agrarian rites were extremely violent and bloody. Their relatives, the Orinoco, put red-pepper in their eyes to propitiate dangerous spirits (p. 268).

From the Mexicans we hear of the custom of sacrificing to the corn with a human sacrifice; the deity honored was known as Zipe Totec, "our Lord the Flayed". He stood for the renewal of vegetation and was represented as clad in a human skin stripped from the body of a sacrificed captive. His chief festival was in spring, when the fresh verdure was appearing, and in the songs there is reference to the changing of a snake's skin. In Petro, the dresses worn by the women are specifically open in front, over another garment, a representation suggesting the wearing of a second skin. Moreover, the dances for the Petro deities are called Quitta sèche: *quita*, in Spanish, means "taken off, removed"; it is from the same root as the French *quitter*, "to part with, to slip off, to take or pull off, to renounce". Bras Chêche and Pied Chêche, which are characterizations of Petro deities likewise give the French *sec* or *sèche*, "dry", suggesting dry bones, dry skin, and the dry sheaf: possibly a sacrificial reference.

At Petro rites the table on which offerings are placed is called a *bila*, and in this connection Maximilien tells of a certain Jerome or Poteau (Aztecan *pou-sto*, fifth of the cardinal points, i.e., the point of the center), who, aided by a Negro, introduced some strange practices. These are said to have come from Europe; however, the description cites small stones sold to the Negroes under the name *maman bila*, which may well be a French transcription of *mapoia* or *maboya*, the name of the great Carib snake deity; or of *mayombo*, a stick which could magically beat any other stick. As already pointed out, the word *maboya* breaks down into *boya*, or *boii*, which in the Carib tongue denoted "snakes" or "priests", and *ma*, meaning "great". The table called a *bila* resembles that in the houses in which the Taino *zemis* were worshipped: a "handsome, round table, made like a dish" (p. 22).

The principal rite of the Indians of Haiti was in honor of their earth goddess, who had several animal heads, and was attended by twin animal-spirits. In modern Haiti, the *baka* are man-eating animals; they have the red eyes of the Petro deities. We do not know what the attendant spirits of the earth goddess were called in Haiti, but in Yucatan the *bacab* were the four deities of the quarters, the earth-guardians, and the guardians of the waters which were symbolized in rites by water-jars with animal or human heads (pp. 137, 143-4 and 154). A magician in Haiti is known as a bocor. The owl, which is the familiar representation of Marinette, Brise, and other Petro deities is, again, a dominant figure of the Indian myths, being, particularly among the Orinocos, a bird of ill-omen (pp. 139, 170, 265, 268 and 274).

But the great patron deity of magic in Voudoun is Simbi, who is said to straddle the Rada and Petro sides. In the Petro context he is associated with Congo Zandor, is represented as a snake, is related to Quitta, and has an owl as familiar. As a kind of cross-roads deity, he is associated with Carrefour (the Petro equivalent of Legba); under their joint patronage talismans and soul-paquets are bound. Simbi is the patron of rains and of drinking waters, and as such duplicates Damballah. Indeed, it is only with difficulty that he can be co-ordinated with the Dahomean deities without overlapping their functions. Moreover, he is not neces- sarily malevolent, but rather magical. He has been traced, tentatively, to the Samba tribe, deep in Africa; but if he is actually of such provenience he would be the only representative of that tribe in Haiti, and this would hardly account for the importance of his position; for he ranks among the highest divinities of Voudoun. Herskovits remarks briefly that Simbi is a Congo deity; but it is not clear whether he means of Congo origin in Africa, or of the Congo nation in the new world (p. 268). The most logical possibility is, that Simbi is a new-world interpolation into the African tradition, derived from the slave-refugees in the Haitian hills, where the Indian *zemi* cult prevailed.

In sum: parallels enough exist, even on first viewing, to support the hypothesis of a powerful Indian strain in the Petro side of Voudoun, and many of the traits of Voudoun are more readily explained in these terms than by reference to Africa.

NOTES

(In these notes, works which are frequently cited are referred to by the author's name only; the title of the work is contained in the bibliography. When Rigaud is cited alone, it refers to the work of Odette Mennesson Rigaud; Rigaud-Denis refers to their joint work: "Ceremonie En l'Honneur de Marinette".)

CHAPTER I

[1] The sense of this anonymous heritage is especially well rendered in a ceremony described by Rigaud. In that instance the invocations to the dead included not only all the dead relatives of the woman (p. 15), but also, at a special rite for the dead, the following phrase: "To those whom I know and to those whom I don't know, to all the dead who belong to my family or who don't belong to my family, to all I give food" (p. 53).

[2] Simpson (I) has described death rites for persons of varying abilities and it is clear that the one for the houngan is the most elaborate. In another connection, he says: "I am sure that dead persons do become *loas*, and that in general those who attain this status are those who were prominent and powerful houngans"; and again: "Perhaps the essential thing is that a *serviteur* for whatever reason or reasons, has made an impression on his relatives or followers which is strong enough to cause them to think that he will surely outrank the ordinary dead and take his place among the important figures in the world which is known only imperfectly to the living" (II, p. 47). Simpson also relates the "degrada-tion" rites, which precede burial, to the special talents or abilities of the person (I). (Most other observers have concerned themselves primarily with death rites relating to the soul of the person and to the loa guardian.) Such special talents would subsequently characterize and determine the nature of the loa into which the ancestor might eventually evolve. Courlander (p. 238) also observes that "Any 'great' man may become one [a *loa*] if his descendants remember to make him one."

[3] Courlander (p. 27) has remarked that modern, or recent loa are generalized in their powers, whereas the ancient loa are more specifically defined in their functions, and that they seem "caricatures of special abilities". This observation would support the process here described. The recent loa would still retain the diversity of human personality whereas, in the case of the ancient loa, the "distillation" into archetype would have taken place.

⁴ The ritual of summoning the loa who is lodged in the govi is per-formed frequently, particularly by houngans and mambos who seek guidance for their work. The quality of the voice which emerges from the govi is truly impressive. Both Maximilien (p. 163) and Courlander (p. 113) have remarked upon it, and the latter has cited a song in which this ritual is mentioned.

⁵ Maximilien maintains that the act of placing a soul in a govi makes it a loa (p. 175). However, the distinction between the mere souls of the dead and the loa proper is that only the latter are able to possess a person. The souls of the dead that were placed in the govis in the cere-mony described in this chapter could not yet possess a person. This statement is emphasized as a condition of becoming loa by both Courlander (pp. 14-15 and 237) and Herskovits.

⁶ Courlander (pp. 14-15) and Herskovits have emphasized the idea that only those who have been possessed by loa can become loa. As an exclusive condition, this formula is virtually meaningless, since the loa are automatically inherited by everyone and it is rare, among those who practice Voudoun, to find people whose loa fail to manifest themselves, unless they have been formally dismissed.

⁷ Dessalines and other historical heroes of Haiti have been mentioned in invocations, but these have been addressed as spirits of the dead and there is no record of any of these historical figures possessing someone as loa. Rigaud cites the case of a woman, Mariline, who was possessed by a personal deity, a Captain Deba. Metraux (in his introductory notes to Rigaud's article, p. 5) says that this Captain Deba seems to have been an early lover of Mariline, who left her and the country a long time ago. Mariline, however, maintained that she did not know of such a person and that she inherited this loa, Captain Deba, from her father.

⁸ As quoted by Rigaud, this song goes on to mention Damballah Gienon (p. 25). Marcelin, however, quotes it with the phrase "Ayizan, old, old", instead of the Damballah reference, and precedes it by a stanza "Grandmother Ayizan, Saluez Legba! This is the moment that silver breaks rocks! We ask: how are you? Salute Legba!" Marcelin translates "argent" (silver) as a reference to money, but this is most unusual in a loa song, and, since it is immediately followed by the mirror reference, it would seem at least as likely to be a reference to the silvering of a mirror (p. 29).

⁹ Marcelin, pp. 42, 128.

¹⁰ Rigaud, p. 18.

¹¹ Herskovits also cites these movements in reverse (p. 183).

¹² Courlander (pp. 26–7) also says that the dead go to "zilet en bas de l'eau" (the island beneath the water); he cites a song that speaks of Grand Bois as master of that island (p. 137), and another speaking of a houngan making ready to go there (p. 110). He also cites the belief that if any one were to see these "beasts of the sea"—that is, the marine or insect forms —this would mean death (p. 27).

¹³ These gestures have been frequently misinterpreted as being a reference to the earth itself, the "Mother Earth" concept.

¹⁴ Maximilien, p. 155 and illustration 20, following p. 42.

¹⁵ Courlander (p. 129) also finds the concepts of the center-post and trees analogous in this connection.

¹⁶ For an illuminating discussion of the crucifixion as a coincidence of opposites, see Campbell (p. 260).

¹⁷ Courlander, p. 41.

¹⁸ Herskovits, pp. 203–4.

¹⁹ Rigaud, p. 56. The only possible explanation for the agelessness of the Marassa is that, being divine from the beginning (as distinguished from loa, which are souls that have become divine after the death of the person), they are not subject to the physical laws of the universe. Moreover, as twins they straddle the divide, and so remain half-human, half-divine, whereas if they were permitted to age and die they would belong exclusively to the world of the Invisibles and would become the same as any loa, thereby losing their special position as twins. Age is a process which would seem to occur to the physical being when, as in ordinary life conditions, it is separated from the metaphysical self.

²⁰ Herskovits (p. 200) particularly notes the close relationship between the Marassa and the Dead, and describes the ritual food offering for the Marassa which is given to children.

²¹ Actually, the Marassa are not considered, precisely, as loa, but as a divine category apart. The phrase cited here is from a ritual described by Rigaud (p. 17). Herskovits (p. 199) describes his efforts to determine which is the most important, the Marassa, the Dead, or the Loa, and receives answers that seem extremely contradictory. If, however, one understands these three as constituting a trinity, that is, three aspects of the same thing, the apparent contradiction between the replies disappears, and the fact that these different answers could be given testifies to the fact that since the three are different aspects of the same thing, there cannot be any definitive gradation in their importance. Several of the sentences

quoted as answers suffice to show the linkage between the three: "Twins
who have been dead a long time become loa"; "Those long dead become
loa"; "The Twins are stronger than the saints [loa]"; "The Twins are the
mother of saints [loa]"; "Everyone serves the Dead [therefore] the Dead
are strongest." Herskovits also cites the fact that in West African belief
the Twins and the Dead were linked as both having "passed through
the womb of woman" (p. 200).

22 The belief that the twins share a common soul is also cited by
Herskovits (p. 204). The Haitian concept of Marassa is comparable to
that of the twin heroes of the Navahos. Here the twins are shown, under
certain circumstances, as a hero and his mirrored reflection in the water.
The magician, or what would be, in Haiti, the soul, is the one in the
reflection, this being analogous to the Haitian belief that the world of the
Invisibles is on the other side of the mirror. Campbell points out that,
characterologically, the twins are distinguished as extra- and introvert;
the doer of deeds and the worker of magic; the killer of enemies and the
child of the water (cf. Jeff King, Maud Oakes, Joseph Campbell,
Where the Two Came to Their Father, The Bollingen Series I, New York,
1943, Plate XI).

23 Lorimer Denis refers to two statuettes, in the possession of the
Bureau of Ethnology, as being Marassa, male and female. The Marassa
vever contains symbols that would seem to represent male and female
principles, and this characteristic is true of the vevers that represent loa
who probably were originally hermaphroditic, such as Legba, etc.

24 Herskovits, p. 204.

25 Herskovits, pp. 89–91; Courlander, p. 104.

26 Maximilien, p. 87.

27 Rigaud, p. 17.

28 In the vever reproduced by Maximilien (illustration 4, following
p. 42) the figure representing the united male-female Marassa is very
similar to the vever for Legba (illustration 1), and it is very probable that
Legba in Africa was not only the loa of fertility but also a hermaphrodite.

29 It is significant that this child, who is actually the first human, is
considered "plus raide" (more powerful, hard, or stern) than the Twins
themselves, just as the houngan is, in a certain sense, more powerful than
the loa, since he can, to some extent, control them. This applies only
when referring to the demiurgic Twins, although the words dossu and
dossa are used for a child following ordinary twins. This is cited also by

Herskovits (p. 202) from his region, and also by observers from other regions.

[30] Courlander quotes such an extension by multiplication in a cere͘mony (p. 55). He also lists, in addition, Marassa Creole (as being Haitian in origin) and Marassa Guinée (of African origin). In another connection (p. 38) he defines Marassa Creole as being of the same sex, and Marassa Guinée as being of different sexes.

[31] According to Metraux the body, soul and spirit are represented by shadows. The regular shadow is the "ombre cadavre"; under certain circumstances of light, there is a double shadow, and this is understood to be the gros͘bon͘ange and the ti͘bon͘ange.

[32] It is an acknowledged fact that "un͘natural" or magic deaths do occur, and that a state of trance, or zombie͘ism, also exists. Walter B. Cannon (*American Anthropologist*, Vol. 44, No. 2, April–June, 1942), in an article entitled "Voodoo Death", cites instances from many regions, including lower Nigeria, of persons being "bewitched" into death. He concludes that it is an actual death which is caused by shock and the effect of fear upon the adrenalin system. Zombie͘ism is apparently recognized by the Criminal Code of Haiti (according to William Sea͘brook, p. 103, who quotes from Article 249 as follows): "Also shall be qualified as attempted murder the employment which may be made against any person of substances, which, without causing actual death, produce a lethargic coma more or less prolonged. If, after the administering of such substances, the person has been buried, the act shall be considered murder no matter what result follows."

[33] Courlander says that a zombie is the "negative after image" which has refused to be separated from the body after death (p. 18) and that the soul is a zombie (p. 26). These statements would seem to imply that the zombie is a spiritual being. This is not the usual understanding, for one of the functions of a zombie is to work as slave laborer in keeping with the belief that the zombie is a physical being without its own spiritual essence, and in the power of another psychic. Metraux, for example, says that a zombie is a person whose gros͘bon͘ange has been stolen and that the possibility of such a theft is one of the dangers involved in en͘trusting one's soul, in a container, to someone else.

[34] Metraux cites an amusing anecdote (pp. 85–6) illustrating the truth͘fulness of the ti͘bon͘ange—sometimes called *ti͘Zange*. He also refers to the belief that it hovers over the corpse for nine days and then goes to heaven, and describes the ceremony intended to restore strength to the *ti͘Zange*.

[35] The fact that the soul and the loa are but different stages of the same essence, that they are both lodged in pots, both called esprits etc., and that their liberation from the corpse is almost simultaneously achieved has created a confusion in scholarly intepretation.

Metraux has interpreted the ceremony as referring exclusively to the loa, with the implication that the gros-bon-ange is self-liberating. Herskovits does not cite such a ceremony in his chapter on the Dead, but says that the loa must be sealed in a jar to prevent it from going under water. Courlander (p. 237) says that the Mystère is put into a canari which is broken nine days later to put the loa at liberty. Simpson speaks of *dessounin* as applying to any special talent, which would be the gros-bon-ange, and tells both of the breaking of a canari at the cross-roads, and, in the case of a houngan's death, of the sealing of a loa into a canari for "transmission".

He specifically disagrees with Herskovits and Courlander about removing the loa in order to prevent the soul from becoming a loa (why would one seek to prevent this?) and believes that it is not the loa which is removed, but the ability to become possessed by loa. (Simpson does not, however, make the logical inference, namely, that the gros-bon-ange represents this ability to become possessed by a loa, or, in other words, is the divine potential of a person.)

My own interpretation is corroborated by Maximilien, who speaks of the function of *dessounin* as the separation of the loa maît-tête from the immortal soul or gros-bon-ange (p. 171). His description of the ceremony he witnessed is the most detailed available and includes an action of the houngan over the navel of the corpse, which would seem to be the moment of the liberation of the loa. (In this connection Campbell's discussion (p. 44) which relates the cross-roads, the navel, and the Yoruba God of Death, Edshu, is especially interesting.) Maximilien recounts that the gros-bon-ange is gathered into the pot-de-tête, the deceased having been an initiate (for non-initiates, having no pot-de-tête, one is made up for this purpose) and this pot is deposited at the cross-roads so that the soul may find its way to the abysmal waters. It is significant that a *mangé Morts* and sometimes a *bruler-zin* preceded this liberation of the gros-bon-ange, as if to feed and warm it in provision for its disagreeable period in the abysmal waters. The confusion in reference to loa being placed in a govi, presumably to be "remitted" or restrained (Herskovits), overlooks the fact that loa are inherited at birth (making Simpson's "remission" unnecessary) and that a govi would hardly suffice to restrain a loa, since that requires special and elaborate ceremonies. My impression is that a govi does not confine a loa, at all, but provides it with a throat, so that it can henceforth be directly invoked for consultations. What is remitted, therefore, is the *voice* of the loa. For both the houngan (in Simpson's account) and the family (which Herskovits describes) such a govi would be a valuable possession as a religious accessory.

[36] This is also cited by Metraux.

[37] Maximilien (p. 9) says that the ancient Egyptian myth of the separation of the waters of the depths from the waters of the surface was conserved in the mythology of the Yorubas, who have contributed much to Voudoun. It would be impossible to determine absolutely whether this is the historical source of the Haitian belief. However, it is clear from the way the Haitian talks about these waters that they are the same as those which, in other mythologies, are termed the "abysmal waters". While a certain confusion with oceanic waters does exist, no Haitian would say that the dead went to the bottom of the Atlantic Ocean and when the Haitian is pressed into localizing and locating these waters, he may give any kind of answer that involves water since, indeed, all waters are related. The loa Simbi-en-deux-eaux, who is considered a particularly powerful figure, and especially related to magical power, is referred to as straddling the two waters. These are explained as being the sweet (he is guardian loa of rain) and the salt. And these are, by extension, the waters above and below the earth, as they are distinguished in Egyptian and other mythologies. A figure with such a span would, logically, be very powerful.

[38] Maximilien (pp. 175 ff) believes that this canopy is actually an element derived from Egyptian rites of resurrection. Although the historical link would be difficult to establish absolutely, the two symbols may well represent the same principle. The idea is one that is common to many mythologies.

[39] Metraux cites a *retirer d'en bas de l'eau* ceremony which is, in many details similar to the one here cited. Particularly, he records an incident where a soul arrives but for whom no govi is available. Maximilien (pp. 177 ff) also records such a ceremony in detail.

CHAPTER II

[1] Herskovits, who seems to have encountered more Christian influence in Mirebalais than other writers working elsewhere, has the most extended references to the prêt-savanne and his functions, particularly in his chapter on Catholicism and Voudoun.

² Leo Frobenius and Douglas C. Fox, *African Genesis*, New York, 1937, pp. 215 ff.

³ Courlander, p. 39 (12).

⁴ Denis, p. 24 (1).

⁵ For a discussion of this High God idea by a number of Christian missionaries, cf. Edwin W. Smith (ed.), *African Ideas of God, A Symposium*, London, 1950.

⁶ Denis, p. 25.

⁷ All writers on Voudoun include lists of saints who have been so identified with the loa. Herskovits particularly has an extended list (pp. 279–80) of such identifications. Since the identifications are made on a superficial basis they obviously differ from locale to locale, and for the same reason, these differences are of only very minor importance.

⁸ They even say that the church bells ring for Legba, so that he will open the way. This phrase is quoted by Herskovits (p. 288) in his chapter on Voudoun and the Church (pp. 267–91). The sense of Herskovits' entire chapter is that Christianity has had a strong influence on Voudoun, but it is difficult to understand how he expects us to follow this conclusion when much of his data, like the phrase quoted above, would seem to indicate the reverse, namely, the assimilation of Christianity by Voudoun. Herskovits' method is to question informants and to base himself upon their formulations. The Haitian peasant, however, has been subject to four centuries of intensive propaganda to the effect that he *ought* to be a Christian; he has been severely punished for practicing Voudoun; and he has been especially impressed with the fact that his practices are "stupid" or "savage", and that he absolutely must not let strangers know about Voudoun. All of this has created in his mind almost a schism between the Christian formulations that he has learned to recite when questioned by authorities or strangers, and his actual beliefs and practices. Even when he has no intention to deceive, his sense of pride, his determination to be "civilized" and "intelligent", lead him, when questioned, to give the answer which he imagines would be respected as "proper" by the one who questions. Or he may, as I have stated in my introduction, "translate" Voudoun concepts into Christian terms without being aware of the discrepancies. The very vocabulary that is used in many of the phrases that Herskovits quotes indicates that most of his peasants were inclined to give him the "proper" answers, not with any intention to deceive, but rather with the intention to impress. And the most "proper" answers are those that they have heard in

church from the only other white men with whom they have had much contact, the Catholic priests.

[9] Rigaud, pp. 14-15.

[10] Simpson cites a ritual for "dismissing" loa ritualistically. They are summoned, fed and sent away.

[11] While the inheritance of loa is automatic (Maximilien, p. 165), it is usually accompanied by rituals of varying degrees of elaboration. (Herskovits, p. 94; Denis, Bulletin, March 1947.)

[12] Denis, p. 1.

[13] These are listed by Herskovits (pp. 18-22; 267-8) and Courlander (p. 3), among others.

[14] Herskovits, p. 140; Courlander, p. 6.

[15] Courlander, pp. 102, 40. Herskovits, pp. 263, 267-8 (16-17).

[16] Courlander, p. 29.

[17] Campbell (pp. 81-5) discusses other mythologies in which daemons, when placated, are good.

[18] Maximilien, pp. 42 ff.

[19] Maximilien, p. 134.

[20] Rigaud-Denis.

[21] Herskovits, pp. 59-61.

[22] Both Herskovits (pp. 220 ff) and Maximilien (p. 149) make a somewhat similar distinction between religion and magic.

[23] This very common practice is also cited by Courlander (p. 22). In this connection, the left hand serves Petro. That is, a vever drawn for Petro will be drawn with the left hand. This is not to be confused with the mirror reversal mentioned in the first chapter, which takes place between the visible and invisible worlds.

[24] This distinction is elaborated by Courlander in his discussions of Haitian dance and music.

[25] Courlander, p. 28.

[26] Courlander refers to Damballah as feathered, or plumed, tracing this to Dahomey, p. 33.

[27] Maximilien (pp. 91-2) comments on the method of religion absorbing various rituals but retaining its own integrity. He speaks of "Indian, European and African" elements as having been fused together into Voudoun. "The African contribution, in spite of the delicacy

necessary to dissociate it from that of the Island aborigines because of the great similarity between the two cultures, seems so important that it may be said that Voudoun . . . is African." He points out that although the Dahomean and Yoruba rituals predominate, those of other tribes are also included.

[28] Rigaud cites another case where a single individual had "ramassé" (gathered) all the loa of the family (p. 11).

[29] The idea of psychic force is sometimes described in the word "poin" (point) which would seem to be a reference to the point of intersection at which the psychic energy from the world of the invisible is transmitted to the visible, material world. To say that a certain loa "marcher sur 'poin' Rada" is to indicate his source, or connection. To speak of a chanson "poin" is to refer to a song that makes some very direct and precise reference, the most explicit kind of contact between a man of this world and a loa of the other world. Courlander (pp. 96–9) has written an excellent exposition of this "poin" concept.

[30] At first glance it may seem erroneous to place the loa of agriculture in a minor position but this is explained and elaborated in the chapter on the pantheon.

CHAPTER III

[1] Most writers on Haiti do, indeed, refer to Voudoun as an animistic religion, but, having done so, do not subsequently elaborate upon it from this point of view. Denis, however, has conscientiously applied the concept to the pantheon (Denis I, p. 21.) and has indeed eliminated major loa in so doing, although he refers to these in other connections. A similar misinterpretation exists in reference to the many ritualistic gestures addressed toward the ground. These, as has been pointed out (p. 36), are addressed not to the spirit *of* the earth, in the Mother Earth sense, but to the waters of the abyss below the earth, which is the source and residence of all loa.

It is possible that other primitive religions have been similarly misunderstood, as animistic in the accepted sense, and that the divinities removed from the pantheons by such Procrustean operations have been consequently lost by mythological record.

For the discussion of trees as *avenues* for the loa, see p. 36.

[2] Levy-Bruhl's discussion of "primitive mentality" is characteristic of the approach which ignores the necessary pragmatism of primitive cultures and fails to concede that the primitive is capable of distinguishing

between principle and phenomena, possibly because that distinction is couched in terms different from those of European culture. He writes: "Their mental activity was a mystic one . . . implies belief in forces and influences and actions which, though imperceptible to sense, are never-theless real . . . the reality is itself mystical . . ." (p. 7) and elsewhere, "The primitive makes no distinction between this world and the other, between what is actually present to sense, and what is beyond. He actually dwells with invisible spirits and intangible forces. To him it is these that are real and actual" (p. 32). Contrast this Hindu statement: "Though He is hidden in all things, that Soul shines not forth; yet He is seen by subtle seers with superior, subtle intellect" (Katha Upanishad, 3 : 12).

³ Levy-Bruhl contrasts the European notion of a world which is "ordered by cause and effect" with that of the primitive, in whose world "all objects and all entities are involved in a system of mystic participa-tions and exclusions; it is these which constitute its cohesion and its order" (p. 35), and "What appears accidental to us Europeans is, in 'reality', always the manifestation of a mystic power which makes itself felt in this way by the individual or by the social group" (p. 43). But to the primitive these "mystic powers" (which are analogous to invisible principles) *are* causes, and, in excluding the possibility of accident, the primitive is much more consistent in a concept of a world completely "ordered by cause and effect", than the European. Levy-Bruhl, in fact, would seem to define as "mystic" any causation which he *understands, believes or knows to be not the true cause.* Logically, then, he would be obliged to term "mystic" those scientifically established causes which subsequent investigation reveals to have been incorrectly or inadequately determined.

Malinowski expresses the primitive idea of pervasive causation—the essential interrelation of all phenomena—as follows: ". . . it brings down a vague but great apprehension to the compass of a trivial, domestic reality. . . . Elements of human error, or guilt, and of mischance assume great proportions. Elements of fate, or destiny and of the inevitable are, on the other hand, brought down to the dimension of human mistakes" (pp. 76-7). This is an excellent statement of the manner in which the concept of a completely integrated and "motivated" universe tends to "level" the significance of all experience, so that the intimate detail ranks with the large phenomenon as being equally an expression of cosmic forces. But Malinowski subsequently would seem to interpret magic as a response to "chance and accident", which is absent "wherever the pursuit is certain, reliable and well under the control of rational methods and technological processes" (p. 81). It would seem necessary, however, to point out that, to the Haitian primitive, at least, "lack of control" results from insufficient *connaissance*—knowledge—of the divine processes involved and of how they might be controlled, rather than from the arbitrary or accidental nature of the universe.

[4] In certain passages Malinowski sees the function of religion as primarily a moral adjustment. "Myth fulfills, in primitive culture, an indispensable function: it expresses, enhances, and codifies belief; it safe-guards and enforces morality; it vouches for the efficiency of ritual and contains practical rules for the guidance of man. . . ." (p. 19). As such, Malinowski considers it "an indispensable ingredient of all culture" (p. 92). But in another connection he seems to assert that it is a com-pensation for inadequate scientific analysis and technological control of the physical universe. "We do not find magic wherever the pursuit is certain, reliable, and well under the control of rational methods and technological processes. . . . The integral cultural function of magic . . . consists in the bridging over of gaps and inadequacies in highly important activities not yet completely mastered by man. . . . Magic is thus akin to science in that it always has a definite aim intimately associated with human instincts, needs and pursuits. . . ." (pp. 81-2). The implication would seem to be that scientific, technological progress would somehow automatically and simultaneously comprehend a moral authority and directive for its benevolent and proper administration and that it would thus eliminate the need for myth or religion as a separate moral system once the technological inadequacies, for which it compensated, were eliminated. This nineteenth-century confidence in the positive moral nature of material progress can almost be formulated, in retrospect, as a belief that science and technology are infused or animated by a benevolent spirit. Such confidence, which the pragmatic, realistic primitive only guardedly extends to the cosmic forces and attends with a complex system of corrective vigilance and persuasion, has unfortunately proven to be completely illusory in reference to man. It is even possible that, in encouraging the devaluation of moral systems as distinctive and valid constructs, this unreserved confidence in science and technology con-tributed to the contemporary situation in which the inadequacy of moral values and authority is the more alarming inasmuch as that every technological progress has created forces for which moral control is more imperatively necessary than ever before.

[5] It has been said that there are seven of each divinity, and this may refer to the original major nations, but the number of aspects of each divinity is now much greater. (Herskovits, pp. 149 and 310; Courlander, pp. 26-47; and Maximilien, pp. 101 and 105, where invocations are cited, list the prevalent nations.) Some family lines would seem to be

indicated in recurrent names such as Dantor, while others may be symbolized by the crab, the owl, the torch (La Flambeau), which may be family totems.

[6] While there remains no explicit reference to Legba as the sun divinity, his functions and character as a whole, as well as vestigial references in songs and rituals, make such an identification logical. He belonged to the Dahomean Sky Pantheon (Herskovits, p. 20), while in certain districts of Haiti a special bonfire is lit for him, and when he possesses a person he is known to walk in fire (Herskovits, pp. 160, 174). The ritual "re-heating" of the sun with bonfires and the identification of the sun and fire are practically universal in mythology, and a similar connection is indicated here. Another common mythological identification is that of the sun, as the supreme cosmic force, with the king, as supreme among humans; which is almost always attended by a taboo, prohibiting the king from being touched by the sun (Frazer, p. 600) and necessitating that the king be covered by canopies or wear a hat out of doors. There exists several references to Legba as king (Marcelin, p. 21, has noted one such example). Moreover, Legba is known to wear always a large hat and this characteristic, in the light of a phrase which occurs in a frequently heard song—"You who wore a hat in Guinée, you who shaded the loa from the sun" (quoted by Marcelin, p. 18, and Courlander, pp. 75-6)—is undoubtedly a reference to the Dahomean version of such a taboo. In invocations to Legba (Maximilien, illustration 1 following p. 42) there occur words such as "claironde" (round brightness?) and "kataroulo" (four wheels of the sun-chariot?), which, in view of all the other indications, would seem to be oblique references to Legba as sun.

[7] It is very common in mythologies for the first or major divinity or principle to be androgynous. Campbell (pp. 152-4) cites instances and discusses them. In Haiti such a concept is related to the Marassa (*supra*, p. 40) and to Ghede, who is sometimes dressed in androgynous fashion. Courlander (p. 10) describes a ceremony in which the drummer was dressed partially in male and partially in female dress, but does not identify the loa involved. The symbol for the Marassa, when presented as united, and that of Legba are sometimes drawn in almost identical fashion. (Maximilien, illustrations 1 and 4, following p. 42). Denis (I, p. 26) quotes a phrase from a prayer: "O Bon Dieu, Maman moin", which extends this androgynous concept even to Christian divinity.

[8] These phrases are from prayers cited by Herskovits (p. 89). References to the opening of gates or roads are formulations specifically related to Legba.

[9] It is agreed by almost all writers that Legba was god of fertility in Africa. Courlander (p. 35) goes into some detail in this connection. It is also possible that the ritualist libation for Legba, which precedes all others, is related to seminal waters.

[10] Maximilien (p. 34) and Marcelin (p. 16) also refer to his relation to the center-post.

[11] These songs, are cited by Herskovits (p. 173) and Rigaud (p. 25), respectively. In this latter song, "learn the secrets" is the translation given the phrase "Sondé miroir" by Rigaud and Metraux, as rendering the true sense of the expression.

[12] Cited by Marcelin (p. 18). Such omniscience is usually attributed to the god of the underworld, Ghede, and, indeed, as will be pointed out, Legba and Ghede are very close together.

[13] Herskovits, p. 30.

[14] One of Legba's titles is *Grand Chemin*, and Courlander (pp. 36 and 82) also interprets this as the road to the other world.

[15] Rigaud (p. 17) and Herskovits (p. 174), respectively.

[16] Herskovits (p. 30) makes Legba a divinity of "accident", on the grounds that he offers a "way out" from worldly destiny. Insofar as Legba is the point of contact with the other world, he is "a way out", but the divine intervention which would be the reward for ritual supplication or the bringing out of daemons by magical invocation, would hardly constitute accident in the eyes of the Haitian, who ascribes everything to the logical action of the Mystères. Herskovits also points out that *Fa* was a divining cult in Dahomey, the divination there being achieved through the patterns of sixteen kernels; but elsewhere mirrors, crystals and other means have been used and these latter may be related to the mirror references in songs to Legba and other loa.

[17] Herskovits, p. 174.

[18] Marcelin, p. 17.

[19] Marcelin, p. 17.

[20] Marcelin, p. 16.

[21] Such a possession is described by Rigaud (pp. 26–7).

[22] A pipe and tobacco are among the inevitable accoutrements of Legba.

[23] In a song cited by Marcelin (p. 16), this statement is made: "Attibon Legba has come to the gate, How old he is! Papa Legba has come to the cross-roads. . . ."

[24] Legba is linked to Grand Bois both by Courlander (p. 44) and in an invocation cited by Maximilien (opposite illustration 1, following p. 42).

[25] Legba Avradra is described as a wandering vagabond (which is a characterization typical of Ghede) by Herskovits (p. 315) and the same idea is implied in a song cited by Marcelin (p. 18).

[26] Courlander, pp. 36 and 99.

[27] Courlander (p. 37) places "Kalfu" under Rada as an aspect of Legba; Maximilien (p. 106) relates Carrefour and Legba, but elsewhere (p. 42, ill. 19) indicates that Carrefour is invoked by the same formula as that used for Simbi. Simpson (II) lists Carrefour as of Haitian (new-world or Petro) origin.

[28] Though such a distinction is not always made, it is present in vevers, at times, and apparent in those reproduced by Maximilien (Illustrations 1 and 19 following p. 42). Another interesting differentiation is observed in the sacrifice of cocks. When killed for Legba, it is customary to use a white cock, and twist its neck. For Carrefour (in at least one hounfor) a black cock is set on fire at the cross-roads (recalling the regenerating bonfire for Legba) at midnight, and let run flaming along the road.

[29] Courlander (p. 22) cites the destruction of a man's virility and a woman's fecundity as among the evils which these daemons can perform.

[30] Herskovits (pp. 225–37) gives a detailed description of the ritual fashioning of such a garde, which, in fact, is generally considered essential.

[31] Although there are minor variations, this seems to be the classic attitude for Carrefour, and is similarly described by Maximilien (p. 134).

[32] Other aspects of Legba have been cited as follows: Legba-Ibo (Denis I); Legba-Petro (Courlander, p. 44); Legba-Congo (Rigaud, p. 22); and Sousou Panman (Simpson II), who would seem to be a malevolent Legba, being also characterized as old, covered with sores, wearing odd, mixed clothing, and having no fixed abode.

[33] According to Herskovits (p. 30), Legba was associated with the soul, as well as, the destiny of man. This indicates that he may have been Lord of the Underworld in Africa.

[34] Rigaud (p. 49). Ghede is sometimes written "Gede" or "Guédé". Nimbo is also written "Nibo".

[35] Rigaud (p. 49). It is also noteworthy that magic under Ghede is undertaken during the period of the new moon (Maximilien, p. 185), which is the rising night sun.

[36] Maximilien (pp. 119–25) believes Ghede to be derived from Egyptian Osiris, and it is significant that one of his names is Khensou, an Egyptian deity. A statue of this Egyptian deity (Khonsu) is at the Cleveland Museum of Art. (F 19 2. 14.)

[37] This is also cited by Maximilien, p. 174.

[38] Cited by Herskovits, pp. 164–5.

[39] Both Rigaud (p. 50) and Herskovits (pp. 194–5) cite this song and comment upon its eerie quality.

[40] Rigaud (p. 48) and others cite this characteristic. It is this indiscretion on the part of Ghede which leads to Herskovits' observation that Ghede is "tolerated rather than favored" (p. 318). He further remarks that the other loa leave at once, should Ghede arrive, and, characterizing Ghede as himself a zombie, attributes this repulsion on the part of both loa and people to a desire not to mingle with the Dead. It is difficult, however, to grasp the logic of this interpretation since, on the one hand, the loa are all spirits of dead ancestors themselves, while the living serviteur is constantly occupied with establishing contact with spirits of the dead. They would not be repelled by the dead, *per se*, but by the falsely dead, malevolent zombies. However, while Herskovits himself cites songs and incidents in which Ghede does not appear as a malevolent figure, his summary portrait of Ghede, in the Appendix, indicates that he does not consider him a full-fledged loa. However, no other writers have considered him so minor a figure. As a matter of fact, the loa will leave whenever they wish to protest against ceremonial disorder *per se*, not only when Ghede may be the cause of such disorder. If Ghede does not appear for competitive or disorderly purposes, if he is quiet and well-behaved (admittedly a rare discretion on his part), his presence is not at all resented.

[41] Maximilien (p. 175) interprets the tail coat as a symbol evolved from the animal skin, which, in Osirian rites, was the winding sheet of the king.

[42] These are his universally recognized identifications, cited by Courlander (pp. 15–17) and others. Simpson (II) says he is armed with a knife for beating people, and this would obviously seem to be a phallic symbol.

[43] Courlander (pp. 16–17) has written a moving description of Ghede in this kind, paternal aspect, and has used the apt phrase, "Death is Positive", in reference to Ghede. This has been my experience, and that of other observers, although Herskovits makes no mention of a benevolent Ghede.

[44] Courlander, p. 88.

[45] Maximilien (p. 185) has a detailed account of the making of such *paquets*.

[46] Ghede is referred to as a heavenly judge by Courlander (p. 87) and his just refusal to dig a grave is cited by Herskovits (p. 247). In Ghede's altar chamber there is sometimes a scale for weighing the soul, and Maximilien makes reference to this. These scales are probably an inter-polation, as symbol, from medieval European magic. Dorsainville, in speaking of Mawu-Lisa says that while Mawu (this divinity is from the Fons) does not partake of life, he does judge after death. This weighing of good and evil proceeds by conceiving of a man as a stick, good on one end and bad on the other, and the stick is balanced at death for judgement. The scales, therefore, may be of African origin, at least in principle, and the straight stick which Ghede often carries as a cane but never leans upon (in the manner of Legba), may be at once a phallic symbol and a means of weighing souls. On the other hand, the entire interpretation of the judgement of souls may stem from the Christian concepts of the observers since, in fact, any soul may be reclaimed from the abysmal waters without undergoing such judgement, and, moreover, the presumably malevolent, or bad, Petro loa were reclaimed under the sign of Ghede and were not made to "suffer for their sins".

[47] Courlander (p. 87) also cites Ghede as a protector of children and cites a song in which his generally protective rôle is apparent in that he is asked "to guard the loa's children". The *maringuin* drum which is particularly related to Ghede, is also known as a children's toy. It is also possible that, as guardian of the history of the race, the continuity of its loa-lines, he is particularly interested in seeing that a child does not die before it has developed a soul which can be immortal. It is significant that in Haiti a child's death is attended by very little ritual or ritual-mourning.

[48] It would appear that Ghede has more aspects than any other loa. Among those listed by Courlander are Gedevi, Gede Mazaca (a possible relation to the agricultural loa Azacca), Ghede Zeclai and Ghede L'Oraille (as possible references to the Sky Pantheon), Baron La Croix and Azagon La Croix (these are mainly related to the cemetery and to magic rather than to eroticism) and Baron Piquant (listed as a Petro, Quitta Chéche loa). Denis lists some dozen Ghedes, among them Brav, Omsou (or probably Khensou), L'Oraille, etc. Maximilien lists Baron La Croix and a Ghede Zariguin (Spider) as Petro aspects. Rigaud identifies Ghede (which she spells Guédé) L'Oraille as a Petro loa (pp. 15–16). Simpson (II) describes a loa Limba which is nude,

lascivious and a glutton, and this would seem to be a malevolent Ghede. Simpson also lists him as being of new-world origin. Herskovits, on the other hand, says that Gede onsu is a Dahomean totem (p. 267) and says elsewhere (p. 318): "There are a number of deities whose names are compounded with the name of Gede—Gedenibo, Gedeonsu, Gedehun —and hence the question whether or not this is a generic term or a specific designation is pertinent." For a discussion of Ghede's origins and history, see the Appendix on Indian influences preceding these notes.

[49] The "bassin" is a pool, constructed specifically for such sacred use, and ranging from a few feet square, inside the hounfor, to swimming-pool size. Marcelin (p. 58) cites several songs referring to the bassin, as does Courlander.

[50] Herskovits (p. 171) cites a case of a Damballah who speaks clearly and a good deal. (The song cited in connection with this possession, however, refers to Shango, usually understood as an Ogoun family loa.) It is conceivable that there exists an articulate aspect of Damballah, but among the many Damballahs I have seen, only a few were capable even of rare, partially intelligible phrases, and other observers concur with my impression. Marcelin (p. 55) cites a Damballah song which specifically states: "The serpent cannot speak . . ." and this seems a highly reasonable assertion.

[51] This is the definition given to this Dahomean word (also written *Dan*) in the Dictionary of Folklore. Marcelin (p. 55) refers to fecundity as one of Damballah's functions and makes the point, as others do, that a devout serviteur, man or woman, will remain chaste on the day dedicated to him. Rigaud (p. 37) makes brief reference to a legendary "affair" with Erzulie. Nevertheless, fecundity in reference to Damballah, has an almost abstract, primal connotation, rather than one of a sexual nature. Chastity, as a form of minor ordeal comparable to fasting, is universally observed, on occasion, for all the major deities and does not constitute a specifically sexual reference.

[52] At the International Folklore Congress in Chicago in 1893 a Mary Alicia Owen reported on "Voodooism" as if it were fairly prevalent in that area and cited the following "Voodoo" myth of origin: That "Old Sun" (the first divinity) "squatted down on the bank of a great river and began to make all sorts of birds . . . and tore a fragment from his body and flung it into the weeds . . . where it became the Great Rattlesnake." Although the tone and form of her report do not conform to modern scholastic form, there is no doubt but that the stories she

quotes are accurately reported, and the incident cited above gives a logical connection to Legba and Damballah.

[53] In the Dictionary of Folklore, Aido Hwedo is defined as a male snake in Dahomey. In Haiti, however, she is definitely a female, and is considered the wife of Damballah. They are almost always represented together. Marcelin cites informants to the effect that a rainbow is under stood as a snake, and, in another connection, quotes a story to the effect that when the rainbow touches the sea it is evidence of Ayida's "affair" with Agwé. This single reference to her promiscuity is not in keeping with her character and her respectable and respected position. A further elaboration of her character, in relation to that of Erzulie, Goddess of Love, is given on pp. 115–16, *supra.* Dorsainville (p. 22) refers to her as "Soleil de la terre."

[54] For an excellent discussion of the World Egg concept in mythology, see Campbell (p. 276).

[55] The drinking of the egg without the use of the hands is unanimously recorded. Rigaud (p. 37) gives a description in which Damballah's head is carefully hidden by a white cloth while he is eating, a practice which I have also observed. Frazer (pp. 198 and 199) cites what is undoubtedly the origin of this practice, a taboo based on the fear that a man's soul might leave or an evil spirit might enter, through the mouth. The Ewe people of the Slave Coast eat and drink in complete privacy. In Loango, it was a capital offense to see the king eat or drink, and the same is true of the king of Dahomey: "when he drinks in public . . . on extraordinary occasions, he hides himself behind a curtain, or handkerchiefs are held up around his head. . . ." Such a tracing of loa sacred practices with ancient royal taboos (the hat of Legba was another) further illuminates the relationship of loa to royal ancestors.

[56] The Wedos would seem to be a royal family. Courlander, for example, cites an Agao Wedo (p. 30) who works in a garden and a Gran Wedo (p. 35) who is his mother.

[57] Sobo and Badé (as Badessy is sometimes called) are both children of Mawu-Lisa and members of what has been termed the Sky Pantheon of Dahomey. In songs they are related to Damballah (Rigaud, p. 11), Agwé (Courlander, p. 32), Gran Erzulie (Marcelin, p. 97) and Agassou (Maximilien, p. 103). Maximilien also cites the invocation to Sobo as identical with that to Damballah, and in the same invocation Agarou Tonnerre is given the family name Wedo (p. 42) and elsewhere (p. 57) is described as an animal "without blood" which climbs trees, i.e. a snake.

[58] The theme of gathering up the past occurs frequently in songs. Rigaud (p. 37) has cited one in which Damballah is requested to "gather the family".

[59] Cited by Courlander (p. 19). Maximilien (illustration 18, following p. 42) which is a cross-roads vever, similar to that for Legba, but contains no serpent.

[60] This is quoted by Maximilien (p. 155) and indicates the order of difference between Rada and Petro, as well as the emotional color of Petro.

[61] According to Herskovits (p. 160-2) this is his major function. Herskovits lists him as a Congo deity (p. 267) and elsewhere includes him in the Baka Squad (p. 241).

This again is evidence of his probably Indian origin, which is discussed in the Appendix on Indian influence.

[62] These relationships are evident in general, and, for specific example, in songs cited by Herskovits (p. 164).

[63] There is considerable disagreement about the overlapping and placement of these names and figures. Maximilien (p. 156), Marcelin (p. 64), Rigaud-Denis (I, p. 14) and Courlander make somewhat conflicting statements. The very existence of such confusion would indicate, it seems to me, that all of these are essentially of the same family and perhaps even the same figure.

[64] Cited in Rigaud-Denis (I, p. 14), again indicating that Petro is not a simple moral opposite to Rada.

[65] Agwé seems to be related to Sobo and Badé (Courlander, p. 31 and in litanies cited by Maximilien, p. 102); Sobo is also related to Agassou (Maximilien, p. 103). Maximilien traces Agwé to an Egyptian king (p. 103). Marcelin (p. 107) speaks of his aspects as admiral and minister of the Navy, and in that connection relates him to Dessalines, Haitian revolutionary hero. He also cites a legend (p. 104) of slaves being able to escape on the back of a fish, presumably Agwé. Denis is the only one who mentions a Petro version of Agwé—Agwé Ge-Rouge—but this seems very illogical since the Petro emphasis on both fire and agriculture would be extremely antagonistic to Agwé's nature. Rigaud cites a phrase "Toni Agwé" (p. 38), which might possibly be a reference to Indian myths (see Appendix B).

[66] Campbell (pp. 87-8) discusses the thunderbolt as symbol of psychic or magic power.

[67] The African mythological origins of Ogoun are given by Courlander (p. 37–8) and Maximilien (p. 13), among others. Herskovits (p. 267) gives his derivation also, and relates him to the African Shango.

[68] The phrase "cord cuts cord", a cryptic suggestion of magical manipulations, occurs frequently in songs about him. (Courlander, p. 78.)

[69] Courlander (pp. 40–1), Herskovits (pp. 280 and 317) and Rigaud (pp. 42–8) all mention the various aspects of Ogoun and characterize them. Rigaud's detailed account of an Ogoun possession includes many keen observations and much information, and is altogether an exceptionally good presentation of Ogoun's character.

[70] Courlander (p. 12) describes a similar possession, with its "period" accessories.

[71] This particular loa was observed in only one hounfor and may have been a personal loa of the mambo, who, significantly enough, was known to enjoy special privileges—in reference to ceremonial permits, etc.—as a result of her political "connections".

[72] This is true at least in the vicinity of Port-au-Prince, which is the political center of Haiti. Such membership seems to be associated somewhat with the sense of priestcraft. It is also in the tradition of the secret societies which were a prevalent African institution and which were undoubtedly maintained, at least as a tradition, in the new world.

On one occasion the vever of Ogoun was accompanied by another vever which consisted of a large hand and other symbols and this was explained as the Masonic symbol of the Hand of God.

[73] Courlander (pp. 45 and 78) cites these Petro Ogouns, and other writers have recorded others, but they all seem to play a relatively minor rôle in the Petro hierarchy.

[74] The linking of Mounanchou to the Ogoun family was first suggested in the characteristic spraying of rum, which is peculiar to the Ogoun family. Furthermore, Courlander (p. 45) lists a Nanchou from the Leogone district, which he identifies as a Petro loa, a warrior deity. Such a linkage is supported by the entire character and function of Mounanchou, who could be logically related to none of the other major divinities.

[75] One of the terms used in the invocation cited by Maximilien (illustration 11, following p. 42).

[76] Herskovits (p. 236) cites a song which contains this phrase, and gives other descriptions of Bossu on pp. 160–2, 164, 170, 197 and 319.

[77] This story is cited by Courlander (p. 31) as a legend collected by Herskovits.

[78] La Sirène, who is understood as an aspect of Erzulie, is specifically related to Agwé, and is pictured as a mermaid. According to Marcelin (pp. 19–22) she is said to steal children and take them to the bottom either of the sea or of a stream, but also is known to bring them up. In Maximilien (p. 101) she is related to Gran Danguy, which would seem to establish her relationship to Ayida, Damballah's female counterpart, the rainbow or snake which goes into the water. Most significantly, however, La Sirène is related to La Balaine (whale), a figure which is rarely elaborated. Marcelin feels that it is a male deity, but Campbell's interpretation of the whale as a sea-womb symbol (pp. 90–4, 207–8) seems to explain La Balaine much more satisfactorily. Courlander also lists an "Ezilie Balianne" (p. 47).

[79] Erzulie is usually identified with the Mater Dolorosa. There are many aspects of Erzulie, however, and these are identified with various saints. La Sirène is identified with Notre Dame de Grâce (Herskovits, p. 279); Gran Erzulie, understood sometimes as a separate aspect of Erzulie and sometimes as an older stage of Erzulie, is identified with St. Anne (Marcelin, p. 93); however, Herskovits (p. 279) identifies with her the Mater Dolorosa, and identifies St. Anne with Adams Wedo (p. 280). Marcelin also lists an Erzulie known as La Vierge Caridad (p. 86), presumably created after that saint.

[80] Erzulie is known for her insistence upon "fraicheur", coolness. Part of her regular equipment is a fan, and she is always being fanned by her devotees and admirers. Maximilien mentions this during his description of an Erzulie possession (pp. 196 ff).

[81] This toilette is her initial key action and is described by many writers, including Marcelin (pp. 81–3) and Maximilien (pp. 196 ff).

[82] Erzulie's beauty is mentioned in many songs, some of which have been cited by Marcelin (pp. 83–4) and Courlander (p. 118).

[83] This characteristic fashion of greeting women (also cited by Marcelin, p. 84) is only one of her ways of indicating her preference for men; and men, rather than women, attend to her various wants.

[84] It is significant that she is not always in favor of the marriage of her woman devotees, possibly because this is frequently accompanied by a "let down" in these various graces of coquetry.

[85] This phrase occurs in a song which is very popular, and is cited by Courlander (p. 118).

[86] In his description of an Erzulie possession, Maximilien (p. 199) also makes a point of this gift giving.

[87] Marcelin (p. 77) mentions the pierced heart and Maximilien has attempted to trace the Erzulie vever to Christian sources in this connection.

[88] All these details of Erzulie's amorous exploits are elaborated in Marcelin's account; Rigaud (p. 37) cites her "affair" with Damballah.

[89] The competition between Ogoun and Agwé is described by Denis (I, p. 35) and others.

[90] Marcelin (pp. 77-80) cites such marriage; Maximilien (pp. 210-11) reproduces such a marriage contract, and an account of such a ceremony is given in Appendix A to this book, pp. 263-71, *supra*.

For a discussion of the general mythological and metaphysical significance of such marriages see Campbell (pp. 350-1, 109-20, 309-10). Many serviteurs who do not go as far as this, remain chaste on the days of the week sacred to her.

[91] Marcelin (pp. 77, 94) quotes a number of Erzulie's songs which deal with her "hard luck, betrayals", etc.

[92] Herskovits (p. 316) has listed Erzulie Ge-Rouge as the wife of Simbi, and has named several other Petro Erzulies (pp. 165-6). Courlander lists a "man-eating" Erzulie Mapionne (p. 42). This is characteristic of the increasing identification of Marinette with Erzulie in her sterner or Petro aspects. "Man-eating" and "man-grinding" are especially associated with the propitiatory ceremonies of the Indian maize, or corn mother. This is the Marinette figure. Erzulie Ge-Rouge, as I have seen her, and I believe that this was the aspect which did derive from the African Erzulie, had a definite rage which was turned in upon itself, to the point where the fingernails drew blood. It was not the extraverted, triumphant, aggressive violence of the consuming corn mother. The corn mother is not unhappy; the tears belong to the African Erzulie—Erzulie Freda Dahomey, as her full name is.

[93] According to one of Marcelin's informants (p. 96), Gran Erzulie (the older Erzulie) repented for the sins of her youth, and having been forgiven, would similarly intercede for the prostitutes as well. Such an interpretation would imply that the younger Erzulie is regarded as sinful, which is inconceivable, inasmuch as she is identified with the Virgin Mary. All interpretations hingeing on "sin" (as in the case of the weighing of souls) would seem to be Christian interpolations and are rarely consistent with the rest of the character of the loa. Erzulie, as a matter of fact, is characterized by purity and the demand for chastity among her devotees

on the days sacred to her. This purity motif has been mentioned by all writers, including Maximilien (pp. 196 ff), Courlander (p. 33) and even by Marcelin himself (p. 80).

[94] One of the explanations advanced to justify the weeping derives from the Mater Dolorosa association. It is said that Erzulie had borne only one child, by Ogoun—a girl named Ursule, who went out in a boat and drowned, and that Erzulie weeps for this lost child. (This explanation is cited by Marcelin, p. 95.) Such an explanation is highly unreasonable inasmuch as the child of two major divinities would not be mortal.

[95] Agassou, whom Dorsainville (p. 22) defines as the guardian of customs and traditions and who is listed as a sacred ancestor and founder of a royal Dahomean sib by Herskovits (pp. 267 and 197), ranks very close to Loco and Ayizan in importance and shares many of their functions and characteristics.

[96] Marcelin (p. 42). Courlander (p. 37) also says that Loco is of the Sky Pantheon.

[97] Herskovits, p. 196.

[98] These titles appear in various songs, some of which are quoted by Marcelin (pp. 41-9).

[99] Frazer (pp. 9-10) makes a point of the fact that the functions of priest and king were often combined in Africa, and in Central America, among the Fans (pp. 85-6), and he cites the prevalence of taboos for such divine kings (p. 169), particularly the restriction noted above (pp. 198-9).

[100] Marcelin, p. 29.

[101] This occurs both in Rigaud (p. 32) and in Herskovits (p. 316), but in general Ayizan is thought of as a woman.

[102] Nanan-bouclou, who is now a loa of herbs and medicines, is presumably an ancient androgynous Dahomean deity, who even preceded Mawu-Lisa (Courlander, p. 39) but neither this loa nor Silibo-Gweto, another of the sacred ancestors (Herskovits, p. 267), plays any prominent rôle today. Both of these ancient loa are related both to Ayizan and Agassou in songs quoted by Courlander (pp. 41 and 78) and by Marcelin (pp. 30-1 and 130-1).

[103] This is cited by Courlander, p. 37.

[104] Both Loco and Agassou are related to a mirror in songs (Marcelin, pp. 42, 128), and it is noteworthy that Agassou is understood to be guardian of springs, which are also the pathways of the loa. On the other

hand, he is said to be Agwé's son (Courlander, p. 31) or his lieutenant, and my own experience has been that, when he manifests himself, he appears to be a sailor.

¹⁰⁵ There is a song about this, quoted by Courlander (p. 89) and Marcelin (p. 45) which says "Ring the bell [asson] there, Papa, I am Ghede; I am coming all in black to meet Loco. . . ." Agassou is said to have brought up Sobo from the abysmal waters (Maximilien, p. 103 and Herskovits, p. 197).

¹⁰⁶ Courlander, p. 31.

¹⁰⁷ The song "Watch the house for me" is quoted by Marcelin (p. 42); Ayizan's palm leaf also purifies the menstruating or pregnant woman, who would not otherwise be able to participate in rituals during that period.

¹⁰⁸ Several writers mention this fact, including Marcelin (pp. 43-4). Agassou is also known for his cures.

¹⁰⁹ This power of protection is mentioned in several songs, and quoted by Marcelin (p. 34).

¹¹⁰ Marcelin (pp. 47 ff) tells of an occasion when the people were having difficulties with a loa, and Loco interceded on their behalf.

CHAPTER IV

¹ Courlander (pp. 82 and 110) quotes songs referring to a houngan being selected by loa.

² The position of the hounsi bossale is elaborated by Courlander (p. 9), Herskovits (pp. 146 and 188) and Maximilien (p. 73). A hounsi bossale may have a *laver tête* ceremony which is understood to give her enough control over the loa to prevent them from arriving at inopportune times or mistreating their "horse".

³ Simpson (II) lists the four stages of elevation as follows: houngans, badjicans (assistants to the houngan), serviteurs (those who become possessed) and fidèles (believers who do not become possessed). Maximilien adds to the hierarchy a "confidant", as a person intimately close to the houngan or mambo.

⁴ One of Miss Owen's statements is of particular significance in this connection. She says that "the inner nature of Voodooism . . . is telepathy, . . . clairvoyance—in a word it is WILL. Its motto is: Control yourself

perfectly and you can control the rest of the world—organic and in-organic ... Alexander doesn't need magic ... Old Grandfather power should make it possible for him to *look* a man dead." She then lists the four degrees and ordeals designed to impart such control: 1st stage—instruction in the use of poisons, remedies, significance of dreams, power; 2nd stage—fasting, withdrawal, ordeals, Dance of the Snake, of Fire and the Moon. The following stages are not clearly differentiated but she indicates that after conquering oneself, one is ready to conquer others, and that such initiates meet in a "Circle"—"a society for the dissemination of knowledge and the trial of strength. Knowledge is principally bio-graphical." She concludes: "Hypnotism is Voodoo's pastime as well as his power." Dorsainville (p. 33) lists "la prise des yeux", explained as clairvoyance, as the fourth and highest step of elevation. This would seem to be a reference to divinatory powers such as derive from a capacity of the eyes, rather than from interpreting fallen kernels, etc. Dorsainville is the only one to refer to such a stage as a ritual step. Herskovits, however, refers to divination by houngans who gaze into crystal balls, etc. (p. 152).

[5] Frazer notes that it is common to many cultures that these three functions should be vested simultaneously in a single individual. It is obvious that the entire structure of the hounfor is an extension of family organization. Herskovits has made a point of this and has included many relevant observations (pp. 125, 145, 213 and 268). Maximilien (p. 70) speaks of the houngan and the mambo in the rôle of kings: this would be compatible with the political function, which, in the new world, was most apparent in their revolutionary rôle, and which now is apparent in their political rôle.

[6] Maximilien also cites the houngan's distinction between "natural" and "supernatural" illness, as well as his calling the loa in the govi for consultation as to treatment. Courlander refers to the houngan as a "pharmacist" (p. 23). It is relevant to point out, in connection with herbal knowledge, that arsenic and digitalis (foxglove) were first used medicinally in the practice of "witchcraft".

[7] Herskovits (p. 134) also speaks of this practice of avoiding an undue display of wealth lest it inspire envy, and cites (p. 95) the slight scarring of a child to prevent the evil eye of envy.

[8] Herskovits (p. 202) also cites the phrase "kembi" as referring to a loa-given illness and notes that the Marassa are said to cause constipation, the loa, dysentery, and the Dead, headaches.

[9] The healing rôle of the houngan is especially stressed by Herskovits, who differentiates between a bocor—a practitioner of magic—and a

houngan or mambo, by the fact that "the loa, of their own accord are believed to have given 'connaissance'—the knowledge of healing and helping—to these latter". He goes on to list the loa, who, in particular, give such healing knowledge (pp. 151 ff). In saying that the "houngan can cure only diseases 'sent by man'—that is, those caused by magic—and by the loa, since against illness sent by God he can do nothing", Herskovits is making a distinction similar to that between "natural" and "supernatural" illness, the "natural" one being caused by God. He also gives a detailed account of the houngan's rôle in aiding during a pregnancy and a delivery (pp. 88 ff).

[10] I am deeply indebted to an article by Dr. Max Jacobson ("Functional Disorders", *Tomorrow Magazine*, March, 1951) for a professional medical analysis of the psychosomatic mechanism which aided me in formalizing and clarifying my own analysis of the houngan's methods. I had begun with the conviction that a poor man is necessarily pragmatic, for he cannot afford to be otherwise, and that therefore the houngan's treatments must be effective. I had been especially interested in what seemed to be psychosomatic disorders among the peasants and had traced it to the basic insecurity of their lives; and I had also understood how the houngan's methods met this problem of morale. My analysis was, however, necessarily that of an amateur, medically speaking. The ideas which Dr. Jacobson advances are especially illuminating in this connection, precisely because, basing himself on experiences far removed from the Haitian scene, his conclusions are so relevant that his analysis constitutes an objective confirmation of the analysis which I had advanced without professional authority. Dr. Jacobson not only discards the idea that psychosomatic projection is "bad" but goes so far as to point out that the typical psychosomatic explosion acts as an automatic safety shield which provides the organism with a "breathing" spell, a relief from unremitting psychic pressures, and so drains off the accumulated tensions before they overcome it entirely. He goes on to suggest that such explosions not only interrupt, or temporarily "black out", destructive pressures, but even release constructive forces. He indicates that "migraine attacks are followed by a deep sense of relaxation and recovery" and that "forces of renewal . . . are released by the recovery". In connection with epileptic attacks, he says that "certain toxic materials are eliminated . . . and that this is an indication that nature may be trying to protect the personality from further damage". He also points out that permitting the explosion to run its course, rather than seeking treatment to terminate it immediately, may be the wise way of getting full benefit out of nature's therapeutic measures. Dr. Jacobson's essay would almost seem to have been based upon careful analysis of Haitian problems and the houngan's

methods. Migraine, which the peasant calls simply a headache, is extremely common among them; epilepsy is also fairly frequent; but most significant, the houngan does not try to rush his treatment through. Most frequently the therapeutic measures take place over a certain period of time, and therefore the curative properties of the "explosion" are fully exploited. The cure is consequently the more sound and lasting, and this is more important than the proud exhibit of spectacular speed.

[11] Courlander (p. 8) also refers to the "mediator" function of the houngan.

[12] Herskovits (pp. 145–6) also sites the "tying" and burying of the loa, and other means of restraining them (p. 167).

[13] Simpson (II) also cites a similar occasion, when a ceremony was performed inside a house while "bal" was being played outside by a small jazz orchestra.

[14] This situation, which might easily lead to destructive competition, is modified by the houngans themselves who are too proud to compete openly for clientele (they habitually avoid seeming over-anxious in any respect) and observe a code of at least ostensible collaboration. Almost inevitably they will invite one or more houngans or mambos to assist them, in positions of honour and prestige, at their own ceremonies, and the prestige of the host houngan is raised or lowered according to the number and importance of the houngans and mambos who "assist" at his ceremony. A certain distinct hierarchy does, actually, exist in such cases and is manifest in the salutations described on pp. 206–7, *supra*.

[15] Herskovits (p. 223) also refers to the fact that his prestige is dependent upon his successes.

[16] Courlander (p. 7) says: "The priest does not control Voudoun . . . he is part of it."

[17] These two terms, cited by Maximilien (pp. 93 and 107), are not in current colloquial usage. Mr. Milo Rigaud, who has read this portion of the manuscript, feels that my translations, or transpositions, into English are inexact; but since there are no precise equivalents for these Voudoun elements in the Christian religion, I have been forced to refer them to the most nearly analogous objects.

[18] This "nom vaillant" is discussed by Maximilien (p. 18).

[19] Maximilien (p. 18) believes this bassin to be of Indian origin.

[20] The pierre-loa (discussed in Chapter I) are often pieces of stone work and flints dating from the aboriginal Indian culture, and are actually closer to the Indian *zemi* (as discussed in Appendix B) than

the thunder stones of African tradition. The stones are believed to contain the spiritual essence of the divinity. Courlander (pp. 27–8) discusses
these stones and relates anecdotes of how they are found, their sale from
person to person, etc.

[21] Both Maximilien (pp. 18 ff) and Courlander (p. 18) have given
full and excellent descriptions of hounfor, peristyle and related objects.
Herskovits (p. 155) has described a family chapel, which, in general,
is related to the hounfor.

[22] The amount of power transferred in the transference of the object
varies in a rather complicated fashion. For instance, one may buy pierre-
loa, and, in so doing, one is buying the actual power as well. If a pot-de-
tête is stolen, deliberately, that is dangerous, for the spiritual essence is
understood to travel with it. On the other hand, if one finds an object and
is innocent of its value, one may not be able to put it to use; however, it
may, under certain conditions, be active against the finder.

CHAPTER V

[1] Maximilien, who concurs in the general belief that the words are
African in origin, quotes (p. 105) M. Le Herisse, who believes that they
may even be Oriental in origin. The litanies and prayers which Maximilien
has rendered (pp. 101–5), word for word, would certainly seem to
contain Spanish and Indian words as well as African.

[2] Maximilien (p. 106) has quoted the words attending this salutation
in the four directions, as follows: east, "A Table"; west, "Dabord";
north, "Olande"; south, "Adonai". Marcelin (p. 44) also quotes words
of address in this connection. The jug which is used for such libations
may be very plain, of clay or china, or it may have been painted and
dedicated to a specific deity. Such objects, which are in constant use and
may be broken during ceremonies, are not treated with great reverence.
On the whole, it is felt that the use of the object is sacred, rather than the
object itself.

[3] Maximilien (p. 97) also describes such libations, beginning with a
circle of water around the poteau-mitan, which he specifies as a salutation
for Legba. Rigaud (p. 23) has also referred to these libations as a means
of leading the loa in on water.

[4] Maximilien (p. 98) speaks of this as a magic circle which protects
the center-post from evil spirits and magicians, but it also serves as an
integrating, unifying element for the vevers which radiate in all directions.

[5] Maximilien (pp. 41–3) believes the vevers to be derived from the Indians and has an extended discussion of their significance. He notes also the presence in them of medieval Christian elements.

Joseph Campbell has pointed out that the vever, in fact, creates a ground altar and that the fire on an altar is in India understood to represent the mouth of the god. This may be the significance of the candle which is required to burn during the entire drawing of the vever and is planted at the foot of the centerpost (or wherever the vevers are drawn), to burn there throughout the ceremony.

[6] Rigaud (p. 20) has described a ceremony including most of these elements. She has pointed out that the permission of the maîthounfor must be asked for any ceremony addressed to another loa. Maximilien (p. 97) describes a ceremony where the laplace and the flags run around the centerpost instead of engaging in the mock competition here described with the houngan.

[7] Two houngans may also salute each other by shaking their assons at each other in a strange, cryptic choreography of movements. Maximilien has cited such a salute (p. 97), as well as other salutes and gradations.

[8] Herskovits (pp. 157–60) also describes a *ceremonie caille* and an *action de grâce*.

[9] Maximilien (pp. 98–100) quotes these prayers at length. He states that "Djo" is an African word signifying "protect", and that although it is addressed to the saints, it is in Creole and langage. The *Litanies des Mystères Djor* which follow are the same as the *Litanies des Saints*, except that they include Legba. Rigaud (pp. 22–3) describes a ceremony in full, giving the order of invocation.

[10] Although this is a very effective moment of the ceremony, I have not found it described in other accounts.

[11] The description which follows is drawn largely from Arada or Rada rites; other rituals—the Petro, Ibo, Congo, etc.—may be different in specific terms, although the general principles would be approximately the same. Maximilien (p. 36) includes a listing of ceremonials.

It should be pointed out that the dating of ceremonies may be arrived at in any one of a number of ways. Certain ceremonies, such as the feast of the Dead (in the last days of October) or the *mangé Marassa* (at harvest or Christmas time) are set by tradition. The general feasting of the loa may be changed every year or every two years, the precise date being determined by convenience and by the need to avoid the rainy season. When an individual feasts his loa, the date may depend upon his ability to accumulate all of the offerings; or it may be forced upon him by his desire to put an end to the misfortunes which result from his neglect of the loa, or the loa may himself specify a date. Ceremonies involving magic gardes take place during the new moon, as do ceremonies referring to the cutting of wood for drums. In other words, the occurrence of ceremonies other than those calendrically prescribed is completely circumstantial and depends upon both the need and the resources of the person.

[12] Rigaud's account of a ceremony includes many observations on the varying practices and beliefs attending the feeding of the loa. She particularly mentions the fact that food consumed by a person while possessed by a loa does not diminish the hunger of the person himself. Herskovits (p. 79) also refers to the belief that it is the essence of the food which is consumed by the loa.

[13] Rigaud has perhaps the most elaborate account of the ritual preparation of the food for the loa.

[14] Herskovits (pp. 79–81) refers to the scattering of the first corn on the fields, and also to the ceremony-yam.

[15] Maximilien (pp. 131–6) has given a detailed description of the *mangé yam* ceremony.

[16] Legba's chicken is white, or sometimes grey; Loco's is yellow; Damballah, Agwé and Erzulie require white; Ogoun requires red; Ghede's animal must be black, etc.

[17] This act also conveys the sense of putting power into, as well as taking evil out of the person.

[18] There seems to be a certain disagreement as to whether "ventailler" refers to the act of passing the chickens over the persons, or to that of swinging them in the air.

[19] If the loa being feasted has meanwhile possessed one of the persons, he may himself perform the sacrifice.

[20] Petro loa often bite off the head of the chicken. Maximilien and Rigaud, in their descriptions of ceremonies, include detailed accounts of the various methods of sacrifice.

[21] Rigaud (p. 35) also mentions such an anointing.

[22] Courlander (p. 54), Maximilien (p. 94) and Herskovits (pp. 162–3) have included descriptions of and observations upon animal sacrifice.

[23] The baptism of the loa is fully discussed in various contexts by Herskovits, particularly in the section, pages 143 ff.

[24] The *laver tête* ceremony is described by Courlander (p. 9) and Herskovits (p. 144).

[25] Maximilien (p. 73) describes this ceremony for a hounsi bossale, including the taking of a pledge. Courlander (p. 14) speaks of a *bruler-zin* for a bossale, which included the breathing of fire.

[26] These ceremonial beads consist of one double strand, joined at every seventh bead (understood as the female strand), and one single strand (the male strand) and are worn, at certain ceremonies, crossed over the shoulders and chest. Maximilien, who has the most extended discussion of these beads, refers to them as being worn in the "manière Africaine" (p. 97). However, that manner of wearing them resembles the Brahminical Thread, as discussed by Campbell (p. 129). The motif of a double strand for the female principle and a single strand for the male principle is also carried out in the decorative stitching found on peasant denim blouses in Haiti. The combining of the two elements is obviously a statement of integrated cosmic totality achieved at the moment of initiation.

[27] Maximilien (pp. 85–6) speaks of the surrender of the "moi personelle" at the moment when the soul is placed in the pot-de-tête, which is akin to the interpretation I have offered here, i.e. that it tokens the fact the individual has become part of the spiritual collective.

[28] This concept of the name as containing the essence of the person is repeatedly noted by Frazer, who notes many name taboos; and the ritual concern with the "signing of name" occurs in reference to Legba (Maximilien, p. 16). Ogoun (Rigaud, p. 42) is mentioned in litanies (Maximilien, p. 100) and in reference to secrecy (Herskovits, p. 95). For a discussion of the general mythological significance of baptism, see Campbell (p. 251).

[29] Maximilien (pp. 75–91) has perhaps the most detailed and elaborate account of the rituals of the hounsi canzo initiation.

[30] Courlander (p. 9) says that "kanzo" means "to tie fire". In daily life when a person is able to handle hot things easily, he is often said to be "canzo".

[31] Maximilien has a very detailed description of *bruler-zin*. Courlander (pp. 10–15) also describes a *bruler-zin* ceremony, citing many of the details mentioned in my account. He notes, however, that there is no *bruler-zin* in the north (p. 48). He cites it as a Rada rite, which is the general understanding (p. 75), but also cites a Quitta song (usually understood as part of the Petro complex) in which there is mention of the boiling zin (p. 145).

[32] Maximilien (p. 93) speaks of the "reception" of the hounsi canzo as being the most important manifestation of the cult, and describes it in considerable detail.

Campbell has pointed out that, inasmuch as the initiation represents the accomplishment of knowledge and control over the loa, it consum-mates the integration of the archetypes of the unconscious with the con-sciousness and corresponds to what Jung calls integration, in the sense that the powers of the psyche which are out of the control of the un-integrated person are under the control of the integrated one. (See Carl G. Jung, *The Integration of the Personality*, Farrar and Rinehart, Inc., New York, 1939.)

CHAPTER VI

[1] This "break" was typical of the Rada and Congo drumming in the Port-au-Prince area but was not heard in Jeremie and is probably not a universal practice.

[2] The drummer may sometimes be possessed by the loa which is being invoked or by the loa Hountor, which is as a loa of the drums; but such possessions occur very rarely.

[3] In addition to Courlander's research on drums, the work by Denis and Paul, and that of Romains (dealing specifically with the assator) includes much detailed information upon the great variety in kinds of drums, shapes, sizes, etc.

[4] The making of drums is accompanied by a number of ritualistic activities. The three Rada drums are all hollowed out of solid tree trunks and oak is the favoured wood; but all wood must be cut on the rising moon, for otherwise it would become worm-infested. After being seasoned, the trunks are dug out by hand, the entire procedure being opened with a small ceremony and accompanied, at intervals, by various rites. These drums are covered with cowhide and are beaten with sticks of various sizes and shapes, except for the maman, which is beaten with one hand and one stick. Almost every hounfor has a set of two Petro drums, which are covered with goatskin and beaten by hand. In a large hounfor there may be Congo, Ibo, Martinique and other drums as well. The drums are usually painted in the color of the loa to whom they are consecrated, and the name is often inscribed upon them. They are some-times profusely decorated, but this decoration is of abstract rather than of representational nature. In addition to the works on drums which have already been mentioned, there is Herskovits' description of drums (p. 182) and an account of a drum baptism (pp. 273-6).

CHAPTER VII

[1] There are a good many misconceptions about possession. The popular supposition relates it to sexual orgies; the clinical supposition is that it is a form of hysteria which liberates inhibitions and is a form of neurotic explosion. The essential fact about possession which stands in contradiction to such concepts is that it does not free the identity of the individual, but, on the contrary, replaces it with a highly formalized, disciplined identity, that of the loa. Herskovits has made some of the best statements in this reference which are available, and inasmuch as my own statements might possibly be construed as a justification of my own experience of possession, I find it preferable to quote from him in this connection.

". . . it is not strange that the untrained observer tends to assess what he sees in almost any terms but those of the underlying discipline that defines all activity in the worship of the gods. A release of psychic tension is undoubtedly afforded those who become possessed . . . nevertheless it must be emphasized . . . that this form of worship of the loa is neither un/ restrained hysteria nor drunken orgiastic satisfaction of the sex drive. The behavior of the participants . . . often seems uncouth, vigorous, violent and even dangerous, when it is merely the expression of a different tradition. And as for the orgiastic aspects of these rites, Haitians have ample opportunity to satisfy their sexual impulses elsewhere without making this a basic and constant element in the worship of their gods. . . ." (pp. 177 ff.)

". . . One must reject an hypothesis which attempts to explain the vodoun cult of Haiti in terms of the neuroses, even when, as in the admirable exposition of Dr. Dorsainvil, the approach neglects neither accepted genetic theory in stressing the inheritance of neurotic tendencies in voduist family lines, nor the important historical forces which have been operative. For in terms of the patterns of Haitian religion, *possession is not abnormal, but normal*; it is set in its cultural mold as are all other phases of conventional living. . . . Hence to consider all possession as something which falls within the range of psychopathology is to approach it handicapped by a fundamental misconception." (pp. 147 ff.)

"Once more it may be emphasized that vodoun is neither the practice of black magic nor the unorganized pathological hysteria it is so often represented to be. The gods are known to their worshippers and the duties owed them are equally well understood. The reward for the per/ formance of these duties is good health, good harvests, and the goodwill of fellow men; the punishment for neglect is corresponding ill/fortune. On the basis of this belief is erected the ceremonial of worship." (p. 153.)

² At times the theory has been suggested that possession is a form of hypnotism and is used by the priest to retain control in the sense that the god would be manifest only at his direction. Nothing could be further from the truth in the Haitian context. The function of the priest, if any, is to control the loa and to protect the serviteur from being ravaged by them. Moreover, the loa may appear in many contexts outside the houngan's province. Possessions in the context of family worship are, if anything, more frequent than in the hounfor. Possessions may even occur under ritualistically informal circumstances, although this is infrequent. The loa may come to give personal advice to the family, or to a person, or may possess a person in sleep, when the loa is experienced as a dream. Such an occasion is cited in Rigaud‑Denis (II).

³ Among people living in close, intimate familiarity with one another it is inconceivable that a man should worship his neighbor. The distinction between the horse and the rider is absolute and complete and without any exception. This means that a person cannot, as himself, benefit from the respect shown the loa which mounted him.

⁴ The possessed person is always looked after very carefully; the women's ear‑rings and money are removed so that they will not be lost; similarly, men's pockets are emptied; and efforts are made not to permit the loa to soil the dress. This vigilance is also cited by Herskovits (p. 170).

⁵ There are many elements in possession which inspire comparison with hypnotism. There is anticipation, tension, and, in the case of possessions occurring during ceremonies and dances, there is the entire weight of atmosphere and rhythmic pressure. Undoubtedly, some of the movements are psychologically designed to induce trance states, by effecting the spinal column, the rate of breathing, etc. The effects of possession are also frequently similar to those induced by hypnotism: an ability to climb impossible heights, or perform other such physical feats, an imperviousness to pain, certain rigidities, etc. But there are other fundamental differences, and among them is the fact that while hypnosis is dependent upon relaxation and agreement, possession takes place in spite of the most active resistance engendered by terror. Moreover, the entire experience of possession is in the opposite direction from that of hypnosis. Hypnosis could be described as going inward and downward, whereas possession is accompanied by a sense of an explosion upward and outward. One might say that hypnosis is the ultimate in self‑negation, whereas possession is the ultimate in self‑realization to the point of self‑transcendence. In hypnosis one accepts the substitution of another human identity in place of one's own; in possession the sense is of being over‑whelmed by a transcendent force.

[6] It is accepted procedure to be warned by such auras and to use every possible method of resisting possession, for any one of a number of reasons. Lack of control is considered indicative of psychic weakness. It has already been pointed out that a houngan or mambo who has specific ritual duties to perform will use all his force to avoid the possession which would make him unable to fulfill his functions.

[7] Possessions are sometimes understood to be contagious by contact. They may also be brought about if a loa spins the person into a reverse pirouette.

[8] It is extremely rare that a person from outside the Haitian culture is "mounted" by a loa, and therefore any additional data which I can provide may be of interest. The first question which may arise in the reader's mind is whether this was a "regular, authentic" possession. The account of the period immediately preceding the "installation" of the loa in the head (and that of the return which follows) is as detailed and exact a description as I have been able to give of the inner experience. (The outer appearance of a possession has been described throughout this book and in virtually all books about Haiti.) The period during which the loa was "installed" is a complete blank in my memory. It is not customary to discuss a possession with the person who was mounted, and this is in keeping with the absolute distinction between the individual himself and the loa, for it serves to prevent any identification between the two or any proprietary attitude which might, for instance, be expressed as "*my* possession by such and such a loa". A group of serviteurs may even discuss the actions of a loa in great detail without thinking to make a single reference as to whose head that loa had entered. However, from the fact that these conventions were observed in my presence (the references were explicitly to Erzulie and not to myself), from such details as were recounted in my presence, and from the reports of persons who had not been present, had heard of the event and had explicitly questioned those who had been present as to the "authenticity" of the loa's manifestation —from all this I infer that it was accepted and understood as an authentic possession by the loa Erzulie and that, in general, it conformed to the pattern of activities which would be expected of her.

In this connection it is important to note the following. The hounfor where this occurred was devoted predominantly to the service of Ogoun, the maît-caille, and Azacca, the maît-tête of houngan Isnard. These loa, along with Ghede, Agassou and several others were the most frequent visitors. Erzulie came rarely to that district altogether, and I had only briefly witnessed her on one occasion. Although I knew her character and personality in general, I was not at all very familiar with the details of her attitudes and actions at this time, and it was only towards the end of my stay in Haiti that I had made sufficient observations to be able to give the description in Chapter III.

The occasion which I have described is not the only time that Erzulie mounted my head. She was understood as my maît-tête, since, not infrequently, she threatened to mount my head and actually installed herself seven or eight times. One of her arrivals was particularly in-opportune. Towards the end of my stay in Haiti I had ordered a set of drums and arranged to have them baptized and "put to sleep" overnight with a special ceremony. I was very anxious to make a wire recording of this relatively infrequent ceremony which I had never seen and which I would not have another opportunity to witness before my departure. I began by making the technical arrangements for recording and, since the drum ceremony would take place after the regular songs of salutation to the loa (which I had already recorded frequently and had no interest in duplicating), I was free to participate in the early part of the ceremony. It was during this period that Erzulie mounted my head. When I regained consciousness, about four hours had passed, and I was in-formed that I was very lucky since Erzulie herself had performed the complete drum ceremony. Inasmuch as these were my own drums, I was justified in asking whether the ceremony was properly executed by her, and the houngan assured me that this was so.

Although Erzulie was my maît-tête, the loa Loco occasionally threatened my head and installed himself once, briefly; and Azacca also threatened my head a number of times. On one occasion this interfered seriously with my efforts to photograph the bull sacrifice and it was then that houngan Isnard recommended a *laver tête* ceremony to strengthen my control over the loa so that they would not impede my activities. (I did not, however, have this ceremony, nor did I ever go through any of the stages of initiation.) It is interesting that although I am more con-cerned with Ghede than with any other loa (because of his impressive metaphysical scope) and although he early pronounced himself my guardian and often came to my house in the head of a visitor or one of my domestics (but never in his boisterous or obscene aspect), he was not one of the loa who ever threatened to mount my head.

There remains, finally, the question which has been posed, and would, I presume, be posed again. Since the loa mounted my head, is this to say that I believe in Voudoun and in Erzulie? In the context of Voudoun, such a question did not occur to me. I would say that, as a metaphysical and ritualistic structure Voudoun *is a fact*, and does exist, and that, as such, it incorporates values with which I am in personal agreement, displays an organizational, psychic and practical skill which I admire, and accomplishes results of which I approve. I would say further, that I believe that the principles which Ghede and other loa represent are real and true, in the sense that it is true, for instance, that nature follows a life-death-life cycle; and the possessions which I have witnessed have seemed to me to be exemplary and absolute personifications of these principles. It was this kind of agreement with, and admiration for the principles and practices of Voudoun which was and is my conscious attitude towards it. Otherwise I simply participated in it to the extent that an average serviteur might, and with the average proportion of pleasure, boredom, and discomfort, according to the circumstances. I observed the appropriate conventions and formalities of the rituals which I attended, sang the songs as I became familiar with them, and danced the dances. In effect, and regardless of what I might think or believe, I *served* the loa and, in so doing, I learned (as I have said in the chapter on the rites) that the effect of the ritual service is upon the doer.

GLOSSARY OF CREOLE TERMS
REFERRING TO VOUDOUN

A

ACTION DE GRÂCE
Catholic ritual and litanies preceding a Voudoun ceremony.

ADORATION
The song which attends the offering of money at ceremonies. The coins are usually placed on a plate which rests on the sacrificed animal and this money may be either buried for the loa, or used for the purchase of some sacred paraphernalia or paid to the officiant for his services.

ANGE
Angel; often used as synonym for a guardian loa; also in phrases ti-bon-ange and gros-bon-ange.

ASSATOR
A very large, ritual drum. There exists a special cult of the assator.

ASSON, AÇON
The sacred rattle of houngans and mambos. It consists of a calabash which has a handle-growth, and it is either filled with seeds or snake vertebrae, or is covered with a loose web of beads and vertebrae. It is usually used in conjunction with a small bell, and for ceremonial pur-poses only. It should be carefully distinguished from the cha-cha, a seed-filled calabash whose function is percussive accompaniment to dances.

B

BAGUETTE
A drum stick.

BAKA
An evil spirit in the form of an animal; a daemon. Not of the same class as a loa.

BANDA
A dance variously assigned to Martinique and African origins. It is a suggestive dance, usually beaten at the request of a loa, often Ghede, who feels like doing a gay dance.

BAPTÊME
Baptism; in Voudoun all sacred objects, areas, etc., are consecrated by baptism.

BARQUE D'AGWÉ
A specially constructed raft, upon which the offerings to Agwé are placed, and which is then set on the sea.

BARRIÈRE, BAYÉ
An entrance way; term used frequently to designate loa to the cross-roads.

BASILIQUE
Basilica; the basil leaves are believed to ward off evil spirits. They are also steeped in water used for ritual cleansings.

BASSIN
A basin for water or a pool; the bassin of Damballah is a pool consecrated to the use of this loa when he arrives.

BATON-LEGBA
The gnarled crutch of the loa Legba.

BATTÉRIE MACONNIQUE
A special beat, produced by clapping hands and beating drums, which, in ceremonies, probably signifies a rapping on the door of the loa world.

BOCOR, BOKOR
A practitioner of magic, not necessarily an initiate of Voudoun, and therefore to be sharply distinguished from the houngan or priest.

BOIS
A single tree, as in "pied bois" (foot of the tree); also a wood, forest. Colloquially, it is sometimes used as a phallic metaphor.

BOSSALE
Wild, untamed, uninitiated.

BOUCAN
In Voudoun, it refers to the ritual bonfires for Legba which are lit immediately preceding the New Year in some regions, and relate to the concept of re-lighting, or re-firing the sun. In Cassell's French-English Dictionary it is defined as "A place used by the American Indians to smoke-dry their meat."

BRULER-ZIN
A ceremony involving the boiling of sacred cooking vessels.

BULA
The smallest of the set of three Rada drums.

C

CAILLE
Hut or house; *caille Mystères* is the house consecrated to the loa.

CALBASSE
A gourd. From the Carib "calabaza".

CAMBÉ, KEMBÉ
To be seized or caught. In Voudoun it refers to pains or illness which an angered loa may cause a person.

CANARI
A jar of red clay, used for holding water; also for lodging the spirits and the loa.

CANZO (KANZO)
Fire ordeal, an important step in initiation. One who has passed through it is called canzo, or hounsi canzo.

CARREFOUR
Crossroads; also the name of the Petro loa of the crossroads.

CASSAVAS
Unleavened, flat, round breads made of coarsely ground maize, a favorite food of the loa Ghede.

CEREMONY-CAILLE
A fairly elaborate and complete feasting of the loa to encourage their favor to the *caille* or "temple" of the hougan.

CHA-CHA
A calbasse rattle used for percussive purposes at dances.

CHARGE
Magical energy or power enabling one to accomplish unusual feats.

CHAUFFER
To warm; to burn rum or zins to warm, enliven and encourage the spirits of the dead or the loa.

CHEVAL, CH'WL
Horse; a person, as a horse, is mounted by a loa, as a rider. This is the metaphor for possession.

CHIRER AYIZAN
A ceremony of protection and purification, under the patronage of Ayizan, which involves the shredding of palm leaves.

CLAIRIN
Raw rum; favorite drink of Ghede.

COLLIER
Necklace; the special ritual necklace worn by initiates.

COMMERE, COMPERE
Godmother, godfather.

CONGO
A nanchon of African origin; the Congo rites, dances and loa are today almost assimilated by Petro.

CONNAISSANCE
Ritual knowledge; refers to herbal cures and control of supernatural forces achieved by those who are advanced in religious training.

COUCHER
To put to sleep; a ceremony in which yams, drums, neophytes, etc. are ritually laid to sleep overnight, as a rite of purification and strengthening.

COUVERT SEC
Synonym for *mangé sec.*

CREOLE
Term used to designate anything native to Haiti—whether persons, loa, plants, language, etc., and as distinguished from African origin.

D

DAHOMEY, DAROMAIN, DAHOMÉ
A kingdom in Africa. Retained in Haiti to designate dances or loa originating from that area.

DANSE DE REJUISSANCE
Dance of celebration. Religious dances may follow a ceremonial or take place independently of a ceremonial. Their form and purpose, however, is religious, not secular.

DÉBÂTMENT
A period of physical movement, sometimes very intense and violent, which reflects the inner conflict between the gros-bon-ange and the loa over the possession of the physical body of a devotee. Once the loa is "installed", this conflict is resolved and subsides.

DESSOUNIN
A portion of the death rites, designed to separate the loa and gros-bon-ange from the body of the deceased.

DOGUÉ, DOGWÉ
Ritual word for the sacrificial goat.

DOSSA
The first child, female, born after twins. Also the female of the Marassa-Trois.

DOSSU
The first child, male, born after twins. Also the male of the Marassa-Trois.

DRAPEAUX
The ceremonial banners of the hounfor *société*, heavily spangled, used during rituals.

E

ENGAGEMENT
A pact between a person and a loa, in which the latter is rewarded for certain services. A magical contract, usually with a malevolent loa.

ESPRIT(S)
The spirits or souls of the dead. Also, colloquially, intelligence. See distinction from Mystères, loa.

F

FARINE
Flour. In Voudoun, used to trace vevers.

FARINE GUINÉE
Powdered ash, used to trace vevers and for other ritual purposes.

FORT
Strong. In Voudoun it specifically means one who knows a good deal about ritual procedure and therefore is powerful in commanding the loa.

G

GAGNIN LOA
To have a loa in one's head or to be possessed by a loa.

GANGAN
Synonym for houngan.

GARDE
Protective charm against magic.

GHUEVO
Small chamber, containing an altar, consecrated to the worship of a loa.

GOVI
Red earthen vessel in which the spirits of the dead or the loa are lodged. This term is used only in reference to such sacred vessels, as contrasted to canari, which refers to all earthen vessels.

GRAN, GRAND
Good, as opposed to *gros*, which means large; also "important". *Gran moun*, means good or important person. It may also mean a very old person, or a grandmother or grandfather.

GRAN MAÎTRE
The original creator deity, the main God, as distinct from the many loa.

GROS⁄BON⁄ANGE
The soul of a person, his metaphysical double.

GUINÉE
Usually understood as Africa, land of origin. Possibly also a reference to South America (see Appendix B).

H

HAUT CHANT
Special song of salutation, either to distinguished visitors or, as *Haut Chant Nago*, for a Nago loa.

HOUNFOR, HUNFOR
The "temple" of a Voudoun priest, including the paraphernalia of the service and understood to include the persons who serve there. When used in juxtaposition to peristyle, it means the actual altar chamber.

HOUNGAN, HUNGAN
Voudoun priest. Literally chief, *gan*, of the spirits, *houn*, from the language of the Fon people.

HOUNGENIKON
A high official of the hounfor, assistant to the houngan, and usually charged with the leading of the singing.

HOUNSIS, HUNSIS
Members of the *société* at various stages of elevation and initiation.

HOUNTOR, HUNTOR
The spirit of the Voudoun drums. Sometimes understood as a loa who may possess the drummer. Also reported as the name of a ritual dance and as the term for the sacrificial goat, in the north of Haiti.

I

IBO
An African tribe; retained in Haiti as the name of a nanchon of loa and a dance.

INSTALLÉ (ER)
Possession by a loa, who *installs* himself in a person. Also refers to the ritual introduction of the loa to a new hounfor, a ceremony of consecration and baptism.

INVISIBLES (LES)
Generic term comprising all the invisible spirits including the loa, the souls of deceased.

J

JUBA
An American nanchon, usually linked with Martinique. Also the name of a dance.

K

KANGA
West African tribe represented in Haiti.

L

LAMBI
Conch shell, used as a horn.

LANGAGE
Sacred language, probably African words, used in ceremonials.

LA-PLACE
An apprentice and assistant to the houngan.

LAVER TÊTE
A ritual washing of the head designed to baptize a loa in the head of a person, or to strengthen his control.

LIMBA, LEMBA
African tribe represented in Haiti; the name of a loa and a dance.

LOA
Deity or deities of Haiti.

LOA ACHETÉ
A "bought" loa, of definitely "lower" class than the major loa.

LOA RACINE
A "root" or very ancient loa.

LOA TRAVAIL
A "work" or immediately functional loa.

LOUP GAROU
Werewolf.

M

MACOUTTE
Straw sack carried by peasants; in Voudoun, associated with Legba and Azacca.

MAÎT'
Master; as in Maît' Hounfor, Maît' Tête (loa, master of the hounfor or the head of a person, the dominant loa).

MAMAN
Mother; also the largest of the set of three Rada drums.

MAMBO
Woman priestess.

MANGÉ (R)
A sacrifice; a feast; to eat.

MANGÉ GUINÉE
A ritual feasting of the loa, of certain specified foods.

MANGÉ MARASSA
Feast of the Marassa.

MANGÉ MORTS
Feast for the Dead.

MANGÉ MOUN
"To eat men"; metaphor for the fatal illness or accident sent by malevolent spirits who "eat men".

MANGÉ SEC
"Dry" offerings, no animal sacrifice.

MARASSA
Contemporary twins; demiurgic, or Divine Twins. See discussion of Marassa, Chapter I.

MARCHER ENSEMBLE
To go together, as when two loa usually are feasted at the same time, or arrive at the same time; referring to a close relationship.

MARRÉ (R)
To tie or restrain, as to "marrer loa", a magical or ritual restraint of a troublesome loa.

MARRON, MARRONAGE
Term used to describe Negroes who escaped from the plantations in pre-revolutionary times and lived in freedom in the hills. Also used, now, in the sense of wild, runaway.

MARTINIQUE
A nanchon and dance closely linked to the Juba.

MASCARON
Mardi Gras secular dance.

MASSISSI
Homosexuals of either sex.

MAZON (NE)
Congo dance of Haitian origin, as opposed to the African Congo dance.

MOMBIN
Leaves of mombin are ritualistically important, and include the idea of African origin as well as purifying properties.

MONTER
To mount, as a loa mounts his "horse", a person.

MORTS
The Dead, as a collective category.

MOUNDONGUE
An African tribe represented in Haiti; a dance and a loa are known by that name.

MYSTÈRES
Les Mystères usually mean the loa, as distinct from the spirits of the Dead; in some contexts it could also be understood as referring to the rituals, in the sense of the "mysteries".

N

NAGO
An African tribe represented in Haiti; a dance; and a loa.

NANCHON
Nation, tribe, cult or clan grouping.

NOM VAILLANT
The "fighting" or ritual name of a houngan.

O

OGAN
The iron piece beaten to accompany the drums for ceremonies and dances.

P

PAQUETS CONGO
A small package, wound around many times, which serves as a magical protection, in effigy, of the person against illness and evil spirits.

PÉ
The altar.

PERISTYLE
The roofed, open-sided area in which most of the ceremonies and dances take place. See illustration 10, facing p. 167.

PETRO
A nanchon of loa; also the word designating the drum beat, dance, etc. Of American origin.

PIERRE-LOA
The smooth, "sweating" stones inhabited by loa.

PILON
Mortar used for grinding and pounding grain.

PLAÇAGE
A relationship similar to common-law marriage.

PLAT⁄MARASSA
Plates of red clay, specifically for offerings to the Marassa. They consist of two or three bowls joined to a single head.

POT⁄DE⁄TÊTE
Earthen jar into which the gros⁄bon⁄ange is ritually placed.

POTEAU⁄LEGBA, POTEAU⁄MITAN
The center⁄post of the peristyle or tonnelle, understood as the avenue by which the loa enter during ceremonies.

POIN, POUIN, POINT
A cryptic but specific reference to a person in a song; the line of force or point of contact with the loa world.

PRÊT⁄SAVANNE
"Bush priest"; a person who reads the Catholic prayers and litanies at ceremonies.

R

RADA
Nanchon of loa, with songs, dances, etc., of Dahomean origin.

RAIDE
Stern, strong; used in characterizing Petro loa.

RAMASSER
Gather together; to collect into one's own heredity and obligation, the loa abandoned by other members of the family.

RARA
Dance festival occurring in spring.

REGLER
To regulate, control; to have command and authority over the loa; to quiet and restrain the loa.

RELER
To call, cry out; in Voudoun songs, to invoke.

RENVOYER
To ritually "send away" a loa.

REPOSOIRS
The circular cement basin enclosing the foot of a tree sacred to loa.

RETIRER D'EN BAS DE L'EAU
Ceremony for reclaiming the souls of the deceased from the waters of the abyss.

S

SAINTS
Saint; used as synonym for loa.

SALANGO
An African tribe; in Haiti, a dance and a loa of the Petro group.

SECONDE
The second, or middle drum of the Rada set.

SERVICE, SERVIR, SERVITEUR
A ritual service of loa; to serve the loa; one who serves the loa.

SERVIR A DEUX MAINS
Serve with both hands, meaning to serve both Rada (right hand) and Petro (left hand) loa.

SIGNALER
To signal; a ritual gesture extending the offering towards the cardinal points while indicating the loa for whom it is intended.

SOBAGUI
The altar. See illustration 1, facing p. 38.

SOCIÉTÉ
An organization; the communal organization underlying a hounfor.

T

TAMBOUR
Drum.

TAMBOUR MARINGUIN
A mosquito drum, associated with Ghede.

TI⁄BON⁄ANGE
The spirit, or conscience, of a person as differentiated from their gros⁄ bon⁄ange, or soul.

TONELLE
A thatched canopy, improvised in the absence of a peristyle, under which the ceremonies and dances take place.

TRAITEMENT
A herbal cure; in Voudoun, one administered by a houngan.

V

VENTAILLER
A ritual gesture of "airing" the sacrificial chickens.

VERSER
To spill; in Voudoun it refers to the ritual pouring of drops of water, coffee, liquor, etc., on the ground for the trinity and the loa.

VEVERS
Symbolic, caballa-like designs drawn on the ground to invoke the loa at ceremonies, made of wheat or maize flour or ashes.

VOUDOUN
The metaphysical principles and the ritual practices comprising the religion of the Haitian masses.

W

WANGA
A magic charm of malevolent intent.

WEDO
Place-name related to loa brought from the Dahomean seaport of Whydah.

Y

YAM (IGNAME)
A root vegetable of ritual importance; the *ceremony-yam* is the major annual agrarian ceremony.

YANVALOU, YENVALO
A dance of the Rada rites.

Z

ZEMI
The fetish or sacred object of the Arawauken Indians who inhabited Haiti; also understood as ancestral spirit. Important evidence of Indian influence in Voudoun, and probable source of words "zombi", and the loa Baron Samedi, and others. See Appendix B.

ZEPAULE
Shoulder dance of the Rada rites.

Z'ILE MINFORT
Island below the water, residence of Agwé.

ZILET EN BAS DE L'EAU
Island below the sea where the souls of the dead go, and also where the loa live.

ZINS
Ceremonial cooking pots, usually of clay, but made of iron for the Nago loa.

ZOMBIE
A soulless body. The soul may have been removed by magic from a living person, or the body of someone recently deceased may have been brought up out of the grave after the soul had been separated from it by regular rites of death. The purpose is to make use of the body as a slave.

REFERENCES

Alexander, Hartley Burr. *Latin-American.* Vol. XI. *The Mythology of All Races.* Boston, 1920.

Bateson, Gregory. *Naven* (A study of the Iatmul culture of New Guinea). Cambridge University Press, 1936.

Bleuler, Dr. Eugen. *Textbook of Psychiatry.* New York, 1924.

Campbell, Joseph. *The Hero With A Thousand Faces.* New York, 1949.
Cannon, Walter, B. *Voodoo Death.* American Anthropologist. Vol. 44, No. 2, April–June, 1942.
Courlander, Harold. *Haiti Singing.* University of North Carolina Press, 1939.

Davis, H. P. *Black Democracy.* New York, 1928.
Denis, Lorimer. *La Religion Populaire.* Bulletin Du Bureau D'Ethnologie. Port-au-Prince, Haiti, March, 1946.
Denis, Lorimer and Paul, Emmanuel C. *Essai Organographie Haitienne.* Port-au-Prince, Haiti, 1948.
Dorsainvil, J. C. *Psychologie Haitienne, Vodou et Magie.* Port-au-Prince, Haiti, 1937.

Fox, Dr. Charles D. *Psychopathology of Hysteria.* Boston, 1913.
Frazer, Sir James George. *The Golden Bough.* (One Volume, abridged edition). New York, 1947.
Frobenius, Leo and Fox, Douglas C. *African Genesis.* New York, 1937.

Herskovits, M. J. *Dahomey.* New York, 1938.
Life In A Haitian Valley. New York, 1937.

Jacobson, Max. *Functional Disorders.* Tomorrow Magazine. New York, March, 1951.

Levy-Bruhl, Lucien. *Primitive Mentality.* New York, 1923.
Leybrun, James G. *The Haitian People.* Yale University Press, 1941.

Malinowski, Bronislaw. *Myth in Primitive Psychology.* New York, 1926.
Marcelin, Milo. *Mythologie Vodou (Rite Arada).* Port-au-Prince, Haiti, 1949.

Mars, Dr. Louis. *La Crise de Possession Dans Le Vaudou.* Port-au-Prince, Haiti, 1946.

Maximilien, Louis. *Le Vodou Haitien, Rite Radas–Canzo.* Port-au-Prince, Haiti, 1945.

Metraux, Alfred. *The Concept of Soul in Haitian Vodu.* Southwestern Journal of Anthropology. Vol. 2, No. 1, Spring 1946. University of New Mexico Press, Albuquerque, New Mexico.

Owen, Mary Alicia. *Voodooism.* International Folklore Congress, Chicago, 1893.

Parsons, Elsie Clews. *Spirit Cult In Hayti.* Paris, 1928.

Pressoir, Charles Fernand. *Debats sur le Creole et le Folklore.* Port-au-Prince, Haiti, 1947.

Price-Mars, Dr. *Ainsi Parla l'Oncle.* Port-au-Prince, Haiti, 1928.

Rigaud, Milo. *Jesus ou Legba.* France, 1933.

Rigaud, Odette Mennesson. *The Feasting of the Gods in Haitian Vodu,* Primitive Man (Quarterly Bulletin of the Catholic Anthropological Conference). Vol. XIX, Nos. 1 and 2, January, and April, 1946.

Rigaud, Odette Mennesson, and Denis, Lorimer. *Ceremonie En L' Honneur de Marinette.* Bulletin Du Bureau d'Ethnologie. Port-au-Prince, Haiti, July, 1947.

Rigaud, Odette Mennesson, and Denis, Lorimer. *La Vie Mystique de Marie Noel.* Bulletin Du Bureau d'Ethnologie. Port-au-Prince, Haiti, March, 1947.

Roumain, Jacques. *Le Sacrifice du Tambour Assator.* Port-au-Prince, Haiti, 1943.

Seabrook, William. *Magic Island.* New York, 1929.

Sylvain, Suzanne. *Le Creole Haitien.* Port-au-Prince. Haiti, 1936.

Simpson, George Eaton (I) *Four Vodoun Ceremonies.* Journal of American Folklore. April–June, 1946.

(II) *Belief System of Haitian Vodoun.* American Anthropologist. Vol. 47, No. 1, January–March, 1945.

(III) *Two Vodoun Related Ceremonies.* Journal of American Folklore. Vol. 61, January–March, 1948.

INDEX

INDEX

abyss, waters of the, concept of, 46, 260-2, Ch I fn 12; African and Indian concepts compared, 65; at foot of cross-roads, 35, 37; communication with, 48, 51, 205; descent to, 30, 35, 45-6, Ch I fn 12; recall from, 46-53, of Ghede by Loco, 149, of Sobo by Agassou, Ch III fn 105

action de grâce, 208, 212

Adja, 137

adoration, 215

African, concepts, 54-5, 107 fn, Ch IV fn 46; compared with Indian, 65-6; in Voudoun, 36, 56-60, 64-70, 82-5; High God, 55; tribes, 58-9; words in Voudoun, 18, 196; see also nanchons

Agaou, 56

Agarou Tonerre, 116

Agassou, 34, 122, 127, 254; Ch III fns 95, 104-5

agriculture, primarily in Petro rites, 110 fn, 137-8 fn, Appendix B pps 280, 285-6; see Azacca, ceremony-yam

Agwé, 56, 89-90, 82-5, 119-30, 137, 142-3, 182-4, 212, 231, 254, 275, 280, Ch III fns 65, 104

Akadja, 137

Alegba, 99; see Legba

Allada, 60

altar, 53, 178; see pé, sobagui

amnesia, during possession, 30, 258-60

ancestors, concept of as psychic heritage, 27-8, 70-1, 81; African and Indian concepts compared, 65, Appendix B; aid to daily life, 72; becoming loa, 28-33, 91, Ch I fns 2, 3, Ch III fns 95, 102; loa principle of, 141; Marassa as

original, 34-40; significance of service for, 27-8

androgynous, principle in myth, 22, Ch III fn 7; in Ghede, 111; in Legba 96; in Loco and Ayizan 146-7; in Marassa 40; in Nanan-bouclou, 55; in Mawu-Lisa, 55; in vever, 41

animal sacrifice, significance of, 213-16, Ch V fn 17; in canzo ceremony, 221, 223; differences according to loa, 63 fn, 119, 128-9, 212, Ch III fn 28, Ch V fns 16, 20

animism, incorrectly applied to Voudoun, 36, 86-7, Ch III fn 1

Aradas, 58

art, anonymous character of in ritual, 227-8; Erzulie, principle of, 140; individual virtuosity in, 229-33; sacred and secular forms compared, 226-7; status of performers, 187, see dance, drummer, houngenikon; use of in hounfor, 120-2, 181-2, 211; in drawing vevers, 204-5

Ashanti, 58

asson, conferred by, 69, 80-1; in Indian culture, 274-5; powers of, 48, 158, 177-8, 206; use in ritual, 48-53, 177-8, 206, 208, 243, Ch IV fn 7

Attibon Legba, 82-5, 99; see Legba

Ayida, 34, 82-5, 115-16, 120-1, 182, 184, 212; see Damballah

Ayizan, 82-5, 93, 146-50, 212, 221-3, Ch I fn 8

Azacca, 82-5, 108-11, 142, 210, 212, 280

Azacca Médé, 109 fn

Aztec, 66; see Appendix B

Badé, 82-3, Ch III fns 57, 65

Badessy, 116

X